Wissenschaftliche Untersuchungen
zum Neuen Testament · 2. Reihe

Herausgeber / Editor
Jörg Frey (Zürich)

Mitherausgeber / Associate Editors
Friedrich Avemarie (Marburg)
Markus Bockmuehl (Oxford)
Hans-Josef Klauck (Chicago, IL)

290

Nicolas Farelly

The Disciples in the Fourth Gospel

A Narrative Analysis of their Faith and Understanding

Mohr Siebeck

NICOLAS FARELLY, born 1978; 2009 PhD, University of Gloucestershire, UK; since 2005 director of the Forum Culturel Protestant, Compiègne, France; instructor in New Testament Theology, Faculté Libre de Théologie Réformée, Aix-en-Provence, France; instructor in New Testament Theology, Institut Biblique, Nogent-sur-Marne, France.

BS
2 615.52
.F37
2010

ISBN 978-3-16-150583-6
ISSN 0340-9570 (Wissenschaftliche Untersuchungen zum Neuen Testament, 2. Reihe)

Die Deutsche Nationalbibliothek lists this publication in the Deutsche Nationalbibliographie; detailed bibliographic data are available on the Internet at *http://dnb.d-nb.de*.

The book was printed by Laupp & Göbel in Nehren on non-aging paper and bound by Buchbinderei Nädele in Nehren.

Printed in Germany.

Preface

The present monograph is a slightly revised version of my thesis, which was submitted in 2009 to the University of Gloucestershire for the degree of Ph.D. More people than can be mentioned here have contributed to my research by providing academic insight, support, inspiration, or encouragement. I owe a special dept of gratitude to my supervisors, Professor Andrew T. Lincoln and Dr. Angus Paddison. I am particularly thankful that, at a time when professional and family responsibilities overwhelmed me and made me question the very rationale for pursuing my research interests, they found the appropriate words of encouragement to help me carry on this project. So many of their ideas on the Fourth Gospel have enriched my understanding of it. Their gracious guidance and insightful suggestions have rendered this thesis better than it could have ever been without them. I would also like to express my gratitude to the editor of this series, Professor Dr. Jörg Frey, for accepting this thesis for publication, and to Dr. Henning Ziebritzki and his wonderful editorial staff for their able assistance. As I worked on the monograph in preparation for publication, I also received the support of Rev. Robert Fossett, a dear friend who accepted to read over the thesis for a final check on my written English. Of course, none of them can be held responsible for the remaining deficiencies in the thesis.

I am very thankful to my parents, Paul and Danielle Farelly, and to my grandparents, Jean and Janine Farelly, for their constant encouragement throughout my life, and for their financial support during my studies.

Two dear friends deserve to be mentioned here as well. Alexander Bukovietski and Rodrigo de Sousa have accompanied me with their friendship during most of my theological and biblical training. Throughout our numerous conversations, their ideas and faith have impacted me more than they will ever know. I am so fortunate to count them as my friends.

Last, but by no means least, my deepest appreciation goes to my wife Alison. But for her love, support, patience, and many sacrifices, neither this thesis nor much that is worthwhile in my life would exist. Together with our three children, William, Elliot, and Aimée, they have brought me joy and continuing encouragement in the past several years, even when so much of my time was spent physically or emotionally away from them. It is with love and gratitude that I dedicate this monograph to them.

Margny-lès-Compiègne, September 2010   Nicolas Farelly

Table of Contents

Abbreviations

AB	Anchor Bible
AcaBib	Academia Biblica
ACR	*The Australian Catholic Report*
AGJU	Arbeiten zur Geschichte des antiken Judentums und des Urchristentums
AJBI	*Annual of the Japanese Biblical Institute*
AnBib	Analecta Biblica
Anton	*Antonianum*
BA	Bibliothèque Augustinienne
BBB	Bonner biblische Beiträge
BBET	Beiträge zur biblischen Exegese und Theologie
BeauR	Beauchesne Religion
BECNT	Baker Exegetical Commentary on the New Testament
BETL	Bibliotheca Ephemeridum Theologicarum Lovaniensium
Bib	*Biblica*
BibInt	*Biblical Interpretation*
BibIntS	Biblical Interpretation Series
BLS	Bible and Literature Series
BNTC	Black's New Testament Commentaries
BRS	The Biblical Resource Series
BSac	*Bibliotheca Sacra*
BTB	*Biblical Theology Bulletin*
BVC	Bible et Vie Chrétienne
BVC	*Bible et Vie Chrétienne*
CahRB	Cahiers de la Revue Biblique
CAR	Cahiers de l'actualité religieuse
CBQ	*Catholic Biblical Quarterly*
CBQMS	Catholic Biblical Quarterly Monograph Series
CI	*Critical Inquiry*
CNTDs	Commentaire du Nouveau Testament; Deuxième série
ColT	*Collectanea theologica*
Did	*Didaskalia*
DRev	*Downside Review*
EBib	Études Bibliques
ER	*Ecumenical Review*
ESV	English Standard Version
ETL	*Ephemerides Theologicae Lovanienses*
ETR	*Études Théologiques et Religieuses*
EvQ	*Evangelical Quarterly*
ExAud	*Ex Auditu*
ExpTim	*Expository Times*

FoiVie	*Foi & Vie*
FRLANT	Forschungen zur Religion und Literatur des Alten und Neuen Testaments
FTS	Frankfurter theologische Studien
FZPhTh	*Freiburger Zeitschrift für Philosophie und Theologie*
GNTS	Guides to New Testament Scholarship
HBS	Herders Biblische Studien
Hok	*Hokhma*
HTIBS	Historic Texts and Interpreters in Biblical Scholarship
HTKNT	Herders theologischer Kommentar zum Neuen Testament
HTR	*Harvard Theological Review*
HvTSt	*Hervormde Teologiese Studies*
ICC	International Critical Commentary
IET	Institut d'Études Théologiques
IJST	*International Journal of Systematic Theology*
Int	*Interpretation*
JBL	*Journal of Biblical Literature*
JCTR	*Journal for Christian Theological Research*
Jeev	*Jeevadhara*
JSNT	*Journal for the Study of the New Testament*
JSNTSup	Journal for the Study of the New Testament Supplement Series
JTS	*Journal of Theological Studies*
KD	Kerygma und Dogma
LCBI	Literary Currents in Biblical Interpretation
LCL	Loeb Classical Library
LD	Lectio Divina
LThPM	Louvain Theological & Pastoral Monographs
LTP	*Laval Théologique et Philosophique*
McMNTS	McMaster New Testament Studies
MdB	Le Monde de la Bible
NABPRSSS	National Association of Baptist Professors of Religion, Special Studies Series
NCB	The New Century Bible
Neot	*Neotestamentica*
NFTL	New Foundations Theological Library
NICNT	The New International Commentary on the New Testament
NIV	New International Version
NovT	*Novum Testamentum*
NovTSup	Novum Testamentum Supplements
NRSV	New Revised Standard Version
NRTh	*Nouvelle Revue Théologique*
NTAbh	Neutestamentliche Abhandlungen
NTL	The New Testament Library
NTTS	New Testament Tools and Studies
NTS	*New Testament Studies*
ÖTBK	Ökumenischer Taschenbuchkommentar zum Neuen Testament
PBM	Paternoster Biblical Monographs
PdD	Parole de Dieu
PNTC	The Pillar New Testament Commentary
PRSt	*Perspectives in Religious Studies*
PT	*Poetics Today*

Presb	*Presbyterion*
PRSt	*Perspectives in Religious Studies*
RNBC	Readings: A New Biblical Commentary
RSR	*Recherches de sciences religieuses*
RTL	*Revue Théologique de Louvain*
RTP	*Revue de Théologie et de Philosophie*
SP	Sacra pagina
Sal	*Salesianum*
SBEC	Studies in the Bible and Early Christianity
SBG	Studies in Biblical Greek
SBib	Sciences Bibliques
SBL	Society of Biblical Literature
SBLDS	Society of Biblical Literature Dissertation Series
SBLMS	Society of Biblical Literature Monograph Series
SBLRBS	Society of Biblical Literature Resources for Biblical Study
SBLSBS	Society of Biblical Literature Sources for Biblical Studies
SE	*Studia Evangelica*
SPNT	Studies on Personalities of the New Testament
StudBibT	*Studia Biblica et Theologica*
SubBi	Subsidia Biblica
THKNT	Theologischer Handkommentar zum Neuen Testament
TNIV	Today's New International Version
TS	*Theological Studies*
TTE	*The Theological Educator*
TU	*Texte und Untersuchungen*
TynBul	*Tyndale Bulletin*
TZ	*Theologische Zeitschrift*
WBC	Word Biblical Commentary
WUNT	Wissenschaftliche Untersuchungen zum Neuen Testament
WW	*Word & World*
ZNW	*Zeitschrift für die Neutestamentliche Wissenschaft und die Kunde der Älteren Kirche*

Chapter 1

Introduction

What originally motivated the study of the present topic were intriguing and recurrent remarks found in scholarly literature on the Fourth Gospel. For instance, Brown, in his commentary's introduction, writes that "the full faith in Jesus which brings life to men is possible only after the resurrection, when men confess him as Lord and God (xx 28)."[1] Likewise, Painter states that "from the narrative confessions, it is clear that authentic faith was not a reality during Jesus' ministry."[2] While these, and many other authors, distinguish pre- and post-resurrection faiths, the nature of the difference is not clearly explicated. If "full faith" leading to life must await the resurrection, how exactly should one consider the faith of those who believed prior to the resurrection? Was, for instance, their faith imperfect because it did not or could not properly understand Jesus' identity, words, and mission?[3] Consequently, were the disciples during Jesus' earthly ministry already in a saving relationship with Jesus?

Questions associated with the nature of faith prior to Jesus' resurrection come to the fore often in this Gospel, generally due to ambiguities in the presentation of the disciples. The evangelist does portray them as believing, confessing, and even witnessing about their faith quite early in the course of the narrative (*e.g.* 1:41, 45, 49; 2:11; 6:68–69). Yet, Jesus apparently considers that the disciples still need to believe (11:15) and even questions whether they do indeed believe (16:31). Finally, the Fourth Gospel's narrative points to a time, after the resurrection, when faith and understanding would be present in them (*e.g.* 2:22; 12:16; 20:8).[4] It follows that the literary and theological coherence of

---

[1] R. E. Brown, *The Gospel according to John*, 2 vols, AB 29 & 29a (Garden City, NY: Doubleday, 1966, 1970), 1:cxviii.

[2] J. Painter, *The Quest for the Messiah: The History, Literature and Theology of the Johannine Community*, 2nd ed. (Nashville, TN: Abingdon, 1993), 414.

[3] So for instance, Painter, *Quest*, 411–12, states that misunderstanding Jesus is a mark of superficial faith. Likewise, R. A. Culpepper, *Anatomy of the Fourth Gospel: A Study in Literary Design* (Philadelphia, PA: Fortress, 1983), 116–18, argues that there is a pattern of misunderstanding in the disciples so that their faith is imperfect and "only [Jesus'] death and resurrection, his glorification, will enable them to understand what he has revealed."

[4] Thus, for Painter, *Quest*, 414: "[…] the words and works of Jesus could not provoke authentic faith in the context of his ministry, but the reminiscence of them in the apostolic witness would." For Painter authentic faith presupposes the glorification of Jesus, the coming of the Paraclete, and the resurrection of Jesus.

the narrative is at stake as readers wonder why the evangelist chose to portray the disciples' faith in such an ambiguous manner. Based on these apparently contradictory statements, many have concluded that the disciples' faith prior to Easter was in some way deficient or faulty. But is this a necessary conclusion? Are the distinctions between pre-Easter faith and post-Easter "full faith" or between pre-Easter inauthentic faith and post-Easter "authentic faith" appropriate? What could be the evangelist's reasons for portraying the disciples' faith in the way he does? The issue deserves to be revisited in a thorough fashion.

It has long been recognized that the themes of faith and understanding play a significant role in the Fourth Gospel. For instance, Mlakuzhyil proposed that "Christocentric faith is one of the most prominent Johannine themes."[5] For Culpepper, the plot of the Fourth Gospel is "propelled by conflict between belief and unbelief as responses to Jesus"[6] and most of the disciples typify a response to Jesus, which he labels "commitment in spite of misunderstanding."[7] Commentaries on this Gospel frequently draw attention to faith and understanding in passing while several scholarly articles and monographs have dealt with particular passages or concepts related to one or other aspect of the overall question.[8] There is also agreement that the disciples are important characters

---

[5] G. Mlakuzhyil, *The Christocentric Literary Structure of the Fourth Gospel*, AnBib 117 (Rome: Editrice Pontificio Istituto Biblico, 1987), 290. More recently, C. R. Koester, *The Word of Life: A Theology of John's Gospel* (Grand Rapids, MI: Eerdmans, 2008), 161–86, has devoted an entire chapter to the theme of faith in his overview of Johannine theology.

[6] Culpepper, *Anatomy*, 97.

[7] Culpepper, *Anatomy*, 147.

[8] On faith in the Fourth Gospel, see *e.g.* A. Schlatter, *Der Glaube in Neuen Testament* (Stuttgart: Calwer Verlag, 1927), 176–221, 486–520, 595–600; J. Huby, "De la connaissance de foi dans Saint Jean," *RSR* 21 (1931): 385–421; M. Bonningues, *La foi dans l'évangile de saint Jean* (Paris/Bruxelles: Office Général du Livre/La pensée catholique, 1955); A. Decourtray, "La conception johannique de la foi," *NRTh* 81 (1959): 561–76; G. F. Hawthorne, "The Concept of Faith in the Fourth Gospel," *BSac* 116 (1959): 117–26; W. Grundmann, "Verständnis und Bewegung des Glaubens im Johannes-Evangelium," *KD* 6 (1960): 131–54; A. Vanhoye, "Notre foi, oeuvre divine, d'après le quatrième évangile," *NRTh* 86 (1964): 337–54; J. Gaffney, "Believing and Knowing in the Fourth Gospel," *TS* 26 (1965): 215–41; R. Schnackenburg, *The Gospel according to John*, trans. by K. Smyth, 3 vols, HTKNT IV/1–3 (London/New York, NY: Burns & Oates/Crossroad, 1968–1982), 1:558–75; L. Walter, "Foi et incrédulité selon Saint Jean" (Thèse de doctorat. Paris: Institut Catholique de Paris, 1975); abbreviated in L. Walter, *L'incroyance des croyants selon saint Jean*, Lire la Bible 43 (Paris: Cerf, 1976); E. Szymanek, "Glaube und Unglaube im Evangelium des hl. Johannes," *ColT* 46 (1976): 97–121; J.-M. Faux, *La foi du Nouveau Testament* (Bruxelles: Institut d'Études Théologiques, 1977), 177–235; D. Mollat, *Études johanniques*, PdD 19 (Paris: Seuil, 1979); Y. Ibuki, "'Viele glaubten an ihn' – Auseinandersetzung mit dem Glauben im Johannesevangelium," *AJBI* 9 (1983): 128–83; R. L. Adkinson, "An Examination of the Concept of Believing in the Gospel of John" (Unpublished Ph.D. Thesis. New Orleans, LA: New Orleans Baptist Theological Seminary, 1990); A. D. Hopkins, "A Narratological Approach to the Development of Faith in the Gospel of John" (Unpublished Ph.D. Thesis. Louisville, KY: Southern Baptist Theological Seminary, 1992); and most recently A. Barus, "The Faith Motif in John's Gospel: A Narrative Approach"

in the narrative of the Fourth Gospel, and research in this domain necessarily mentions something about their faith and understanding. Yet, though discipleship has become the focus of increased interest in the last several decades,[9] Culpepper's 1983 remark that "the role of the disciples in John has escaped the intense interest that has recently been turned on their role in Mark"[10] remains true overall today. Clearly, the door is still open for further research on discipleship and on the faith and understanding motifs in the Fourth Gospel. More to the point, and quite surprisingly given the dilemma briefly exposed above, there remains to be written a substantial work fully dedicated to the disciples' faith and understanding in the Fourth Gospel. Therefore, this study will seek to establish how and why the characterisation of the disciples has been presented

---

(Unpublished Ph.D. Thesis. Aberdeen: University of Aberdeen, 2000). On faith as it relates to signs in the Fourth Gospel, see *e.g.* R. Bultmann, *The Gospel of John: A Commentary*, trans. by G. R. Beasley-Murray (Oxford: Blackwell, 1971), 69, 131; M. de Jonge, *Jesus, Stranger from Heaven and Son of God: Jesus Christ and the Christians in Johannine Perspective*, trans. by J. E. Steely, SBLSBS 11 (Missoula, MT: Scholars Press, 1977), 117–40; F. J. Moloney, "From Cana to Cana (Jn. 2:1–4:54) and the Fourth Evangelist's Concept of Correct (and Incorrect) Faith," *Sal* 40 (1978): 817–43; M.-É. Boismard, "Rapport entre foi et miracles dans l'évangile de Jean," *ETL* 58 (1982): 357–64; C. R. Koester, "Hearing, Seeing, and Believing in the Gospel of John," *Bib* 70/3 (1989): 327–48; G. H. Twelftree, *Jesus the Miracle Worker: A Historical and Theological Study* (Downers Grove, IL: InterVarsity Press, 1999), 189–238.

[9] See R. M. Chennattu, *Johannine Discipleship as a Covenant Relationship* (Peabody, MA: Hendrickson, 2006), 1–22, for a helpful overview of research on the Johannine discipleship motif since 1970. Particularly influential studies in this area are: Schnackenburg, *John*, 3:203–17; de Jonge, *Stranger*, 1–17; M. Vellanickal, "Discipleship according to the Gospel of John," *Jeev* 10 (1980): 131–47; J. S. Siker-Gieseler, "Disciples and Discipleship in the Fourth Gospel: A Canonical Approach," *StudBibT* 10 (1980): 199–227; F. F. Segovia, "'Peace I Leave with You; My Peace I Give to You': Discipleship in the Fourth Gospel," in *Discipleship in the New Testament*, ed. by F. F. Segovia (Philadelphia, PA: Fortress, 1985), 76–102; M. M. Pazdan, "Nicodemus and the Samaritan Woman: Contrasting Models of Discipleship," *BTB* 17 (1987): 145–48; C. L. Winbery, "Abiding in Christ: The Concept of Discipleship in John," *TTE* 38 (1988): 104–20; R. F. Collins, *These Things Have Been Written: Studies on the Fourth Gospel*, LThPM 2 (Louvain/Grand Rapids, MI: Peeters/Eerdmans, 1990), 46–55; J. A. du Rand, "Perspectives on Johannine Discipleship according to the Farewell Discourse," *Neot* 25 (1991): 311–25; W. H. Gloer, "'Come and See': Disciples and Discipleship in the Fourth Gospel," in *Perspectives on John: Methods and Interpretation in the Fourth Gospel*, ed. by R. B. Sloan and M. C. Parsons, NABPRSSS (Lewiston, NY/Queenston/Lampeter: Edwin Mellen, 1993), 269–301; M. R. Hillmer, "They Believed in Him: Discipleship in the Johannine Tradition," in *Patterns of Discipleship in the New Testament*, ed. by R. N. Longenecker, McMNTS (Grand Rapids, MI: Eerdmans, 1996), 77–97; D. G. van der Merve, "Towards a Theological Understanding of Johannine Discipleship," *Neot* 31 (1997): 339–59; A. J. Köstenberger, *The Missions of Jesus and the Disciples according to the Fourth Gospel: With Implications for the Fourth Gospel's Purpose and the Mission of the Contemporary Church* (Grand Rapids, MI: Eerdmans, 1998), 141–98.

[10] Culpepper, *Anatomy*, 115. For a treatment of discipleship in Mark, with a recent bibliography, see S. W. Henderson, *Christology and Discipleship in the Gospel of Mark*, SNTSMS 135 (Cambridge: Cambridge University Press, 2006), 3, n.2.

in the way it is in the Fourth Gospel. Simply stated, recognizing the exegetical and theological obscurities still facing Johannine interpreters, this study
proposes to investigate how one should consider the faith and understanding of
Jesus' disciples before and after the resurrection.

Given the limited space available, a wide-ranging exploration of the topic
from the mutually illuminating perspectives of literary, historical, and theological analyses cannot possibly be undertaken. Although the study will at times
refer to the manner in which questions have been answered from a historical
and theological point of view,[11] its primary interest is in the literary, and only
secondarily in the theological. Indeed, this study will propose that a narrative
understanding of the disciples' faith and understanding may give new breath to
further historical and theological examinations. Arguably, of the three perspectives, the literary task is primary, as the investigation of what the text says and
how it functions both within itself and in relation to its readers is essential for
questions of the text's meaning. As Lee argues, "What lies behind the text is
important, yet it is always dependent on, and secondary to, what lies within."[12]
Only when questions have been formed on this level, however tentative they
may be, is it possible to employ the text properly as a resource for enquiries
into 'the world behind the text' and 'the world in front of the text.'[13] It should
be noted that a literary approach is neither necessarily a-historical, nor does it
exclude theological explorations. It is rather that the emphasis and focus of the
questions posed by literary critics are different from those posed by historians
and theologians.[14] For instance, literary analysts attempt to appreciate a story
apart from its referential function, *i.e.*, its ability to refer to the real world: "the
story world is to be entered and experienced rather than evaluated in terms of
historicity."[15] But this is not to say that a degree of historical or theological
analysis is not necessary to the literary task. It remains useful, for instance, to
understand historically what was going on during the Jewish feasts to better
grasp how the narrative of the Fourth Gospel functions within itself.

This study will employ narrative criticism in its focus on the disciples' faith
and understanding. Narrative criticism or narratology is interested both in the
content and the form of the text. Its development began around 1970, and ad-

---

[11] See especially chapters 4 and 5. These questions are essentially the following: *Did* the
disciples believe prior to Jesus' glorification and *what* would such belief have entailed? *Could*
the disciples believe prior to Jesus' glorification?

[12] D. A. Lee, *Flesh and Glory: Symbolism, Gender, and Theology in the Gospel of John*
(New York, NY: Crossroad, 2002), 5.

[13] See *e.g.* E. S. Malbon, "Texts and Contexts: Interpreting the Disciples in Mark," *Semeia* 62 (1993): 82, n.3, for whom it is necessary to view the text as both window and mirror
in order for the interpretive task to be fully carried out.

[14] For M. A. Powell, *What Is Narrative Criticism?*, GNTS (Minneapolis, MN: Fortress,
1990), 8, literary critics "bracket out questions of historicity in order to concentrate on the
nature of the text as literature."

[15] Powell, *Narrative Criticism*, 8.

vanced with the works of literary critics such as Genette, Iser, Chatman, Booth, and Ricoeur.[16] As such, it can still be considered a recent method of analysis. But in the last forty years, it has been very productive. For instance, though the resources of earlier approaches have certainly not been exhausted, literary approaches have moved beyond the traditional narrative and reader-response criticisms, to, for example, poststructuralist, deconstructive, or ideological criticisms.

Biblical scholars rapidly learned to use the tools of narrative analysis,[17] so that in 1983 Culpepper's seminal study *Anatomy of the Fourth Gospel* introduced Johannine scholars to this method of analysis.[18] At the time, its main import was to show that the Fourth Gospel's narrative, taken as a unified whole, was inherently meaningful regardless of its sources or composition history. Needless to say, Culpepper began a revolution of sorts in Johannine studies. His monograph convinced many that new insights could be gained through a narrative analysis of this Gospel, and so paved the way for the publication of diverse narrative studies, such as Duke's *Irony in the Fourth Gospel* and O'Day's *Revelation in the Fourth Gospel* respectively only two and three years

---

[16] G. Genette, *Figures III*, Poétique (Paris: Seuil, 1972); G. Genette, *Nouveaux discours du récit* (Paris: Seuil, 1983); W. Iser, *The Implied Reader: Patterns of Communication in Prose Fiction from Bunyan to Beckett* (Baltimore, MD: Johns Hopkins University Press, 1974); W. Iser, *The Act of Reading: A Theory of Aesthetic Response* (Baltimore, MD: Johns Hopkins University Press, 1978); S. Chatman, *Story and Discourse: Narrative Structure in Fiction and Film* (Ithaca/London: Cornell University Press, 1978); W. C. Booth, *The Rhetoric of Fiction*, 2nd ed. (Chicago, IL: University of Chicago Press, 1983); P. Ricoeur, *Temps et récit. Tome I: L'intrigue et le récit historique*, Points-Essais (Paris: Seuil, 1983); P. Ricoeur, *Temps et récit. Tome II: La configuration dans le récit de fiction*, Points-Essais (Paris: Seuil, 1984); P. Ricoeur, *Temps et récit. Tome III: Le temps raconté*, Points-Essais (Paris: Seuil, 1985); W. C. Booth, *The Company We Keep: An Ethics of Fiction* (Berkeley, CA/Los Angeles, CA/London: University of California Press, 1988).

[17] See the works of pioneers of biblical narrative criticism, such as N. R. Petersen, *Literary Criticism for New Testament Critics* (Philadelphia, PA: Fortress, 1978); R. Alter, *The Art of Biblical Narrative* (New York, NY: Basic Books, 1981); D. Rhoads and D. Michie, *Mark as Story: An Introduction to the Narrative of a Gospel* (Philadelphia, PA: Fortress, 1982); J. D. Kingsbury, *Matthew as Story* (Philadelphia, PA: Fortress, 1986); R. C. Tannehill, *The Narrative-Unity of Luke-Acts: A Literary Interpretation*, 2 vols, Foundations and Facets (Philadelphia, PA: Fortress, 1986–90); J.-N. Aletti, *L'art de raconter Jésus Christ*, Parole de Dieu (Paris: Seuil, 1989); S. D. Moore, *Literary Criticism and the Gospels: The Theoretical Challenge* (New Haven, CT: Yale University Press, 1989); or Powell, *Narrative Criticism*. More recently, see J. L. Resseguie, *Narrative Criticism of the New Testament: An Introduction* (Grand Rapids, MI: Baker Academic, 2005).

[18] Culpepper, *Anatomy*. If Culpepper's essay is a watershed in Johannine literary studies, precursors to his *Anatomy* are H. Leroy, *Rätsel und Missverständnis; ein Beitrag zur Formgeschichte des Johannesevangeliums*, BBB 30 (Bonn: P. Hanstein, 1968); D. Wead, *The Literary Devices in John's Gospel* (Basel: Friedrich Reinhardt Kommissionsverlag, 1970); or de Jonge, *Stranger*.

later.[19] This new trend in Johannine studies reached its height in the 1990s, with the publication of an issue of *Semeia* entitled *The Fourth Gospel from a Literary Perspective*,[20] and several important monographs such as Stibbe's *John as Storyteller* and *The Gospel of John as Literature*,[21] Davies' *Rhetoric and Reference in the Fourth Gospel*,[22] Tovey's *Narrative Art and Act in the Fourth Gospel*,[23] and Resseguie's *The Strange Gospel*.[24] Most recently, Thatcher and Moore published a collection of essays seeking to recount the history of narrative analysis of the Fourth Gospel and to project the future of such an approach to this Gospel, thus showing that this area of research is still alive and well.[25]

Thus this study will make use of basic narratological terminology[26] in its focus on the story-as-discoursed.[27] Throughout, it will seek to read the text as the implied reader. Clearly, to the extent that the implied reader is an idealised abstraction only perceptible in clues suggested by a narrative, this goal is never perfectly attainable. Even more, actual (real) readers are each influenced by their own reading conventions and competences, by their knowledge of other texts (such as Synoptic Gospels), and by their location in space and history. Thus, it

---

[19] P. D. Duke, *Irony in the Fourth Gospel* (Atlanta: John Knox, 1985); G. R. O'Day, *Revelation in the Fourth Gospel: Narrative Mode and Theological Claim* (Philadelphia, PA: Fortress, 1986). See also J. L. Staley, *The Print's First Kiss: A Rhetorical Investigation on the Implied Reader in the Fourth Gospel*, SBLDS 82 (Atlanta, GA: Scholars Press, 1988), though he uses reader-response criticism rather than narrative criticism.

[20] R. A. Culpepper and F. F. Segovia, eds., *The Fourth Gospel from a Literary Perspective*, Semeia, vol. 51 (Atlanta, GA: Scholars Press, 1991).

[21] M. W. G. Stibbe, *John as Storyteller: Narrative Criticism and the Fourth Gospel* (Cambridge/New York: Cambridge University Press, 1992); M. W. G. Stibbe, *The Gospel of John as Literature: An Anthology of Twentieth-Century Perspectives*, NTTS 17 (Leiden/New York: Brill, 1993).

[22] M. Davies, *Rhetoric and Reference in the Fourth Gospel*, JSNTSup 69 (Sheffield: Sheffield Academic Press, 1992).

[23] D. Tovey, *Narrative Art and Act in the Fourth Gospel*, JSNTSup 151 (Sheffield: Sheffield Academic Press, 1997).

[24] J. L. Resseguie, *The Strange Gospel: Narrative Design and Point of View in John*, BibIntS 56 (Leiden/Boston, MA: Brill, 2001).

[25] T. Thatcher and S. D. Moore, eds., *Anatomies of Narrative Criticism: The Past, Present, and Future of the Fourth Gospel as Literature*, SBLRBS, vol. 55 (Atlanta, GA: Society of Biblical Literature, 2008). See also G. Hallbäck, "The Gospel of John as Literature," in *New Readings in John: Literary and Theological Perspectives. Essays from the Scandinavian Conference on the Fourth Gospel in Aarhus 1997*, ed. by J. Nissen and S. Pedersen, JSNTSuppS 182 (Sheffield: Sheffield Academic Press, 1999), 31–46.

[26] See Chatman, *Story*, for a thorough explanation of the theoretical model that is most often used by narrative analysts. His model is then expressed through a diagram on p. 267. See also the diagrams (derived from Chatman) used by Culpepper, *Anatomy*, 6; Powell, *Narrative Criticism*, 27; or Barus, "Faith", 21.

[27] Chatman, *Story*, 19. Chatman distinguishes the "what" (the story) from the "how" (the discourse) of a narrative.

may never be possible for them to perfectly read the text as the implied reader.[28] Yet, the following question, though implicit, will continually beg answering in much of the following research on the disciples' faith and understanding in the Fourth Gospel's narrative: "Is there anything in the text that indicates how the reader is expected to respond *to the characterisation of the disciples*?"

Indeed, since this study attempts to clarify issues surrounding the faith and understanding of Jesus' disciples in the narrative of the Fourth Gospel, it is a study of their characterisation.[29] Characterisation is arguably the most interesting element of the story. In fact, for Culpepper "Much of the power of the Fourth Gospel comes from its vivid characterizations and their effects upon the reader."[30] It is all the more surprising that this area of narrative analysis has not produced a larger array of studies on the Fourth Gospel's characters. Nevertheless, since Culpepper's section of his *Anatomy* on the topic,[31] one that is still of much use and continues to influence new generations of Johannine scholars, several studies have made a significant impact in the field, laying the groundwork for further research in the area. These are best represented by Beck's *The Discipleship Paradigm* and Conway's *Men and Women in the Fourth Gospel.*[32]

---

[28] See discussion in Powell, *Narrative Criticism*, 19–21.

[29] On characterisation in literature, see especially E. M. Forster, *Aspects of the Novel* (San Diego, CA/New York, NY/London: Harcourt, Inc., 1955), 43–82; W. J. Harvey, *Character and the Novel* (Ithaca, NY: Cornell University Press, 1965); Chatman, *Story*, 96–145; T. Docherty, *Reading (Absent) Character: Towards a Theory of Characterization in Fiction* (Oxford: Clarendon, 1983); B. Hochman, *Character in Literature* (Ithaca, NY/London: Cornell University Press, 1985); J. Phelan, *Reading People, Reading Plots: Character, Progression, and the Interpretation of Narrative* (Chicago, IL/London: University of Chicago Press, 1989); S. Bar-Efrat, *Narrative Art in the Bible*, BLS 17 (Sheffield: Almond, 1989), 48–92; On characterisation in biblical literature, see D. Rhoads and K. Syreeni, eds., *Characterization in the Gospels: Reconceiving Narrative Criticism*, JSNTSup, vol. 184 (Sheffield: Sheffield Academic Press, 1999); P. Létourneau and M. Talbot, eds., *Et vous, qui dites-vous que je suis? La gestion des personnages dans les récits bibliques*, SBib, vol. 16 (Montréal/Paris: Médiaspaul, 2006); or E. S. Malbon and A. Berlin, eds., *Characterization in Biblical Literature*, Semeia, vol. 63 (Atlanta, GA: Scholars Press, 1993).

[30] Culpepper, *Anatomy*, 7.

[31] Culpepper, *Anatomy*, 99–148.

[32] D. R. Beck, *The Discipleship Paradigm: Readers and Anonymous Characters in the Fourth Gospel*, BibIntS 27 (Leiden/New York, NY: Brill, 1997); C. M. Conway, *Men and Women in the Fourth Gospel. Gender and Johannine Characterization*, SBLDS 167 (Atlanta, GA: SBL, 1999). In addition to these, particularly relevant to the present study are N. R. Petersen, *The Gospel of John and the Sociology of Light. Language and Characterization in the Fourth Gospel* (Valley Forge, PA: Trinity Press International, 1993); A. Fehribach, *The Women in the Life of the Bridegroom: A Feminist Historical-Literary Analysis of the Female Characters in the Fourth Gospel* (Collegeville, MN: Liturgical Press, 1998); M. M. Beirne, *Women and Men in the Fourth Gospel. A Genuine Discipleship of Equals*, JSNTSup 242 (Sheffield: Sheffield Academic Press, 2003); A. Marchadour, *Les personnages dans l'évangile de Jean: miroir pour une christologie narrative*, Lire la Bible 139 (Paris: Cerf, 2004); B. B. Blaine Jr., *Peter in the Gospel of John: The Making of an Authentic Disciple*, AcaBib 27 (Atlanta, GA: SBL, 2007).

It should also be added that two books were released after the completion of this monograph, so that interaction with them was impossible: Bennema's *Encountering Jesus*, and Hylen's *Imperfect Believers*.[33]

In a narrative work, implied readers learn about characters primarily through discovering their role in the plot. In the fourth chapter of the study, on the basis of the conclusions reached in its two preceding chapters, the relationship between plot and characterisation will be discussed thoroughly, but at this point Abrams' definition of 'plot' may already prove useful. For Abrams, "the plot in a dramatic work is the structure of its actions, as these are ordered and rendered toward achieving particular emotional and artistic effects."[34] Consequently, characterisation emerges in the web of events and relationships that make up the plot. The implied author may reveal, define, and shape character by a variety of means that are best categorised as 'showing' and 'telling.' Within these categories, what characters do or what they say reflect the showing aspect, while comments made about them by the narrator (also called 'inside views'[35]) or by other characters in the story reflect the telling aspect.[36] It follows that showing may be less precise or reliable than telling.[37]

Most Johannine scholars agree that the narrator of the Fourth Gospel speaks from the ideological and temporal (in this case, retrospective) vantage point of the Johannine community, as evidenced through the use of "we" language in 1:14, 16 and 21:24. As such, his evaluative point of view is not impartial. In fact, it has been proposed that one of his roles in the narrative is to "prejudice the reader toward or away from certain characters, claims, or events and their implication."[38] Yet, such a narrator is clearly meant to be trusted for he "is established not only as omniscient and omnicommunicative but also entirely *reliable*."[39] The narrator generally speaks in the third person, which

---

[33] C. Bennema, *Encountering Jesus: Character Studies in the Gospel of John* (Milton Keynes/Colorado Springs, CO/Hyderabad: Paternoster, 2009); S. E. Hylen, *Imperfect Believers: Ambiguous Characters in the Gospel of John* (Louisville, KY: Westminster John Knox, 2009).

[34] M. H. Abrams, *A Glossary of Literary Terms*, 3rd ed. (New York, NY: Holt, Rinehart and Winston, Inc., 1971), 127.

[35] Culpepper, *Anatomy*, 22–25, provides a list of these in the Fourth Gospel.

[36] On this terminology, see Booth, *Fiction*, 3–20; Powell, *Narrative Criticism*, 52–53.

[37] Powell, *Narrative Criticism*, 52: "The reader must work harder, collecting data from various sources and evaluating it in order to figure out the implied author's view of the character. One must consider the reliability of the character whose point of view is presented."

[38] Culpepper, *Anatomy*, 32.

[39] Culpepper, *Anatomy*, 32 (italics original). Culpepper further explains that "The reliability of the narrator (as defined by Booth and used as a technical term by literary critics) must be kept distinct from both the historical accuracy of the narrator's account and the 'truth' of his ideological point of view" (p. 32). A similar statement may be proposed regarding the vantage point of the so-called Johannine community. As used in a narrative analysis, such a designation does not refer to any historical community, but to a literary construct. On this aspect of the narrative, see also Davies, *Rhetoric*, 31–38.

emphasises the sense that he bears the voice of an observer, but as omniscient, he is able to give readers inside (or psychological) views of characters such as Jesus (6:61, 64; 13:11; 16:19), and the disciples (2:11; 2:17; 2:22; 12:16; 20:9; 21:4).[40] As the references just given illustrate, this omniscience is particularly important for the present study, which focuses on internal dispositions such as belief and understanding.[41] Because of the narrator's ability to give inside views of characters, he does not have to suggest them merely from their actions and behaviour. His omniscience, moreover, is not limited to what characters could have known, and as such he is able to provide readers with what none of the characters in the story would have been able to convey. In this sense, he is "free to tell the reader whatever is vital for the progress of the story."[42] Yet, part of the difficulty in the interpretative task is that "the narrator does not make profound or prolonged plunges into any of the characters."[43] Since he is not interested in exploring or detailing the exact state of mind or the psychological phenomena experienced by the characters, including Jesus' disciples, the present study's exegesis will necessarily entail many deductions and conjectures from the narrative's telling and showing aspects of the disciples' characterisation.

Such an observation should lead narrative analysts to humility in their task and in the conclusions they reach. Yet, the Fourth Gospel does not encourage bystanders but, in the words of O'Day, it invites "readers to enter into the revelatory dynamic themselves."[44] In fact, the narrative indicates that readers are being led to make a judgement of their own on the issues at stake in the narrative.[45] As such they are meant to be neither neutral nor detached observers, but have to make up their own minds while being involved, included, and guided, as they are, within the narrative. Regarding characterisation proper in the Fourth Gospel, Lincoln asserts that readers

[…] are judges who assess the attitudes and actions of all characters […]. They are judges who are expected to be familiar with the basic facts of this case and to be in sympathy with the stance and witness of its main character.[46]

---

[40] G. Genette, *Figures III* (Paris: Seuil, 1972), 203–211, speaks of "focalisation interne" (as opposed to "focalisation externe" and "focalisation zéro") when the narrator orientates readers to the internality of characters.

[41] Culpepper, *Anatomy*, 23. It is also of interest for the present study that very few of these inside views are of *individual* disciples. Rather, with the exception of Judas (12:4, 6, 18:2) and the Beloved Disciple (20:8), these inside views are about the *group* of the disciples.

[42] Culpepper, *Anatomy*, 26. See also Davies, *Rhetoric*, 31.

[43] Culpepper, *Anatomy*, 24, continues: "Most of the comments are aesthetically or rhetorically motivated; they involve disclosures which establish characters and explain responses."

[44] O'Day, *Revelation*, 95.

[45] A. T. Lincoln, *Truth on Trial: The Lawsuit Motif in the Fourth Gospel* (Peabody, MA: Hendrickson, 2000), 173, quotes Aristotle: "The object of rhetoric is judgment [κρίσις]," and "he who has to be persuaded is a judge."

[46] Lincoln, *Truth*, 174.

This, in essence, is the genius of the Fourth Gospel's rhetoric: its readers are jurors who have already come to a basic conclusion on the issues at stake,[47] but who are invited to revisit the issues throughout the narrative, with the goal of confirming and strengthening their initial conclusion, all the while setting aside any potentially defective judgment.

The present study, then, is concerned with the manner in which the Fourth Gospel's implied author fashioned the characters of the disciples, focusing on the particular aspects of their portrayals that are their faith and understanding. What this study seeks to clarify is the implied author's ideological and temporal points of view on the disciples' faith and understanding. Further, it seeks to understand *why* the implied author chose to portray these features in the way he does, that is, what rhetorical strategy produced this characterisation. To put it another way: What are implied readers supposed to gain from interacting textually with the Fourth Gospel's disciples? To that end, the key questions this study seeks to address regarding the disciples' characterisation are the following:

– How does the implied author's evaluative point of view shape the presentation of the disciples' faith and understanding in the Fourth Gospel's narrative?
– How does the presentation of the disciples' faith and understanding function rhetorically within the narrative of the Fourth Gospel?
– How does the implied author's temporal perspective shape the presentation of the disciples' faith and understanding?

The study will proceed in the following manner. After this introductory chapter, the second and third chapters constitute the bulk of the study. They will approach the disciples' faith and understanding in two complementary ways. Chapter 2 will investigate the overall development of the faith of the disciples *as a group* in the sequence of the entire narrative. In turn, chapter 3 will sequentially analyse the faith and understanding of key *individual* disciples in the order in which they appear in the narrative: Peter, Judas, Thomas, the Beloved Disciple, and Mary Magdalene.

These two chapters will complement each other, as comparisons will be possible between the group of the disciples and key representatives of this group. For instance, such comparisons will demonstrate whether issues faced by individual disciples mirror the issues experienced by the group as a whole or whether they are unrelated. Inevitably, the group of the disciples reveal aspects of the faith and understanding that the entire group experienced and struggled with, while individual disciples display more personal aspects of experience and struggle. Thus, the group of disciples and individual disciples may not

---

[47] See chapter 4 for an expanded explanation of this statement.

function in the same way throughout the narrative. The manner in which implied readers are to respond to either the group or each of the individual disciples is not necessarily similar; different shades of responses may be expected from them.

The five individual disciples were selected because they appear at different times of the story, so that developments in their faith and understanding may potentially be noted. Moreover, they display particularly important aspects of faith and understanding, especially, though not exclusively, in relation to Jesus' resurrection. For instance, Thomas is well known for his reluctance to believe the testimony of his fellow disciples regarding Jesus' resurrection, and Peter for both his inspiring confession of faith in 6:69 and for his lapses, especially his threefold denial of Jesus, followed by his 'reinstatement' after the resurrection. In this light, the choice of Judas in a study related to issues of faith and understanding may appear odd. Though he appears several times in the course of the narrative, he is never said to believe, and indeed, disappears from the narrative before the resurrection. Yet, Judas is clearly identified as one of Jesus' disciples (6:70–71), and his characterisation will prove particularly helpful in illustrating the dramatic differences between his own experience and that of the disciples who do believe and seek to follow Jesus during his earthly ministry, albeit imperfectly. Likewise, Mary Magdalene is not always thought of as one of Jesus' disciples. But this common understanding of what is a disciple results more from a knowledge of the Synoptic tradition and its listings of the twelve male apostles than from the Fourth Gospel proper. As will be argued in the beginning of the first chapter, the title "the Twelve" appears only 4 times in the narrative of the Fourth Gospel and does not play a prominent role. The term "disciples" (μαθηταί), however, is used almost 60 times in the Gospel, so that the Twelve may be thought of as a group distinct from, but included in, the overall group of Jesus' disciples. Mary Magdalene is certainly to be considered a member of this larger group of disciples. Her encounter with the risen Jesus in the garden, moreover, will prove particularly beneficial in delineating issues of faith and understanding both before and after Jesus' resurrection. Surely, this is not an exclusive list: other characters in the story could have been studied as well. For instance, it might have been beneficial to analyse the characterisation of Nicodemus (3:1–21; 7:43–52; 19:38–42), the Samaritan woman (4:4–42), or the man born blind (9:1–38). Yet, these characters, who come to faith in Jesus in the story, can hardly be called "disciples" since they do not appear to follow Jesus during his earthly ministry. Moreover, the Samaritan woman and the man born blind receive significant narrative space, but their characterisation is each limited to only one section of the narrative, so that an analysis of the development of their faith and understanding throughout the narrative could not be undertaken. Finally, none of these characters appear after Jesus' resurrection, so that the impact the resurrection had upon their faith and understanding in the story cannot be noticed. For these reasons, it was thought best to leave them out of the thorough analysis of individual characters.

To study the disciples' faith and understanding in the *sequence* of the narrative was considered necessary in order to note the development, changes, and struggles (*e.g.* misunderstandings, doubts) they experienced regarding the person of Jesus, his message and his mission.[48] Such analysis can be done on its own, but a study of the contrasts between the disciples' and other characters' attitudes towards Jesus will also prove useful. How do the disciples, as a group or as individuals, appear in relation to other characters in this or other scenes of the Gospel? The goal of this narrative analysis is to provide an overview of the author's treatment of the disciples' faith, and thus to clarify the nature of such a faith both leading up to Jesus' resurrection and following it. Therefore, in each of the episodes being analysed, an appreciation of the nature or state of the disciples' faith and understanding will be given, as well as an evaluation of the way their characterisation contributes to meaning in the narrative as a whole. Finally, focus will be maintained on potential patterns of presentation in the characterisation of the disciples' faith and understanding, since these patterns may prove relevant to an appreciation of the implied author's rhetorical intentions.

Following these two chapters, chapter 4 stands as an extended reflection on the issues raised by the findings of its two preceding chapters. It is in this chapter that answers to the three literary questions posed above will be proposed. Thus, based on the findings of chapters 2 and 3, chapter 4 will suggest first a way to understand the plot and the purpose of the Fourth Gospel's narrative, together with the manner in which the characterisation of the disciples fits and serves both the plot and the purpose. In turn, this will lead into a more precise formulation of the rhetorical function of the disciples' faith and understanding in the Fourth Gospel, and into a discussion on the temporality (narrative time) of this narrative.

Thus, the decision was made to deal with the narrative analysis of the text before laying down literary reflections regarding the relationship of the plot with characterisation, the rhetorical functions of characterisation, or aspects of temporality in narratives. Yet, although a narrative analysis is performed first in this study, this is neither the only way to proceed, nor does it reflect exactly how the reading of the Fourth Gospel's narrative advanced for this interpreter in the course of his research. This study does not make the claim to have come at the narrative by means of an objective critical description, and then to have moved

---

[48] In other words, this sequential analysis is not an attempt to read the text naïvely, as a first time reader. Arguably, such a naïve reading is impossible for those who have already read this Gospel numerous times. Thus, this study is a *critical* reading, an engagement with the text from a research standpoint, seeking deeper comprehension of the text. On the process of reading, see especially P. Ricoeur, *Interpretation Theory: Discourse and the Surplus of Meaning* (Fort Worth, TX: Texas Christian University Press, 1976), 71–88.

on to the application of these findings. Rather, as research was conducted on the topic at hand, questions and prior research related to literary theory, characterisation theory, or narrative time were continually in the background and influenced in varied ways the findings of the second and third chapters. It is nonetheless preferable to await chapter 4 to draw conclusions related to these matters, since they will therefore benefit from the surer foundation of narrative analysis of the disciples' faith and understanding.

Finally, chapter 5 constitutes the conclusion of this study. It is an attempt to move from narrative analysis to more explicitly theological questions. Using Bultmann's numerous works on the Fourth Gospel, it will dialogue with his conclusions to answer the basic question: what is the relationship between faith and understanding according to the Fourth Gospel?

Chapter 2

The Faith and Understanding of the Disciples as a Group in the Sequence of the Fourth Gospel's Narrative

Introduction

The disciples of Jesus in the Fourth Gospel are part of a narrative that is inextricably linked with the person and activity of the protagonist, Jesus. In the Fourth Gospel, the disciples very seldom appear by themselves, and when they do, Jesus is still somehow present since he is the focal point of the decisions they make and interactions they have.[1] It is through the disciples' relationship, discussions, and involvement with Jesus that readers learn to know them. Indeed, if they are an interesting topic of inquiry, it is because of their multi-faceted relationship to the one protagonist Jesus. This, of course, is not to say that the disciples are insignificant characters in the Fourth Gospel. On the contrary, the simple fact that they accompany Jesus throughout the whole of his earthly ministry, that they participate in his work (*e.g.* 4:2, 38; 6:12–13) and that the risen Jesus appears to them in order to commission them (20:19–23), strongly suggest that the disciples are much more than mere background characters.[2]

Since in this monograph it is proposed to study the faith and understanding of the disciples in the Fourth Gospel, several introductory notes on the characters examined are necessary. The term μαθητής occurs 78 times in the Fourth Gospel, more than in each of the Synoptic Gospels (Matthew: 73, Mark: 46, and Luke: 37). The plural μαθηταί is applied to the followers of Jesus 59 times in the Gospel (32 times in chapters 1–12, and 27 times in chapters 13–21), and the singular μαθητής appears 15 times (exclusively in chapters 18–21), and essentially referring to the Beloved Disciple.[3] This high frequency does not

---

[1] Even though the present study will focus on the faith and understanding of the disciples, we do not agree with J. Zumstein, *L'apprentissage de la foi. À la découverte de l'évangile de Jean et de ses lecteurs* (Poliez-le-Grand: Moulin, 1993), 58–60, for whom the plot of the Fourth Gospel is not first about the destiny of the protagonist Jesus, but about the motif of faith, through the different faces 'faith' has in the narratives. However, we do agree that the theme of faith is inextricably linked to the plot of the Fourth Gospel and its three-stage movement centred on Jesus (commission, complication, resolution). See Lincoln, *Truth*, 19: "What moves the plot along is how [Jesus] achieves his goal and the responses to him as he does so."

[2] Köstenberger, *Missions*, 145.

[3] The remaining four uses of the term μαθητής in the Fourth Gospel refer not to Jesus' followers but to John's disciples (1:35, 37; 3:25) and to "the Jews" claiming to be Moses' disciples (9:28).

necessarily mean that this notion is more important for the Fourth Gospel than for the other Gospels, but it does require one to treat these recurring terms with care. Who are the disciples for the Fourth Gospel? What is the relationship between Jesus' disciples and "the Twelve?" Does the term refer to a group larger than the characters described as having walked with and followed Jesus during his earthly ministry?

Most modern readers of the Fourth Gospel, no doubt influenced by the Synoptic Gospels' accounts and by two thousand years of tradition, inevitably think of Jesus' disciples as the twelve apostles. But in John, the expression "the Twelve" occurs very infrequently (6:67, 70, 71; 20:24) and the word "apostle," found only once in 13:16, does not carry the connotations that the term has in the Synoptic Gospels or in Acts.[4] In fact, nothing is said about the formation of the circle of "the Twelve" and readers need to wait until 6:67, 70–71 before this group is explicitly mentioned. Since "the Twelve" are mentioned without explanation of their exact identity (though several names are mentioned in connection with the term: Peter and Judas in 6:67–71, and Thomas in 20:24), it is likely that the author of the Fourth Gospel assumed that readers were already acquainted with the identity of "the Twelve," possibly through knowledge of one or more Synoptic Gospels.[5] It is also likely that "the author of the Fourth Gospel was concerned to identify specific followers or to refer to the 'disciples' generally, but not to give an important place to 'the Twelve' as such."[6] In the same vein, Köstenberger warns against overstating the importance of "the Twelve" in the Fourth Gospel's narrative:

The inclusion of these passages [*i.e.* 6:67–71; 20:24] in the Fourth Gospel indicates that the Fourth Evangelist recognised the historical configuration of twelve disciples who were especially chosen by Jesus (cf. 6:70). Nevertheless, in light of the scarcity of the expression in John's Gospel, care should be taken not to place an undue emphasis on the Johannine characterization of the twelve. Rather, it appears that John's Gospel, being a Gospel, assumes this important part of the tradition and refers to it incidentally without pursuing any elaborate literary strategies of characterization.[7]

Köstenberger is correct, but in no way should this restrain readers from seeing "the Twelve" as a group distinct from, though included in, the group of Jesus' disciples. What transpires from the Fourth Gospel are both that "the Twelve" are part of a larger group of disciples (a proposition which 6:66–67 favours),

---

[4] Collins, *These Things*, 69, believes that "to speak of the twelve apostles or Jesus' twelve disciples is a manner of speaking that is foreign to the tradition of the Fourth Gospel."

[5] Collins, *These Things*, 85. Collins simply thinks of 'the Twelve' as an element of the tradition with which John had to deal. See also R. Bauckham, "John for Readers of Mark," in *The Gospels for All Christians: Rethinking the Gospel Audiences*, ed. by R. Bauckham (Edinburgh/ Grand Rapids, MI: T. & T. Clark/Eerdmans, 1998), 167; and A. T. Lincoln, *The Gospel according to Saint John*, BNTC 4 (Peabody, MA/London: Hendrickson/Continuum, 2005), 26–39.

[6] Hillmer, "Discipleship," 80.

[7] Köstenberger, *Missions*, 147.

and therefore that "*hoi mathetai* are not simply equivalent of *hoi dodeka*, the Twelve."[8]

Since the term μαθητής is not restricted to "the Twelve" in the Fourth Gospel, the exact identity of Jesus' μαθηταί is at times ambiguous. For instance, in 4:1, we read that Jesus was baptizing "more disciples than John," and in 6:60, 66, "many of his disciples" were scandalized and ceased to accompany him. This last group is explicitly distinguished from "the Twelve" and could possibly be identified with "the crowd" (6:2), a group of adherents (7:3), or more naturally a group which, up to this point in the narrative, was considered to be comprised of followers of Jesus. Whether they were part of an inner-circle or of a larger group of followers, it is difficult to assess. By considering how and with whom the disciples are contrasted in the Fourth Gospel, their identity may become clearer.[9] For instance, Jesus' disciples are portrayed as different from the followers of John the Baptist (1:36–51), "the Jews" (esp. in 9:22; 12:42; and 16:2, that is, the instances where the Gospel refers to the removal of believers from the synagogue), "the world" (esp. 8:23; 17:14), and "the crowd" (6:2, 5, 22, 24, 7:12, 31, 40–43; 11:42, 12:9, 12, 17–18, 29, 43). But if this contrasting of the disciples with other characters allows one not to confuse them, the fact remains that the exact identity of the disciples is never clearly defined in the Gospel.

The terms μαθητής and μαθηταί thus refer to different characters in the Fourth Gospel. At times, they appear to refer to characters belonging to Jesus' inner circle (2:2, 11, 17, 22; 3:22; 4:2, 8, 27, 31; 6:3, 8, 12, 16, 22, 24; 9:2; 11:7, 8, 12, 54, 12:4, 16; 13:5, 22, 23; 16:17, 29; 18:1, 2; 19:26; 20:18, 19; 20:25, 26) or to a larger group of followers (4:1; 60:60, 61, 66; 7:3; 9:27, 28; 18:17, 19, 25; 19:38). But other referents of the term are more difficult to assess (18:15, 17, 25; 20:2, 3, 4, 30).[10] For Schnackenburg, the reason for such vagueness in the use of these terms is that "the concept has already been used, extended and

---

[8] C. Brown, ed., *The New International Dictionary of New Testament Theology*, 4 vols (Grand Rapids, MI: Zondervan, 1976), s.v. "Disciple" by W. Bauder, 1:487. J. J. Gunther, "The Relation of the Beloved Disciple to the Twelve," *TZ* 37/3 (1981): 142, suggests, in the same vein, that the Beloved Disciple was "a member of both the Twelve and another group, such as his family and their friends."

[9] See also R. E. Brown, *The Community of the Beloved Disciple: The Life, Loves, and Hates of an Individual Church in the New Testament* (New York, NY/Mahwah, NJ: Paulist Press, 1979), 59–91.

[10] Another classification is that of Marchadour, *Personnages*, 207–13, who proposes that the term 'disciple' has these diverse senses in the narrative of the Fourth Gospel: the sociological disciples (when the term is used in a relatively neuter sense), the disciples in formation (those who are beneficiaries of Jesus' pedagogy), the reticent disciples (those who are reluctant to engage with Jesus' teaching), the individual vocations (when the individual disciples are addressed in the narrative with the second person singular), the believing disciples (the post-resurrection disciples who believe), and the true disciple (namely, the Beloved Disciple).

applied to a new situation,"[11] such as in 8:31: "If you continue in my word, you are truly my disciples."[12] For Schnackenburg, while this statement is applied to Jews who have believed in Jesus in the narrative, it is also a statement made to the Christian readers of the gospel, that is, later believers.[13] Whether this is the primary reason for such 'vagueness' on the part of the Fourth Evangelist remains to be seen. At this point, however, suffice it to say that even though the Fourth Gospel does not contain a list of names or any clear description of those who belong to Jesus' inner circle, it is this particular group, including "the Twelve," which will be the subject of the following inquiry.[14] It should also be noted that the following enquiry will not focus only on passages where the terms μαθητής and μαθηταί appear,[15] since the disciples are at times present and active in the narrative even when these terms are not mentioned.[16]

There is no real consensus on a structure for the Fourth Gospel, but space does not permit that we engage in the debate about its structural analysis. Therefore, Brown's classic structure will be used as a framework for the analysis of the faith and understanding of the disciples in the sequence of the Fourth Gospel's narrative.[17]

---

[11] Schnackenburg, *John*, 3:206.

[12] Unless otherwise noted, the Bible translation used in this study is the English Standard Version (ESV).

[13] Schnackenburg, *John*, 3:206–9. For him, there are possibly three different referents to the term μαθητής in the Fourth Gospel: Jesus' close companions, his (serious) adherents, and later believers. On the widening of the term μαθητής in the Fourth Gospel, see also Köstenberger, *Missions*, 149–53, esp. 150: "However, as has been argued, the twelve, as well as the μαθηταί of John's Gospel in general, besides retaining their historical point of reference, also function as representatives of Jesus' messianic community."

[14] Marchadour, *Personnages*, 207, speaks of this group as "la troupe de Jésus."

[15] This would be the approach of Gloer, "Come and See," 269–301.

[16] For instance, the terms do not appear in chapters 10, 14, and 17, but these chapters are arguably all about the disciples or discipleship. It is also important to study the prologue, which does not explicitly mention the disciples, but which, as will be seen shortly, contains relevant data for the present study.

[17] Brown, *John*, 1:CXXXVIII–CXLIV and 2:541–42. Such a structure appears to us adequate in its simplicity and respect for basic pericopes (such as 2:1–4:54). It should be noted that Segovia, "Peace," 79–80, sees the characterisation of the disciples as progressing in four basic stages throughout the Fourth Gospel: (*Stage 1*) the gathering of the elect and the initial incomprehension of "the world" (John 1–3); (*Stage 2*) the elect on "the way" and the growing rejection of "the world" (John 4–12); (*Stage 3*) the farewell to the elect and the exclusion of "the world" (John 13–14); (*Stage 4*) the vindication of the elect and the judgment of "the world" (John 18–20). Segovia, however, does not treat the Gospel as it presently stands, but according to his reconstruction of an earlier, unrevised version of the Fourth Gospel. Because of this perspective, he leaves out several important passages in which Jesus is addressing the disciples directly (*e.g.* 13:1b–3, 12:20, 34–35; 15–17; 21). Since the publication of that article, Segovia has manifested a shift in his methodological approach to the Fourth Gospel and has studied it from a literary perspective. See F. F. Segovia, "The Journey(s) of the Word: A Reading of the Plot of the Fourth Gospel," *Semeia* 53 (1991): 23–54 and F. F. Segovia, "The Final Farewell of Jesus: A Reading in John 20:30–21:25," *Semeia* 53 (1991): 167–90.

A. The Prologue: 1:1–18

B. The Book of Signs: 1:19–12:50
    1.   The Opening Days and the Revelation of Jesus (1:19–1:51)
    2.   From Cana to Cana (2:1–4:54)
    3.   Jesus and the Principal Feasts of the Jews (5:1–10:42)
    4.   Jesus Moves Toward the Hour of Death and Glory (11:1–12:50)

C. The Book of Glory: 13:1–20:31
    1.   The Last Supper (13:1–17:26)
    2.   The Passion Narrative (18:1–19:42)
    3.   The Risen Jesus (20:1–29)
    4.   Conclusion (20:30–31)

D. The Epilogue: 21:1–25

As will become clear, the issues of belief and understanding play an important role in the characterisation of the group of Jesus' disciples. The following sections will therefore study Jesus' disciples by analysing the implied author's perspective on their faith and understanding throughout the narrative

A. The Prologue: 1:1–18

It is generally accepted that the prologue of the Fourth Gospel was designed to enable readers to understand the message of the Gospel.[18] Narrative analysts have also shown that in these eighteen verses the author plainly presents his perspective on the person of Jesus by disclosing his identity, his origin, and his role. Readers are therefore given necessary christological elements needed to understand the subsequent story. They are 'in the know,' and have a positive impression of Jesus. In being taken into the confidence of the narrator, they are made to feel superior to those with whom Jesus will later interact and who do not share this ideological perspective.[19]

The prologue tells readers of the Word's mission, but also, in advance, of the general reception it would experience, something that is highly relevant to the present study: "He was in the world and the world was made through him, yet the world did not know him. He came to his own (εἰς τὰ ἴδια ἦλθεν), and his own people (οἱ ἴδιοι αὐτὸν) did not receive him" (1:10–11, echoed in

---

    [18] R. H. Lightfoot, *St. John's Gospel: A Commentary* (Oxford: Oxford University Press, 1963), 11.
    [19] Culpepper, *Anatomy*, 89.

12:37).[20] According to Pryor, 1:11 represents a narrowing of the scope of 1:10, so that Jesus' ἴδιοι are not humanity in general, but more precisely Israel. Pryor goes further and rightly shows that, while this conclusion is correct, the relationship between these two verses is subtler: "While it is true that there is no absolute overlap between Israel and the world, it is also clear that in many references it is Israel who is representative of the world."[21] In the next two verses, the narrator balances out the overall negative reception of the Word, even from the Word's own:

But to all who did receive him, who believed in his name, he gave the right to become children of God, who were born, not of blood nor of the will of the flesh nor of the will of man, but of God (1:12–13).

Thus, while "his own" as a whole did not receive him (1:11: οὐ παρέλαβον), some did receive him, that is, "believed in his name" (πιστεύουσιν εἰς τὸ ὄνομα αὐτοῦ). In these verses, readers of the Fourth Gospel are told what is the correct response to the Word: in order to receive the Word, one must believe in his name. In turn, such an attitude results in being given the power, right, or authority to become children of God (ἔδωκεν αὐτοῖς ἐξουσίαν τέκνα θεοῦ γενέσθαι), and to be born of God (ἐκ θεοῦ ἐγεννήθησαν).[22]

These four verses (1:10–13) have correctly been considered as a summary of the whole Gospel, so that the themes of faith and unbelief as opposite responses to the Word play a significance role throughout the narrative.[23] Clearly, both believers and unbelievers are introduced in these four verses of the prologue, and the implied readership is encouraged to read the rest of the narrative with these two opposite responses in mind. This, for Barus, is the first step toward the characterisation of the Fourth Gospel: the characters of the narrative will either be representatives of belief or unbelief.[24] Therefore, even though the disciples are not explicitly mentioned in the prologue, the perspective of the two opposite categories of responses to Jesus sets the ground for implied readers

---

[20] As W. Carter, "The Prologue and John's Gospel: Function, Symbol and Definitive Word," *JSNT* 39 (1990): 39, mentions: "The negative response is first stated in v. 5 in the image of darkness (σκοτία antithetical to φῶς), and the verb κατέλαβεν."

[21] J. W. Pryor, "Jesus and Israel in the Fourth Gospel-John 1.11," *NovT* 32 (1990): 218 (see, for instance, 7:1, 7; 8:23; 9:39).

[22] For a theological discussion on this verse, see H. N. Ridderbos, *The Gospel of John: A Theological Commentary*, trans. by J. Vriend (Grand Rapids, MI: Eerdmans, 1997), 46–48; and D. A. Carson, *The Gospel according to John*, PNTC (Leicester/Grand Rapids, MI: Apollos/ Eerdmans, 1991), 126, 181–82.

[23] Culpepper, *Anatomy*, 87. For Lincoln, *John*, 102, 1:11 previews the first half of the narrative (1:19–12:50) where Jesus receives a predominantly hostile response from the nation's leaders, and 1:12–13 previews the second part of the narrative (13:1–17:26), where Jesus is portrayed with those who did receive him and who are called "his own" (13:1).

[24] Barus, "Faith", 61. Against this view, see C. M. Conway, "Speaking Through Ambiguity: Minor Characters in the Fourth Gospel," *BibInt* 10 (2002): 324–41, and for an assessment of these positions, see chapter 4 below.

to assess their later appearances. Implied readers will necessarily ask if they should consider the disciples in the narrative to be on the side of those who did not receive Jesus, or on the side of those who received him. In subsequent chapters, it will become apparent that deciding on which side of the divide they fall is not necessarily easy, but the prologue at least sets the stage for the question to be asked regarding the characters of the disciples as well as any other character encountered throughout the narrative.

Another character mentioned in the Prologue, John, is characterised by his witnessing activity. Sent by God, he bears witness to the "light," so that all may believe through him (1:6–7). The narrator quickly cautions the readers not to identify John with the protagonist, Jesus: "He was not the light, but came to bear witness about the light" (1:8). Just as the prologue sets the stage for the belief/unbelief dichotomy to be kept in mind in the narrative's presentation of its characters, the prologue also sets the stage for further mention of John in the narrative (1:35–39; 3:22–36), where his activity as a witness influences other characters to either follow Jesus or reject him. For Boismard, witness is "la fonction essentielle du Baptiste: il est venu pour rendre témoignage à un autre."[25]

Finally, note should be made of the "we" language used in 1:14, 16. For readers who were acquainted with the author(s) of the Fourth Gospel, such "we" language was not ambiguous. To modern readers, whether or not one or more disciples is to be understood as part of this "we" remains to some extent speculative, though the Beloved Disciple, if he is understood to be involved in the writing of the Fourth Gospel (as 20:24 suggests), is very probably included in it.[26] In any case, this is a retrospective view on the events of the whole Gospel narrative. Readers need to await further narration to understand when the Word's glory was seen and recognized (*e.g.* 2:11). Moreover, such language needs to be considered as a rhetorical device used by the implied author. Lincoln proposes that the "we" language in 1:14 and 16 invites readers to share the implied author's perspective in including them "as among those who have true insight into the main character of the trial [*i.e.* Jesus]."[27] As noted earlier, Lincoln claims that implied readers are therefore made to be "judges who as-

---

[25] M.-É. Boismard, *Du baptême à Cana (Jean 1:19–2:11)*, LD 18 (Paris: Cerf, 1956), 26.

[26] Carson, *John*, 128, may be overly confident in his affirmation: "In the context of the incarnation, the *we* who saw the Word's glory must refer to the evangelist and other Christians who actually saw Jesus in the days of his earthly life." On this, we appreciate Culpepper, *Anatomy*, 213: "In 1:14, in the phrase 'and he dwelt among us,' the word 'us' may be a reference to mankind in general, a group of eyewitnesses, or a community within which there are some who saw 'the Word.' The 'we' which follows is not necessarily coterminous with the previous 'us.' Furthermore, it may or may not include the readers. The readers may or may not be part of the group for which the narrator speaks, but they at least know the narrator (evangelist) and the group he represents."

[27] Lincoln, *Truth*, 172.

sess the attitudes and actions of all characters [...]. They are judges who are expected to be familiar with the basic facts of this case [*i.e.* the trial] and to be in sympathy with the stance and witness of its main character."[28] While implied readers may, potentially, still have to make up their own mind on the issue at stake (mainly, the identity of Jesus), they are already involved in the narrative and sympathetic not only to the protagonist, but also to the characters who will later receive him by believing. In addition, Lincoln's point fits well with the view that 1:10–13 encourages implied readers to pose the question of whether or not the characters encountered in the narrative have received Jesus. Through the prologue of the Fourth Gospel, readers are not only introduced to the person of the Word, but also given interpretive clues on the characters who will later appear in the narrative.

Narrative analysts have given much attention to the beginnings of stories, and Gospels' beginnings in particular, for the important functions they fulfill.[29] The beginnings of narratives can give a great deal of information to readers by introducing characters, issues, and problems, and by raising questions which the remaining narrative will answer or resolve. In so doing, beginnings of narratives have a primacy effect in constituting a hermeneutical frame which readers need to understand the remaining narrative, and which inevitably shapes or influences their interpretation of the narrative.[30] It appears that the Fourth Gospel's prologue is no exception to this rule.

B. The Book of Signs: 1:19–12:50

1. The Opening Days and the Revelation of Jesus (1:19–1:51)

The first appearance of Jesus' disciples will come in this section. However, the first disciples mentioned are not Jesus', but John's (1:35, 37). There, two of John's disciples hear him proclaim, upon the sight of Jesus walking by

---

[28] Lincoln, *Truth*, 174.

[29] See, for instance, Genette, *Figure III*, 77–121; M. C. Parsons, "Reading a Beginning/ Beginning a Reading: Tracing Literary Theory on Narrative Openings," *Semeia* 52 (1990): 11–31; W. H. Kelber, "The Birth of a Beginning," *Semeia* 52 (1990): 121–44; R. C. Tannehill, "Beginning to Study 'How Gospels Begin'," *Semeia* 52 (1990): 185–92.

[30] On the meaning of 'primacy effect,' see the discussion in Chennattu, *Discipleship*, 23, n.125, who uses the explanation given by M. Perry, "Literary Dynamics: How the Order of a Text Creates Its Meanings," *PT* 1 (1979): 35–64. For Perry, the 'primacy effect' is the tendency of what comes first in the story to control readers' understanding of what follows and 'recency effect' is the tendency of the most recently read to influence readers' understanding. Relevant to this area of study is the concept of 'exposition.' See Chatman, *Story*, 67, for whom the concept of an exposition's function is "to provide necessary information concerning characters and events existing before the action proper of a story begins. Its emphasis is strongly explanatory. Exposition is traditionally done in the summary mode. Nineteenth-century novels typically introduce such summaries in a lump at the very outset (characteristically in the perfect tense)."

"Behold, the Lamb of God!,"and immediately begin to follow (ἀκολουθέω) Jesus.[31] The witnessing activity of John, mentioned in the prologue (1:7), is here illustrated with positive results.

John had already used the title "Lamb of God" to speak of Jesus, even adding "who takes away the sin of the world" (1:29), and such a title seems to have been John's title of choice for Jesus.[32] Although the two disciples could not have foreseen the death of Christ on the cross, and although it is impossible to know exactly what the disciples understood by such a title at this time in the narrative, contemporary Judaism interpreted "Lamb of God" either as a substitutionary offering for sin (*cf.* Is. 53:5) or as the apocalyptic warrior lamb who would bring judgment (1 Enoch 90:9–12; T. Jos. 19:8; T. Ben. 3:8).[33] As will shortly become clear, these two disciples saw in Jesus the expected Messiah (1:41).

Noticing that these two were following him, Jesus speaks for the first time in the Fourth Gospel, posing them a question: "what are you seeking?" (Τί ζητεῖτε – 1:38). Though the words of Jesus could have two meanings, implied readers cannot miss the force of this 'existential' question.[34] Beneath the surface, it challenges the disciples as well as the implied readers to consider what it is they are looking for. The following dialogue, too, must be understood on different levels. The disciples switch allegiance from John to Jesus in calling the latter "Rabbi" (1:38), a title that serves as an introduction to their answer (also in the form of a question to their new teacher): "where are you staying?" (ποῦ μένεις – 1:38). While the disciples probably did not mean anything more than Jesus' physical place of lodging, the Evangelist continues to introduce terms and concepts that will be developed throughout the narrative

---

[31] Even though the explicit mention of Jesus having his own disciples will only come in 2:2, readers can already consider that these two have become Jesus' disciples. Boismard, *Baptême*, 73, puts it well: "'Suivre' quelqu'un, marcher derrière lui, était synonyme de se mettre à son école, se faire son disciple. En 'suivant' le Christ, André et son compagnon font le premier pas qui va les attacher à Jésus."

[32] S. E. Porter, "Can Traditional Exegesis Enlighten Literary Analysis of the Fourth Gospel? An Examination of the Old Testament Fulfilment Motif and the Passover Theme," in *The Gospels and the Scripture of Israel*, ed. by C. A. Evans and W. R. Stegner, JSNTSup 104 (Sheffield: Sheffield Academic Press, 1994), 396–428, argues that the paschal motif is prominent throughout the Fourth Gospel.

[33] A. J. Köstenberger, *John*, BECNT (Grand Rapids, MI: Baker Academic, 2004), 66–67. See also, Brown, *John*, 1:59; Carson, *John*, 150; and H. K. Nielsen, "John's Understanding of the Death of Jesus," in *New Readings in John: Literary and Theological Perspectives. Essays from the Scandinavian Conference on the Fourth Gospel in Aarhus 1997*, ed. by J. Nissen and S. Pedersen, JSNTSuppS 182 (Sheffield: Sheffield Academic Press, 1999), 250–53, who argues that this title refers to a soteriological understanding of Jesus' death.

[34] Jesus will, after his resurrection, pose a similar question to Mary Magdalene "Who are you seeking" (20:15). Chennattu, *Discipleship*, 29: "The first words of Jesus Τί ζητεῖτε, can have two meanings: (1) the surface meaning: what do you want? (2) the deeper meaning: what are you searching/longing for? It is necessary to listen to the Fourth Gospel with both ears: one for the literal and the other for the symbolic sense."

(here, μένω).[35] Now, Jesus "officially" calls them in the form of an invitation and a promise: "come and you will see" (ἔρχομαι, ὁράω – 1:39), two terms being used in the Fourth Gospel to speak of belief.[36] It is therefore likely that Jesus, in his call to the disciples, is primarily calling them to believe in him. The disciples respond positively to Jesus' call ("so they came and saw" – 1:39), and the narrator explains that "they *stayed* with him that day, for it was about the tenth hour." Staying or abiding (μένω) is an aspect of discipleship that will receive extensive treatment in the narrative (15:1–17). Though such mention of 'abiding with Jesus' seems to be only a hint of what will be developed later in the narrative, it already introduces an important concept. Its significance, in the context of verses filled with such prominent Johannine terms, can hardly go unnoticed.

The narrator, who had kept the two disciples anonymous up to this point, chooses to introduce one of them: "Andrew, Simon Peter's brother" (1:40). The identity of the second disciple has been the subject of many inquiries and hypotheses, but no consensus has ever been reached on this issue.[37] The exact identity of such a disciple is not necessarily important for the present study, and the fact that the narrator kept him anonymous indicates that his name is not necessary for the reader's interpretation of the narrative. The character of Andrew, however, is developed, as he begins his own witnessing activity[38] in finding and telling his brother: "We have found the Messiah" (1:41). Such a testimony may shed light on the verse that just preceded it, most notably the question of what exactly Andrew and the other disciple saw as they abided with Jesus. Certainly, they saw more than Jesus' place of lodging, for it resulted in Andrew's witness about Jesus as "the Messiah." Such a title presupposes knowledge of Jesus, as though Jesus' promise in 1:39 had already been partially fulfilled.[39] Andrew

---

[35] Bultmann, *John*, 99–100: "It is essential to know where Jesus 'lives'; for in the place where Jesus is at home, the disciples will also receive his dwelling (14:2)."

[36] C. H. Dodd, *The Interpretation of the Fourth Gospel* (Cambridge: Cambridge University Press, 1953), 186. On the theme of 'coming to Jesus', see *e.g.* 3:21; 5:40; 6:35, 37, 45; and on 'seeing Jesus,' see 6:40.

[37] Some have seen in him Philip, such as Boismard, *Baptême*, 72, or J. Colson, *L'énigme du disciple que Jésus aimait* (Paris: Beauchesne, 1969), 14. However, it is difficult to agree with this identification since Philip will be introduced, apparently for the first time, in 1:43. Others have preferred to see in him the Beloved Disciple: J. H. Charlesworth, *The Beloved Disciple: Whose Witness Validates the Gospel of John* (Valley Forge, PA: Trinity, 1995), 326–30 (Charlesworth also concludes that the Beloved Disciple is Thomas); Brown, *John*, 1:73–74. But this view is also far from predominating, and has been criticized by scholars such as F. Neirynck, "The Anonymous Disciple in John 1," *ETL* 66 (1990): 5–37, who concludes: "The other disciple is still unknown and is 'sachlich und theologisch uninteressant.'"

[38] Every time Andrew is mentioned in the Fourth Gospel, he is described as witnessing about Jesus to someone (6:8; 12:22). See L. Morris, *Reflections on the Gospel of John* (Peabody, MA: Hendrickson, 2000), 43–49.

[39] Chennattu, *Discipleship*, 33.

then brings his brother Simon to Jesus, who implicitly welcomes him and gives him a new name: "Cephas (which means Peter)" (1:42).[40] Peter remains silent throughout this section, but the rapidity with which he seems to follow his brother to come to Jesus, together with Jesus' apparent acceptance and inclusion of him among his followers, implicitly indicates that Peter has found validity in Andrew's depiction of Jesus. Therefore, at the end of the day, Jesus had three disciples, each of whom, it is presumed, welcomed Jesus' invitation to believe in him and recognised in him the Messiah, the Anointed One, the Christ.

The next day (1:43), Jesus goes to Galilee and continues to gather disciples around him. He first finds Philip, who was from Bethsaida (where Andrew and Peter were also from), and ordered him to follow him: "Ἀκολούθει μοι" (1:43). Next in the narrative, Philip begins his own witnessing activity. He finds Nathanael,[41] and tells him: "We have found him of whom Moses in the law and also the prophets wrote, Jesus of Nazareth, the son of Joseph" (1:45).[42] A quite surprising announcement for somebody who has just met Jesus!

Nathanael's readiness to follow Jesus is not immediate and his response to Philip quite sarcastic: "Can anything good come out of Nazareth?"[43] The irony cannot go unnoticed,[44] but Nathanael's rhetorical question is taken as a challenge by Philip who, as a good disciple, is (already) an imitator of his rabbi:

---

[40] Chennattu, *Discipleship*, 33, sees in Jesus' words both an affirmation and a promise regarding his future mission.

[41] For Brown, *John*, 1:82, Nathanael is a symbol of Israel coming to God. On the symbolic value of Nathanael, see also T. L. Brodie, *The Gospel according to John: A Literary and Theological Commentary* (Oxford/New York, NY: Oxford University Press, 1993), 168–69, and C. K. Barrett, *The Gospel according to St. John: An Introduction with Commentary and Notes on the Greek Text*, 2nd ed. (Philadelphia, PA: Westminster, 1978), 183–84. Different traditions have identified Nathanael with other characters (*e.g.* Simon the Cananean, Bartholomew, Matthew), but with Brown, "it is better to accept the early patristic suggestions that he was not one of the Twelve" (p. 82).

[42] It should be noted how Jewish is the disciples' manner of speaking about Jesus up to this point ("Rabbi" in 1.38; "Messiah" in 1.41; and here "him of whom Moses in the law and also the prophets wrote"). For some, this means that their faith has not yet grasped the reality of the Johannine Jesus (F. J. Moloney, *Belief in the Word: Reading the Fourth Gospel, John 1–4* (Minneapolis, MN: Fortress, 1993), 53–76), but this remains to be seen.

[43] A. Destro and M. Pesce, "Kinship, Discipleship, and Movement: An Anthropological Study of John's Gospel," *BibInt* 3 (1995): 267, propose that Philip's social identification of Jesus as "Jesus of Nazareth, the son of Joseph," is the basis of Nathanael's sarcasm. Brown, *John*, 1:184, indicates that such a statement in Nathanael's mouth may express an existing rivalry between the two neighbouring towns (Nathanael comes from Cana; 21:2). See also K. E. Dewey, "Paroimiai in the Gospel of John," *Semeia* 17 (1980): 90–91. Though it may be so, a stronger case can be made for understanding Nathanael's question in the fact that Nazareth does not figure in Scriptural prophecies as a city of origin for the Messiah (see 6:42; and especially 7:41–42).

[44] Duke, *Irony*, 54–55.

Just as Jesus finds Philip, Philip finds Nathaniel. Just as Jesus wins the attention of enquirers with the enticing 'Come and see', so Philip attracts Nathaniel with the same words, 'come and see'.[45]

In these words, Philip invites Nathanael to believe, just as Jesus had invited Andrew and the other disciple to do in 1:39. In seeing Nathanael approaching, Jesus announces: "Behold, an Israelite indeed, in whom there is no deceit" (1:47).[46] Jesus addresses Nathanael as a faithful Israelite, but readers are immediately struck by the apparent arrogance of Nathanael: "How do you know me?" (1:48)! Jesus' answer, in turn, is unexpected, as he proceeds by telling him that he had seen him, under a fig tree.[47] Jesus' knowledge of this event impresses and convinces Nathanael that Jesus is indeed "the Son of God", "the King of Israel" (1:49). These identifications illustrate Nathanael's belief, as acknowledged by Jesus: "Because I said to you: 'I saw you under the fig tree,' do you believe?" (1:50). This is the first explicit mention of a character's belief in the narrative, and it comes from Jesus' mouth. However, to this assessment, but arguably without downgrading his belief, Jesus adds the promise that Nathanael as well as the other disciples[48] will witness greater things than a display of Jesus' surprising knowledge. Jesus' revelation has just begun. Soon, the disciples' faith will be based on more: "you will see heaven opened, and the angels of God ascending and descending on the Son of Man" (1:51).[49] Yet, the narrative already suggests that at least Nathanael, and certainly the other disciples as well, believe. Jesus has gathered disciples around him who have seen in him the Messiah, and have put their faith in him.[50]

---

[45] M. W. G. Stibbe, *John*, RNBC (Sheffield: JSOT Press, 1993), 41. The fact that Philip was persistent in wanting Nathanael to meet Jesus already indicates a certain degree of persuasion about Jesus' identity.

[46] Many have seen in the expression "an Israelite in whom there is no guile/deceit" a clear reference to the patriarch Jacob (see Gen. 27:35). Whatever we make of this, Jesus is here complimentary towards Nathanael who is truly without guile. This, as mentioned by B. Witherington, *John's Wisdom: A Commentary on the Fourth Gospel* (Louisville, KY: Westminster John Knox, 1995), 71, is also an "essential trait of a good witness."

[47] There has been much speculation regarding the image of the fig tree. It is important, however, not to be distracted from the major thrust of this passage: Jesus has impressed Nathanael with his knowledge of this event, and such a knowledge will play a part in the comparison in v. 50 where Jesus promises that greater things would later be seen. For further discussion, see J. Jeremias, "Die Berufung des Nathanael," *Angelos* 3 (1928): 2–5; C. F. D. Moule, "A Note on 'Under the Fig Tree' in John 1:48, 50," *JTS* 5 (1954): 210–11.

[48] The ESV, in its literalness, gives the impression that Jesus only has Nathanael in mind as he speaks to him in 1:51: "And he said to him (sg.: αὐτῷ): Truly, truly, I say to you (pl.: ὑμῖν), you will see heaven opened, and the angels of God ascending and descending on the Son of Man."

[49] J. H. Neyrey, "The Jacob Allusions in John 1:51," *CBQ* 44 (1982): 586–605, shows that 1:51 alludes to Gen. 28:12 (Jacob's ladder) and argues that it is not Jesus who is compared to Jacob, but the disciples: "[Jesus] is not seeing a vision; he is offering one" (p. 589).

[50] Segovia, "Peace," 81, puts it thus: "The promise presents two fundamental aspects: on the one hand, it points to the fact that Jesus' revelation has barely begun, that there are 'greater

To conclude this section, three comments can be made on this first appearance of the disciples in the narrative. First, it is striking how many christological confessions are given by Jesus' new disciples: the Messiah (1:41), the one written about in the Mosaic Law and in the prophets (1:45), the son of God, and the King of Israel (1:49). Though this issue will be dealt with later, the recurrence of christological confessions raises key issues: how much is the depiction of the disciples so far meant to be plausible or realistic? How much is post-resurrection faith already being attributed to the disciples? Moloney sees all these confessions as bound to the disciples' culture, history, and religion.[51] Others see in the title 'Son of God' the full Johannine christological meaning.[52] With Moloney, we agree that it is implausible that Jesus' new disciples had grasped the full Johannine meaning of these confessions at this point of the narrative, but implied readers, however, do know them and agree with the disciples. In any case, Jesus positively identified Nathanael's confession as an indication of his belief.[53] Several commentators have seen in Jesus' remark after Nathanael's confession either an indication that the disciples' faith must still be deepened,[54] or that "La reconnaissance du Messie qu'ils ont 'trouvé,' si elle est pour les disciples une avancée vers la lumière, n'est pas encore le 'voir' qui leur est promis,"[55] that is, possibly not faith at all.[56] However, while it is true that Jesus infers that the disciples' faith will be fed by other, greater things, such a qualified appreciation is not necessarily meant to denigrate their new faith. Jesus, on the contrary, could be showing his appreciation for the disciples who

---

things' yet to come; at the same time, it also makes clear that, in light of this outstanding revelation, the preceding confessions must give way to and be understood solely in terms of a further acceptance of Jesus' claim as the Father's unique representative." Yet, if more revelation is to come, it does not necessarily follow that what has already been confessed, accepted, and believed should be seen negatively. The disciples' lack of certain knowledge and understanding (which could only come later) does not qualify negatively their belief in Jesus, but calls for further and deeper knowledge and understanding. See also Brodie, *John*, 168.

[51] Moloney, *Belief*, 72–73.

[52] Brown, *John*, 1:88; S. Pancaro, *The Law in the Fourth Gospel: The Torah and the Gospel, Moses and Jesus, Judaism and Christianity according to John*, NovTSup 42 (Leiden: Brill, 1975), 288–304.

[53] *Pace* X. Léon-Dufour, *Lecture de l'évangile selon Jean*, 4 vols (Paris: Seuil, 1988–1996), 1:201; and especially Moloney, *Belief*, 73: "Instead of a blessing, Nathanael is chided for the limitations of his faith [...] Nathanael's faith, limited to what the best of Jewish hopes has produced, is the result of Jesus' supernatural knowledge." However, it does not appear that Jesus 'chides' Nathanael here. Jesus' question suggests that the basis for Nathanael's belief will be superseded.

[54] Barus, "Faith", 95.

[55] Léon-Dufour, *Lecture*, 1:201.

[56] See also J.-M. Sevrin, "Le commencement du quatrième évangile: prologue et prélude," in *La Bible en récit. L'exégèse biblique à l'heure du lecteur*, ed. by D. Marguerat, MB 48 (Genève: Labor et Fides, 2003), 345: "En fait, la confession de Nathanaël va être marquée par Jésus d'un coefficient d'inadéquation, en étant dépassée par une énigme."

barely know him but who nonetheless believe. Jesus thus receives positively their confessions, and points the disciples to the fact that their knowledge and understanding of him will, and needs to, be enhanced by what they will witness during his ministry.

Second, "witnessing" (μαρτυρέω) is of obvious importance in this section of the narrative. John the Baptist witnesses to his disciples as well as to 'the Jews' inquiring about him (1:19–34). Two of Jesus' disciples, Andrew and Philip, witness to Peter and Nathanael respectively, who, in turn, become followers of Jesus. Beside this parallelism mentioned by commentators between 1:35–42 and 1:43–51,[57] the whole passage brings to the forefront this important Johannine theme. Witness is needed in order to bring people to belief in Jesus, even though witness does not always lead to belief, as John's witness to the priests and Levites illustrates (1:19–28). Moreover, this theme associated with discipleship shows that discipleship results in actions (*i.e.* witnessing and bringing people to Jesus). As will become evident, witnessing is that for which Jesus is preparing his disciples throughout the narrative.

Third, Collins mentions that in 1:35–51 so much is said about important elements of discipleship that will later be developed (*i.e.* call, human testimony, hearing, following, seeking, finding, coming and seeing, abiding with Jesus) that this section of the Gospel could easily be considered "an interlude on the nature of discipleship."[58] Vellanickal goes further in proposing that John 1 summarises the whole process of discipleship.[59] Chennattu, however, prefers to see in the call stories "only the initial stage of the discipleship journey of the first disciples."[60] These propositions need not be opposed to one another. Though the narrator takes the implied reader into what it means to be a disciple in these stories, they only recount the beginning of the disciples' journey with Jesus. Chennattu thus correctly states that "the discipleship motif is developed gradually and progressively as the Johannine story unfolds,"[61] beginning with 1:35–51. Though the disciples are portrayed as only beginning their journey with Jesus, the journey has begun already.

At the end of this section, implied readers have a positive view of Jesus' disciples. These new followers have quickly recognized in Jesus the expected Messiah and they have put their faith in him. Jesus makes clear that this is only the beginning of his ministry and of his disciples' journey with him, but his promise that they will see "greater things" provides implied readers with the positive idea that the disciples may be 'in it for the long run,' that their 'abiding' with Jesus will continue. The disciples have not yet come to a point where they could confess their faith in Jesus in as full an understanding as the prologue has

---

[57] *E.g.*, Stibbe, *John*, 39.
[58] Collins, *These Things*, 54.
[59] Vellanickal, "Discipleship," 131–47.
[60] Chennattu, *Discipleship*, 7.
[61] Chennattu, *Discipleship*, 49.

given. They may neither know nor understand yet anything about Jesus' mission, but the narrative depiction of their coming to, seeing, abiding, following, and confessing of Jesus certainly sheds a positive light on them.[62] Moreover, it is possible that the narrative also already shows a certain progress in their knowledge and understanding of Jesus, even so early in their discipleship (*i.e.* Andrew's recognition of Jesus first as Rabbi in 1:38 and as Messiah in 1:41).[63] So far in the story, they clearly fall on the side of those who received him and believed in his name (1:12). They are Jesus' new disciples.[64]

2. From Cana to Cana (2:1–4:54)

The first section under consideration in this portion of the narrative is 2:1–12, a pericope also known as "The wedding at Cana." This section is well-known and has been the subject of many interpretations, some of them very hypothetical and allegorical. As Carson mentions, this is probably due to the fact that, unlike other signs in the Fourth Gospel, this one is not tied to a discourse which explains its significance.[65]

This is not the place to exegete the entire pericope, but simply to look at the characterisation of the disciples, focusing on their faith and understanding. The disciples appear both at the beginning of this pericope: "Jesus also was invited to the wedding with his disciples" (2:2), and at the end: "And his disciples believed in him. After this he went down to Capernaum, with his mother and his brothers and his disciples, and they stayed there for a few days" (2:11–12). As this last verse indicates, they are not the only characters mentioned in this section: together with Jesus and the disciples, we find the mother of Jesus (2:1, 3–5, 12), the servants at the wedding banquet (2:5, 7–8), the master of ceremonies (2:9–10), the bridegroom (2:9–10), and the brothers of Jesus (2:12). Among these other characters, particular attention should be given to the mother of Jesus because she is quite possibly to be considered a 'disciple' of Jesus by the implied author. Though she will not be mentioned again in the course of the narrative before 6:42 (as an allusion) and 19:25–27, her presence with Jesus

---

[62] R. M. Chennattu, "On Becoming Disciples (John 1:35–51): Insights from the Fourth Gospel," *Sal* 63 (2001): 496, concludes (probably hastily at this stage of the narrative) her study of the disciples' call stories as such: "On the basis of this study of 1:35–51, we can reasonably conclude that discipleship is a process of becoming, a process of growth. It is a vocation to which one has never responded fully in a final and definitive way."

[63] Chennattu, *Discipleship*, 45.

[64] Certain scholars do not agree, *e.g.* de Jonge, *Stranger*, 13: "The pericope of 1:35–51 is little more than a prelude to what follows in chapters 2–12. To 'the greater things' belong the σημεῖα as revelation of Jesus' δόξα; the disciples who are present when Jesus changes water into wine in Cana in Galilee come to believe in him. The Cana-event, indicated as the 'beginning of the signs,' obviously also marks the real beginnings of discipleship for the small band who follows Jesus around […]."

[65] Carson, *John*, 166.

at the banquet, coupled with her remaining and following Jesus in Capernaum (2:12), indicate that she must be considered as a potential disciple, a member of Jesus' inner circle of followers.[66]

In the short narrative of 2:1–12, Jesus' mother plays an important role in the plot. After having set the scene (2:1–2), the narrator presents a problem or complication: "the wine ran out" (2:3), which pushes Jesus' mother to turn to her son: "They have no wine" (2:3). Apparently, she understands Jesus' ability or power to resolve this issue, but Jesus rebuffs her sharply: "Woman, what does it have to do with me? My hour has not yet come" (2:4).[67] Then, the reaction of Jesus' mother is expressed very briefly in her ordering of the servants: "Do whatever he tells you" (2:6). The remaining story (2:6–11) narrates Jesus changing water into wine and the apparent consequence of such a sign (the belief of the disciples in 2:11).[68] Jesus and his mother's dialogue, together with their actions in this short narrative, remain puzzling to many. Did she implicitly ask him to perform a miracle, or did she simply want to inform Jesus in 2:3? Why did Jesus rebuke her so harshly?[69] And finally, why did he perform a sign after such a rebuke?

Of greatest interest to the present study is the nature of the mother's response or attitude after Jesus' rebuke: "His mother said to the servants, 'Do whatever he tells you'" (2:5). Could this response be equivalent to belief in Jesus' word? Moloney believes so: "The command of the mother of Jesus to the

---

[66] Even though Jesus' brothers also accompany him in 2:12, nothing else is said about them in this pericope. They will appear again in 7:1–10, where their unbelief will be mentioned explicitly.

[67] This verse has been described as one of the most difficult in the Fourth Gospel by F. M. Braun, *La mère des fidèles: esssai de théologie johannique*, CAR (Tournai: Casterman, 1953), 49. The translation and meaning of Τί ἐμοὶ καὶ σοί, γύναι; are notoriously difficult. Literally, such a sentence does not make much sense in English ("What to you and to me, woman?"). Most likely, this expression means something like "What concern is that to you and to me" (see Lincoln, *John*, 171; and Boismard, *Baptême*, 145–49, for lengthy discussions). Moreover, the term γύναι is not the normal manner with which a son addresses his mother, but it is not necessarily disrespectful since Jesus addresses other women that way in the Fourth Gospel (4:21; 8:10), and at least one of them, affectionately (20:15). Yet, the use of such a term towards one's mother clearly suggests distancing (see Lincoln, *John*, 127). Regarding the reason for such an address, J. M. Howard, "The Significance of Minor Characters in the Gospel of John," *BSac* 163 (2006): 66–67, is correct that "the key to understanding this enigma seems to lie in His word: 'My hour has not yet come.'" For Howard, Jesus is here making clear that the governing will of his life is not his mother's any more, but his and his Father's.

[68] Moloney, "Cana," 826. See also Giblin, "Suggestion, Negative Response, and Positive Action in St. John's Portrayal of Jesus (John 2:1–11; 4:46–56; 7:2–14; 11:1–44)," *NTS* 26 (1980): 197–211.

[69] On this question, see esp. Lee, *Flesh*, 144–45, who proposes three elements explaining Jesus' rebuff of his mother: to introduce the motif of the 'hour,' a test of faith, and the theological point that Jesus works at his own timing, "which is divinely ordered and therefore different from that of human beings" (p. 145).

attendants […] is a communication of the Mother's unconditional trust in the word of her son." Even more, Moloney goes on: "The woman, the mother of Jesus, is the *first* person, in the experience of the reader, to manifest trust in the word of Jesus."[70] Beyond the fact that the present study has argued that Jesus' disciples seem to have already responded to Jesus' words with faith (1:39), are implied readers truly meant to assess the mother's words in 2:5 in such a positive manner?[71] Moloney is probably correct that Jesus' mother responds to his rebuke in a positive manner, at the very least with perseverance and possibly with faith.[72] Moreover, she may have heard a promise in Jesus' negative answer to her, the promise that he would act.[73] She appears to have confidence in her son's wisdom and power, even though Jesus' response has made clear that her understanding is limited.[74] It is also possible that Jesus' mother is taken aback by Jesus calling her 'woman.' Nevertheless, she does not turn away from him in anger or discouragement but rather acknowledges that her son has control of the situation. She trusts him in spite of her lack of understanding and possible humiliation.[75] All in all, it is therefore very plausible[76] that Jesus' mother,

---

[70] Moloney, *Belief*, 84 (italics original). For him, therefore, "Her relationship with Jesus transcends the limitations displayed by the disciples, who attempted to understand him within their own categories in 1:35–51."

[71] J. Becker, *Das Evangelium nach Johannes*, 2 vols, ÖTBK 4/1–2 (Gütersloh/Würzburg: Gerd Mohn/Echter Verlag, 1979, 1981), 1:110, certainly goes too far in the opposite direction, writing "Ihre Reaktion ist […] unwichtig."

[72] However, Moloney's concern to show that true faith (such as the one he believes Jesus' mother exemplifies) is not based on signs but on Jesus' words, forces him to overstate his case, which is apparent later in his article, where he makes the surprising suggestion that the disciples do not come to faith as a result of seeing the sign, but as a result of the faith of Jesus' mother: "I would understand 2:11 as a consequence of the 'faith in the word' of the mother of Jesus, leading to the faith of others" (Moloney, "Cana," 842).

[73] Ridderbos, *John*, 106; Köstenberger, *John*, 96; Conway, *Men and Women*, 74. According to this interpretation, Jesus saying to his mother "My hour has not yet come" (2:4) is both a refusal and a promise to act. The remaining verses in this passage will show that, though the hour remains future (referring to end of Jesus' mission), Jesus, at times, reveals his glory and thus anticipates his hour: "Since the hour is an hour of glory and the narrator will explicitly state that in this sign Jesus revealed his glory (v. 11), the turning of water into wine should be seen as one of those proleptic eschatological moments" (Lincoln, *John*, 128).

[74] See Witherington, *John*, 79, and especially J. Ashton, *Understanding the Fourth Gospel* (Oxford: Oxford University Press, 1993), 268–69: "Jesus' mother […] is as a representative of […] those for whom misunderstanding is not a permanent obstacle to discipleship."

[75] Beirne, *Discipleship*, 52. Beirne notes that the faith of Jesus' mother precedes the sign so that she is open to receiving the gift of divine life, and it enables her to see Jesus' glory (pp. 53–54). This could also explain why Mary is following Jesus with the disciples in 2:12. See also Boismard, *Baptême*, 159; and J. McHugh, *The Mother of Jesus in the New Testament* (London: Darton, Longman & Todd, 1975), 442,

[76] Clearly, we cannot be certain that Jesus' mother ought to be considered as a believer. Indeed, R. G. Maccini, *Her Testimony Is True. Women as Witnesses according to John*, JSNT-Sup 125 (Sheffield: Sheffield Academic Press, 1996), 193, argues that the lack of any explicit

in saying to the servants "ὅ τι ἂν λέγῃ ὑμῖν ποιήσατε" (v. 5), expressed her belief in Jesus, even though it is difficult to tell exactly what content such faith may have had. As already mentioned, Jesus' mother will accompany him to Capernaum in 2:12, thus possibly identifying herself, at least for some time, as one of Jesus' followers.

If certain doubts remain regarding the status of Jesus' mother as a member of Jesus' troop of followers, the disciples of Jesus, mentioned explicitly as such for the first time in the narrative (2:2), are obviously members of such a group. It seems that they have "accepted Jesus' claims and remain bound to him in a continuing bond."[77] In 2:2, at least five disciples are present (Andrew, the anonymous disciple, Peter, Philip, and Nathanael). Having depicted the call of a few representative disciples, the narrator can now treat 'the disciples' as a larger group whose number is generally unspecified (except when the narrator mentions 'the Twelve' explicitly).[78] Interestingly, 2:2 mentions that Jesus was invited to the wedding at Cana *with his disciples*. There is no need to put too much weight on this, but it is possible that Jesus and his disciples were already considered a group, a unit, so that Jesus could not be invited without them.

The disciples play no particular role in the story of the wedding at Cana, even though they are beneficiaries of Jesus' first sign: "Ταύτην ἐποίησεν ἀρχὴν τῶν σημείων ὁ Ἰησοῦς ἐν Κανὰ τῆς Γαλιλαίας καὶ ἐφανέρωσεν τὲν δόξαν αὐτοῦ, καὶ ἐπίστευσαν εἰς αὐτὸν οἱ μαθηταὶ αὐτοῦ" (2:11). The text does not say that the disciples *saw* the sign. Their presence with Jesus at the wedding (2:2), coupled with the concluding remark that they "believed in him" after Jesus manifested his glory (2:11), seems to favour the reading of καὶ ἐπίστευσαν εἰς αὐτὸν οἱ μαθηταὶ αὐτοῦ as implicitly explaining that the disciples received the witness of the servants and/or Jesus' mother about the sign. Yet, since the evangelist chose not to tell his readers how the disciples knew about the sign, it may also be that the unexplained reference to their faith simply makes them representative of the appropriate response to a sign. In any case, doubts regarding the reality of the disciples' faith can now be abandoned: the disciples *believed in him*, as Jesus manifested his glory.[79] Indeed, it is

---

reference to Mary's faith indicates the probability that she is a non-believer.

[77] Segovia, "Peace," 79.

[78] For Barrett, *John*, 190: "it is probably this complete group [the Twelve] to which John here [2:2] refers."

[79] This study argued that Jesus' disciples were already considered as believing prior to 2:11. But as already alluded to, many disagree and prefer to see 2:11 as the beginning of the disciples' faith. See, *e.g.* B. F. Westcott, *The Gospel according to St. John. The Authorized Version with Introduction and Notes* (Grand Rapids, MI: Eerdmans, 1981), 38; Stibbe, *John*, 44; F. J. Moloney, *The Gospel of John*, SP 4 (Collegeville, MN: Liturgical Press, 1998), 69. However, others prefer to understand the faith of the disciples as being *strengthened* or *confirmed* by the revelation of Jesus' glory in 2:11. See, *e.g.* Ridderbos, *John*, 113; G. R. Beasley-Murray, *John*, WBC 36 (Waco, TX: Word, 1987), 33; M. C. Tenney, "Topics from the Gospel of John. Part IV: The Growth of Belief," *BSac* 132 (1975): 347; Lincoln, *John*, 131. For L. Morris, *The Gospel*

possible to argue that it is because they already believed that they were able to "see" Jesus' glory through the sign, and so believe.[80] The significance of Jesus' first sign, therefore, is that it manifested his glory. This mention of Jesus' glory brings implied readers back to 1:14, where the glory is that of the Word made flesh, that of "the only Son from the Father, full of grace and truth."[81] But 2:11 also points implied readers forward to the hour of Jesus' death and exaltation (17:5), when his glory would be fully manifested.[82] In 2:11, the disciples witnessed the first realisation of that glory.[83] Jesus' first sign pointed the disciples to something that was beyond the miracle itself; in this sign, they saw that Jesus was more than a mere man, and they believed, which is the most appropriate response to the sign. Jesus had announced to the disciples that they would see "greater things" (1:50), and in 2:11 this promise begins to be fulfilled.[84]

Jesus' sign at Cana was the means through which the disciples "beheld his glory" (to use the expression of 1:14) and believed. For the second time (after 1:50), the relation between Jesus' miraculous power and belief is mentioned in the narrative. Much has been written about this issue,[85] and so far in the narrative, it appears that the implied author has no intention to devalue a faith that

---

according to John, Rev. ed., NICNT (Grand Rapids, MI: Eerdmans, 1995), 164: "Nathanael has already been recorded as a believer (1:50), and now others join him."

[80] R. Kysar, *John, The Maverick Gospel*, Rev. ed. (Louisville, KY: Westminster John Knox, 1993), 84: "Hence, in order for signs to provoke faith they must be experienced from a perspective that already presupposes faith – at least to a minimal degree." Likewise, Koester, "Hearing," 332, proposes that: "The sign they saw at Cana did not evoke an initial faith. Rather, the sign confirmed and was perceived by a faith that had been engendered through hearing." More recently, Koester makes the same point in Koester, *Theology*, 165.

[81] For Bultmann, *John*, 119, Jesus' "revelation of his δόξα is nothing more nor less than his revelation of the ὄνομα of the Father (17.6)." One could add that 'glory' is Jesus' status as the Father's only Son (in addition to 1:14, see 5:44; 12:41, 43).

[82] Lincoln, *John*, 131.

[83] Before his death and exaltation, Jesus will again manifest his glory through signs (*e.g.* the resurrection of Lazarus in 11:4, 40), and 12:37–43 indicates that all of Jesus' signs revealed his glory.

[84] *Pace* W. R. G. Loader, "John 1:50–51 and the 'Greater Things' of Johannine Christology," in *Anfänge der Christologie: Festschrift für Ferdinand Hahn zum 65. Geburtstag*, ed. by C. Breytenbach and H. Paulsen (Göttingen: Vandenhoeck & Ruprecht, 1991), 255–74, who argues that the 'greater things' refer exclusively to the cross and resurrection. Loader is certainly correct to point to the cross and resurrection as the ultimate 'greater things.' However, just as Jesus' hour is future but at times anticipated by Jesus during his ministry through manifestations of his glory, the same can arguably be said of the greater things of 1:51.

[85] See Y.-M. Blanchard, *Des signes pour croire? Une lecture de l'évangile de Jean*, Lire la Bible 106 (Paris: Cerf, 1995); Boismard, "Rapport," 357–64; X. Léon-Dufour, "Les miracles de Jésus selon Jean," in *Les miracles de Jésus selon le Nouveau Testament*, ed. by X. Léon-Dufour (Paris: Seuil, 1977), 269–86; W. Nicol, *The Sēmeia in the Fourth Gospel: Tradition and Redaction*, NovTSup 32 (Leiden: Brill, 1972). For a brief overview and proposition, see also Twelftree, *Miracle*, 230–33.

is either based on or reinforced by Jesus' sign.[86] However, one may ask if the disciples' belief in 2:11 does not indeed reflect a certain growth of belief and of knowledge/understanding on their part. For Gloer, this is precisely the case:

The sign became an occasion for the deepening of their understanding of who Jesus really was, and they 'believed in him' (2:12) [*sic*]. This is how the signs will function for Jesus' disciples. As they 'follow' him, as they 'abide' with him, they will come to 'see' the signs as pointers to his identity.[87]

This assessment is probably correct. Nevertheless, it is highly probable that the disciples, though they "beheld" Jesus' glory, though they caught a glimpse of his identity as "the only one Son from the Father," (1:14) still did not fully understand what they saw.[88] Up to that point, they may not have understood much more about Jesus than the fact that he was Messiah and had extraordinary powers. Readers, however, have reasons to expect that the disciples, if they go on following Jesus, if they remain with him until his "hour" (2:4), will also continue to witness "greater things" and thus grow in their knowledge and understanding of his person and mission.

As already mentioned, the disciples, together with Jesus' mother and brothers, continued their journey with Jesus, and went down to Capernaum where they stayed for several days (2:12). The time of the Passover festival was at hand, and Jesus went to Jerusalem (2:13). There, he provoked a confrontation with the religious authorities of the temple. Jesus first 'cleansed'[89] the temple (2:14–17), which resulted in a dialogue between him and "the Jews" (2:18–21). Both of these small sections, as they will now be studied, conclude with pregnant asides regarding the disciples' remembering (2:17, 22). The first remembering on the part of the disciples comes immediately following Jesus telling the dove sellers: "Take these things away; do not make my Father's house a house of trade" (v. 16). The text then says that: "His disciples remembered (ἐμνήσθησαν) that it was written, zeal for your house will consume me" (2:17). After Jesus' dialogue with "the Jews," where Jesus answered their demand for a sign with a cryptic saying ("Destroy this temple, and in three days I will raise

---

[86] *Contra* E. Lohse, "Miracles in the Fourth Gospel," in *What About the New Testament?*, ed. by M. Hooker and C. Hickling (London: SCM, 1975), 65, for whom the author of the Fourth Gospel "points to a critical assessment of a faith born out of miracle; indeed, he denies such faith both permanence and value."

[87] Gloer, "Come and See," 280.

[88] It would be to go too far to understand the content of Jesus' glory in 1:14 as that which the disciples believed in 2:11. Obviously, the Fourth Gospel's prologue reflects the faith of the implied author, not that of the disciples at this point of the narrative.

[89] For two opposing views regarding the legitimacy of continuing to call this event 'the cleansing of the temple,' see, among others, E. P. Sanders, *Jesus and Judaism* (London/Philadelphia, PA: SCM/Fortress, 1985), 61–76, and C. A. Evans, "Jesus' Action in the Temple: Cleansing or Portent of Destruction?," *CBQ* 51 (1989): 237–70.

it up" – 2:19)[90] which they obviously did not understand (2:20),[91] the narrator first explains what Jesus meant by the word "temple" ("he was speaking of the temple of his body" – 2:21) and then makes use of a prolepsis regarding the disciples: "When therefore he was raised from the dead, his disciples remembered (ἐμνήθησαν) that he had said this, and they believed (ἐπίστευσαν) the Scripture and the word that Jesus had spoken" (2:22).

Several issues need to be considered regarding vv. 17 and 22. First, the relationship between the two verses needs to be clarified. Indeed, they are very similar, even though 2:22 adds elements not present in 2:17. In 2:17, the disciples "remembered" a verse of the Scriptures (Ps. 69:9), and in 2:22 they are once more said to remember, but also to "believe" as a result of it. The question that needs to be asked is whether 2:17 should be considered a prolepsis like that of 2:22, or whether it is an indication of the disciples' remembering at the time of the incident. This ambiguity raises the key issue of how far the post-resurrection temporal perspective of the implied author impacts the characterisation of the disciples. Scholars' answers diverge on this question. For instance, Ridderbos comments on 2:17:

> The idea that we have here a later reflection (as in vs. 2:22 and 12:16) is not suggested by the text itself. […] But this is not to deny that in Jesus' violent and authoritative resistance against the misuse of the temple the disciples saw the spirit of prophecy moving in him – and that in that context they learned to understand his conduct also during his lifetime (cf. 14:25).[92]

Carson goes in the same direction, adding that what the disciples remembered was the "zeal" Jesus exercised, rather than the consumption.[93] Moreover, for Moloney, the text shows a progression between these two verses. The disciples remembered in 2:17, but such remembering was insufficient since it fell "short of a correct understanding of Jesus' passion for the ways of his Father."[94] In turn, 2:22 indicates that there will be a time, after Jesus' resurrection, when the disciples will exercise a deeper remembering, which would lead them to "believe and rightly understand the word of Scripture and the word of Jesus."[95] To

---

[90] Brown, *John*, 1:115, argues that Jesus failed to give them a sign, but M. A. Matson, "The Temple Incident: An Integral Element in the Fourth Gospel's Narrative," in *Jesus in Johannine Tradition*, ed. by R. T. Fortna and T. Thatcher (Louisville, KY: Westminster John Knox, 2001), 149, argues that Jesus does offer a sign, one that would later come in his death and resurrection (2:19).

[91] The Jews' answer to Jesus exposes both their misunderstanding of Jesus' word and their rejection of Jesus. Sarcasm is obviously present in 2:20: "It has taken forty-six years to build this temple, and will you raise it up in three days?" In this, their response to Jesus starkly contrasts with that of the disciples so far in the story, and such a contrast will continue during Jesus' stay in Jerusalem (2:21–25; 3:1–21).

[92] Ridderbos, *John*, 117.

[93] Carson, *John*, 180. Yet, it is certainly incorrect to assert such a point. In fact, it is likely that the disciples remembered the whole of the quotation, and not just the "zeal."

[94] Moloney, *John*, 79.

[95] Moloney, *John*, 79.

these three authors' case, one could also add the fact that, apparently, the two rememberings have different objects: in 2:17 the disciples remember Ps. 69:9, while in 2:22, they remember the words of Jesus, which lead them to believe in "the Scripture" and "the word that Jesus had spoken."

Several arguments, however, can be proposed against their views. First, although these scholars correctly propose that the most natural reading of the text up to that point does not lead one to read 2:17 as a prolepsis, *i.e.* a later remembering on the part of the disciples after Jesus' resurrection, it appears that a strict sequential reading of this passage may not be appropriate. Rather, it is likely that implied readers are meant to read 2:17 *in light of* 2:22, since these two verses are so similar and closely situated.[96] The second mention of the disciples' remembering adds new elements, not present in 2:17, thus enriching the readers' understanding of 2:17. Second, in the context of the story, "the Scripture" alluded to in 2:22 is most probably Ps. 69, already mentioned to in 2:17,[97] while the "word that Jesus had spoken" is probably found in 2:19. In fact, as is often noted, Ps. 69 was a favourite psalm of the early Church to explain Jesus' suffering and death as a fulfilment of the Scriptures.[98] Finally, the meaning of this Jewish Scripture's reference adds a futurist dimension to the whole episode: "zeal for your house *will* consume me." The Hebrew original and the LXX[99] state this in the past tense, but the Fourth Evangelist chose to quote this verse using the future tense. This verse, therefore, not only emphasises Jesus' "zeal" for the temple, but also that his zeal would lead him to be consumed, *i.e.*, to be destroyed in death.[100] In so quoting this verse, the implied author certainly wanted to introduce implied readers to the reason for, and the

---

[96] So R. B. Hays, "Reading Scripture in Light of the Resurrection," in *The Art of Reading Scripture*, ed. by E. F. Davis and R. B. Hays (Grand Rapids, MI/Cambridge: Eerdmans, 2003), 222: "We should understand this [2:22b] as a summary comment about the whole narrative unit (vv. 13–22a)."

[97] *Pace* P. M. Hoskins, *Jesus as the Fulfillment of the Temple in the Gospel of John*, PBM (Milton Keynes/Waynesboro, GA: Paternoster, 2006), 192–93, n.49, for whom the Scripture mentioned in 2:22 must not only refer to Jesus' death but also to his resurrection, thus ruling out Ps. 69:9 as its referent. Yet, Hoskins unnecessarily separates Jesus' death and resurrection for the narrative of the Fourth Gospel presents Jesus' glorification as a unit.

[98] Lincoln, *John*, 138. See, for instance, the use of Ps. 69:4 in Jn. 15:25, and of Ps. 69:21 in 19:28–29; Matt. 27:34, 48; Mk. 15:36 and Lk. 23:36.

[99] See J. H. Bernard, *A Critical and Exegetical Commentary on the Gospel according to St. John*, 2 vols, ICC (Edinburgh: T. & T. Clark, 1953), 1:92, for a discussion on the LXX's variants of PS. 69:9 (Ps. 68:10 LXX).

[100] As mentioned by L. J. Kreitzer, "The Temple Incident of John 2:13–25: A Preview of What Is to Come," in *Understanding, Studying and Reading. New Testament Essays in Honour of John Ashton*, ed. by C. Rowland and C. H. T. Fletcher-Louis, JSNTSuppS 153 (Sheffield: Sheffield Academic Press, 1998), 97: "It is the ambiguity of the crucial verb 'to consume' which is often missed when we read the story in English translation. [...] The Hebrew verb לכא can mean 'to consume' in the sense of 'to destroy', and by implication can be taken to mean 'to cause to be put to death.'"

manner of, Jesus' death. But it is very unlikely that the disciples, at this point of the story, would have been able to identify Jesus' action in the temple as one that would bring him to his death. In the following verses (2:20–22), however, the implied author links this implicit mention of Jesus' death with Jesus' resurrection, implicitly saying that the resurrection would shed fresh light on the whole incident of 2:13–21 and lead to the disciples' belief in "the Scripture and the word that Jesus had spoken." Therefore, though Ridderbos, Carson, and Moloney (to name but a few) propose a plausible case, we prefer to understand 2:17 as a prolepsis which serves as a link between 2:13–17 and 2:18–22, and which implicitly indicates that the disciples did not understand the meaning and implications of Jesus' action in the temple at the time of the incident.[101]

This first conclusion leads us to the second issue that needs to be considered regarding 2:17, 22, *i.e.* the nature of the remembering, and by implication, the belief of the disciples. Zumstein has written extensively on the issue of remembering and belief in the Fourth Gospel.[102] In several articles, he studies the different "prolepses de la mémoire" found in the narrative (12:16; 20:9 in addition to 2:22),[103] and shows how these prolepses (*i*) "mettent en exergue le fait que le passé fondateur ne livre pas de lui-même sa signification. Il fait l'objet d'une rétrospection illuminatrice qui se cristallise dans le *tournant pascal*."[104] Thus, the past is foundational only retrospectively, when after Easter the disciples are able to interpret, in light of the resurrection, the events of the life of Christ. (*ii*) Second, Zumstein shows that these prolepses "alertent sur le fait que la mémoire pascale, qui crée le sens, est à la fois interprète de l'*Écriture* et structurée par elle."[105] For Zumstein, the Scripture in question is obviously the Jewish Scripture (2:17, 22; 12:16), but it is also the words of Jesus (2:22; 14:26; 16:4).[106] Zumstein concludes: "Nous sommes confrontés ici à un phénomène extrêmement intéressant: la mémoire est à la fois témoin des paroles de Christ

---

[101] Among those who agree that the Fourth Evangelist meant that the disciples came to understand the meaning of the temple incident only after the resurrection are Brown, *John*, 1:123, and Lincoln, *John*, 138–39.

[102] See J. Zumstein, "Mémoire et relecture pascale dans l'évangile selon Jean," in *La mémoire et le temps. Mélanges offerts à Pierre Bonnard*, ed. by S. Amsler et al., MB 23 (Genève: Labor et Fides, 1991), 153–70 [republished in J. Zumstein, *Miettes exégétiques*, MdB 25 (Genève: Labor et Fides, 1991), 299–316]; J. Zumstein, "Le processus de relecture dans la littérature johannique," *ETR* 73 (1998): 161–76.

[103] These retrospective comments ("prolepses de la mémoire") are part of a larger group of prolepses in the Fourth Gospel, the "historical prolepses" (15:18, 20, 21; 16:2, 3, 4, 21:18).

[104] Zumstein, "Mémoire," 163 (italics original).

[105] Zumstein, "Mémoire," 163 (italics original).

[106] As noted by Lincoln, *John*, 141: "It is significant that for the narrator Scripture and Jesus' word can be spoken of in the same breath as the object of belief [...] With regard to the Scripture, it is not just that a proof-text, whose detail fits later Christian belief, can be found, but that in the light of the resurrection Jesus can now be seen as the speaker of the psalm, as the righteous one, whose zeal for God's cause leads to his suffering but later vindication."

et leur interprète pascal."[107] The present of the believing community is both being "fed" by the past and it "illuminates" the past.[108] To conclude, according to 2:22, the disciples did not, at the time of the event, understand the meaning of Jesus' action in the temple. After the resurrection, they remembered these events, interpreted them appropriately, and "they believed the Scripture and the word that Jesus had spoken." Thus, this first conclusion leads to three remarks: (*i*) so far in the narrative "faith does not presuppose understanding."[109] This at the very least is true of the disciples since they clearly have not understood the purpose of Jesus' mission yet, but as the narrator expressed in 2:11, they did believe in Jesus. But (*ii*) as 2:22 makes clear, the disciples will also experience belief that is based on understanding (remembering and proper interpretation of the Scripture and the words of Jesus) after the resurrection of Jesus. Thus, implied readers are left with the impression that if the disciples are already in a "state" of belief (2:11), this does not mean that their faith involves all possible and proper propositions about Jesus, his person, and his mission. In this regard, there is room for growth in their faith. (*iii*) Finally, and more positively, the two asides of 2:17, 19 already indicate to implied readers that the disciples will continue in their discipleship, even after Jesus' death.[110]

In 2:23, Jesus is still in Jerusalem and will remain in the city until 3:22. There, he performs signs which draw "many" to believe (πιστεύειν) in his name (2:23–25).[111] However, he does not entrust (πιστεύειν) himself to them.[112] Through the narrator's use of this inside view, readers learn that Jesus did not entrust himself to them because "he knew all people" (2:24).[113] The text neither says if Jesus' lack of entrusting himself to them became evident to people around him, nor whether these many people followed Jesus or sought to remain with him. It is apparent, however, that these "many" contrast with the disciples, whose confessions of Jesus were welcomed by him (1:49–51), and whose belief was not questioned by the narrator.[114] Similar comments could be made re-

---

[107] Zumstein, "Mémoire," 163.

[108] Zumstein, "Mémoire," 170. See also Iser, *Implied Reader*, 144.

[109] Petersen, *Sociology of Light*, 39. Petersen adds: "According to 10:38, belief makes understanding possible. […] So before the resurrection [the disciples] 'believed in' him, and afterwards they 'understood' things about him."

[110] A point made by Culpepper, *Anatomy*, 116.

[111] The same expression "to believe in his name" is used in 1:13 and 3:18 to speak of adequate faith (*Pace* Westcott, *John*, 45, who contrasts 'in his name' with 'on him').

[112] For two contrasting views on this paradox, see Z. C. Hodges, "Problem Passages in the Gospel of John. Part 2: Untrustworthy Believers – John 2:23–25," *BSac* 135 (1978): 139–52, and N. Farelly, "John 2:23–25: What Kind of Faith This?," *Presb* 30 (2004): 37–45.

[113] See Lincoln, *John*, 145: "In this case, as the elaboration makes plain, Jesus' omniscience includes knowing what goes on inside a person, and therefore being able to discern whether their outward confession comes from an authentic or inauthentic faith."

[114] For a majority of scholars, this text shows that there is something inherently wrong with a faith based on signs. But such a conclusion is unwarranted. Later in the narrative, Jesus will

garding the dialogue between Jesus and Nicodemus (3:1–21). Given the literary
links found between 2:23–25 and 3:1–2,[115] it is likely that Nicodemus is meant
to illustrate the "many" of 2:23, culminating in Jesus' ironic question of 3:10
and his statement regarding the unbelief of Nicodemus and the Jews he represents in 3:12.[116] The remaining section (3:11–21), in contrast, will develop what
adequate belief means from the perspective of Jesus and, through the use of the
first person plural in 3:11, of a larger group also. One might expect that Jesus is
speaking of himself and the disciples who were present with him.[117] However,
this "we" is probably simply a continuation of the manner with which Nicodemus addressed Jesus in 3:2 ("Rabbi, we know").[118]

Jesus and his disciples left Jerusalem to go to and remain for a while in the
Judean countryside, where Jesus was baptising (3:22). There, a conversation
between John and his own disciples, sparked by their asking about the success Jesus was receiving across the Jordan and culminating in John's statement
"he must increase, but I must decrease" (3:30), is followed by the evangelist's
reflections on Jesus' superiority (3:31–36). But Jesus soon left Judea because
he learned that the Pharisees apparently saw his "making and baptizing more
disciples than John" as a threat (4:1). As an aside, the narrator then mentions
the group of Jesus' disciples in 4:2 in order to clarify that, in fact, "Jesus himself did not baptise but only his disciples." On their way to Galilee, the group
stops in Sychar, a Samaritan town (4:4–6). As will now be argued, this episode
of Jesus' ministry between Judea and Samaria (4:1–42)[119] is very instructive in
regard to the characterisation of the disciples.[120]

The disciples are not the primary characters in this section, the Samaritan
woman and Jesus are. However, they function in very specific ways, especially
as they contrast both with Jesus and the Samaritan woman. They appear three
times in the section: in 4:1–2, and within two sub-sections, that concerning

---

exhort his hearers to believe in the works he has done (10:38), the narrator will link Jesus' signs
with 'glory' in 12:37–43, and most importantly 20:30–31 will express the purpose of the signs
such as they were written in this Gospel as to produce belief. Clearly, the signs of Jesus are not,
in and of themselves, inadequate bases for adequate faith since they are meant to evoke belief.

[115] The term ἄνθρωπος is used in both 2:25 and 3:1, and the "signs" play a significant role
in the two pericopes (2:23; 3:2).

[116] In 3:11, the 'you' is plural.

[117] For F. P. Cotterell, "The Nicodemus Conversation: A Fresh Appraisal," *ExpTim* 96
(1985): 238, the "we" present in 3:2 is due to the improbability "that Nicodemus, an eminent
Rabbi, should be walking about Jerusalem without any of his disciples in attendance. It is similarly unlikely that Jesus would be without any of his disciples."

[118] Carson, *John*, 198–99.

[119] As the following argument will show, it is important to consider the figure of the disciples
in 4:1–2 in connection to the other places where they appear in 4:1–42.

[120] Most pertinent to the present study are the two important articles by É. Cuvillier, "La figure des disciples en Jean 4," *NTS* 42 (1996): 245–59; and É. Cuvillier, "La femme samaritaine
et les disciples de Jésus. Histoires de rencontres et de malentendus. Une lecture de l'évangile
de Jean 4,1–43," *Hok* 88 (2005): 62–75.

the Samaritan woman (4:8, 27) and that concerning the Samaritan people of Sychar (4:31–38). First, in 4:2, readers learn that the disciples, not Jesus, were baptising. This seems to be in direct opposition to 3:22, 26, where Jesus is said to be baptising in Judea. But this aside makes sense in the context of what was just written about Jesus' superiority over John. The narrator wants to distance Jesus' activity from John's, so as to make clear that Jesus is not simply continuing John's task after John has left the narrative.[121] In turn, 4:2 gives the sense both that the disciples have received a sort of ecclesial function even during Jesus' ministry, but also that baptism is only secondary to Jesus' "making disciples" (4:1).[122] It is difficult to assess what this baptising activity says about the disciples' faith and understanding, though their participation in Jesus' ministry appears to show that they have fully dedicated themselves to a "spreading Jesus-movement."[123]

The disciples are mentioned next in 4:8, where they are said to have "gone away into the city to buy food." Though Lenglet sees in this aside only a literary device allowing Jesus to spend time alone with the Samaritan woman,[124] it can be added that such activity on the part of the disciples is pertinent to the rest of the narrative and will be taken up again in Jesus' dialogue with them about 'food' (4: 27, 31–34).[125] The fact remains that Jesus is left alone with the Samaritan woman and that as a result of their lengthy conversation the woman will become an effective witness to Jesus' identity, inviting fellow Samaritans to "come and see" Jesus (4:29). When the disciples come back to Jesus (4:27), the woman leaves her water jar, giving the impression that the disciples are responsible for breaking the conversation.[126] After having left, she goes into town to witness to its citizens (4:28). The disciples can therefore take no credit for what is happening, that is, both the woman coming to realise that Jesus was someone special,[127] and witnessing to her fellow citizens.[128]

---

[121] Lincoln, *John*, 171. It could also be said that this aside could apply retrospectively to the other mentions of Jesus' baptising in 3:22, 26 or that "Jesus baptized only by using his disciples as the agents" (Carson, *John*, 215; see also Ridderbos, *John*, 152–53).

[122] So Cuvillier, "Figure," 251: "Comme précédemment pour Jean-Baptiste, la supériorité de Jésus sur les disciples est ainsi exprimée dans le texte; ici par cette séparation des tâches: Jésus 'fait' les disciples, les disciples baptisent."

[123] Moloney, *John*, 116.

[124] So *e.g.* A. Lenglet, "Jésus de passage parmi les Samaritains. Jn. 4/4–42," *Bib* 66 (1985): 499.

[125] Segovia, "Peace," 82.

[126] So F. F. Bruce, *The Gospel of John. Introduction, Exposition and Notes* (Grand Rapids, MI: Eerdmans, 1983), 112.

[127] The text never explicitly says that she believed in Jesus, but her actions (witnessing, leaving the water jar behind, openness to speak about her past) certainly show a positive response to her conversation with him. Moloney, "Cana," 838, speaks of her as a "model of partial faith" in opposition to John the Baptist and the Samaritans, who are "models of complete faith," but this terminology is not substantiated by the text.

[128] Cuvillier, "Figure," 252, makes a lot of this: "La présence de disciples en Samarie est

The disciples, as they came back to Jesus, were "astonished" that Jesus was speaking with a Samaritan woman. This statement parallels the surprise of the Samaritan woman that a Jewish man would talk to her (4:9), with the difference that the disciples never voiced their amazement: "No one said, 'What do you seek?' or, 'Why are you talking with her?'" (4:27). The text does not explicate why the disciples refused to engage Jesus on these points, but the result is that implied readers see the disciples' reaction negatively, which contrasts with the Samaritan woman's openness to dialoguing with Jesus.[129] The disciples did begin to address Jesus, but on a different level, urging him to eat (4:31), which conformed to the purpose of their "mission" in this section (4:8). Just as Jesus dialogued with the Samaritan woman on the topics of "drinking" and "water" (4:10–15), he will now speak to the disciples on the topics of "eating" and "food" (4:31–34), with similar ironies and subsequent misunderstandings. For the disciples, this is sparked by Jesus' statement that "I have food to eat that you do not know about" (4:32).[130] This statement does not mean that the disciples had no knowledge whatsoever that Jesus was on a mission, but instead that they were ignorant both of the nature and extent of this mission.[131] Once more, the disciples did not respond to Jesus' statement in engaging him in further dialogue. Rather they "said to one another, 'Has anyone brought him something to eat?'" This question, in addition to setting up Jesus' explanation in 4:34–38, may give the impression that "ils s'enferment sur eux-mêmes évitant que le Révélateur ne les questionne et ne les emmène où ils ne voudraient pas aller."[132] In any case, the true meaning of Jesus' statement remains obscure for the disciples.

But Jesus continues to speak to them, in spite of their apparent reluctance to engage in conversation.[133] Thus begins Jesus' short speech to his disciples

---

marquée par la stérilité: elle ne sert pas la tâche missionnaire." Thus, Cuvillier disagrees with Lenglet, "Samaritains," 499, for whom the disciples' absence is at the same time their presence in the town.

[129] Cuvillier, "Samaritaine," 71: "Les disciples sont ici qualifiés par rapport à la Samaritaine."

[130] Cuvillier, "Samaritaine," 71: "Jésus affirme cependant que les disciples ne *connaissent* ou ne *savent* pas (*ouk oidate*) quelle est sa nourriture (par opposition, cf. 4,25: la femme *sait – oida* – que le Messie doit venir; de même en 4,42, les Samaritains *savent – oidamen* – que Jésus est le sauveur du monde). Les disciples sont donc caractérisés par un non-savoir confirmé par leur incapacité à comprendre la portée symbolique des paroles de Jésus."

[131] D. A. Lee, *The Symbolic Narratives of the Fourth Gospel: The Interplay of Form and Meaning*, JSNTSup 95 (Sheffield: Sheffield Academic Press, 1994), 87, argues that "the conversation between Jesus and the disciples enables the evangelist to set the story of the Samaritans within its proper theological setting. It is a story about mission which, in the process, discloses theological insights. Jesus is finally revealed as ὁ σωτὴρ τοῦ κόσμου (v. 42)."

[132] Cuvillier, "Samaritaine," 71–72.

[133] F. Vouga, *Le cadre historique et l'intention théologique de Jean*, BeauR 3 (Paris: Beauchesne, 1977), 33, remarks: "Même si les interlocuteurs de Jésus ne comprennent pas où il veut en venir ni qui il est, Jésus tente toujours à nouveau, par ses propos, de les amener à mettre

regarding the nature of his mission: "My food is to do the will of him who sent me and to accomplish his work" (4:34). Most likely, this dialogue is first intended to show that the disciples had no idea that Samaria was on the map of Jesus' mission, so that Jesus had to tell them that the harvest was already taking place, even there: "Look, I tell you, lift up your eyes and see that the fields are white for harvest" (4:35). Jesus confirms to the disciples that, though they have not yet understood the nature and possibly the extent of his mission, they must somehow be involved in it (4:35–38) and thus obey the Father as he is obeying his Father's will (4:34). This is made clear by the harvest imagery used by Jesus. In this illustration, Jesus reaps and is already "receiving wages and gathering fruit for eternal life." This "reaping" occurs in fulfilment of the "sowing" of his predecessors.[134] But Jesus now refers to the inclusion of the disciples in his work of harvesting: "I sent you to reap that for which you did not labour. Others have laboured, and you have entered in their labour" (4:38).[135] In context, the harvest seems to refer to the Samaritan believers (4:39–42), but later in the narrative, 17:18 and 20:21 will remind implied readers that Jesus' sending of his disciples to harvest must await his own glorification.[136] Thus, even though the disciples have so far taken no part in this harvest, Jesus nonetheless invites and prepares them to participate in bringing people to eternal life and to rejoice with him.[137]

In this long pericope (4:1–42), the implied author has been able to develop the two themes that he set up in 4:1–2. (i) Jesus makes disciples, such is the mission he has received from his Father, and this mission expands even to Samaria. (ii) The disciples baptise and are invited to "enter" into the labour of Jesus and his predecessors (4:38). The time will come when they will be sent to harvest that for which they did not labour through the exalted Jesus. But implied read-

---

en question l'objet de leur recherche, leur compréhension de l'existence et leur mode d'être."

[134] Potentially a reference to the Old Testament prophets up to John (see Köstenberger, *Missions*, 182–83, for arguments in favour of this understanding).

[135] Köstenberger, *Missions*, 181, argues that the aorist ἀπέστειλα "may be viewed from a global aspect and not necessarily as referring to a past time ('I send you'; 'you enter')." But others, such as T. Okure, *The Johannine Approach to Mission: A Contextual Study of John 4:1–42*, WUNT 2/31 (Tübingen: Mohr Siebeck, 1988), 158–59, argue on the basis of a past time understanding of ἀπέστειλα that 4:38 reflects the post-resurrection standpoint of the Gospel's redaction. Both propositions are possible, and chapter 4 below will deal more precisely with this temporal perspective issue. In any case, Jesus is not here speaking of the disciples *already* harvesting.

[136] Köstenberger, *Missions*, 184, adds: "The present passage is consistent with the message of 14:12 that it is ultimately the exalted Jesus who will continue his mission through the disciples. There a comparison is made between the works of the earthly Jesus and those of the exalted Jesus through his followers."

[137] Lee, *Symbolic*, 89–90, correctly contrasts the Samaritan woman and the disciples in that the woman is actually engaged in the apostolic task of sowing, while the disciples neither understand nor share this task.

ers realise that, before then, the disciples still need to grow in their understanding of the nature of Jesus' mission in order to better collaborate with him.

Jesus remained in Sychar for two days with the new Samaritan believers (4:40, 43), and continued on his way to Galilee. There, the Galileans "welcomed him" (ἐδέξαντο) as a result of what they had seen him do in Jerusalem,[138] and where an official[139] came to Jesus requesting that Jesus heal his son (4:47, 49). Jesus, in a pattern similar to that which occurred in the first Cana sign (2:1–12: request/rebuke/positive response), promises that his son would live (4:54), which results in the official and his household's belief (4:54). This second sign ends this section of the Fourth Gospel (2:1–4:55).

Throughout, implied readers have been faced with the interesting phenomenon of Jesus' disciples being confirmed as believers, together with an increasing sense that the disciples are far from having a well-rounded understanding of Jesus' identity and mission: the meaning of his death and resurrection (2:17, 22), the nature of his work (4:32–34), and his gathering of the crop (4:34–38). While implied readers had the suspicion that the disciples' bold confessions in 1:41, 45, 49 could not possibly match the high Christology presented in the Prologue (1:1–18), the depth of the disciples' understanding is now explicitly in question. But Jesus, far from giving up on them, teaches them (4:34–38), gives them tasks to accomplish (4:2), and invites them to take part in the harvest (4:38). As the disciples continue to 'follow' him and 'abide' with him, Jesus' promise that there would be "greater things" for them to see (1:50) is already being fulfilled (2:11), even though Jesus' 'hour' has not yet come (2:4, 16, 19). The constant contrast between their responses to Jesus and that of unbelievers (2:20; 3:12, 23–25; 4:48) underlines the fact that their discipleship is secure and not to be confused with the status of unbelievers. This, in addition to the prolepses according to which there will be a time when the disciples will remember, understand, and believe (2:17, 22), comes to reinforce, in the implied reader's mind, the fact that the disciples will not only remain disciples, but also grow in their discipleship, throughout Jesus' earthly ministry and beyond.[140] A strong distinction is therefore underlined so far in the narrative between the disciples' faith and their knowledge/understanding.

3. Jesus and the Principal Feasts of the Jews (5:1–10:42)

The disciples, in this section of the narrative, do not appear explicitly again until the story of the feeding of the five thousand (6:1–15). However, it can be pre-

---

[138] But quickly this apparently positive response to Jesus is counter-balanced by 4:48: "Unless you (pl.) see signs and wonders you will not believe," indicating that their reception of Jesus is similar to that of the "many" in 2:23–25.

[139] See A. H. Mead, "The βασιλικὸς in John 4.46–53," *JSNT* 23 (1985): 69–72, for a discussion of the meaning of that word: "He is a Gentile officer, perhaps in the service of Herod Antipas, but quite probably, I would suggest, in the service of Rome" (p. 71).

[140] Ridderbos, *John*, 167.

sumed that they were with Jesus when he went up to Jerusalem (5:1), healed an invalid man at the pool of Bethesda (5:2–17), and responded to the Jews' accusations (5:18–47). More importantly, Jesus presents four witnesses in 5:30–47: John the Baptist (5:33–35), Jesus' works (5:36), the Father (5:37–38), and the Scriptures (5:39–40). These witnesses create textual links with the disciples' basis for coming to believe in Jesus in the narrative thus far: the first of Jesus' disciples came to Jesus as a result of the Baptist's witness (1:36–37); the disciples believed as a result of Jesus' sign at Cana (2:11); and they believed after remembering Jesus' word[141] and the Scripture (2:22).[142] If this is correct, it suggests that the evangelist wished to present the disciples not only as believing, but as having responded to the different means intended to lead to faith.

The disciples play an important role in John 6.[143] In 6:1–15, the story of Jesus feeding five thousand people, Jesus is sitting on the mountain with his disciples, and seeing a large crowd coming towards him (6:5),[144] he begins a dialogue with his disciples. First, he asks Philip: "where are we to buy bread, so that these people may eat?" (6:5). The narrator, as an aside, tells readers that "he said this to test him, for he himself knew what he would do" (6:6). Given the section of the narrative studied above (4:31–38), the nature of the test proposed by Jesus cannot be mistaken. The test was to determine whether Philip (probably representative of the disciples) would remember Jesus' earlier teaching about real food and, by extension, mission.[145] The following verses indicate that the disciples had not understood Jesus' teaching yet. First, Philip overlooks Jesus' question ("*where* are we to buy food?") by giving a monetary estimate for feeding such a crowd, implicitly telling Jesus that even if they found a place to buy food for everyone, they could never come up with enough money to buy

---

[141] U. C. von Wahlde, "The Witnesses to Jesus in John 5:31–40 and Belief in the Fourth Gospel," *CBQ* 43 (1981): 390, understands the witness of the Father mentioned in 5:37–38 as "precisely the word of the Father which he has given to Jesus and which Jesus gives to the world."

[142] von Wahlde, "Witnesses," 404.

[143] See J. D. Crossan, "It Is Written: A Structuralist Analysis of John 6," *Semeia* 26 (1983): 4, who proposes, as internal indications of the unity of chap. 6, the inclusion between the handling of the disciples in 6:1–15 and the Twelve in 6:67–71, and the general parallel structure within the chapter:

| (a) Jesus and the crowds | 6:1–15 | 6:22–59 |
| (b) Jesus and the disciples | 6:16–21 | 6:60–71 |

[144] The narrator's mention in 6:2 that the large crowd was following him "because they saw the signs that he was doing on the sick" is reminiscent of 2:23–25. As we noted earlier, such a response to Jesus was then inadequate. Few commentators (though see Léon-Dufour, *Lecture*, 2:105) note that Jesus "lifting up his eyes" in 6:5 is reminiscent of 4:35, where the disciples were also to lift up their eyes, "and see that the fields are white for harvest." Jesus, therefore, sees this crowd as his "mission field."

[145] M.-J. Lagrange, *Évangile selon Saint Jean*, EBib (Paris: Gabalda, 1925), 162, speaks of a "test of faith."

it (6:7). Andrew does answer the question, but with similar helplessness (6:9). Neither of these two disciples give any indication that they believed Jesus could potentially be the solution to his own question, that Jesus had the resources to meet the full spectrum of human needs such as he had already proven (2:7–10; 4:49–54; 5:6–9). They operate on a purely human level and "despite their previous exchange on the subject of 'food', they do not see the present gathering in terms of mission."[146] The disciples failed the test.

The following verses (6:10–13) present Jesus both ending the conversation with the disciples, and performing the sign as the disciples help with sitting people down (6:10) and gathering leftovers (6:12). The response to "the people" as they saw Jesus' sign seems very positive at first: "This is indeed the prophet who is to come into the world!" (6:14), but the next verse shows that Jesus had to withdraw from them because they wanted to make him king by force.[147] So "Jesus withdrew again to the mountain *by himself*" (6:15). It is difficult to know how much weight to put on these last words (αὐτὸς μόνος), but it is possible that Jesus' disciples are thus understood as part of "the people," at least in their inadequate understanding of the nature of Jesus' kingship (see also 1:49, 18:36–37) and mission.[148] Nevertheless, Jesus in these fifteen verses has acted as the disciples' teacher (6:3; 6), one who desired to see them progress in their understanding.[149]

When evening came, the disciples went down to the sea by themselves and got into a boat to cross the sea to Capernaum (6:16–17). The narrator gives this information: "It was now dark,[150] and Jesus had not yet come to them" (6:17). This aside could indicate (*i*) that the disciples were expecting Jesus to join them;[151] (*ii*) that "Jesus had directed the apostles to meet Him at some point on

---

[146] Segovia, "Peace," 83.

[147] This inside view from the narrator is a reminder that propositions that make up Christological confessions, even if they are true to the ideological perspective of the implied author, do not necessarily reflect a proper understanding of the person and work of Jesus by the persons who confess them. For a brief discussion on the content of the present confession as reflecting Jewish eschatological expectations, see Ridderbos, *John*, 215–16. For discussions in favour of and against this confession reflecting a first-century messianic interpretation of Deut. 18:15–18, see respectively W. J. Bittner, *Jesu Zeichen im Johannesevangelium: Die Messias-Erkenntnis im Johannesevangelium vor ihrem jüdischen Hintergrund*, WUNT 2/26 (Tübingen: Mohr Siebeck, 1987), 155–58; and U. Schnelle, *Antidocetic Christology in the Gospel of John: An Investigation of the Place of the Fourth Gospel in the Johannine School* (Minneapolis, MN: Fortress, 1992), 103–04.

[148] This point is proposed by Gloer, "Come and See," 283, and Beasley-Murray, *John*, 89.

[149] The didactic or catechetical nature of this text has been noted most particularly by L. T. Witkamp, "Some Specific Johannine Features in John 6.1–21," *JSNT* 40 (1990): 50–51.

[150] *Pace* Carson, *John*, 274, it is very unlikely that the mention of darkness (σκοτία) symbolises in this verse the state of unbelief in which the disciples found themselves, since the implied author has not put their belief in question since 2:11.

[151] Lincoln, *John*, 218, while agreeing that the disciples were waiting for Jesus to come to them, also remarks that the lack of information regarding the exact expectation of the disciples

the eastern shore on their way to Capernaum;"[152] and (*iii*) "that now also the darkness separated them from him and he therefore had to come to them in the dark."[153] In this verse, the narration appears to be done from the perspective of the disciples, thus emphasising a sense of expectation on their part. When Jesus showed up, the disciples probably recognised him: "they saw Jesus walking on the sea and coming near the boat, and they were frightened" (6:19). What frightened them was arguably not that *Jesus* was walking towards them, but that Jesus was *walking on water*. This seeing, according to Ridderbos, is reminiscent of 1:14, and the fear experienced by the disciples is that which "fills a person confronted with the revelation of God or the divine [...]."[154] Jesus' words in the next verse come to reinforce this impression: "I am (ἐγώ εἰμι); do not be afraid."[155] Whether or not the disciples understood Jesus' words as a declaration that he was one with God in deed and words, the text does not say. Jesus' words, however, alleviated the disciples' fear and they wished to welcome (λαβεῖν) him into the boat.[156] Finally, in what appears to be another miracle, the boat immediately reached dry land where they were going (6:21).

The next section of the narrative, 6:22–59, is also known as "the bread of life discourse." But before Jesus delivers it, an introduction in which the disciples are mentioned three times (6:22 2x, 23) provides the setting of this discourse. The crowd went after Jesus to Capernaum (6:25), and readers learn at the end of the discourse that in Capernaum, Jesus spoke "in the synagogue" (6:59). The "bread of life discourse" in this chapter is an exposition of scripture passages that took the form of an exchange between Jesus and the crowd, a dialogue with questions and answers.[157] Jesus' teaching was not received by the crowd,

---

should favour an interpretation that reads this clause "as a narratorial aside for the benefit of readers, who are being informed that the disciples are still alone."

[152] Westcott, *John*, 98; Morris, *John*, 308.

[153] Ridderbos, *John*, 217.

[154] Ridderbos, *John*, 217.

[155] While on the surface level, Jesus' saying is a recognition formula that could be translated by "It is I; do not be afraid," Lincoln, *John*, 219, shows how Jesus in this verse "is being presented as the embodiment of the God who walks on the water and whose self-proclamation is 'I am; do not be afraid." As Lincoln further shows, Deutero-Isaiah LXX uses eight times the formula "ἐγώ εἰμι" in an absolute way for God's self-identification as the one true God (Is. 41:4; 43:10, 25; 45:18; 46:4 (twice); 48:12; 51:12), and throughout this section of the book there are also frequent exhortations not to fear (40:9; 41:10, 13; 43:1, 5; 44:2; 43:4). See also D. M. Ball, *'I Am' in John's Gospel. Literary Function, Background and Theological Implications*, JSNT-Sup 124 (Sheffield: Sheffield Academic Press, 1996), 74, 181–185, for further discussion.

[156] Could this reception/welcome of Jesus by the disciples reflect 1:12: "But to all who did receive him, who believed in his name, he gave the right to become children of God"? Nothing is sure, but it would not be the first time in the narrative that the disciples believe as a result of one of Jesus' miraculous displays (*cf.* 2:11). See J. P. Heil, *Jesus Walking on the Sea: Meaning and Gospel Functions of Matt. 14:22–33; Mark 6:45–52 and John 6:15b–21*, AnBib 87 (Rome: Biblical Institute Press, 1981), 148–49, for a discussion on this issue.

[157] See Lincoln, *John*, 223, who shows that "the exchange with 'the Jews' has in all

as they "grumbled about him" (6:41), questioned his teaching on his divine origins (6:42),[158] and "disputed among themselves" about it (6:52). Such negative reactions to Jesus could explain the change from characterising this group as "the crowd" (6:24) to "the Jews" (6:41, 52).[159] "The Jews" were unable to respond to Jesus with belief. Throughout its interaction with Jesus, this group of ("the crowd"/"the Jews") remained limited by its sight (6:26) and understanding (6:31, 42, 52).

Once the discourse has ended, another dialogue begins and clearly emphasises two distinct responses to Jesus' teaching and self-revelation. Once more, the name of Jesus' dialogue partners has changed, as he is now addressing a group characterised as "many of his disciples" (6:60, 61, 66).[160] The exact identity of these "disciples" is difficult to assess. The fact that this new dialogue builds on the preceding interaction between Jesus and the crowd/"the Jews" potentially indicates that the disciples were a distinguishable part of the crowd without necessarily being "the Jews" referred to in 6:41,52.[161]

The response of these disciples is disconcerting as they act similarly to "the Jews." The fact that the narrator could speak of these "many disciples" as grumbling (6:61), finding Jesus' words "hard" and being offended by them (6:60–61), not believing (6:64), and finally turning back and no longer walking with Jesus (6:66) is, to say the least, puzzling.[162] However, if we assume

---

probability been built up from material in the form of a synagogue homily with its typical midrashic features of commentary on a scriptural text, found here in v. 31."

[158] W. E. Sproston, "'Is not this Jesus, the Son of Joseph…?' (John 6.42). Johannine Christology as a Challenge to Faith," *JSNT* 24 (1985): 91–92: "We then see that it is precisely the claim to divinity of Jesus son of Joseph which challenges all who encounter him to acceptance or rejection, and that their reaction to his challenge will mean for them salvation or condemnation."

[159] Thus for J. Painter, "Tradition and Interpretation in John 6," *NTS* 35 (1989): 421, there is here a change of genre from quest (6:1–36) to rejection (6:41–59) stories. Note also how Jesus' "I am" sayings (6:35, 41, 48, 51) seem to be what triggered "the Jews'" negative reactions to Jesus.

[160] Painter, "Tradition," 421–22, observes parallelisms in this chapter between changes of genres and changes of audiences, time, and location. From the *crowd* at Capernaum (6:22–36: *quest story*), the narrative moves to "*the Jews*" in the synagogue at Capernaum (6:41–59: *rejection story*), to the disciples in an unspecified location (6:60–66: *rejection story*), and finally to the Twelve (6:67–71: *commendation story*).

[161] So for instance, L. Schenke, "Johannine Schism and the 'Twelve' (John 6:60–71)," in *Critical Readings of John 6*, ed. by R. A. Culpepper, BibIntS 22 (Leiden/New York, NY/Köln: Brill, 1997), 207, proposes that "6:26–58 presupposes the disciples as hearers, but not as discussion partners." For Lincoln, *John*, 236, however, "the primary function of this group may […] be to represent later followers of Jesus who were unable to go all the way with the viewpoint on Jesus represented by the evangelist."

[162] For K. Quast, *Peter and the Beloved Disciple: Figures for a Community in Crisis*, JSNTSup 32 (Sheffield: Sheffield Academic Press, 1989), 46: "What is significant is that belief in Jesus has become the watershed for eternal life and the category of discipleship is not identical to the category of those who believe."

that these "many disciples" were a distinguishable part of the crowd, a rapid survey of the narrative's flow up to this point seems to indicate that the implied author never considered their discipleship to be anything more than a physical following (6:2, 24) of a man they thought was a prophet and a potential king (6:14–15) who could provide them with food (6:26). If this is the case, they had neither understood his teaching nor his signs (6:26–27) and 6:60–66 concludes in showing that this ongoing lack of understanding led to defection.[163] Jesus' comment in 6:65 comes to reinforce this conclusion and theologically makes sense of their upcoming defection: "This is why I told you that no one can come to me unless it is granted him by the Father" (6:65). Belief, for these "many disciples," was impossible for the Father had not granted it to them.[164]

Though the text never explicitly says so, it is possible that more than just the Twelve stayed with Jesus after the defection of the many disciples.[165] In any case, it is now exclusively them whom Jesus addresses in 6:67.[166] His question to them, "Do you want to go away as well?" (6:67), reflects the fact that Jesus has seen the number of his auditors and followers shrink dramatically in a short span of time, but it is unlikely that it betrays his nervousness that the Twelve will also part from him. Jesus "knew from the beginning who those were who did not believe, and who it was who would betray him" (6:64). Rather, Jesus gives the Twelve, in the midst of a crisis within the larger group of Jesus' followers, an opportunity to reaffirm their belief in him and their willingness to continue to follow him.[167] Thus Peter, speaking for the Twelve,[168] gives this rich confession of faith: "Lord, to whom shall we go? You have the words of eternal life, and we have believed, and have come to know, that you are the Holy One of God" (6:68–69). The question Peter asks is obviously rhetorical and prepares the way for the next sentence in the confession.[169] It is clear to him that there is no other alternative, for Jesus has "the words of eternal life" and is thus worthy of their allegiance.[170] As is often noticed, Peter echoes Jesus' own words

---

[163] The disciples apparently wanted Jesus to conform to their expectations (6:62), but such an approach to Jesus is "fleshy" as indicated by 6:63 (so Moloney, *John*, 228).

[164] See also 6:37, 44. Lincoln, *John*, 238, puts it well: "The mystery of belief or unbelief is ultimately in the hands of God. Just as the Spirit has to be at work for humans to be able to transcend their own categories and come to true recognition of Jesus, so the Father is the one who grants such believing recognition."

[165] So Schenke, "Schism," 210.

[166] This is the first time the Fourth Gospel distinguishes the Twelve as a particular group of disciples.

[167] So Carson, *John*, 303.

[168] Peter addresses Jesus with the first person plural in 6:68–69, and when Jesus replies, it is not to Peter alone, but to the Twelve (6:70). For Léon-Dufour, *Lecture*, 2:187: "Pierre apparaît comme le responsable du groupe."

[169] Schnackenburg, *John*, 2:75.

[170] Note also that Peter here takes on the same verb (ἀπελευσόμεθα) that was used to speak of the disciples' defection (ἀπῆλθον).

in 6:63: "The words that I have spoken to you are spirit and life." Peter thus shows that he has assimilated these words from Jesus, though how much he understood from this (and the entire preceding discourse) is once more difficult to assess.[171] More importantly, in his confession Peter shows that Jesus' words did not become for the Twelve the stumbling block that it had been for the disciples in 6:66. The Twelve had continued to believe and know that Jesus was "the Holy One of God" (6:69).[172] The perfect tense of the verbs πεπιστεύκαμεν and ἐγνώκαμεν indicates belief and knowledge that began in the past and continue in the present, and it is also properly "stative," *i.e.* expressing the state of the disciples' belief and knowledge.[173] As for the sequencing of these two verbs, it is certainly incorrect to state that it reflects a development from belief to knowledge, for these verbs can be used interchangeably in the Fourth Gospel (*cf.* 17:3, 8) and, in the case of 16:30, in reverse order.[174] Interestingly, Peter in his confession repeats none of the terms used by Jesus to describe himself in the preceding discourse (bread of life/living bread, Son of Man). However, he declares "*you are* (σὺ εἶ) the Holy One of God," which could be interpreted as Peter's confirmation of Jesus' prior and controversial "ἐγώ εἰμι" declarations.[175] Moreover, the title "Holy One of God" speaks of Jesus' divine origins, and of his being set apart by God.[176] Thus, this confession makes for an interest-

---

[171] For Léon-Dufour, *Lecture*, 2:188: "Implicitement, c'est tout le contenu du discours, jugé inadmissible par les disciples, que Pierre accepte sans réserve. Certes, au niveau du récit évangélique, le sens plénier des paroles de Jésus lui échappe encore, mais sa confiance se risque sur l'essentiel: le message de Jésus est porteur de vie éternelle."

[172] Indeed, the Twelve's reaction to Jesus words is an important aspect of their characterisation in this chapter. The Twelve are the only ones in the audience to accept these claims and to realise that Jesus has the words of eternal life (6:68). Thus for Quast, *Figures*, 50: "The ἡμεῖς is emphatic, and this is probably stressed in order to contrast the Twelve with the unbelieving disciples as described in vv. 60–66."

[173] See S. E. Porter, *Verbal Aspects in the Greek of the New Testament, with Reference to Tense and Mood*, SBG 1 (Bern: Peter Lang, 1989), 251–59. See also, M. Zerwick, *Biblical Greek Illustrated by Examples* (Rome: Pontificii Instituti Biblici, 1963), 96, for whom the perfect tense is used for "indicating not the past action as such but the present 'state of affair' resulting from the past action." Barrett, *John*, 306, paraphrases Peter's confession as such: "We are in a state of faith and knowledge; we have recognized the truth and hold it."

[174] *Pace* E. C. Hoskyns, *The Fourth Gospel*, Rev. ed. (London: Faber and Faber, 1947), 303. For Léon-Dufour, *Lecture*, 2:188–89, the order of the verbs does not mark a progress from simple faith to intelligent faith (contrary to many Church Fathers), but renders explicit what makes true faith: not an abstract knowledge, but an existential relation such as that which unites the good shepherd and his sheep (10:14), which, for him, is the biblical sense of the verb γίνωσκω.

[175] So Heil, *Walking*, 169.

[176] See W. R. Domeris, "The Confession of Peter according to John 6:69," *TynBul* 44 (1993): 155–67; and H. L. N. Joubert, "'The Holy One of God' (John 6:69)," *Neot* 2 (1968): 57–69, for overviews of the debate regarding the connotations to be given to this expression (basically, Jesus as divine or Jesus as Messiah/agent). For Joubert (p. 64), "there can be no doubt that 'ὁ ἅγιος τοῦ θεοῦ' is a title by which Jesus, in a very real sense, is put on the side of God."

ing reformulation of much of Jesus' teaching in the "Bread of Life" discourse. In short, one might say that Peter confesses to Jesus that the Twelve desire to remain with him because of his divine identity and self-revelation that leads to eternal life.

But Jesus' reply to such a full confession is unexpected. Instead of congratulating Peter or rejoicing in the Twelve's continuing discipleship, Jesus reminds the disciples that *he* chose them (echoing prior statements made in 6:37, 44–45, 65),[177] and announces that one of them is a devil.[178] Jesus here wished not to invalidate Peter's declaration but to stress his sovereign choice of his followers (see also 13:18; 15:16), *including* Judas who, he knew (6:64, 70), was going to betray him! Thus for Conway, such a declaration from Jesus' mouth "dispels any notion that inclusion among the twelve is equivalent to faithful discipleship."[179] In and of itself, this argument is obviously correct, but when Conway adds that "an element of suspicion lingers around the twelve,"[180] she may be going too far since the "devil" is explicitly identified as Judas Iscariot (6:71), and not as any of the other eleven. The last two verses of this section bring back to the forefront of the narrative (after 2:17 and of course the bread of life discourse), but through a different angle, the upcoming death of Jesus.[181] The Twelve, though they have expressed their faith to Jesus in this pivotal time of his ministry, have yet to be tested in a profound manner. One of them, readers are already aware, will inevitably fail.

In the following section of the narrative (Jn. 7) Jesus' disciples are not mentioned, except when Jesus' brothers exhort him to go to Judea so that "your disciples also may see the works that you are doing" (7:3). For implied readers, the mention of Jesus' disciples in Judea is somewhat of a surprise, since the

---

And then p. 66: "We conclude: this confession makes it clear that the eternal Sonship of Jesus is the soul of his Messiahship: in every detail of the Messiah-figure there beats the mighty pulse of the deity." For Schenke, "Schism," 216–17, this Christological title "far surpasses the belief in the Messiah to which Peter has already attained (cf. 1:41f.)."

[177] However, in 6:70 Jesus (and not the Father) is doing the choosing. Nevertheless, as noted by R. Kysar, "The Dismantling of Decisional Faith: A Reading of John 6:25–71," in *Critical Reading of John 6*, ed. by R. A. Culpepper, BibIntS 22 (Leiden/New York, NY/Köln: Brill, 1997), 178: "The theme of God's role in originating the faith response runs through the whole discussion and is represented in the dialogue with each group of participants."

[178] Readers learn the identity of this "devil" through the narrator's aside in 6:71, an aside which builds on a prior one in 6:64.

[179] Conway, *Men and Women*, 169.

[180] Conway, *Men and Women*, 169. See also E. Haenchen, *A Commentary on the Gospel of John*, trans. by R. W. Funk, 2 vols, Hermeneia (Philadelphia, PA: Fortress, 1984), 1:308.

[181] For Moloney, *John*, 229–30, such a comment requires of readers to ponder the fragility of human responses to Jesus, even that of believers: "The confession of Simon Peter is excellent ... so far! How will this expression of faith survive in the difficult moments that will bring this story to an end?" Here again, this point is good and well taken, but one should not forget that here Jesus is speaking of only one of the Twelve. Even more, the narrator identifies him, and does so potentially to dispel any unnecessary suspicion of the eleven others.

narrative has not mentioned their existence so far. Jesus has performed signs in Jerusalem (2:23; 3:2; 5:1) and "many believed in his name" (2:23), but Jesus' visits in Judea had mostly resulted in threats and persecutions from the Jews (4:1–3; 5:16–18). What 7:3 seems to imply is that even though the general response to Jesus was negative, there were still people who identified themselves as his disciples in Judea (*cf.* Mary, Martha, and Lazarus in chap. 11). Nevertheless, these "disciples," are not mentioned any longer in the narrative.[182] For the narrator, Jesus' brothers insistence that he should go to Jerusalem for the Feast of the Booths, together with their reprimand that "no one works in secret if he seeks to be known openly" (7:4) show that they did not believe in him (7:5).[183] Jesus' brothers had misunderstood the nature of Jesus' mission since for them the success of such a mission entailed that Jesus would perform his "works" before a public platform constituted of his Judean followers, but also before "the world" (7:4). For Lincoln, "they fail to recognize that Jesus' mission is not congenial to the world and that his aim is not to achieve publicity for himself but to do the will of the one who sent him."[184] In spite of his announcement that he would not go to the Feast (7:8), he does go to Jerusalem, first secretly (7:10), but then teaching openly in the temple (7:14). This teaching received very contrasted responses: marvel (7:15), accusation (7:20, 46–49), confusion and division (7:25–27, 35, 40–44, 46), threats to arrest and kill him (7:30, 32), a defence (7:50–51), and finally belief (7:31). Yet, the belief of these many people is once more reminiscent of that of 2:23–25, so that implied readers do not take this aside at face value. They have learned that the implied author could use such a term to refer to what may appear as true belief but actually is not so.[185]

On the last day of the feast (7:37–39), Jesus' proclamation is relevant to our study of the disciples' characterisation: "If anyone thirsts, let him come to me and drink, and let him who believes drink. As the Scripture has said, 'out of his belly shall flow rivers of living water.'"[186] Following Jesus' call for anyone

---

[182] In the whole of chapter 7, Jesus seems to be alone, without his disciples, before "the Jews" (7:1, 11, 15, 35) and other groups such as "the crowd" or "many people" (7:12, 31, 40, 41, 43), "some of the people of Jerusalem" (7:25), "the authorities" (7:26), the "Pharisees" and "high priests" (7:32, 45, 47, 48), and the "officers" (7:32, 45). Only Nicodemus is treated as an individual, and as one dissonant voice among the Pharisees (7:50–52).

[183] In retrospect, we could thus say that when Jesus' brothers followed him from Cana to Capernaum in 2:12, such a following did not entail true discipleship.

[184] Lincoln, *John*, 244. See also L. Devillers, *La saga de Siloé. Jésus et la fête des Tentes (Jean 7,1–10,21)*, Lire la Bible 143 (Paris: Cerf, 2005), 52–53.

[185] See 2:23; 8:30; 10:42; and 12:42.

[186] Here we part with most Bible translations, such as the ESV: "if anyone thirsts, let him come to me and drink. Whoever believes in me, as the Scripture has said, 'out of his heart will flow rivers of living water.'" Though the two translations are possible, it makes better sense to see the "belly" as being that of Christ (see 19:34) rather than that of the believers. For thorough treatments of exegetical, syntactical, and theological issues surrounding this most disputed passage, see Lincoln, *John*, 253–58; Devillers, *Saga*, 79–94; and esp. G. Bienaimé, "L'annonce

(τις) to believe in him and thus to receive "rivers of living waters," the narrator explains: "Now this he said about the Spirit, whom those who believed in him were to receive, for as yet the Spirit had not been given, because Jesus was not glorified" (7:39). The narrator declares retrospectively that those who believed in Jesus during his earthly ministry would receive flows of living waters (the Spirit) during or after his glorification. Thus, Jesus and the narrator seem to disconnect the possibility of believing in the narrative from the gift of the Spirit. This poses important questions regarding (*i*) the nature of this gift of the Spirit[187] and (*ii*) the implications of this gift for faith and life, and in our case for the faith and the life of the disciples.[188] At this point of this sequential study, however, we are not in a position to give definitive answers to these questions, but only to point out difficulties. A later dealing with the implied author's temporal perspective will address these issues in a more detailed fashion (see chapter 4 below).

In chapter 8, Jesus' disciples are not mentioned.[189] In this chapter, however, Jesus gives an important criterion for true discipleship that shapes the way im-

---

des fleuves d'eau vive en Jean 7, 37–39," *RTL* 21 (1990): 281–310. The strongest defences of the "traditional" view probably come from Carson, *John*, 321–28; and J. B. Cortés, "Yet Another Look at John 7:37–38," *CBQ* 29 (1967): 75–86. For a "mediating" position, understanding the primary meaning of the imagery as referring to Christ, but secondarily to discipleship, see C. R. Koester, *Symbolism in the Fourth Gospel: Meaning, Mystery, Community*, 2nd ed. (Minneapolis: Fortress, 2003), 13–14, 192–200.

[187] How are implied-readers to understand other, prior occurrences of the Spirit in the narrative in light of such a stark comment? Indeed, though it is never explicitly stated, in Jesus' dialogue with Nicodemus the Spirit seems to be a present possibility (3:5–6). Likewise, Jesus proclaims to the Samaritan woman: "the hour is coming, and is now here, when the true worshipers will worship the Father in Spirit and truth" (4:23). Of course, it is unclear whether "Spirit" should take a capital S or not in these verses. Carson, *John*, 195, commenting on 3:5, writes: "the focus is on the impartation of God's nature as 'spirit' [*cf.* 4:24], not on the Holy Spirit as such." For many interpreters, 7:39 indicates that the Spirit had not yet been given "in the full, Christian sense of the term" (Carson, *John*, 329; Léon-Dufour, *Lecture*, 2:239) or in a "new way" (C. Bennema, "The Giving of the Spirit in John's Gospel – a New Proposal?," *EvQ* 74 (2002): 212: "John 7:39 promises a new way of the Spirit being active/available, which is dependent on the *start* of Jesus' glorification (the cross) and finds its fulfilment in 19:30 and 20:22").

[188] For instance, if the Spirit has not yet been given and if the Spirit is that which gives or sustains life (4:14; 7:38), it may be asked how Jesus could announce: "whoever hears my words and believes him who sent me has eternal life" in 5:24? Two options are most often proposed: (*i*) "what was in fact experienced after the resurrection is retrojected into the time of Jesus and thus in the story line anticipates the post-resurrection period" (Lincoln, *John*, 258). (*ii*) The gift of the Spirit in 20:22 for instance (Jesus breathing on his disciples and saying: "receive the Holy Spirit") "secures and sustains the adequate belief and the life-giving relationship the disciples already had with Jesus through the Spirit" (Bennema, "Giving," 208; and de Jonge, *Stranger*, 10).

[189] The present study chooses to pass over the infamous adulterous woman pericope (7:53–8:11). The overwhelming textual ground to deny its authenticity is laid out in B. M. Metzger,

plied readers understand the standing of the group of Jesus' disciples. First, Jesus declares "I am the light of the world. Whoever follows me will not walk in darkness, but will have the light of life" (8:12). This declaration regarding discipleship and its consequences triggers a new heated interaction with the Pharisees/"the Jews" (8:12–29), and once more "many believed in him" (8:30).[190] This narratorial comment may in fact simply prepare readers for the exposure both of a criterion for true discipleship, and thus also of the many deficiencies of these so-called believers.[191] Jesus tells the "Jews who had believed in him, 'if you abide in my words, you are truly my disciples, and you will know the truth and the truth will set you free'" (8:31), which results in an ever more heated debate (8:32–58) culminating in "the Jews" wanting to stone Jesus (8:59).[192] For Jesus, the test of true discipleship is continuing allegiance to his teaching, to truth that liberates from sin (8:34) and death (8:24).[193] Such allegiance constitutes one as a member of God's household (8:35; see also 1:12). As 8:36 makes clear, this liberating truth is none other than God's revelation embodied in Jesus (see also 14:6). In other words, one might say that true discipleship entails a *continuing* following (8:12) and abiding with Jesus, that is, a continuing belief in what Peter declared for the Twelve in 6:68–69. The Jews

A Textual Commentary on the Greek New Testament, 2nd ed. (Stuttgart: Deutsche Bibelgesellschaft/United Bible Societies, 1994), 187–89. It should be noted that, while recognising this section's inauthenticity in the original text of the Fourth Gospel, Beck, *Discipleship*, 101–2, makes a case for its inclusion in any literary analysis of the Fourth Gospel narrative since "it is part of the text of the Fourth Gospel as read by most readers, from ancient time until now, within the interpretive communities of faith adherents in which they participate" (p. 101).

[190] S. Motyer, *Your Father the Devil? A New Approach to John and 'the Jews'*, PBM (Carlisle: Paternoster, 1997), 157, suggests that faith here could be understood against the legal background of the passage to mean that "impressed by [Jesus'] appeal to God as witness, 'many' are prepared to accept his claims [...]. So the 'many' who believe are those who accept that Jesus is 'the Prophet', prompted to faith by his calling God to witness, and moved by the warnings attached to rejecting both." See Deut. 13:1–11 and 18:21 for OT backgrounds to this idea.

[191] Hoskyns, *Fourth Gospel*, 338, correctly argues: "The purpose of this discourse is to expose this false belief and to reveal its compatibility with murderous action." *Pace* Westcott, *John*, 132–33, there is no distinction between πιστεύω εἰς of 8:30 and πιστεύω with the dative of 8:31, as though true believers were spoken of in 8:30, while those of 8:31 were not. J. Swetnam, "The Meaning of πεπιστευκότας in John 8,31," *Bib* 61 (1980): 106–09, correctly understands the perfect participle πεπιστευκότας as serving as a pluperfect. Thus, instead of understanding these Jews as still believing in 8:31, they could instead be "those who had believed him – but no longer do."

[192] This passage is certainly where the debate around Jesus' identity is most heated in the whole Gospel. Indeed, it is here that we find the harshest accusations, coming both from 'the Jews" and Jesus' mouths (8:37,40, 44, 48).

[193] Chennattu, *Discipleship*, 76. On "abiding" (μένειν), see also D. A. Lee, "Abiding in the Fourth Gospel: A Case Study in Feminist Biblical Theology," *Pac* 10 (1997): 123–36; K. Scholtissek, *In Ihm Sein und Bleiben: Die Sprache des Immanenz in den johanneischen Schriften*, HBS 21 (Freiburg: Herder, 1999).

who believed in Jesus in 8:30 were unable to stand this test of allegiance.[194] Indeed, Jesus' words in 8:31, 35–35 "freinent leur progrès dans la foi: ils se montrent réticents face à cet homme qui prétend être le seul accès à Dieu, à la vérité, à la liberté."[195] Their discipleship was thus not 'true' but similar to that of the "many disciples" in 6:60.

In chapter 9, the disciples reappear[196] very briefly in the narrative as they pose a question to Jesus that sets up the following events.[197] The question is about "a man blind from birth" that Jesus and his disciples notice as they pass by: "Rabbi, who sinned, this man or his parents, that he was born blind?" (9:2). By this question, the disciples display their "savoir implicite"[198] of the relation between sin and blindness, but such understanding will be shown to be wrong.[199] Jesus had alluded to light and darkness in the narrative in 8:12: "Whoever follows me will never walk in darkness, but will have the light of life" so that a parallel could be made between "darkness" and spiritual blindness (*cf.* 3:19–21). The disciples, however, did not think of integrating this earlier teaching with their implicit understanding of physical blindness. As such they show "that in their understanding they remain close to that of the Pharisees themselves"[200] because the Pharisees held similar assumptions about physical blindness (9:34). Jesus will thus seek to teach the disciples and those involved in the story about the blindness and sight he is most concerned about (see 9:39; 41). To do so, he first answers the disciples' question briefly and negatively in 9:3, and tells them that the ensuing events are meant to reveal God's works: "It was not that this man sinned, or his parents, but that the works of God might be displayed in him."[201] Jesus then performs a healing on the blind man (9:6–7), which will trigger interrogations from the man's neighbours (9:8–12), and a trial before the Pharisees.[202] From such a trial will result the blind man's implicit acknowledgement

---

[194] See J. H. Neyrey, "Jesus the Judge: Forensic Process in John 8,21–59," *Bib* 68 (1987): 520–35.

[195] Devillers, *Saga*, 115. See also Lincoln, *Truth*, 90.

[196] The troupe of the disciples has not been mentioned since 6:70.

[197] See J. W. Holleran, "Seeing the Light. A Narrative Reading of John 9; Part I: Background and Presuppositions," *ETL* 69 (1993): 10–11; and U. C. von Wahlde, "Literary Structure and Theological Argument in Three Discourses with the Jews in the Fourth Gospel," *JBL* 103 (1984): 578, n.8, for questions of structure and extent of this particular story.

[198] A. Dettwiler, "Fragile compréhension. L'herméneutique de l'usage johannique du malentendu," *RTP* 131 (1999): 379.

[199] This is not the place to research historically the Jewish understanding of blindness and its causes in first century Palestine (see Léon-Dufour, *Lecture*, 2:334–35, for a brief discussion). What is striking, on a literary level, are the simple options presented by the disciples to Jesus. Blindness must necessarily come either from one's parents' sins or from one's own sin.

[200] Segovia, "Peace," 84.

[201] Thus Segovia, "Peace," 84, points out that Jesus, in presenting the blind man as another occasion for his and their mission (9:3–5), shows that "the disciples have also failed to see the illness at hand in terms of the ongoing harvest."

[202] For a literary study of this trial, see Howard, "Significance," 63–78; and especially

of his discipleship before the Pharisees (9:27),[203] his apparent excommunication from the synagogue (9:34, ἐξέβαλον), and the confession of his belief in Jesus as the "Son of Man" (9:35–39). This new "disciple", however, is not mentioned again in the narrative (except as a reference in 10:21 and 11:37), and however important his place in this section of the narrative may be, he cannot be considered to be part of the troupe of Jesus' disciples.[204] In any case, beginning with the disciples' somewhat naïve question about blindness, Jesus was able to display God's works and gained a new disciple.

The disciples have remained with Jesus in spite of the Jews' attempt to stone Jesus, and they continue to follow and work with Jesus. Indeed, Jesus associates them in his task (9:4: "*We* must work the works of him who sent me while it is day"), so that they can be considered his co-workers.[205] Jesus' motivation for including the disciples in his task should not be missed: "night is coming, when no one can work. As long as I am in the world, I am the light of the world" (9:4–5). Several scholars have proposed that Jesus associates his disciples in his works so that night would not happen, so that the light would continue to be present in the world even after Jesus' departure. This could only happen through the continuing work and presence of the disciples in the world.[206] If this proposal is correct,[207] this would be the first time Jesus implicitly teaches his disciples about their continuing task *after* his departure.[208] It would also necessarily give implied readers additional reasons to trust in the continuity of their discipleship even after his departure.

In the meantime, Jesus will give a most important teaching (10:1–38), which, though addressed to the Pharisees and "the Jews," has implications for his disciples.[209] In this well-known "Good Shepherd" discourse, Jesus uses a

---

Lincoln, *Truth*, 96–105; J. L. Staley, "Stumbling in the Dark, Reaching for the Light: Reading Characters in John 5 and 9," *Semeia* 53 (1991): 55–80.

[203] Such acknowledgment triggers this interesting response by the Pharisees: "You are his disciple, but we are disciples of Moses" (9:28). This is an example of Johannine irony, as Jesus in 5:46 has already told "the Jews" that "if you believed Moses, you would believe me; for he wrote of me."

[204] Siker-Gieseler, "Disciples," 207–08: "After this scene [6:67–71], there are others who express faith in Jesus ('the Jews who had believed,' 8:31; the man born blind, 9:38; Martha, 11:27) but they are not portrayed as 'disciples' who accompany Jesus, as are 'the twelve,' the apparent referent of 'disciples' in 11:7–12, 54 and 18:1, 2. Thus, the Fourth Gospel seems to present a wider group of believers who do not actually accompany Jesus, and a smaller group of believers, the twelve, who do accompany Jesus."

[205] Moloney, *John*, 291, puts it well: "They are associated with the task of Jesus, to work the works of the one who sent him."

[206] Moloney, *John*, 291–92; Devillers, *Saga*, 147.

[207] For a critique, see Ridderbos, *John*, 334–35.

[208] To our knowledge, however Köstenberger, *Missions*, does not even consider such a proposal. Much of the farewell discourse, culminating in Jesus' prayer in 17:18, will also serve this very purpose.

[209] With J. L. de Villier, "The Shepherd and his Flock," *Neot* 2 (1968): 91, we understand

figure of speech (παροιμίαν, 10:6) to speak of himself as "the door of the sheep" (10:7) and the "good shepherd" who "lays down his life for the sheep" (10:11). Later at the Feast of Dedication (10:22–39), Jesus is answering "Jews" who requested that he be more open and less suspenseful about his real identity: "If you are the Christ, tell us plainly" (10:24). But Jesus continues to answer with his figure of speech and points his interlocutors to his "works" (10:25, 32, 37–38) that, in turn, point to his union with the Father. Beyond the question of Jesus' identity, though it is intimately related to it, Jesus' words regarding his "sheep" and his "flock" are relevant to the present study. Implied readers necessarily understand Jesus' flock/sheep to refer to his disciples (present, 10:27, and also future, 10:16). He speaks of them as "his own" (10:3–4, 14),[210] those who have been given him by the Father (10:29), who "know" him (10:4, 14),[211] and for whom he lays down his life (10:11, 15, 17) so that they may have life abundantly (10:10, 28). Thus, his disciples starkly and positively contrast with 'the Jews' to whom Jesus says: "you do not believe because you are not part of my flock" (10:26).[212] Jesus' true disciples are members of Jesus' flock, and will forever remain so. Just as their belief was not of their own doing, they will be kept in the secure hand of their "good shepherd."

In this part of the narrative (5:1–10:42), what strikes readers most as far as Jesus' disciples are concerned is their faithfulness, their commitment to remain with and follow Jesus even though they have been tested in many ways. Their understanding was tested by Jesus himself (6:1–15) but more importantly, their faith in and allegiance to Jesus was tested through a series of events: many disciples abandoning Jesus (6:66); Jesus' declaration that one of them is a devil (6:70); "the Jews" and the Pharisees' repeated attempts to kill him (7:1; 8:59; 10:31); and the apparent excommunication of the blind man (9:34). Nevertheless, the disciples have remained with Jesus, as the beginning of the next part

---

the connection between Jn. 9 and Jn. 10 as follows: "A signal instance of the failure of hireling shepherds, in this case the Pharisees, has been given; instead of properly caring for the blind man, the Pharisees have cast him out, 9:34. Jesus, on the other hand, as the good Shepherd, found him, ευρων, 9:35, and so brought him into the true fold." Therefore, the discourse concerns the whole of Jesus' disciples (whether they are physically following him or not), including the man born blind.

[210] Jn. 13:1 will validate the claim that the disciples were in view in chap. 10, since Jesus speaks of his disciples as "his own."

[211] Ridderbos, *John*, 361, notes that "the people's knowledge of God means that they know him as *their* God and themselves as adopted and called by him and, accordingly, that they act in faith, in the consciousness of being called, in obedience."

[212] The circularity of Jesus' argument has been noted by scholars. See for instance Lincoln, *John*, 312: "Jesus' interrogators are told they do not believe because they do not belong to his sheep, yet they are still invited to believe and are held responsible for not doing so. His followers believe because they are the sheep whom God has given to Jesus and who have been enabled to recognise his voice."

of the narrative makes clear (11:7).[213] Thus, one might say that in this part they fulfil Jesus' criterion for true discipleship, to abide in his word (8:31). More, as they were in the midst of people abandoning Jesus (6:66), they confessed their faith in Jesus in a new manner, recognising Jesus' divine identity and his having the words of eternal life (6:68–69). Finally, in this period Jesus also continued to include them in his task (6:10–14; 9:4), which, as will be seen in chapter 4, may have significant rhetorical intents. Such a positive depiction of the disciples in their belief, understanding, and allegiance to Jesus should however not make us lose sight of the upcoming defection of one of them (6:70–71) as well as their recurrent lack of understanding (6:5; 9:2). The implied author thus continues to present as threads both their ongoing faith and discipleship (for all those represented in the band of the disciples, minus Judas) as well as their ongoing mis-(or deficient)-understandings.

But implied readers notice an interesting phenomenon in this regard. The implied author appears to have set a pattern where (*i*) the disciples show a deficient understanding on an issue that has already been addressed by Jesus in the narrative; (*ii*) the disciples' deficient understanding triggers further teaching by Jesus; and (*iii*) Jesus includes the disciples further in his task. Thus, in 6:1–15, after Philip and Andrew fail the test of understanding the present gathering in term of mission (even after Jesus' teaching in 4:43–38), Jesus implicitly shows them that he himself is the solution to human needs. In so doing, he uses the disciples to feed the crowd and gather the leftovers (6:10, 12). Later, the disciples' poor understanding of sin and blindness in 9:2 (*i.e.* 8:12) is taken up by Jesus to perform a miracle and reveal the true nature of guilt (9:39–41). There, Jesus reminds his disciples that they too are included in his mission (9:4). Therefore, one wonders if these particular deficient understandings, on the part of the disciples, should not be interpreted as literary devices used by the implied author for the purpose of clarifying or expanding Jesus' teaching on a given issue.[214] As Jesus continues to involve his disciples in his mission, the implied author shows that these deficient understandings should not be considered as threats to their discipleship. In fact, nothing will "snatch them out of [Jesus'] hand" for Jesus is giving them eternal life (10:28). He lays down his life for them (10:15, 17).

4. Jesus Moves Toward the Hour of Death and Glory (11:1–12:50)

The next section of the narrative (the Lazarus story) has been the focus of a significant amount of literary studies in recent years.[215] This story is particularly

---

[213] Culpepper, *Anatomy*, 118.

[214] Note that the disciples, after Jesus' teaching on these matters, show no immediate sign of better grasping his teaching. Thus, it appears that the role of the mis-(or lack of)-understandings in this section of the narrative is simply to trigger Jesus' teaching, but not necessarily to show how the disciples' understanding is progressing.

[215] Most notably, W. Wuellner, "Putting Life Back into the Lazarus Story and its Reading:

important for the plot of the Fourth Gospel since the conclusion of the episode presents Caiaphas' prophecy (11:49–50) and the plans of the Council to kill Jesus (11:53).[216] Early in this chapter, readers learn that Lazarus of Bethany, the brother of Martha and Mary, was ill, so his sisters relayed to Jesus that "he whom you love is ill" (11:1–3). Jesus then announces: "This illness does not lead to death. It is for the glory of God, so that the Son of God may be glorified through it" (11:4), and decides to stay "two days longer in the place where he was" (across the Jordan, *cf.* 10:40).[217] The disciples appear on the scene once Jesus tells them "let us go to Judea" (11:7) which may indicate that he wishes once again to include them in his mission. To this invitation, they respond: "Rabbi, the Jews were just now seeking to stone you, and you are going there again?" The disciples were of course aware of the danger Jesus would face in Judea, and their question points to their surprise for what they interpret as "Jesus' courting of death."[218] Jesus answers his disciples' hesitation and incomprehension in the form of another question: "Are there not twelve hours in the day?" (11:9); and proceeds to explain the sense of this question.[219] In this explanation, Jesus contrasts the danger of death that he incurs to the danger of "stumbling" incurred by those walking in the darkness (11:9–10). Jesus switches the disciples' preoccupation from his death to the real danger that is

---

The Narrative Rhetoric of John 11 as the Narration of Faith," *Semeia* 53 (1991): 113–31; M. W. G. Stibbe, "A Tomb with a View: John 11.1–44 in Narrative-Critical Perspective," *NTS* 40 (1994): 38–54; R. Hakola, "A Character Resurrected: Lazarus in the Fourth Gospel and Afterwards," in *Characterization in the Gospels. Reconceiving Narrative Criticism*, ed. by D. Rhoads and K. Syreeni, JSNTSuppS 184 (Sheffield: Sheffield Academic Press, 1999), 223–63; J. Zumstein, "Foi et vie éternelle selon Jean," in *Résurrection: L'après-mort dans le monde ancien et le Nouveau Testament*, ed. by O. Mainville and D. Marguerat, MB 45 (Genève: Labor et Fides, 2001), 215–35; F. J. Moloney, "Can Everyone be Wrong? A Reading of John 11.1–12.8," *NTS* 49 (2003): 505–27; F. J. Moloney, "The Faith of Martha and Mary. A Narrative Approach to John 11,17–40," *Bib* 75 (1994): 471–93; A. T. Lincoln, "The Lazarus Story: A Literary Perspective," in *The Gospel of John and Christian Theology*, ed. by R. Bauckham and C. Mosser (Grand Rapids, MI/Cambridge: Eerdmans, 2008), 211–32.

[216] Of course, this is not the first time in the narrative that humans want to put Jesus to death (10:31 being the latest attempt), but here "the depiction of Caiaphas' words as prophecy already indicates that the human decision has been co-opted for God's purposes and is part of the divine resolution of Jesus' mission" (Lincoln, "Lazarus," 214).

[217] At first, it may appear strange that somebody who loved these sisters and their brother (11:5) should decide to not go urgently to Bethany to care for Lazarus. A closer look at the story, however, shows that this is Jesus' way of expressing his love, as the "therefore" (οὖν) at the beginning of v. 6 indicates. The explanation for this unusual display of love is given by Jesus himself in v. 4: "Jesus is operating according to a divine timetable and plan for his mission that involves his and the Father's glory" (Lincoln, *John*, 319).

[218] Lincoln, *John*, 320.

[219] This question is reminiscent of one of his earlier teachings in 9:4: "We must work the works of him who sent me while it is day, night is coming where no one can work." This could be showing that the disciples still do not understand that Jesus, and by implication they also, are engaged in a mission and must go on doing God's work while it is day.

their stumbling. The disciples must remain with Jesus (the light), so that they would not fear Jesus' upcoming death, and so would not stumble. Since Jesus has already decided to go back to Judea, the real issue is whether the disciples will accept to accompany him in this dangerous endeavor or will falter in the face of danger. As Jesus seems to imply: "The preventive measure is to see and have within oneself the light embodied in Jesus, the light of life that overcomes the darkness of death."[220]

So far, the disciples have been portrayed as lacking a certain amount of courage, but when Jesus tells them "our friend Lazarus has fallen asleep but I go to awaken him" (11:11), they also manifest blatant misunderstanding: "Lord, if he has fallen asleep, he will recover" (11:12). For Stibbe, the disciples are portrayed here as "people who are unable to understand even the most transparent of metaphors."[221] However, if their misunderstanding is obvious (and attested by the narrator in 11:13), it is possible that implied readers are meant to see the link between their lack of courage and their inability to interpret (or rather, to *accept*) this obvious metaphor.[222] Jesus thus has to tell it as plainly as possible ("Lazarus has died"), and quickly adds: "and for your sake I am glad that I was not there, so that you may believe" (11:14). In other words, Jesus is glad that Lazarus died, because such a death will serve the disciples' believing. In 11:4, Jesus had already alluded to the consequences of Lazarus' condition: "It is for the glory of God, so that the Son of God may be glorified through it." This connection encourages readers to interpret what follows (the raising of Lazarus) as a sign which will display Jesus' glory.[223] Indeed, the mention of the disciples believing (reminiscent of 2:11) reinforces this outlook. Such a believing, as the narrative has made clear so far, is not one that is non-existent in the disciples so that what is at stake is rather to confirm their belief or to give them "a further boost to the process of believing."[224] Given the context of this verse, *i.e.* the disciples' reluctance to let Jesus go to Judea as well as their misunderstanding regarding "sleeping" and "death", implied readers are led to interpret that what the disciples lack is an understanding and belief in the necessity of Jesus' death and resurrection.[225] Jesus, in performing the following sign, will reveal further

---

[220] Lincoln, "Lazarus," 228. See also Koester, *Symbolism*, 163.

[221] Stibbe, "Tomb," 46. Stibbe adds: "They fail to understand a metaphor which was so common it was almost *cliché*."

[222] Note a different interpretation by Ridderbos, *John*, 392: "From the way Jesus speaks of Lazarus 'falling asleep' and of 'awakening him' they conclude that whatever had come over Lazarus had apparently taken a turn for the better. They see this as all the more reason to persist in their objection to the dangerous trip to Judea."

[223] Zumstein, "Foi et vie," 221: "Le miracle annoncé n'a donc ni sa fin, ni son intelligence en lui-même. Il doit être lu comme un signe renvoyant à la gloire de Dieu et à la glorification du Fils."

[224] Lincoln, *John*, 321.

[225] Lee, *Symbolic*, 200, argues that "The disciples misunderstand the symbolic meaning of Jesus' intended journey to Bethany (vv. 8, 16). They do not understand that, on a deeper level, Jesus is to give life to Lazarus through his death."

what his identity and mission entail, and will do so for the sake of his disciples' faith.[226] This section ends with Thomas' response to Jesus urging the disciples once more to go with him to Judea:[227] "Let us go also, that we may die with him" (11:16). Beside Thomas' oft-noticed resigned bravado,[228] his words may have spoken more than he knew. Jesus' sign at Bethany is meant to enhance the disciples' faith, and with that deepened faith would come the possibility of martyrdom.

The rest of the Lazarus story does not mention the disciples again, so readers do not know what the true impact of this sign was on their faith.[229] Other characters in the narrative benefit from this sign: "many of the Jews therefore, who had come with Mary and had seen what he did, believed in him" (11:45).[230] However, some of them went to the Pharisees to tell them what Jesus had done (11:46; 12:11), and the issue of more and more people believing in Jesus is precisely what worried the Jewish authorities (11:48; 12:11). In the face of mounting anger on the part of the authorities, Jesus moved to Ephraim, where

---

[226] So Segovia, "Peace," 84: "the journey, given its real purpose, is presented explicitly as an occasion for their own belief to develop further (v. 15) – that is, Lazarus' raising is meant to be an anticipation for his own approaching glorification."

[227] Jesus says: "But let us go to him" (11:15). Thus, the already noticed pattern of mis-(or lack of)-understanding on the part of the disciples, further teaching on the part of Jesus, and inclusion of the disciples in Jesus' task is once more present here.

[228] Of course, this resigned bravado is only comical to readers already acquainted with the Fourth Gospel and the disciples' general abandonment of Jesus during his crucifixion. In this regard, Stibbe, "Tomb," 46, has particularly harsh words towards the disciples: "Thomas and Peter [see 13:37] are the embodiments of a certain kind of false discipleship: the kind which promises much in word (in this case, martyrdom) but delivers little in deed (where are Thomas and Peter when Jesus is crucified?). Thomas' words to his fellow disciples in 11:16 are not indicative of a positive characterization." However, Thomas' words are more ambivalent than this. Implied readers can recognise the courage of the disciples at this point of the story: they are indeed ready to go with Jesus and die. Only later will implied readers recognise that the disciples were not ready to die with Jesus.

[229] The rhetorical effect of the disciples' characterisation in this passage is thus apparently first to prepare implied readers for the following narrative, which will in turn seek to persuade them to grow in their belief. See Lincoln, "Lazarus," 231–32.

[230] Note that in the story proper (11:1–53), the narrator does not show how Martha and Mary react to the restoration of their brother to life. It is rather their reactions to his death that figure prominently. In dialoguing with Jesus, they actually serve to highlight important elements of the story (*e.g.* Martha triggers Jesus' saying "I am the resurrection and the life" in 11:25), as well as showing deep faith in Jesus in the face of death and sorrow. For negative views of Martha and Mary's faith, see T. E. Pollard, "The Raising of Lazarus (John XI)," in *SE 6 (TU 112)*, ed. by E. A. Livingston (Berlin: Akademie Verlag, 1973), 440; Moloney, "Martha and Mary," 471–93, and more recently Moloney, "Wrong," 513–19. *Contra* these positions, see S. M. Schneiders, *Written That You May Believe: Encountering Jesus in the Fourth Gospel*, 2nd ed. (New York, NY: Crossroad, 2003), 180, n.26: "Like Peter, who did not fully understand the bread-of-life discourse, Martha believes not in *what* she understands but in the *one* who has the words of eternal life" (italics original).

he stayed with his disciples (11:54). But Jesus came back to Bethany "six days before the Passover" (12:1; see also 11:55–57 regarding the general atmosphere in Jerusalem at the time). There, Mary showed him, in an extravagant display of devotion (pouring a pound of expensive ointment on Jesus' feet and wiping it with her hair), that she accepted by faith[231] that Jesus was willing to go to his own death and thus that the day for his burial was at hand.[232] As such, her belief seems to be a direct consequence of Jesus' actions in the preceding episode (see 11:4, 15). Readers do not have the band of the disciples' reaction with which to compare Mary's act, but so far in the story the disciples have not shown such an acceptance of the necessity of Jesus' death.[233] A reaction to Mary's action in this passage comes from Judas Iscariot, but it can hardly be considered representative of what the other disciples thought since Judas is singled out. Judas complained that the ointment was not sold to care for the poor (12:5), and his reaction is interpreted very negatively first by the narrator (Judas was "about to betray him," he was a "thief" who did not care for the poor, 12:4, 6), then by Jesus who harshly tells him to "leave her alone," explains the significance of Mary's act (12:7), and finally underlines the fact that the time left before his death and departure is short, while the presence of the poor will continue.[234]

The disciples are present, "the next day" (12:12), when Jesus enters Jerusalem on a donkey (12:14) as a fulfilment of the prophecy of Zech. 9:9. A large crowd (12:12) was expecting Jesus and went to meet him (12:18) with branches of palm trees and cries of "Hosanna! Blessed is he who comes in the name of the Lord, even the King of Israel" (12:13). The disciples "did not understand these things at first, but when Jesus was glorified, then they remembered that these things had been written about him and had been done to him" (12:16). Arguably, what the disciples did not understand was both that this particular event was a fulfilment of prophecy, and that the meaning and significance of

---

[231] As Hoskyns comments (followed by Brown, *John*, 1:454) regarding the two opposite reactions to the Lazarus' story: that of the Jewish authorities who in "a supreme act of ignorant unbelief" decree that Jesus should die, and that of Mary who in "a supreme act of intelligent belief" shows her loving devotion to Jesus (Hoskyns, *Fourth Gospel*, 413–17). So also Lee, *Symbolic*, 219.

[232] As Lincoln, *John*, 339, mentions, the term ἐνταφιασμός and its cognate verb can refer not only to burial itself, but also to preparation for burial. Thus, Jesus explains her gesture as such: "the purpose was that she might keep it for the day of my burial preparation" (12:7). Other commentators are uneasy about seeing the anointing by Mary as an embalming of Jesus, so Barrett, *John*, 409, who suggests that it is rather a royal anointing.

[233] R. Bauckham and T. A. Hart, *At the Cross: Meditations on People Who Were There* (Downers Grove, IL: InterVarsity Press, 1999), 17, probably are correct: "No more than any of the disciples does Mary understand *why* Jesus' death should be God's will for him. It is simply that Mary sees that Jesus himself fully accepts his coming death as the destiny he has to fulfil."

[234] It is the contrast between the lengths of time, that of Jesus' remaining presence and that of the poor, which is the issue, not any lack of concern for the poor on the part of Jesus. See Ridderbos, *John*, 420.

this event lay in Jesus riding a young donkey.[235] The nature of Jesus' kingship is the focal point of this narratorial aside: Jesus' kingship was both real and representative of God's kingship, but also carried out by the weakness of the cross. It is only after Jesus' glorification by means of the cross that the disciples remembered both what "had been written about him" (Zech. 9:9) and what "had been done to him."[236] Obviously, this aside is strongly reminiscent of 2:17, 22, where the post-resurrection perspective of the narrator on the disciples' understanding is also present.[237] As a result of Jesus' hour, after the completion of Jesus' mission through his death and exaltation, the disciples will remember the events of 12:12–15 and be able to interpret them appropriately.

In the next section of the narrative, some Greeks (probably God-fearers) who were present at the feast came to Philip and asked him: "Sir, we wish to see Jesus" (12:20–21).[238] The text does not say what Philip answered them, but simply that he went to Andrew and that together they went and told Jesus (12:22). These two disciples have already been singled out in the narrative (first in the call stories in 1:40–46 and more recently in the story of the feeding of the five thousand in 6:5–9), so that this new appearance is not simply caused by their names being distinctly Greek,[239] but also because they seem to have distinctive intermediary roles in the narrative. Just as they have already acted as witnesses between Jesus and other potential disciples in the story (1:41, 45), they are now the links between Jesus and these potential Greek disciples.[240] What commentators have not noted is the possible evolution between these two disciples' lack of understanding of theirs and Jesus' mission in 6:5–9, and their apparent openness to bringing these potential *Greek* disciples to Jesus. Could it be that these two were recognizing the universal (and not only national) scope of Jesus' mission? Such a hypothesis is obviously difficult to assess, and opposite interpretations could easily be proposed.[241] In any case, Jesus will ap-

---

[235] Lincoln, *John*, 344.

[236] Ridderbos, *John*, 425: "That it was specifically the humility of the donkey-riding king over which his own should rejoice – *that* they would understand only in the light of Scripture" (emphasis original).

[237] The difference being that in 12:16, no mention of "belief" is made, while in 2:22, the disciples remembered *and* believed the scripture and Jesus' words. Structurally, Gloer, "Come and See," 285, notes that the aside in 2:22 was found just after the first mention of Jesus' hour (2:4), while here it comes immediately before Jesus' announcement that his hour has come (12:20–22).

[238] As many commentators have noted, *e.g.* Brown, *John*, 1:466: "'To see' may have the sense of 'to visit with, to meet' […], as in Luke viii 20, ix 9. Yet, in the Johannine theological context, 'to see' may well mean 'to believe in.'"

[239] So *e.g.* Brown, *John*, 1:470; Moloney, *John*, 352.

[240] Lincoln, *John*, 348–49.

[241] So Segovia, "Peace," 85, proposes the exact opposite hypothesis: "… the hesitation shown by both Philip and Andrew with respect to the coming of the Greeks to see Jesus seems to indicate a failure to interpret such a request in terms of the mission or harvest."

parently not consent to meet with these Greeks, but will rather identify this request as the beginning of his "hour" (12:23), an "hour" which necessitates his death (12:24–25). More, Jesus explains that just as a seed must fall to the ground and die in order to bear much fruit, he too will die and bear much fruit, which implies that Greek or Gentile believers will be part of these fruits (see 12:32).[242] But this teaching, as Jesus explicitly states, is also a call to discipleship: "If anyone serves me, he must follow me; and where I am, there will my servant be also. If anyone serves me, the Father will honour him" (12:26). As Lincoln puts it: "One who serves Jesus will follow him in self-giving, even if that leads to death. But just as Jesus' death will be his glory, so that pattern will be reproduced for his followers."[243] Such is the promise Jesus is making to his true disciples.[244]

The disciples do not appear again in the rest of the so-called Book of Signs (1:19–12:50), which has told the story of Jesus' public ministry before his Passion. A conclusion to this ministry is given in two parts: in 12:37–43 (the narrator's summary of the general response to Jesus in negative terms) and 12:44–50 (Jesus' summary of the theological issues at stake in the response to him and his word).

As this important section of the narrative ends, several comments can be made regarding the disciples' faith and understanding. The disciples have been present throughout this section, though at times their presence can only be presumed (*e.g.* 5:1–47; 7:1–8:59).[245] From an early stage of the narrative, Jesus has called to himself (1:39, 43, 51) and chosen (6:70) a group of followers who have been characterised as believers ever since (1:50; 2:11), once re-affirming their faith explicitly (6:68–69). More, these disciples are included by Jesus in his task (4:2, 38; 6:10, 12; 9:4), and they continue to follow him even as they face difficulties and danger.[246] Already, through a series of comments speaking of the post-resurrection belief and understanding of the disciples

---

[242] Thus, the Greeks do not need to see Jesus at this point (see also 20:29). See Barrett, *John*, 422: "Here John does not represent Jesus in direct conversation with the Greeks; this however is not careless writing, for the rest of the chapter winds up the ministry of Jesus to the Jews in order that the true and spiritual 'conversation' of Jesus with the Greeks may begin – on the other side of the crucifixion."

[243] Lincoln, *John*, 351.

[244] M. Morgen, *Afin que le monde soit sauvé. Jésus révèle sa mission de salut dans l'évangile de Jean*, LD 154 (Paris: Cerf, 1993), 181: "L'ensemble du verset constitue une promesse: celui qui sert sera honoré par le Père; mais cette promesse est ancrée dans une mise à la suite du Christ."

[245] The following comment by Morgen, *Salut*, 182–83, may therefore be overstated: "Les disciples occupent une place de moins en moins significative du chapitre 1 au chapitre 12. [...] Les disciples, à partir de ce logion de révélation [1:51] deviennent moins importants."

[246] This positive outlook on the disciples should not lead one to forget that the disciples have also been characterised by their fear and lack of courage in the narrative (6:19–20; 11:8). The point remains, however, that so far in the narrative, they have been able to face these fears and have continued to follow Jesus in spite of them.

(2:17, 22; 12:16), implied readers are aware that the disciples will remain so even after Jesus' death and exaltation. As such, the disciples strongly contrast with "the Jews," the Pharisees, and other Jewish authorities who outwardly reject Jesus and seek to kill him (5:18; 7:1; 10:31; 12:27–36).[247] However, as we have noted throughout this study, while the disciples' belief and discipleship are never questioned (except for Judas – 6:71; 12:4), their understanding is very limited, so that at times it is on a similar level to that of unbelievers (2:19–22; 8:27; 9:3, 34). Indeed, the theme of the disciples' lack of understanding, first mentioned in 2:13–22, broadens throughout the narrative so that it can be considered a major theme of their characterisation.

But these gaps in understandings are not left at that in the narrative. Segovia shows that each failure to understand on the part of the disciples is "directly and systematically counterbalanced" by Jesus through further teaching or action.[248] In other words, the disciples' deficient understanding matters and Jesus is not content for the disciples to lack in this area. As will become evident in the following chapters (Jn. 13–17), Jesus is preparing his disciples for a time when he will not be with them anymore and when they will have to continue to live as disciples and witnesses to Jesus.[249] It is thus crucial that the disciples are ready to take on that task. As two narratorial asides have made clear, the disciples' understanding will not be complete (at least as far as the issues at stake in these passages are concerned) before Jesus' glorification (2:22; 12:16), but in spite of this, implied readers are reminded that their belief in Jesus has not been questioned so far in the narrative.[250] Therefore, though the group of Jesus' disciples is overall portrayed positively by the narrator, their characterisation is not free from ambiguities.

C. The Book of Glory: 13:1–20:31

1. The Last Supper (13:1–17:26)

With this new section of the narrative begins what could also be called the "farewell materials." The first episode studied is Jesus washing his disciples' feet

---

[247] Note, however, that if at several points "the Jews" accuse Jesus and seek to kill Jesus, at other times, they wonder about him and his claims (6:52; 7:15, 35; 8:22; 10:24) and apparently believe (8:30) even though such a belief cannot be considered authentic. Moreover, certain Jewish leaders are portrayed more positively than others: Nicodemus defends Jesus (7:50–52); some are divided among themselves regarding the value to be accorded to Jesus' signs (9:16–17); and many of the authorities "believed" but refused to confess it because of their fear of excommunication and their love of glory that comes from humans (12:41–43).

[248] Segovia, "Peace," 85–86.

[249] See A. T. Lincoln, "'I am the Resurrection and the Life': The Resurrection Message of the Fourth Gospel," in *Life in the Face of Death. The Resurrection Message of the New Testament*, ed. by R. N. Longenecker, McMNTS (Grand Rapids, MI/Cambridge: Eerdmans, 1998), 132.

[250] So Culpepper, *Anatomy*, 118; Hillmer, "Discipleship," 85–86.

(13:1–20),[251] of which the first five verses are particularly important because they provide implied readers with a variety of temporal indicators, characters, themes, and actions that will be indispensable for a proper understanding of the text. In these verses, Jesus is having supper (13:2) with his disciples "before the Feast of the Passover." Most importantly for this study, through the narrator's inside view of Jesus, implied readers learn that Jesus is aware that his time to depart out of this world to the Father has now come and that, "having loved his own who were in the world, he loved them to the end" (13:1). The mention of the Passover and of the "end" (τέλος) thus propels the death of Jesus into view: from this point on "the end" will be narrated, "the hour" of Jesus has come, and Jesus needs to instruct his disciples further.[252]

During the supper, Jesus rises and begins to wash his disciples' feet (13:4–5).[253] Once more, there is more to this scene than is immediately evident. Interestingly, early in the story the narrator gives an aside according to which "the devil had already put it into the heart of Judas Iscariot, Simon's son, to betray him" (13:2). This is of no surprise to implied readers since they have already been informed of Judas' intentions (6:71).[254] This aside, however, after the mention of Jesus' love for his own, reminds implied readers that Judas cannot properly be called a true disciple of Jesus and should therefore not be understood as one of Jesus' own.

When Peter's turn arrives to have his feet washed by Jesus, a significant dialogue takes place between them (13:6–11). Peter, apparently embarrassed that Jesus (his κύριος) desires to perform such menial service to him, asks him: "Lord, do you wash my feet?" (13:6). But as Jesus will make clear in the ensuing dialogue, this is more than mere hospitality on his part, and the meaning of his action cannot be understood by Peter now, "but afterward [μετὰ ταῦτα], you will understand" (13:7).[255] There is an obvious future dimension to μετὰ

---

[251] John 13:1–20 is structured basically in three parts: 13:1–5: narrative introduction; 13:6–11: dialogue; 13:12–20: discourse. See J. C. Thomas, *Footwashing in John 13 and the Johannine Community*, JSNTSup 61 (Sheffield: Sheffield Academic Press, 1991), 78.

[252] As is often noticed, "In John 13–20, the speed of the narrative is reduced dramatically, virtually grinding to a halt the events of Jesus' hour" (D. F. Tolmie, *Jesus' Farewell To the Disciples: John 13:1–17:26 in Narratological Perspective*, BibIntS 12 (Leiden/New York, NY/Köln: Brill, 1995), 157).

[253] For many, this scene is analogous to the Lord Supper institution in the Synoptics (*e.g.* Brown, *John*, 2:558–59; Koester, *Symbolism*, 130–34). For Schneiders, *Written*, 189: "it functions as the symbol and catechesis of Jesus' approaching death, his handing over of himself for and to his disciples."

[254] Thus, the implied author continues to guide readers to interpret Judas from the perspective of the struggle between darkness and light (so Tolmie, *Farewell*, 193).

[255] For M. M. Thompson, "'His Own Received Him Not': Jesus Washes the Feet of His Disciples," in *The Art of Reading Scripture*, ed. by E. F. Davis and R. B. Hays (Grand Rapids, MI/Cambridge: Eerdmans, 2003), 265, Peter had grasped, at least in part, the significance of Jesus' act as he assumed the role of a servant rather than that of a teacher and Lord.

ταῦτα, so that for most commentators it must refer to the period following Jesus' crucifixion and resurrection (similarly to 2:17, 22; 12:16),[256] while others
also stress that one must reckon with the more immediate explanation to Jesus'
action in 13:12–17. With Thomas, it is certainly best to take μετὰ ταῦτα as
having a double referent.[257] If Jesus does begin to explain the meaning of his
action, it is only after the hour, after he serves his own in a most powerful way,
that the disciples will understand what Jesus was teaching them through the
footwashing. Yet, Peter rejects Jesus' comment and, impulsively, exclaims "you
shall never wash my feet." Jesus thus has to be just as categorical: "if I do not
wash you [sg.], you have no share [μέρος] in me."[258] For the evangelist, receiving this action is not optional as μέρος certainly makes reference to eternal life
as an inheritance. Thus, Jesus indicates that appropriating the meaning of the
footwashing and the values it refers to are necessary for the disciples to abide
continually in Jesus.[259] This rebuke from Jesus immediately changes Peter's attitude toward this act and he asks Jesus to not only wash his feet, but in essence
his entire body as well (13:9). Such a reversal is also a sign of Peter's deficient
understanding of Jesus' action so that Jesus now needs to explain to the entire
group of disciples something of great relevance to this study: "The one who has
bathed does not need to wash, except for his feet, but is completely clean. And
you [pl.] are clean, but not every one of you" (13:10).[260] Scholars disagree on
the referent to the bath in question. For most, ὁ λελουμένος is the person who
has appropriated the salvific effects of Jesus' death.[261] If one holds to such a

---

[256] R. A. Culpepper, "The Johannine Hypodeigma: A Reading of John 13," *Semeia*
53 (1991): 138; Ridderbos, *John*, 459; Carson, *John*, 463; Brown, *John*, 2:552; Bultmann,
John, 467.

[257] Thomas, *Footwashing*, 92: "The disciples are given an explanation immediately (v. 12)
but understand fully after the Passion." See also Köstenberger, *John*, 406; Morris, *John*, 548.

[258] *Pace* Tolmie, *Farewell*, 195, it is unlikely that Peter is here characterised as a leader/
spokesperson to the group of disciples, since, contrary to 6:68–69, Peter seems to speak for
himself and Jesus replies to him only.

[259] Lincoln, *John*, 369. See also R. B. Edwards, "The Christological Basis of the Johannine
Footwashing," in *Jesus of Nazareth: Lord and Christ. Essays on the Historical Jesus and New
Testament Christology*, ed. by J. B. Green and M. Turner (Grand Rapids, MI/Carlisle: Eerd-
mans/Paternoster, 1994), 375.

[260] The words εἰ μὴ τοὺς πόδας are debated by textual critics. For many, later copyists
added "except for the feet" after "need to wash" to solve the problem of further forgiveness of
sin after baptism (so, *e.g.*, P. Grelot, "L'interprétation pénitentielle du lavement des pieds," in
L'homme devant Dieu: Mélanges offerts au Père Henri de Lubac, Théologie 56 (Paris: Aubier,
1963), 1:75–91, Moloney, *John*, 378–79). Others argue that it is original, such as *e.g.* Metzger,
Textual Commentary, 204, followed by Thomas, *Footwashing*, 19–25. The arguments proposed
by Metzger are convincing: "the words εἰ μὴ τοὺς πόδας may have been omitted accidentally
(or even deliberately because of the difficulty of reconciling them with the following declaration, ἀλλ᾽ἔστιν καθαρὸς ὅλος)."

[261] See *e.g.* Köstenberger, *John*, 406–07. For Brown, *John*, 2:945–52, it is likely that the
water and blood flowing from Jesus' side in 19:34 refer back to this washing.

view, the feet still needing to be washed even as one is clean [καθαροί] refer to subsequent sins needing to be washed after the fundamental cleansing provided by Christ on the cross.[262] However, if the effects of Jesus' death are in view here, the last part of 13:10 cannot make sense, since Jesus tells the disciples that they are *already* clean.[263] To this, several commentators reply that baptism must therefore be in view,[264] but in the Fourth Gospel, baptism is not presented as an element of the disciples' belief.[265] The most likely solution is that ὁ λελουμένος is the person who already believes and who already has fellowship with Jesus. As already indicated in 13:8, what the footwashing points to are the values which will enable one to continue in this fellowship, namely the pattern of glory through humiliation that Jesus will exemplify at the cross.[266] This interpretation makes sense of the last verse of this section (13:11), where the narrator explains that Jesus' mention of the one who is not clean (13:10) indicates that Jesus knew who was about to betray him, that is, the unbeliever Judas.

The following verses (13:12–20), as already mentioned, serve to explain the meaning of Jesus' act of footwashing. Just as he washed his disciples' feet, so should they wash each other's feet, for he has given them a "model" (ὑπόδειγμα) to imitate. The model in question seems at first to indicate simply a role reversal from master to servant, a model of humble service. But as mentioned by Coloe, the solemnity of the occasion, the imminence of the 'hour,' together with Jesus' words about having a "part with him" suggest a second, deeper meaning related to the cross.[267] More, in what many consider to be a parallel passage in 13:31–35, where the verb δίδωμι also features, Jesus' instruction to "love one another just as I have loved you" (13:34) suggests that Jesus' act of footwashing should also be understood as an act of love – and that too will find its fulfilment and climax at the cross.[268] Jesus, in washing his disciples'

---

[262] So Carson, *John*, 465; I. H. Marshall, *New Testament Theology: Many Witnesses, One Witness* (Downers Grove, IL/Nottingham: InterVarsity Press/Apollos, 2004), 505.

[263] Thompson, "His Own," 272, seems to disregard this as she claims that "at this point of the narrative, Peter scarcely stands on firmer ground than Judas, than the disciples who deserted Jesus, than the Jews who did not believe, or than the world that 'did not know him.' Like the uncomprehending Nicodemus, Peter needs the 'birth from above.'"

[264] For instance, Brodie, *John*, 452; F. J. Moloney, *Glory not Dishonor: Reading John 13–21* (Minneapolis, MN: Fortress, 1998), 14–15. For Thomas, *Footwashing*, 103, footwashing then signifies the removal of sin that might accumulate after baptism.

[265] Lincoln, *John*, 370.

[266] Lincoln, *John*, 369. This claim is substantiated later in the narrative (15:3–4), where Jesus makes a similar statement: "Already you are clean [καθαροί] because of the word I have spoken to you. Abide in me, and I in you."

[267] M. L. Coloe, "Welcome into the Household of God: the Footwashing in John 13," *CBQ* 66 (2004): 410.

[268] Coloe, "Footwashing," 410; and especially Y. Simoens, *La gloire d'aimer: Structures stylistiques et interprétatives dans le discours de la Cène (Jean 13–17)*, AnBib 90 (Rome: Biblical Institute Press, 1981), 92.

feet, has given them a model of service and love that prefigures his crucifixion. Such a model puts upon the disciples demands that are inherent to discipleship, and will result in the disciples' blessedness: "If you know these things, blessed are you if you do them" (13:17), says Jesus.[269] Just as Jesus' knowledge led him to action (13:1–5), so must it be for the disciples' knowledge: it must flow into actions of service and love.[270] The context of such acts on the part of the disciples is that of their mission: "Truly, truly I say to you, a servant is not greater than his master, nor is a messenger greater than the one who sent him" (13:16). Jesus is here referring to the time when the disciples will not have Jesus with them and will be his authorised representatives. Then, their imitation of the Master will be of crucial importance for their own blessedness, but very certainly for the success of their mission as well (*cf.* 13:35).

This episode ends in 13:18–20 with the announcement that one of the disciples will betray him. Jesus announces it in advance so "that when it does take place you may believe that I am" (13:19). The fulfillment of this particular prediction will serve to reinforce the disciples' belief (*cf.* 6:69) that Jesus is indeed one with God (ἐγώ εἰμί).[271] Such a belief, according to Jesus in 13:20, will also qualify the disciples to be sent as witnesses to Jesus. Just as Jesus is fully qualified and authorised to be sent by the Father, so are the disciples. Even more, the success of their mission will result in people 'receiving' both Jesus and the Father. All in all, the disciples, qualified by their belief, are sent to represent Jesus' example of self-sacrifice and love in their mission. Their task as agents of Jesus is to be characterised by the same principles and actions.

The narrator, after having mentioned several times already the one who would betray him (6:71, but also no later than 12:2; 13:2), recounts now Jesus' own comments according to which one of the Twelve was to betray him (13:21–30). If readers are aware of the betrayer's identity, this is not true of the disciples. All they have heard in the story are hints that one of them will betray Jesus (6:70; 13:10, 18). Surprisingly, the discussion between Jesus and his disciples in 13:21–30 will not, in fact, serve the disciples' knowledge of the betrayer's identity. Even after Jesus answers the Beloved Disciple's question regarding such identity, "no one at the table knew why he had said this" (13:28). Even in the context of Jesus speaking of his betrayer, and then charging him

---

[269] Tolmie, *Farewell*, 197.

[270] F. J. Moloney, "A Sacramental Reading of John 13:1–38," *CBQ* 53 (1991): 244, puts it well: "The first section of Jesus' encounter with his disciples in the upper room (vv. 1–17) is both an indication of the total gift of Jesus for 'his own,' through the footwashing, and a call upon them to be so caught up in the new 'knowledge' which has been given to them through this gesture of love that they will 'do' this in their own lives."

[271] As mentioned by Lincoln, *John*, 374, "… at the point at which the fulfilment will take place (18.2–3), Jesus also reveals himself as 'I am' (18.6, 8), and his audience fall to the ground in the reaction that would be expected to a theophany."

("what you are going to do, do it quickly" – 13:27),[272] the disciples remain in the dark. Implied readers understand that the disciples could not have imagined that Judas would do such a thing. This must have come as a shock to them when they finally realised that Judas, their fellow disciple, was the betrayer.[273]

In 13:31, Jesus continues to speak with his disciples after the departure of Judas, and thus begins the farewell discourse proper.[274] First, he foretells his own departure to the Father in "a little while" (13:33). As already noted, Jesus thus prepares his disciples for the time when he would not be with them anymore in giving them a new love commandment, one that would qualify them for their mission as well as identify them in the eyes of the world as disciples of Jesus (13:35). There follows a moving account of Jesus' dialogue with Peter. Peter, probably reflecting the concerns of the group, neither understands where Jesus is going nor why the disciples cannot go with him. Indeed, Peter is distressed about the idea of not being with Jesus anymore. He is ready to follow him anywhere, even if it means fighting and laying down his own life for Jesus (13:37). But he does not understand the implications of what he says, nor does he understand that Jesus is to die willingly. Jesus must here give another prediction, this time about the denials of Peter (13:38). Peter will fail, but his characterisation is very different from Judas'. Indeed, implied readers are not concerned about Peter abandoning or betraying Jesus like Judas because Jesus has just promised him "you will follow me later (13:36).[275] Moreover, in the context of Jesus' teaching about "love," implied readers understand that displaying this love for Jesus is not going to be easy for the disciples, and Peter is about to discover it.[276] The narrator does not recount Peter's immediate reaction to such a prediction, but most likely he and the other disciples were distraught by this particular announcement.[277] This gives Jesus an opportunity to comfort them, as well as teach them, regarding both his departure and their future state and mission.

---

[272] For Tolmie, *Farewell*, 199, Jesus last appeals to Judas by love, through a gesture of oriental hospitality, in 13:26. This is unlikely, however, for the narrative portrays Jesus as knowing not only the intentions of Judas (intentions that could potentially be overcome by Jesus' appeal to Judas), but as knowing that Judas would indeed betray him (13:22).

[273] Interestingly, nothing is said either regarding the Beloved Disciple's knowledge of the identity of the betrayer, or about his eventual reporting back to Peter and the other disciples about it. Thus, the dialogue between the Beloved Disciples and Jesus is certainly more for the sake of readers than for the sake of the plot (see Lincoln, *John*, 379).

[274] The "Farewell discourse" can be structured in two parts: 13:31–14:31 and 15:1–16:33.

[275] Tolmie, *Farewell*, 202.

[276] Lincoln, *John*, 400.

[277] All in all, J. A. du Rand, "Narratological Perspectives on John 13:1–38," *HvTSt* 46 (1990): 379, is correct to assert that "the ideological issue at stake in John 13 is to understand Jesus' identity in the framework of his departure and the disciples' remaining behind," and "it is Jesus' knowledge and the disciples' ignorance that dominate the flow of the narratives in chapter 13."

Interestingly, Jesus' message of reassurance in 14:1[278] is coupled with an exhortation to believe: "Believe in God; believe also in me."[279] This is not anodyne, as in the rest of this passage, Jesus will elaborate on his relation to his Father in such a way as to show that having faith in God necessarily entails believing in Jesus as the One sent by God, and *vice versa*.[280] Even more, comfort and faith are interrelated in such a way that both "point to and reinforce one another."[281] The disciples' consternation must be overcome through a renewal of their faith in God and in Jesus.[282] But the disciples can only take up such an exhortation if Jesus further explains his upcoming departure. Jesus will first reassure his disciples by making a promise to them (14:2–3). If he must depart from them to go to his Father in heaven, he will come again and take them to be with him. Jesus' departure is beneficial because he will prepare places for them there "so that where I am you may be also" (14:3). According to Jesus, the disciples already know the "way" to his destination (14:4), presumably referring to what he has just told them.[283] For the disciples, however, the confusion is comprehensive, and they voice it through Thomas: "Lord, we do not know where you are going. How can we know the way?" (14:5). Jesus responds with this famous self-revelation that will clarify both why the disciples already know the 'way' and why they fail to realise it: "I am the way, the truth, and the life. No one comes to the Father except through me. If you have come to know me, you shall know my Father also. From now on, you do know him and have seen him" (14:6–7).[284] Thus, Jesus makes clear that his destination is the Father and that it is only through himself that the Father is knowable. Indeed, because of their faith and knowledge of Jesus, the disciples already know the Father and see him authentically. Yet, there is clearly a futurist element in Jesus' declaration, for implied readers know that the truth and life he embodies in his person will be revealed most climactically through his death and exaltation.[285] Thus,

---

[278] F. F. Segovia, *The Farewell of the Word: The Johannine Call to Abide* (Minneapolis, MN: Fortress, 1991), 81, prefers to speak of "a call to courage."

[279] The first part of this discourse is marked by an *inclusion* with "do not let your hearts be troubled" appearing both in 14:1 and 27.

[280] Lincoln, *John*, 389.

[281] Segovia, *Farewell*, 82.

[282] Moloney, *Glory*, 32–33.

[283] Lincoln, *John*, 390.

[284] On 14:6, see especially I. de la Potterie, *La vérité dans Saint Jean*, 2 vols, AnBib 73–74 (Rome: Biblical Institute Press, 1977), 1:252–53, who shows that the first καί must be understood as epexegetical: Jesus is the way *because* he is the truth and the life. On 14:7, the choice was here made to read this verse as a real condition, implying a promise (choosing the variants ἐγνώκατέ/γνώσεσθε instead of ἐγνώκειτέ/ἤδειτε) rather than a contrary-to-fact condition, implying a reproach (*e.g.* the ESV reading: "If you had known me, you would have known my Father also"). This is also the choice made by *e.g.* Moloney, *Glory*, 37, and Barrett, *John*, 458–59, though Segovia, *Farewell*, 87 n.52, disagrees.

[285] In fact, the disciples should also know this, for Jesus has given instructions throughout

it is Jesus as a whole that is the way to the Father, in his person just as in his present and future works.[286]

Still, the disciples' confusion remains, so Philip requests: "Lord, show us the Father, and it is enough for us" (14:8). Once more, such a request from the disciples is revelatory regarding the state of understanding of the disciples, for Jesus has just expressed that it was already granted to them. It shows that the disciples have yet to understand the concepts of knowledge and sight of God used by Jesus in 14:7. This is not to say that they do not already know God and see him, but only that they do not recognise that they do: they do not recognise that in Jesus God is known to them and seen by them (*cf.* 1:14, 18; 12:45). What the disciples want is a direct access, a full display of the Father himself, so that their attitude is placed on a similar level to that of the unbelieving Jews of 2:18.[287] Carson is correct to assert that "to the extent that this is beyond them, they do not know Jesus himself very well."[288] But as often in the narrative of the Fourth Gospel, the disciples' lack of understanding will foster an expansion of the theme through Jesus' teaching.

Jesus needs to rebuke Philip for such an erroneous request, revealing his lack of recognition of Jesus despite the time he and his fellow disciples have spent with him: "Whoever has seen me has seen the Father. How can you say: 'Show us the Father'?" (14:9). Jesus does not expect an answer, but will rather explain this still confusing concept for the disciples in the form of a reproach and in terms of indwelling: "Do you not believe that I am in the Father and the Father is in me?" (14:10). Jesus' authority rests in the fact that the Father dwells in him and works through him.[289] Therefore, if the disciples do not believe Jesus on account of his words, they should at least believe on account of his works. This challenge to believe is similar to what is found in 5:36 and 10:38, where Jesus was speaking to non-believers. Thus, though the disciples' situation is obviously not one of unbelievers, it appears that so far in the farewell discourse, they are placed in a similar situation as that of outsiders during Jesus' public ministry as far as their understanding of Jesus is concerned.[290] That their posi-

---

his ministry about his departure to go the Father as his lifting up (3:14; 8:28; 12:32) and as his death (10:16–18; 11:4; 13:31).

[286] Carson, *John*, 493: "If we retain *From now on* [as opposed to 'assuredly,' a possibility given the fact that the contracted pair of words *ap'arti* could be read in one word], the reference is to the time the disciples have come to know Jesus during his ministry, and especially through the hour of his death and resurrection, now immediately upon them."

[287] Segovia, *Farewell*, 88 n.55.

[288] Carson, *John*, 494.

[289] This concept of indwelling should also be understood in terms of Jesus' mission. Jesus is the authorised agent of the Father, and thus completely represents the one who sent him (see Lincoln, *John*, 391).

[290] Lincoln, *John*, 391–92. *Pace* Moloney, *Glory*, 37, for whom the problem lies in the disciples' lack of faith. On the contrary, Jesus here takes their faith for granted, and teaches them to grow in their knowledge/understanding of his person and work.

tion of believers is not in question in this passage is reaffirmed next by Jesus in 14:12–14. Indeed, Jesus simply assumes[291] that his disciples are believers and will do greater works than Jesus himself because he is going to the Father (14:12).[292] Through their future ministry, the Father will continue to be glorified in the Son after Jesus' departure.

Just as the importance of believing for the future ministry of the disciples has been emphasised, Jesus now stresses the response of love (14:15, 21, 23–24, 28) and such love for Jesus involves keeping his word/commandments: "If you love me, you will keep my commandments" (14:15).[293] If the disciples love Jesus, they will also receive a number of promises. First, the Paraclete (παράκλητος). John 14:16–17 is the first Paraclete saying of Jesus in the Fourth Gospel.[294] Jesus promises that he will send another Advocate,[295] also called the "Spirit of truth," to be with the disciples forever. This implies that Jesus was the first Paraclete and thus also had a role of advocacy in his ministry.[296] After his physical departure, a new Paraclete will continue his forensic role in the ongoing trial, revealing truth, "advocating and prosecuting both God's and his own case in the trial of truth with the world."[297] This replacement is obviously to the advantage of the disciples in the difficult ministry that will be theirs, aiding them in their own witnessing activity (15:18–27). Moreover, and most importantly, the Paraclete will be given to the disciples *because* they are not of the world, thus emphasising once more their believing status. Just as the disciples have received and believed in Jesus while the world has not, so they already "know" the Spirit who "dwells" with them while "the world cannot receive [him] because it neither sees nor knows him" (14:17). Again, such a declaration on Jesus' part raises the question of the post-resurrection perspective of the implied author: if the Spirit was not yet given because Jesus was not yet glorified (*cf.* 7:39), how do the disciples already know him?

Another promise given by Jesus to those who love him is that he will not leave them as orphans (14:18). Jesus will manifest himself to them after his

---

[291] Lincoln, *John*, 392.

[292] The nature of these greater works is debated, but with A. J. Köstenberger, "The 'Greater Works' of the Believer According to John 14:12," *Did* 6 (1995): 36–45, these are most certainly 'greater' not because they are more astounding, but because they are one step closer to the fulfilment of salvation.

[293] Lincoln, *John*, 393, remarks that "Talking of Jesus' farewell instructions as his commandments may well be meant to recall the Mosaic law as the summation of the divine commandments and to suggest Jesus' teaching as the new norm for the disciples."

[294] See also 14:26; 15:26; 16:7–15.

[295] Lincoln, *Truth*, 111, and Lincoln, *John*, 393–94, argues on the basis of semantics that the meaning "Advocate," rather than, *e.g.* "Encourager" or "Exhorter" is to be preferred. Moreover, such forensic overtones fit the trial motif in the Fourth Gospel.

[296] See R. E. Brown, "The Paraclete in the Fourth Gospel," *NTS* 13 (1966–67): 113–32; Segovia, *Farewell*, 95.

[297] Lincoln, *John*, 394.

death (14:18–20) and forever after that (14:21–24). First, in 14:18–20, Jesus makes a reference to the time, in "a little while" (14:19), on "that day" (14:20) when he will manifest himself to the disciples, arguably referring to the time immediately following his resurrection. Such manifestation will demonstrate that he lives, but also that the disciples will live (14:19). More, it will demonstrate the mutual love and indwelling of Jesus in the Father, the disciples in him, and he in them (14:20).[298] Once more, Jesus' teaching triggers a question by one of the disciples. Judas (not Iscariot), takes up a distinction made by Jesus in 14:19 and poses a question that will foster further claims by Jesus: "Lord, how is it that you will manifest yourself to us, and not to the world?" (14:22).[299] For Jesus, such manifestation will be the Father dwelling with believers who love him and keep his words. Thus, the presence of the Father is not true only in heavenly dwelling places, but can already be experienced by believers. Most likely, such experience will be mediated by the presence of the Paraclete in the disciples.[300]

It will be the role of the Paraclete to "teach you all things and bring to your remembrance all that I have said to you" (14:26), thus stressing the continuity between the two advocates in the lives of the disciples.[301] Jesus has been teaching these things to the disciples so that they would have peace, *his* peace, so that they would be neither troubled nor afraid (14:27). More, the rejoicing and belief of the disciples are the fundamental purposes behind Jesus' teaching: "If you had loved me, you would have rejoiced" (14:28) and "I have told you before it takes place, so that when it does take place you may believe" (14:29). For some commentators, the first of these clauses is meant as a reproach to the disciples for *not* loving Jesus.[302] Others prefer to speak of a lack in this area, which is likely.[303] Certainly, the disciples already love Jesus, but they must

---

[298] Thus, as noted by Lincoln, *John*, 395, the focus of this promise is not on external appearances, but on internal relationships.

[299] Here more than elsewhere before, the question is most certainly a literary device to keep the narration lively and enhance Jesus' teaching on the issue at stake.

[300] Lincoln, *John*, 396: "This suggests that the coming of Jesus and the Father are mutually interpretative. [...] If earlier in the narrative the incarnate Logos, Jesus, was the location of God's presence as the new temple, in the period after Jesus' departure the believing community becomes the temple of God in the Spirit."

[301] Examples of such a remembering by the disciples after the resurrection of Jesus (and implicitly the coming of the Paraclete) have already been narrated in 2:17, 22; 12:16. From these examples, it is clear that the remembering in question is not simply a recollection of the words, but rather of their significance. See, *e.g.* Segovia, *Farewell*, 105–06.

[302] *E.g.* Carson, *John*, 506–07.

[303] Tolmie, *Farewell*, 210. For Brown, *John*, 2:651, 654: "The unreal condition, 'If you loved me...,' is meant not to deny that the disciples love him, but to indicate that their love is possessive rather than generous." Ridderbos, *John*, 494, 511, however, goes too far in his comparison between 14:28 and 14:7, for here, εἰ in the conditional clause, coupled with ἄν in the consequence clause expresses a contrary to fact condition. See W. Bauer and others, *Greek-*

grow in their love for him. Thus, "their love for Jesus should lead them to re-joice in what will happen *for Jesus* in his departure to the Father who is greater than he is."[304] Likewise, the second clause is not meant as a reproach to the disciples for not yet believing in Jesus. Rather, Jesus foretold these events in order that their occasion may ensure, nurture, and reinforce the faith of the disciples. These clauses, moreover, are not independent from the rest of Jesus' prior speech: "Love for Jesus and belief in his word should make [upcoming events] occasions for further belief."[305]

In the second and longer part of the farewell discourse (15:1–16:33), the disciples remain silent until 16:17. In the meantime, much of Jesus' teaching concerns their discipleship. As is often noted, such teaching is not completely new, but rather repeats and expands on prior themes.[306] Thus the three sections that make up the second part of the discourse build upon the themes of Christian community and the love that should unite the disciples to Jesus and to one another (15:1–17), the hatred of the world for Jesus and the disciples (15:18–16:4a), and the happenings surrounding Jesus' departure and return (16:4b–33).[307] These three sections contain important thematic links with the first part of the discourse,[308] but as a whole, its direction is different. For Zumstein, if the first part of the discourse (13:31–14:31) underlines "la thématique christologique de la séparation,"[309] the second part is essentially ecclesiological

---

English Lexicon of the New Testament and Other Early Christian Literature, 3rd ed. (Chicago: University of Chicago Press, 2000), s.v. "εἰ," 277.

[304] Moloney, *John*, 411 (italics original).

[305] Moloney, *John*, 411.

[306] On this important literary phenomenon, see J. Zumstein, "L'adieu de Jésus aux siens. Une lecture intertextuelle de Jean 13–17," in *Raconter, interpréter, annoncer. Parcours de Nouveau Testament. Mélanges offerts à Daniel Marguerat pour son 60e anniversaire*, ed. by E. Steffek and Y. Bourquin, MB 47 (Genève: Labor et Fides, 2003), 207–22;

[307] See Brown, *John*, 587.

[308] As Zumstein, "Adieu," 216–18, shows, there are important "rapports de sens" between 15:1–8 and 14:20 (abiding); 15:7b–8, 16 and 14:13–14 (answers to prayers in relation to 'fruits'); 15:9–17 and 14:15–24, 34–35 (love for Jesus, now expanded to the love the disciples must have for one another); 15:10 and 14:15–31 (to obey the commandments); 15:11 and 13:28 (joy); 15:18–16:4a and 14:17, 19, 22, 27 (the world); 15:26–27 and 14:16–17, 25–26 (the Paraclete, now expanded from the perspective of the disciples' witness in the world). As for the "rapport de sens" between 16:4b–33 and 13:31–14:31, it has been noticed by many scholars such as Brown, *John*, 589–93, and A. Dettwiler, *Die Gegenwart des Erhöhten. Eine exegetische Studie zu den johanneischen Abschiedsreden (Joh 13,31–16,33) unter besonderer Berücksichtigung ihres Relecture-Charakters*, FRLANT 169 (Göttingen: Vandenhoeck & Ruprecht, 1995), 278–83. This third section of the second part of the discourse is often considered a re-reading of 13:31–14:31 because these two sections are structurally similar, speaking of the imminent separation of Jesus from his disciples, giving rise to reactions from the disciples and concluding with the themes of peace (14:27; 16:33b), Christ's sovereignty (14:30–31; 16:32–33), and consolation (14:27d; 16:33d). Even more, the link between Easter and the Paraclete is underlined in both sections (14:15–26; 16:7–24). See Zumstein, "Adieu," 218 for a summary.

[309] Zumstein, "Adieu," 215.

in nature and "décrit comment la communauté est appelée à affronter le temps post-pascal."[310]

Besides the many calls for the disciples to abide in Jesus and in his love, to bear fruit and glorify the Father, to keep the commandments and love one another, to recall the status of being the chosen people of God (15:1–17),[311] and beside the reminder of the world's hostility towards the disciples (first expressed in general terms in 15:18–25, and later more specifically in 16:1–4a), a world in which the disciples will bear witness to Jesus by virtue of having been with him from the beginning (15:26–27),[312] this second section of the discourse remains a monologue up to 16:17, where the disciples will relate their confusion to one another. Their reaction is different to that of Peter, Thomas, and Philip in 13:31–14:31, for there it was Jesus' destiny that gave rise to their questions. In 16:17–18, the narrator rather underlines the disciples' own distress about this upcoming situation.[313] At first, the disciples are depicted as perplexed regarding Jesus' teaching, so perplexed that they do not even ask Jesus to explain the meaning of his words. They do not understand what he means by "in a little while and you will not see me, and again a little while, and you will see me" (16:16, 17), so Jesus takes the initiative to tell them what he meant. In his answer, he underlines the future lament and sorrow of the disciples (16:19) that will be turned into joy when, implicitly, Jesus would appear to them again after his resurrection (16:22, *cf.* 20:20).

In 16:23a, Jesus thus promises the disciples that they will ask nothing of him "in that day," and in 16:25, he contrasts the way he has been speaking to the disciples in this discourse and how he will communicate with them in the future: "the hour is coming when I will no longer speak to you in figures of speech but will tell you plainly about the Father" (16:25). These two verses are thus significant regarding the present and future understanding of the disciples in the story:

Thus the implied reader is led to understand that the disciples' poor performance will be countered by the things that will happen in Jesus' hour. Furthermore, this promise also enables the implied reader to understand why the disciples have not been able to understand Jesus up to that

---

[310] Zumstein, "Adieu," 214.

[311] Chennattu, *Discipleship*, 112. Zumstein, "Adieu," 211, remarks that these preoccupations are *ad intra* (15:1–17 speaks of the community from the perspective of the link that unites it to Jesus), while the end of the second section will underline the *ad extra* situation of the community in its relations to the "world" (15:18–16:4).

[312] Lincoln, *John*, 412, rightly asserts: "This puts them in a position to provide witness to the significance of Jesus' mission as a whole." With R. Bauckham, *Jesus and the Eyewitnesses: The Gospels as Eyewitness Testimony* (Grand Rapids, MI/Cambridge: Eerdmans, 2006), 150–51, 389–90 (but *pace* Köstenberger, *Missions*, 150–51) this also highlights the special status of Jesus' close group of disciples as *witnesses*, in contrast to later disciples, in the aftermath of his death and resurrection.

[313] Zumstein, "Adieu," 218.

point in the narrative text: full understanding of Jesus will only become possible once Jesus has been resurrected and has returned to the disciples.[314]

In the last verses of chapter 16, Jesus also reiterates the fact that the disciples' relationship with the Father will be one of greater intimacy (16:26–27) after his imminent departure, based on the fact that "the Father himself loves you, because you have loved me and have believed that I came from God" (16:27). Following these announcements, and on the basis of Jesus' teaching since 16:17–18, the disciples are now confident that they have attained an adequate level of knowledge: "Now we know that you know all things and do not need anyone to question you; this is why we believe that you came from God" (16:30). But their confession is ambiguous as the implied author seems to hint at the fact that the disciples' confidence is ill-founded.[315] Their confidence is based mainly on the exchange in 16:16–19 rather than on the core of Jesus' teaching in the farewell discourse (the new situation that will be brought about by Jesus' departure to his Father).[316] If the disciples only believe that Jesus has come from God on the basis on Jesus' omniscience, such a basis is not far from that of those who, throughout the Gospel, believed on the basis of Jesus' miraculous works (2:23; 3:2; 4:45).[317] Once more, such a basis is not necessarily inadequate in and of itself (*e.g.* 11:15), but it obviously misses the mark here. Thus, the disciples' confession does not eliminate the fact, mentioned by Jesus himself, that they do love and believe in Jesus,[318] but rather implicitly highlights their poor integrating of Jesus' teaching throughout the farewell discourse.[319] Moreover, it serves to remind implied readers that knowledge and understanding of Jesus apart from his "hour" is necessarily imperfect.[320]

---

[314] Tolmie, *Farewell*, 220. Of course, implied readers are already aware of this since 2:22 and 12:16.

[315] Tolmie, *Farewell*, 220, is correct in his assessment that: "In this segment [16:29–33] the implied author uses the reaction of the disciples to drive home the point made in verses 23a and 25: the disciples will only be able to understand fully after the resurrection of Jesus."

[316] Lincoln, *John*, 427. It is thus surprising that Dettwiler, *Gegenwart*, 258–63, considers such a confession of faith a climactic expression of faith.

[317] Moloney, *Glory*, 97.

[318] Chennattu, *Discipleship*, 129, rightly reminds that "For the Fourth Evangelist the basic identity of the disciples does not merely depend on their profession of faith. [...] The true sign of discipleship resides in their abiding covenant relationship with God (15:8) and keeping the commandments or loving one another (8:34–35). This relationship and journey of faith is a dynamic and ongoing process."

[319] For Segovia, *Farewell*, 271: "In effect, such failure to address the full character of this relationship casts further doubt on the parameters of the given confession concerning origins. [...] These full and confident affirmations, therefore, reveal an even greater lack of understanding than before. Sorrowful silence and an admission of ignorance finally give way to obvious misunderstanding." It is likely that Segovia goes a bit too far in considering such confession as expressing "obvious misunderstanding." Such a judgment is not warranted by the text.

[320] Gloer, "Come and See," 288.

This perspective allows implied readers to understand Jesus' response to the disciples in its proper light. The interpretation of his short question "Do you now believe?" (16:31) has been understood either as "Jesus' recognition and appreciation of the faith professed by the disciples"[321] or as a claim "that sharply undermines the entire response of the disciples, not only questioning the claim to belief itself but also sharply underscoring the ironic nature of their response."[322] But contrary to these opposite propositions, it is neither likely that Jesus is here questioning the claim to belief of the disciples (especially after 16:27, and before 17:8), nor that he is showing appreciation for it. What is at stake for Jesus is the disciples' lack of understanding of the present discourse's themes. It is because the disciples have failed to integrate Jesus' teaching with their belief in him that they will abandon him in his hour of need (16:32). The disciples believe that Jesus has come from God, but they do not seem to understand what it implies in terms of Jesus' departure back to his Father. Overall, if Jesus is therefore questioning anything in 16:31, it is the overconfidence of the disciples, which will lead them to "be scattered each in his own home."[323]

However grave the consequences of their lacunae may be, Jesus ends this part of his discourse with encouragement (16:33). Jesus told them "these things" (*i.e.* the whole discourse) so that the disciples may have peace in him, so that in spite of the tribulation that will be theirs in "the world", they may remember that Jesus has overcome the world (16:33). Thus, Jesus predicts a time of hardship for the disciples, a time when the meaning of his discourse will come to their rescue and give them peace. When the disciples will endure suffering in the world, Jesus' decisive victory will have been won and this will make a difference for the disciples' understanding. But interestingly, Jesus speaks in 16:33 of the story's future events as having already taken place ("Take heart: I have overcome the world"). This study will treat the temporal perspective of the implied author in more detail in chapter 4. At this point, however, O'Day's explanation is worth mentioning.[324] For her, here "the voice of the risen Jesus" asserts that "the 'future' victory is in fact the present reality."[325] In so doing,

---

[321] Chennattu, *Discipleship*, 130.

[322] Segovia, *Farewell*, 272.

[323] Léon-Dufour, *Lecture*, 3:264: "Ici, les disciples se montrent trop sûrs d'eux, alors qu'ils n'ont pas compris le sens des paroles de Jésus et raisonnent à partir de leurs propres déductions." Likewise, M. de Jonge, "The Radical Eschatology of the Fourth Gospel and the Eschatology of the Synoptics: Some Suggestions," in *John and the Synoptics*, ed. by A. Denaux, BETL 101 (Leuven: Leuven University Press, 1992), 483: "Here Jesus tells his disciples that this will happen and that, in fact, it has already started; it is necessary to say this, because they are under the wrong impression that the hour of full faith and clear insight has already arrived (vv. 29–30 in contrast with vv. 27–28)."

[324] G. R. O'Day, "'I Have Overcome the World' (John 16:33): Narrative Time in John 13–17," *Semeia* 53 (1991): 162.

[325] O'Day, "Narrative Time," 163. *Contra* Tolmie, *Farewell*, 221, for whom "the only way in which these statement can be understood narratologically is by assuming that Jesus is speak-

Jesus gives the disciples theological tools to interpret both present and future events:

> By placing the promises and words of assurance before the Passion narrative, not after, the Fourth Evangelist emphasizes that these words are part of present reality for the disciples rather than part of some distant future. [...] The words of promise and assurance are available in advance of the moment of crisis.[326]

It is likely, based on what Jesus has already said (*e.g.* 16:23, 25), that the disciples were unable to use these tools before the coming of the Paraclete who assisted them in interpreting Jesus' words, so that these words are to be interpreted primarily as comfort for implied readers.

Jesus' prayer in 17:1–26 can be understood as a restatement of the Gospel as whole as well as the farewell's discourse.[327] As such, it is not only a prayer directed to the Father, but also a continued teaching for the disciples: it prepares them for Jesus' upcoming death and exaltation.[328] Three parts make up Jesus' prayer (17:1–5; 6–19; 20–26), the second being most interesting for this study since there Jesus prays for his present disciples. He makes important claims regarding their response to God's initiative in their lives: "they have kept your word" (17:6); "now they know that everything that you have given me is from you" (17:7); "they have received [the words that you gave me] and have come to know in truth that I come from you and they have believed that you sent me" (17:8). Jesus thus reformulates, after the disciples' confession in 16:29–30, that they are believers who know Jesus' identity and origin. In the perspective of this prayer, the disciples can only understand themselves as having a special status and living a special relationship with the Father and the Son.[329] Indeed, Jesus presents them as the locus of his glorification (17:10b), implying that his identity as God's manifestation is made visible in the disciples. As such, they are to become God's visible presence in the world after Jesus' return to the Father (17:11–19).[330] There is thus no doubt, since this is coming from Jesus' own mouth, that he himself considers them as believers, united to him and his Father, faithful to the Father's calling, and this even before what implied readers know will happen in the next chapters of the narrative, namely, the scattering of the disciples and the denials of Peter.

---

ing 'as if' these events had already taken place – a technique that puts across the notion that Jesus knew for a fact that these things would happen." This, however, seems to be only part of the way to understand this verse narratologically.

[326] O'Day, "Narrative Time," 164.

[327] Carson, *John*, 550–51. Thematic links between this prayer and what precedes it in the Gospel are, *e.g.*, the pre-existence of the Son, the relation of love and unity between him and the Father, the glory of the Son and the Father, the upcoming departure of Jesus, the disciples' future mission, and the necessity of love for one another.

[328] Lincoln, *John*, 432.

[329] Lincoln, *John*, 436.

[330] Chennattu, *Discipleship*, 132–33.

If from this prayer (as from the narrative so far) implied readers know that the status of the disciples is secure (except for Judas Iscariot, *cf.* 17:12), they are nonetheless aware that true difficulties are only about to begin for the disciples. This is why Jesus prays for them. Soon, he will not be with them, but they will remain in a hating world (17:14) and thus must be protected from the "evil one" (17:15). Implied readers know that being in the world implies that the *faith* of the disciples will be under attack. It is primarily for this faith (17:7–8) that Jesus is asking protection, so that the Father would "keep them in [his] name" (17:11) and "consecrate them in the truth" (17:17). Only if they remain attached to Jesus and the Father will the disciples be able to witness about the significance of Jesus' identity and mission.

2. The Passion Narrative (18:1–19:42)

The Fourth Gospel's Passion narrative can be divided into five sections: (*i*) Jesus' arrest (18:1–11); (*ii*) his interrogation by Annas (18:12–27); (*iii*) his trial before Pilate (18:28–19:16a); (*iv*) his crucifixion and death (19:16b–37); and (*v*) his burial (19:38–42). Throughout these sections, certain disciples play secondary but important roles. However, since it is often more in their individuality that they are present rather than as a group, this section of the study will pass briefly through this part of the narrative.

In the first section, the disciples are present with Jesus in the garden (18:1), and among them, the two most important characters are Judas (even though he could hardly be called a disciple anymore), and Peter. Both are portrayed negatively, though with varying degrees. First, Judas is twice said to be the one "who betrayed him" (18:2, 5). Moreover, the fact that he knew where to find Jesus "because Jesus often met there with his disciples" (18:2), emphasises that this betrayer was "one of Jesus' inner group of trusted followers,"[331] but also that Judas has "officially switched sides."[332] Jesus, though he is sovereign over his own arrest (18:6), lets himself be arrested, but asks that the soldiers let the disciples go (18:8) in order to fulfil words spoken earlier: "of those whom you gave me I have lost not one" (18:9).[333] But Peter refused to let Jesus be apprehended so easily. Probably convinced that the Messiah's glorification would come through a sort of military victory (and so not through his death),[334] he

---

[331] Lincoln, *John*, 443

[332] Köstenberger, *John*, 505

[333] 6:39; 10:28–29; 17:12. For I. de la Potterie, *La passion de Jésus selon l'évangile de Jean*, Lire la Bible 73 (Paris: Cerf, 1986), 59–60, Jesus' intent is not only to save the disciples from arrest and potential death, but on a deeper level, to protect their spiritual salvation.

[334] A. J. Droge, "The Status of Peter in the Fourth Gospel: A Note on John 18:10–11," *JBL* 109 (1990): 310, however, goes too far when he asserts, against M. M. Thompson, *The Humanity of Jesus in the Fourth Gospel* (Philadelphia, PA: Fortress, 1988), 87–115, that Jesus' death, since it is his glorification, does not also entail suffering and humiliation in the Fourth Gospel. Moreover, Droge asserts, in light of 18:36, that the author of the Fourth Gospel "has leveled a

"drew his sword and struck the high priest's servant and cut off his right ear" (18:10). This event serves to vindicate Peter's earlier honesty (13:38): he was indeed willing to fight and potentially die for Jesus. This is however the extent of the revolutionary fight for the Messiah. Jesus immediately stops the hostilities, rebuking Peter: "Shall I not drink the cup that the Father has given me?" (18:11). Once again, Peter has not comprehended what is happening. Though Jesus spent a significant amount of time explaining his upcoming death and departure to the disciples, Peter is not willing to let it happen. The narrative only describes Peter's attitude faced with the arrest of Jesus, and though the other disciples did not begin to fight, their understanding at this point is probably similar to that of Peter.[335]

In the next section, Peter is once again present. He follows Jesus with "another disciple" (18:15), who has traditionally been identified as the Beloved Disciple.[336] Thus, Peter appears at first to be faithful to Jesus as he follows him and does not wish to abandon him, contrary to the other disciples who are not mentioned and can only be assumed to have either scattered or stayed together away from the action. But while in the high priest's court, Peter denies being one of Jesus' disciples three times (18:17, 25, 27). What is striking in this section is not only that Peter disowned his Lord, but that he did so as an intimate disciple of Jesus.[337] As noted by Carson, this has the double effect of demonstrating Jesus' advance knowledge of the events surrounding his passion (*cf.* 13:38), but also of underlining the fact that, during these events, Jesus was isolated and abandoned by even his most faithful followers.[338] Peter's characterisation is not meant, however, to be representative of the group of disciples. Clearly, it is his own struggle that is depicted here.[339]

After this portrayal of Peter's denials, neither he nor any other disciples of Jesus will be mentioned until 19:25–27. Jesus will go through his trial and crucifixion alone. But once he is crucified, five relatives and disciples of Jesus join him and stand by the cross, the Beloved Disciple being the only male repre-

---

devastating indictment at Peter", for in fighting, Peter shows that he is not a "subject" of Jesus' heavenly kingdom (p. 311). This too is to go too far. Peter certainly does show deep misunderstanding of Jesus' kingship when he begins to fight, but it does not logically follow that he is not a subject of Jesus' kingdom.

[335] Segovia, "Peace," 88, n.57, is correct to assert that the figure of Peter is "representative of the reaction and/or attitudes of the wider group." Later in 18:19, the high priest will question Jesus about his disciples, which may indicate that he was concerned about the possible threat that they might pose, thus possibly referring to Peter's violent reaction (see Gloer, "Come and See," 288).

[336] Such an identification is today questioned on several grounds. See discussion in Carson, *John*, 581–82. The characterisation of this "other disciple" in this section is very limited as it mainly serves to introduce Peter's own struggles and denials.

[337] Culpepper, *Anatomy*, 120.

[338] Carson, *John*, 581.

[339] Segovia, "Peace," 88, n.56

sentative from the group of the disciples. Just before Jesus "gave up his spirit" (19:30), he gave what appears to be his last will and testament to his mother and the beloved disciple: "Woman, behold your son!" and to the disciple "Behold, your mother!" (18:26–27). Theologically as well as symbolically, this is very significant.[340] As mentioned by Lincoln, it is probable that the Beloved Disciple is, "from that hour," given the charge to be Jesus' human successor, though not as the Paraclete would be his successor. His role, after Jesus, is to instruct Jesus' future followers about discipleship.[341] Thus, it may be that Jesus' mother "represents all who are receptive to salvation from Jesus, perhaps believing Jews in particular, who are now referred to the disciple who is the witness par excellence, the founding figure of the evangelist's community."[342] The image of the family chosen by Jesus will again come to the fore after the resurrection, when the ἀδελφοι of Jesus are no longer simply the members of his physical family, but his disciples (20:17) and the members of the community (21:23).[343] It is only after Jesus had secured his cause in such a manner that he knew that everything was "completed" (τετέλεσται).

Even though up to that point they were not explicitly linked with the band of disciples who followed Jesus during his earthly ministry, Joseph of Arimathea and Nicodemus took care of Jesus' body after his death, and buried it according to proper Jewish customs, placing his body in a new tomb of a close-by garden (19:38–42). Interestingly, Joseph is said to be a "disciple of Jesus, but secretly for fear of the Jews" (19:38).[344] His action in these verses no doubt serves as an implicit, but clear, attempt to confess his allegiance. Likewise, Nicodemus who, up to that point had been ambiguously portrayed in the story (3:1, 10; 7:50), chooses to identify himself as a disciple of Jesus.[345] The text does not say what happened to them after this, whether they went back to their homes or joined Jesus' disciples. What is certainly most important as far as the present study is concerned, however, is that these two men, *and not Jesus' close followers*, took care of giving a proper burial to Jesus' body. Once again, the absence of the disciples can hardly go unnoticed.

---

[340] See especially Lee, *Flesh*, 154–59, and Köstenberger, *John*, 548, n.47, for propositions and overviews of the different positions on the symbolism of this section.

[341] Lincoln, *John*, 476–77. Lincoln uses 1 Macc. 2:65 as parallel to make this point.

[342] Lincoln, *John*, 477.

[343] Lee, *Flesh*, 154. To explain why the mother of Jesus and the Beloved Disciple are not given to each other as brother and sister but as mother and son, Lee interestingly proposes that it is because in the Fourth Gospel Jesus served as the Beloved Disciple's mother (p. 155).

[344] This is certainly a reference to 12:42–43, where "Nevertheless many, even of the authorities, believed in him. But because of the Pharisees they did not confess it, for fear that they would be put out of the synagogue; for they loved human glory more than the glory that comes from God." (NRSV).

[345] As mentioned by many commentators, this is certainly meant to be an encouragement to the so-called crypto-Christians (7:13; 9:22; 12:42–43). See *e.g.* Moloney, *Glory*, 149, n.79.

3. The Risen Jesus (20:1–29)

As implied readers reach this point of the narrative, one might say that the story of Jesus accomplishing the task given him by the Father has come to a satisfying conclusion, but many issues, not least of which is the status of the band of disciples, remain unresolved.[346] Implied readers are hopeful, however, for "of those you gave me, I have lost no one" (18:9). The remaining part of the narrative will thus bring a sense of resolution to these issues.

On the "first day of week," Mary Magdalene came early to the tomb, where she discovered that the stone had been taken away (20:1). She ran to Peter and the Beloved Disciple to tell them that "They have taken the Lord out of the tomb" (20:2).[347] The two disciples thus ran to the tomb, but the Beloved Disciple outran Peter and reached the tomb first (20:4).[348] He stopped at the entrance of the tomb, took a look inside, but did not go in. When Peter reached the tomb, however, he entered the tomb, and also witnessed the linen cloths lying there (20:6–7). It is only at this point that the other disciple went in and "saw and believed; for as yet they did not understand the Scripture,[349] that he must rise from the dead" (20:8–9).[350]

Interestingly, the narrator does not specify what the Beloved Disciple believed, nor whether Peter also believed.[351] It is very unlikely that the Beloved Disciple only believed Mary Magdalene's earlier news,[352] for this would be quite anti-climactic. More plausible is the idea that he believed Jesus to be

---

[346] Moloney, *Glory*, 153.

[347] Here it is clear that Mary has no thought of the resurrection; she rather thinks that the body has been stolen. *Cf.* Köstenberger, *John*, 562.

[348] Whether or not implied readers should find significance in the Beloved Disciple's outrunning Peter is still debated. For *e.g.* Brodie, *John*, 561, it symbolically stresses the Beloved Disciple's superior discipleship. Though this certainly lacks warrant, later narrative remarks potentially go in this direction: the Beloved Disciple is the first to believe on the basis of what he sees – or does not see! – in the tomb in 20:8, and he later is the first to recognize Jesus standing on the shore in 21:7.

[349] Most scholars propose that the scripture in question is Ps. 16:10; Hos. 6:2; or Is. 53:10–12, while others think that the entirety of Scripture is in view here. This, however, has no bearing on our interpretation.

[350] Köstenberger, *John*, 565, probably makes too much of the fact that the Beloved Disciple's belief was based on "seeing." It is unlikely that he is here portrayed as sharing with Thomas "his position as follower of Jesus during his earthly ministry, which must be transformed through the Spirit-Paraclete subsequent to Jesus' glorification." Rather, the Beloved Disciple is quite unique as he believes on the basis of the physical *absence* of Jesus' body in the tomb (not on the basis of seeing Jesus' resurrected body), and not on the basis of others' testimony (see Lincoln, *John*, 491). This 'seeing' must therefore be understood as spiritual in nature.

[351] The lack of information on this second point certainly leads implied readers to think that Peter *did not* reach such a belief himself, and thus contrasts negatively with the Beloved Disciple.

[352] So Conway, *Men and Women*, 189–90.

resurrected from the dead.[353] And yet, the following narratorial aside about the disciples' understanding of the scripture is ambiguous: does it serve to exclude Jesus' resurrection from such a belief, or rather to highlight the Beloved Disciple's belief in the resurrection of Jesus? Given the circumstances, *i.e.* the disciples witnessing the actual body of Jesus missing in the tomb, it is far more likely that a belief in his resurrection is meant here. Moreover, the mention of Scripture brings implied readers back to 2:22 and 12:16 where the narrator explains that it is only after the resurrection that the disciples remembered the Scripture, understood it, and believed it (as it pertains to Jesus' resurrection). Thus, the Beloved Disciple's belief is highlighted because it is independent from any such interpretation and understanding on the part of the disciples as a whole.[354]

The following verse could lead readers to think that the Beloved Disciple may not have worked out entirely the implications of such a belief, for he and Peter simply went back to their homes (20:10) without witnessing about what they had seen (and in the case of the Beloved Disciple, believed). As mentioned by Lee, the Beloved Disciple's believing has no immediate narrative impact.[355] In the next section, however (20:11–18) Mary Magdalene, after having seen and recognised Jesus outside the tomb (20:16), is sent by Jesus to announce to the disciples a message from him: "go to my brothers[356] and say to them, I am ascending to my Father, to my God and your God" (20:17). In addition to Jesus' message, Mary Magdalene announced to the disciples "I have seen the Lord," which, as far as the plot is concerned, is more interesting than a potential "I have believed that the Lord is risen" by the Beloved Disciple. Mary is thus not only the first character to witness Jesus' bodily resurrection, but also the first to testify to others about it.

But since Mary Magdalene is at this point the lone witness to the risen Jesus, her testimony will have to be corroborated by others.[357] This will happen in the

---

[353] So *e.g.* Brown, *John*, 2:987; Carson, *John*, 638–39; Witherington, *John*, 325; Köstenberger, *John*, 564.

[354] Lincoln, *John*, 491. *Pace* I. de la Potterie, "Genèse de la foi pascale d'après Jn. 20," *NTS* 30 (1984): 30–31, for whom 20:8 does not "exprime la plenitude de la foi pascale [...] Il s'agit d'une foi encore initiale et imparfaite."

[355] D. A. Lee, "Partnership in Easter Faith: The Role of Mary Magdalene and Thomas in John 20," *JSNT* 58 (1995): 39.

[356] As mentioned by *e.g.* Lincoln, *John*, 494, calling the disciples "brothers" highlights his solidarity with his disciples in the new family relationship. More, "The intimacy of Jesus' relationship to God is now made available to believers." This of course serves to show that the disciples, though they have not been with Jesus during his Passion, continue to be considered believers by Jesus himself. Their status is not in question. More, it also comes to show the completion of Jesus' glorification (see 14:18–21: "I will not leave you as orphans; I will come to you [...]. And he who loves me will be loved by my Father, and I will love him and manifest myself to him."

[357] Several commentators (*e.g.* Beasley-Murray, *John*, 372; Hoskyns, *Fourth Gospel*, 540) argue that her testimony had to be corroborated, not because she was alone when she witnessed

next sections (20:19–23, 24–29) when Jesus appears to his disciples. There, behind closed doors for fear of the Jews, "Jesus came and stood among them and said to them, 'Peace be with you.'" As in the case of Mary Magdalene earlier, it is possible that the disciples did not at first realise that it was he. Indeed, it is only after Jesus showed them his hands and his side that "then" (οὖν), the disciples rejoiced to see the Lord (20:20). Jesus' presence brought joy to the disciples, thus replacing their fear (*cf.* 6:19–21; 16:22). Though nothing is explicitly said about the disciples' belief or understanding in this section, it is clearly impossible to speak of the disciples' unbelief at this point, for they "see" the risen Lord.[358] As far as their understanding is concerned, the Fourth Gospel has made clear that it is after the resurrection that they would understand the Scripture's testimony about Jesus' hour (2:22; 12:16; 20:9). At this point of the narrative, however, joy takes over comprehensive understanding and intellectual knowledge. Jesus is risen!

If Jesus' earthly mission is now completed, that of the disciples is not, and they will have to carry on such a task: "As the Father has sent me, even so I am sending you" (*cf.* 17:18). Just like Jesus, they will have to bear witness to the truth in the world (*cf.* 18:37).[359] But as was explained earlier (15:26–27), the Spirit will have to come alongside them for this task, thus fulfilling the law's requirement for double witness.[360] This is why,[361] as the glorified Lord, Jesus now breathes on his disciples, saying: "Receive the Holy Spirit" (20:22; *cf.* 7:38–39). The particular task of the disciples to witness to the truth can thus fully begin as they are accompanied by the presence and activity of the Paraclete.[362]

---

the risen Jesus, but because she was a woman. This view has been criticised by Maccini, *Testimony*, 225–33.

[358] Likewise, nothing is said about the disciples' reception of Mary Magdalene's announcement to them in 20:18. It is possible that their reaction was similar to that of Thomas later in the narrative (unbelief), though it is impossible to ascertain this.

[359] As Léon-Dufour, *Lecture*, 4:215–16, noticed, in his interaction with the disciples, Jesus follows a similar pattern to that which he used during his interaction with Mary Magdalene: Jesus initiates the action, the disciples recognise him, and Jesus commissions them.

[360] Lincoln, *John*, 498.

[361] The significance of the giving of the Spirit is not exhausted by this understanding of the Paraclete as Helper. Indeed, the manner with which Jesus confers the Spirit is reminiscent of Gen. 2:7 and Ezek. 37:5, 9–10 so that "The bestowal of the Spirit by the risen Jesus here in 20:22, therefore, signals the eschatological new creation. The God who endowed humanity with life is now through Christ's gift to the disciples endowing humanity with new life" (Lincoln, "Resurrection," 139). See also M. M. Thompson, "The Breath of Life: John 20:22–23 Once More," in *The Holy Spirit and Christian Origins. Essays in Honor of James D. G. Dunn*, ed. by G. N. Stanton, B. W. Longenecker, and S. C. Barton (Grand Rapids, MI/Cambridge: Eerdmans, 2004), 69–78.

[362] Segovia, "Peace," 89, thus proposes that "As a result complete understanding concerning not only the events of 'the hour' but also their own role after 'the hour' is now possible for the disciples."

The narrator does not list the disciples who were present in the locked room when Jesus appeared to them. However, in 20:24 he explains that "Thomas, one of the Twelve, called the twin, was not with them when Jesus came." Like Mary Magdalene in 20:18, the disciples declare to him that they have seen the Lord (20:25), to which Thomas famously replies that his belief in such a declaration would only be possible on the basis of certain conditions: seeing and touching the injured body of Jesus. Thomas' perspective could only change through an encounter with the risen Jesus. Otherwise, said Thomas: "I will never believe."[363] Thus, as the disciples begin their task of witnessing to the truth, even to one of their own, they receive adamant refusal to believe on their account only!

A more detailed study of Thomas' characterisation, focusing on his faith and understanding, will come later. At this point, however, it is important to note that his characterisation in this passage should not be understood apart from the context of Jesus' purpose in carrying out his will for the disciples.[364] Though the narrator in no way downplays Thomas' individuality, his personal doubts and unbelief, the important point to grasp in this passage is that Jesus wants Thomas to believe because he, as a disciple of Jesus, must take on the task of witnessing to others about Jesus.[365] Thus, Jesus graciously offers himself to Thomas in 20:26, inviting him to see and touch his wounds, but not as an answer to Thomas' challenge.[366] Rather, "Jesus is fully aware of Thomas' situation and comes specifically to remedy it according to his own purpose."[367] That is, he comes to prepare and send Thomas on a mission, and for this he must offer himself to Thomas.[368] Implied readers are not told whether Thomas actually proceeded to touch Jesus' wounds, but this is unlikely for Jesus immediately summons him to "not disbelieve, but believe" (20:27).[369] Thus, Jesus insists that Thomas must

---

[363] Lee, "Easter Faith," 43, proposes that such a demand on Thomas' part is indicative of a positive desire to meet the risen Jesus in faith, but this is unlikely. What transpires from Thomas' answer is more a negative demand for proof; or even a "sarcastic expression of unbelief" (W. Bonney, *Caused To Believe: The Doubting Thomas Story at the Climax of John's Christological Narrative*, BibIntS 62 (Leiden/Boston, MA: Brill, 2002), 159–60).

[364] Bonney, *Doubting Thomas*, 142.

[365] Bonney, *Doubting Thomas*, 144.

[366] *Pace* Beasley-Murray, *John*, 385.

[367] Bonney, *Doubting Thomas*, 165.

[368] This underlines the fact that Thomas' unbelief will be turned into belief through a gracious act on the part of Jesus: "The reader here sees Jesus revealed as the agent of Thomas' change" (Bonney, *Doubting Thomas*, 168). Jesus is thus both the agent and the object of faith. The disciples' testimony to Jesus is not enough to bring about belief in the people they witness to. Jesus, through his successor the Paraclete, will continue to be the agent of belief (*cf.* 16:8–11).

[369] For R. E. Brown, *A Risen Christ in Eastertime: Essays on the Gospel Narratives of the Resurrection* (Collegeville, MN: The Liturgical Press, 1990), 79: "[…] if Thomas had examined and touched Jesus' body, he would have persisted in a disbelief that he had already demonstrated and would have ceased to be a disciple." Thomas needed a change of perspective, and believe not on the basis of his own condition, but on the invitation of Christ.

change, become believing, in order to take on the task given him. The object of the belief requested by Jesus is probably not only the fact of the resurrection, but much more, the implications and significance of the resurrection: to believe in Jesus as the actual source of life (1:3), as "the resurrection and the life" (11:25).[370] Compelled by the visible evidence of the risen Christ, as well as by Jesus' challenge, Thomas immediately responds with the fullest Christological confession of the narrative: "My Lord and my God" (20:28).[371]

Again, this change in Thomas' attitude toward Jesus involves more than his personal belief,[372] since Jesus immediately shifts the focus from Thomas' faith to the faith of those who would believe on the basis of the disciples' testimony to Jesus' resurrection: "Have you believed because you have seen me? Blessed are those who have not seen and yet have believed" (20:29). As Lincoln mentions, "the force of Jesus' final words to Thomas can be seen as, 'have you believed their testimony because you have seen me? Blessed are those who have not seen and have believed their testimony.'"[373] It is difficult not to see a reproach in Jesus' statement. Thomas should have believed on the basis of the other disciples' testimony of the resurrected Jesus, for he himself will testify and call people who have not seen to believe nonetheless.[374] At the same time, it should also be noted that Thomas' role as witness presupposes his having seen the risen Christ.[375]

4. Conclusion (20:30–31)

This last claim of Jesus immediately leads to the narrator's statement of purpose for the entire narrative. Everything that has been narrated has been written

---

[370] Thus, it would be incorrect to state that Thomas was simply an "unbeliever" throughout the narrative, but became a believer only when he witnessed the bodily resurrection Jesus. Rather, the belief to which Jesus summons Thomas goes beyond the belief held by the disciples through the narrative prior to his crucifixion. Thomas must now take into account Christ's resurrection and work out the theological implications of this fact.

[371] As mentioned by M. Baron, "La progression des confessions de foi dans les dialogues de Saint Jean," *BVC* 82 (1968): 43: "Sa confession de foi est la plus claire, la plus explicite, celle où se reflète le plus parfaitement la foi même de l'évangéliste qui a affirmé en tête de son livre: *Le Verbe était Dieu* (1,1)." And here again, it is clear that the faith of Thomas has come as a result of Jesus' action and according to his plan for salvation (so Bonney, *Doubting Thomas*, 171).

[372] Bonney, *Doubting Thomas*, 168, speaks of Thomas' "conversion," but this is certainly not the most appropriate terminology in this case.

[373] Lincoln, *John*, 503.

[374] In addition to this reproach, this verse is probably meant also to encourage future believers, instilling in them the confidence that their faith is not inferior to that of those who have seen the resurrected Christ (see *e.g.* Bonney, *Doubting Thomas*, 170; Moloney, *Glory*, 178).

[375] Bonney, *Doubting Thomas*, 170. These two propositions are not contradictory. Though Thomas' future witness necessarily involves having witnessed the resurrected Jesus, his attitude of unbelief regarding the other disciples' testimony was unacceptable.

down as the record of the disciples' witness of Jesus, from the beginning to his resurrection, in order to enable the readers who have not seen Jesus to believe. This link with the preceding dialogues should not be missed. Throughout the narrative, and more specifically in the so-called book of Glory (chaps. 13–20), Jesus has been training his disciples so that they would take the task of witnessing to Jesus upon themselves. In the present book, the implied author thus puts into practice the task given him.

There is a long-standing debate on the interpretation of 20:31, as to whether this book was written down in order to produce belief or to produce continuance in belief, thus implying that the intended readers were already Christians. Most scholars tend to choose the second option today, and this would seem most convincing.[376] Indeed, just as the disciples have been characterised as believers from very early on in the narrative but still needed to grow in their understanding, especially of the significance of Jesus' mission and identity, so the intended readers of the narrative are correspondingly nurtured in their faith and understanding through the depiction of the disciples. The story has thus come full–circle. It opened with the narrator's open statement to implied readers about Jesus' identity and work, and ends with Thomas' high Christological confession. Now, the narrator explains that his chief concern in telling this story was the belief of his readers (*cf.* 19:35). These readers who have not seen Jesus and yet believe are told that this account of the life and works of Jesus has been written especially for them, so that they may go on believing further. Belief is no doubt important for the implied author, but not as an end in itself: "For the evangelist it is essential to have the right belief about Jesus' identity *in order to* experience eternal life (20:31)."[377]

D. The Epilogue: 21:1–25

Though the narrative has already come full circle, there are still several issues that the implied author wishes to address, not least the status of Peter after his threefold denial. Jesus appears once more to a group of disciples by the sea of Tiberias (21:1). The disciples are listed: Simon Peter, Thomas (called the Twin), Nathanael of Cana in Galilee, the sons of Zebedee, and two others (21:2). It is quite surprising to find the disciples fishing in Galilee after having been commissioned by Jesus in chapter 20, so that for several commentators, the disciples' fishing is an "aimless activity undertaken in desperation,"[378] or even "apostasy!"[379] Yet, it is far more likely that the narrator is here setting up a

---

[376] This issue will be treated at greater length later in this study (see chapter 4, below).

[377] Lincoln, *John*, 507 (emphasis added).

[378] Brown, *John*, 2:1096.

[379] Hoskyns, *Fourth Gospel*, 552.

second, and very symbolic, call to mission.[380] Even more surprising in this section is the disciples' failure, one more time, to recognise Jesus in 21:4. Again, it is the Beloved Disciple who will first reach the conclusion about Jesus' identity: "That disciple whom Jesus loved therefore said to Peter, 'it is the Lord'" (21:7). But such insight comes only after Jesus performed a miracle, allowing the disciples to catch a miraculous amount of fish.[381] This is certainly significant: as the disciples obey Jesus' command to cast their net on the other side of the boat, they receive fish in abundance. In this section, "There is no longer any resistance to Jesus' command or questioning of his plans and predictions."[382] Later, the narrator tells readers that the number of fish caught was 153 and that the net did not break (21:11), which, in addition to attesting to the miracle, probably also attests to the completeness and unity[383] of those drawn in by the disciples' mission.[384] Thus, one could say that this event is symbolic of the disciples' involvement in the mission/task Jesus has given them as they will draw people to him through their witness.[385] After this catch of fish, the disciples had breakfast with Jesus, and though they were apparently timid in his presence, they "knew it was the Lord" (21:12).

The disciples are therefore portrayed, early in the epilogue, as potential successful witnesses. But what about Peter's earlier failures? His threefold denials of Jesus (18:15–27) cannot be ignored, but they will be overcome by his threefold professions of love for Jesus (21:15–17). It is on the basis of this love that

---

[380] C. Claussen, "The Role of John 21: Discipleship in Retrospect and Redefinition," in *New Currents in John: A Global Perspective*, ed. by F. Lozada Jr. and T. Thatcher, SBLRBS 54 (Atlanta, GA: SBL, 2006), 61, proposes another literary explanation, that the small number of disciples present in Galilee (seven) indicates that they may have viewed themselves as far too powerless to obey Jesus' commission in 20:21. Such experience of shortcoming represents the human condition before God (see similar experience in 2:3; 6:9). This interpretation, however, appears rather far-fetched since nothing in this section seems to warrant it.

[381] Thus for Bonney, *Doubting Thomas*, 171: "Jesus himself is to be recognized in the work of the church."

[382] T. Wiarda, *Peter in the Gospels: Pattern, Personality, and Relationship*, WUNT 2/127 (Tübingen: Mohr Siebeck, 2000), 139.

[383] The unbroken net has received several other symbolic explanations: *e.g.* the preservation of what is caught (Witherington, *John*, 355) or the limitless number of Christian converts (Carson, *John*, 673).

[384] Lincoln, *John*, 512–13. In fact, the verb "to draw" or "to haul" (ἑλκύω) is the same verb that Jesus used earlier to say: "No one can come to me unless the Father who sent me draws them" (6:44, *cf.* also 13:32). The number "153" has been given numerous symbolic explanations (see *e.g.* Brodie, *John*, 587–88), but several scholars are doubtful that it is possible to give it a symbolic meaning (Brown, *John*, 2:1075–76; Staley, *Print*, 113).

[385] Okure, *Mission*, 220. For Schneiders, *Written*, 226: "Whatever one makes of such interpretations, it seems fairly clear that the enormous catch, which became possible only at Jesus' command, represents the universal mission of the church carried out by those who without Jesus can do nothing (see 15:5) but who will be fruitful as long as they abide in him and obey his commands."

Peter is reassured by Jesus himself, as far as his status of disciple is concerned, through Jesus' entrusting him with a mission to shepherd the sheep and through the declaration that he would die as a faithful follower of Christ, laying down his life for the sheep (21:18–19). Even more, implied readers are here reminded that love for Jesus is essential, for Peter as for any other disciple, in order to take up the task of witnessing in the world.[386]

Then, Peter "turned and saw the disciples whom Jesus loved following them" (21:20) and asked Jesus about what the future held for him. Jesus was not willing to answer Peter's question directly, but rather pointed Peter back to his own role in the mission, and the necessity to follow him (21:22). Implied readers then understand that Jesus is saying that "each disciple should fulfil the role assigned him by his Lord while not questioning the role of the other."[387] Thus, in their mission, the disciples have different, though complementary roles within the believers' community and in their ministry in the world. While Peter's primary role will be to follow Jesus and care for the sheep,[388] the Beloved Disciple's role is to bear witness to Jesus, a role that he will put into practice in the writing of the present narrative (21:24), "and we know that his testimony is true" (21:24).[389]

The Book of Glory, together with the epilogue has treated the manner in which Jesus has trained and taught his disciples about their task of witnessing in a hostile world. Throughout this second half of the Fourth Gospel, their faith has been taken for granted, though once more, they have shown a considerable amount of inadequate understanding, at times even blatantly so, and with dire consequences. At the end of the narrative, the overall sense gained by the implied readers is that, though they are still weak and still lack certain insights (insights that they will gain, in part through the remembrance and re-reading of Scripture – 2:22; 12:16 – aided by the Spirit-Paraclete), the disciples are ready to take on the task given them by Jesus. More, as they are sent once more by Jesus, with particular ministries to fulfil, implied readers realise that their ministry will be successful, as their representatives Peter and the Beloved Disciple will respectively die a God-glorifying death (21:18–19) and witness about the truth of Jesus as the Christ in a written Gospel (21:24).

---

[386] Köstenberger, *John*, 596.

[387] Köstenberger, *Missions*, 159.

[388] As noted by Köstenberger, *Missions*, 159–60, this shepherding role is not merely pastoral in the sense of nurturing believers only: "Rather, as in the case of Jesus, the role of a shepherd also entails his bringing to the flock yet other dispersed sheep (cf. 10:16). Thus 21:15–23 transcends mere nurture of believers to include outreach to unbelievers."

[389] Here, as in 1:14, 16, the implied author uses the second person plural language in a confessional context (see Lincoln, *Truth*, 20–21).

Chapter 3

The Faith and Understanding of Key Individual Disciples

A. Peter

As this study moves from the characterisation of the disciples as a group in the Fourth Gospel's narrative to the study of five individual disciples, it is fitting that it begins with Peter. Indeed, apart from the protagonist Jesus, Peter is certainly the most significant male character of the Fourth Gospel, appearing in nine different passages of the narrative.[1] He is referred to by a variety of names: Peter (17 times),[2] Simon Peter (17 times),[3] Simon (2 times),[4] Simon son of John (4 times),[5] and Cephas (1 time).[6] As noted by Beck, these names all appear successively in the space of only three verses in 1:40–42.[7] Though Peter, after being introduced in 1:40–42, comes on the scene again in a very significant passage of the "Book of Signs" (*i.e.*, 6:67–69), his character is particularly prominent in the "Book of Glory" as well as in the Epilogue of the Fourth Gospel. Peter is the most complex of the disciples of the Fourth Gospel,[8] as the following analysis of his faith and understanding through the narrative will show.[9]

1. "You shall be called Cephas" (1:40–42)

The first passage under consideration is the account of Peter's calling. Interestingly, the name of Peter, in this context, appears before his character does, since his name serves as a means of identifying Andrew: "Andrew, Simon Peter's

---

[1] *Cf.* 1:40–42; 6:68–69; 13:6–9; 13: 24; 13:36–38; 18:10–11; 18:15–18, 25–27; 20:2–10; 21:2–22.

[2] 1:42, 44; 13:8, 37; 18:11, 16 (twice), 17, 18, 26, 27; 20:3, 4; 21:7, 17, 20, 21.

[3] 1:40; 6:8, 68; 13:6, 9, 24, 36; 18:10, 15, 25; 20:2, 6; 21:2, 3, 7, 11, 15.

[4] 1:41, 42.

[5] 1:42; 21:15, 16, 17

[6] 1:42.

[7] Beck, *Discipleship*, 47. In the ensuing narrative, this character is usually called "Simon Peter" when he first appears in a scene, with either name occurring in later references in the same scene (see R. E. Brown, K. P. Donfried, and J. H. P. Reumann, eds., *Peter in the New Testament: A Collaborative Assessment by Protestant and Roman Catholic Scholars* (Minneapolis, MN: Augsburg, 1973), 129, n.275).

[8] Culpepper, *Anatomy*, 120.

[9] Marchadour, *Personnages*, 48, speaks of Peter's characterisation in the Fourth Gospel as "L'histoire d'une fidélité difficile."

brother" (1:40).[10] The fact that Andrew needs to be identified in connection with his brother suggests that Peter was better known to the intended readership of the Fourth Gospel. But in this episode, it is his brother Andrew who is given the more prominent role. Peter is not the first character to become a disciple of Jesus, as before him Andrew and another disciple begin to follow Jesus (1:37–40).[11] Moreover, Andrew is first to confess that Jesus is the Christ,[12] and it is as a result of his initiative and testimony ("We have found the Messiah" – 1:41) that Peter is led to Jesus (1:42).

Once in his presence, Jesus looks at Peter and promises him that his name would change: "You shall be called Cephas (which means Peter)" (1:42). Not every scholar agrees that Jesus' words here refer to a promise. For instance, *pace* Bultmann,[13] Brown argued that the future tense κληθήσῃ was not intended to be understood as a prophecy about a future event (as in Matt. 16:18), since it is "part of the literary style of name changing, even when the name is changed on the spot."[14] Brown is probably correct as far as the literary style is concerned, but his conclusion does not fit the Fourth Gospel's account. Indeed, in the ensuing narrative Jesus almost never addresses directly his disciple by one of his names, but when he does, it is with his initial name: "Simon, son of John" (21:15, 16, 17). Conversely, the narrator consistently refers to Simon as "Peter" or "Simon Peter," but never as "Simon, son of John," which indicates that at the time of the writing of the Fourth Gospel, his new name was in use, and so introduced back into the narrative. The function of this name change thus probably serves to underline Jesus' foreknowledge that Simon son of John would later be called "Peter."

Even though the significance of such a promise is not explicitly stated in this passage, two main options can be proposed to explain it: (*i*) Jesus perceived Peter's future potential for stable and solid leadership,[15] or (*ii*) Jesus knew how fickle and obtuse Peter would be.[16] One may argue that the second proposition reflects Peter's character in the ensuing narrative, but it is unlikely that this is what Jesus desired to convey.[17] Rather, Jesus promised that this new

---

[10] See, *e.g.*, Quast, *Figures*, 30. Conway, *Men and Women*, 164–65, goes further and proposes that Andrew's entrance into the narrative before his brother is "an indication of Peter's diminished status in the Fourth Gospel" compared with the Synoptic accounts. Though this is possible, the reference to "Andrew, brother of Simon Peter" might on the contrary serve to alert readers to the importance of the character about to be introduced in the narrative (so Marchadour, *Personnages*, 49).

[11] Compare with Mk. 1:16–18; Matt. 4:18–20.

[12] Again, compare with the Synoptic accounts (Mk. 8:29; Matt. 16:16; Lk. 9:20).

[13] Bultmann, *John*, 101, n.5.

[14] Brown, *John*, 1:80.

[15] So, *e.g.*, Schnackenburg, *John*, 1:312–13; Brown, *John*, 1:80; Beasley-Murray, *John*, 80.

[16] So Droge, "Peter," 308.

[17] One might even say, with O. Cullmann, *Saint Pierre. Disciple - Apôtre - Martyr*, Bibliothèque Théologique (Neuchatel/Paris: Delachaux & Niestlé, 1952), 26, that "ce caractère

name would someday reflect Peter's role.[18] As mentioned by Köstenberger, it is "not that Peter is worthy of such an epithet in himself; rather, the new name is proleptic of the new man whom God would someday create."[19]

What is most striking in this short episode is that, as Peter enters the narrative, he remains completely passive and the narrator provides almost no individual characterisation for him.[20] Not only is he found (εὑρίσκει) and told about Jesus by Andrew, but he is also brought (ἤγαγεν) to Jesus, who looks at him, identifies him, and promises to rename him.[21] Throughout, Peter remains silent, which contrasts with the other characters who have come to and have given titles to Jesus in this chapter (*cf.* 1:29, 36, 41, 45, 49). Peter is therefore introduced into the narrative in a particularly unremarkable fashion, but his lack of characterisation may be intended to underline Jesus' own characterisation: the focus is on Jesus as the one who knows his disciples intimately and calls them authoritatively.[22]

Almost nothing can be said concerning the faith and understanding of Peter at this stage of the narrative. Indeed, Peter is never explicitly said to have begun following Jesus, except that in the midst of the other call stories, it can be assumed. So far, one might simply say that Peter has been called by Jesus and has become one of the disciples, but much of his personality remains unknown to implied readers.

2. "You have the words of eternal life" (6:67–69)

The next passage in which Peter appears comes at the end of a controversy between Jesus and "the Jews" about his claim to be "the bread of life" (6:35–59). Such a controversy caused a division within the disciples of Jesus, so that many of them turned back and no longer followed him (6:66). If Peter contrasted earlier with some of his fellow disciples in that he did not confess Christ in his first appearance in the narrative, he now becomes the voice of the Twelve and confesses: "Lord, to whom shall we go? You have the words of eternal life, and

---

même, avec ses contradictions prononcées, faisait peut-être de Pierre le disciple psychologiquement le plus propre d'entre ses pairs à être le « Roc » [...]. L'inconstance et la faiblesse de Pierre ne seraient alors que le revers de ses qualités."

[18] So Lincoln, *John*, 119; A. Marchadour, "La figure de Simon-Pierre dans l'évangile de Jean," in *Raconter, interpréter, annoncer. Parcours de Nouveau Testament. Mélanges offerts à Daniel Marguerat pour son 60° anniversaire*, ed. by E. Steffek and Y. Bourquin, MdB 47 (Genève: Labor et Fides, 2003), 186.

[19] Köstenberger, *John*, 77–78.

[20] Although Petersen, *Sociology of Light*, 26, rightly argues that "naming is one way of constructing characters." Thus, we can say that Jesus naming Simon and promising him a new name contributes to Peter's characterisation in showing that this character, though he is passive in this passage, will become important. See also Bultmann, *John*, 72, n.2.

[21] Conway, *Men and Women*, 165.

[22] Carson, *John*, 156.

we (ἡμεῖς) have believed, and have come to know, that you are the Holy One of God" (6:68–69). As was already noted in the study of the group of the disciples in the narrative, Peter's confession first takes the form of a rhetorical question (6:68a), and is followed by a two part confession first affirming the person and teaching of Jesus (especially of chapter 6[23]), and secondly declaring that the Twelve have believed and have known (the verbs in this confession are in the perfect tense) that Jesus had divine origins.[24] Peter, in his "solemn declaration of belief,"[25] appears to have assimilated and accepted without reservation Jesus' words, though at this point of the narrative it cannot be assessed exactly how much he understood from the entire preceding discourse.[26] If Peter has, together with the disciples, put his faith in Jesus, the plenary sense of Jesus' discourse still escapes him.[27] Thus, Culpepper rightly proposes that: "He has grasped the importance of Jesus' words, his glory, and the life his words give. Paradoxically, the words of life may also require death, and this Peter has not yet grasped."[28] This will become evident in the rest of the narrative.

After the call stories (1:35–51), implied readers have here the confirmation that Peter is indeed a member of the group of Jesus' disciples. However, Peter in these verses also appears as much more than one of the Twelve, since the narrator presents him as a representative or spokesperson of the group, thus giving more depth to a characterisation that was thus far marked by passivity. Peter now takes a leading role within the group of the disciples. Moreover, his declaration of faith can only be taken at face value. It does not follow from Jesus' statement about one of the Twelve being a "devil" (6:71) that Peter's confession is overshadowed by "dubiousness."[29] If Judas is identified as the "devil," it is because he *contrasts* with the other disciples who remain faithful to Jesus while many are falling away (6:66).[30] Thus, the implied author did not wish to communicate that the faith of the other disciples was untrustworthy because of Judas' upcoming betrayal.[31]

---

[23] *Cf.* 6:27, 33, 40, 47, 50–51, 63.

[24] Joubert, "Holy One," 66; Marchadour, *Personnages*, 53.

[25] B. Lindars, *The Gospel of John*, NCB (Grand Rapids, MI: Eerdmans, 1981), 275.

[26] For Collins, *These Things*, 40: "Indeed, according to John, the acknowledgment of Jesus' messiahship seems to derive from an acceptance of Jesus as revealer."

[27] Léon-Dufour, *Lecture*, 2:188.

[28] Culpepper, *Anatomy*, 120.

[29] As Haenchen, *John*, 1:308, proposed, followed by P. Perkins, *Peter: Apostle of the Whole Church*, SPNT (Columbia, SC: University of South Carolina Press, 1994), 97 and Conway, *Men and Women*, 169.

[30] Quast, *Figures*, 163.

[31] That said, Conway, *Men and Women*, 169, correctly asserts that Judas' identification as a devil "immediately dispels any notion that inclusion among the twelve is equivalent to faithful discipleship."

3. *"Not my feet only, but also my hands and my head!" (13:6–11)*

In the "Book of Glory," Peter will be characterised in a much more ambiguous manner. Indeed, his portrayal during the Footwashing scene begins a series of "trials"[32] for the disciple, where his difficulties in following Jesus appropriately will come to the fore.

During the meal (13:2), Jesus rises and begins to wash his disciples' feet. Peter's reaction, when his turn has come, is very informative as to the state of his belief and understanding at this point of the narrative: "Lord, do you wash my [μου][33] feet?" (13:6). Clearly, Peter could not fathom how his κύριος could lower himself in such a way before his own disciples. Peter, at this time, did not understand the meaning of this menial and demeaning act, and Jesus acknowledges this: "what I am doing you [sg.] do not understand now, but afterward, you will understand" (13:7).[34] As was argued in chapter 2, Jesus will begin to explain the meaning of his gesture immediately after (13:12–17), but most likely his words also refer to a time, after his resurrection, when Peter would adequately understand it.[35] And yet, Jesus' promise of a future understanding is not enough for Peter, and he simply refuses to let Jesus perform what he considers to be an unworthy task, insisting: "you shall never wash my feet" (13:8). On the one hand, Peter is obviously well intentioned here. He has very high regard for his Lord, and cannot possibly, out of respect for Jesus, let him wash his feet.[36] But as well intentioned as he may be, Peter's refusal is a consequence of his poor understanding of the person and mission of Jesus. On the other hand, Peter's adamant resistance may also mean that he understands more than he articulates:

Peter realizes that, by transcending the inequality between himself and his disciples and inaugurating between them a relationship of friendship, [Jesus] is subverting in principle all structures of domination, and therefore the basis for Peter's own exercise of power and authority.[37]

Jesus must therefore make clear to Peter that his refusal to let him act in such a manner is tantamount to a rejection of his person and work. For Bultmann, Peter refuses "to see the act of salvation in what is lowly, or God in the form of a

---

[32] Marchadour, *Personnages*, 53.

[33] Here, it is Peter as an individual who speaks, as nothing indicates that he is again speaking on behalf of the Twelve (*pace* Tolmie, *Farewell*, 195). Clearly, it is possible that Peter voiced what others were feeling, but it is not as their representative that Peter speaks.

[34] Of course, Peter had grasped something of the significance of Jesus' act as he assumed the role of a servant rather than that of a teacher and Lord, but he failed to understand why (*cf.* Thompson, "His Own," 265).

[35] Thomas, *Footwashing*, 92.

[36] For Conway, *Men and Women*, 171: "Peter's own brand of incomprehension [of a different type than that of Nicodemus, the Samaritan woman, and Martha] is marked by a particular passion that will also be evident in his exchange with Jesus later at the meal (13:37)."

[37] Schneiders, *Written*, 195.

slave."[38] This is the meaning of Jesus' reproach to his disciple: "if I do not wash you [sg.], you have no share in me" (13:8). Only if Peter accepts this service will he be able to abide continually in fellowship with Jesus.[39] Bultmann goes on and explains that if Peter has now understood something of the importance of the footwashing act, he has not yet understood in what way it is important: "For now, his refusal turns into the opposite: he demands more than what he has already received."[40] Peter is already "clean" (καθαροί) according to Jesus, he is already in fellowship with Jesus,[41] but he needs the footwashing proposed by Jesus in order to *continue* in this fellowship, for this menial act points to values necessary for Peter's perseverance in belief: the pattern of glorification through humiliation that Jesus will exemplify climactically on the cross, and that the disciples ought to imitate (13:15).[42]

Once more, that this is true of Peter is clear from the contrast proposed by Jesus between his faithful disciples and Judas (though his name is not mentioned): "and you [pl.] are clean, but not every one of you" (13:10). Thus, throughout this exchange, Peter's belief in Jesus has been emphasised both by his passionate refusal to let Jesus wash his feet, and by Jesus' insistence that he ought to let his Lord perform this task: if Peter needs the footwashing, it is because he is already clean (contrary to Judas), because he already stands in a faithful relationship with Jesus. But this dialogue also indicates that to put faith in Jesus does not necessarily entail a proper understanding of Jesus and his mission. Indeed, at this point in the story, Peter cannot fathom the self-abasement of Jesus, who does not fit his understanding of what the Messiah ought to be.[43] The disconnect between his faith and understanding is thus very apparent at this point.

4. "Simon Peter motioned to him to ask Jesus" (13:23–26)

After 6:67–69 and 13:6–11, the next mention of Peter in 13:23–26 appears again in connection with the issue of Judas' betrayal. Though readers are aware of the Betrayer's identity, this is not so for the disciples because Judas' name has not been mentioned to them in connection with the upcoming betrayal of one of the Twelve (6:70; 13:10, 18). This is why Peter tells the Beloved Disciple, who was reclining at the table close to Jesus, to ask Jesus about the identity of this Betrayer (13:24). At the end of this section, however, though Jesus has made known to the Beloved Disciple who the betrayer was (13:26), there

---

[38] Bultmann, *John*, 468.

[39] Lincoln, *John*, 369.

[40] Bultmann, *John*, 469.

[41] *Pace* Thompson, "His Own," 272.

[42] Lincoln, *John*, 369; J. D. G. Dunn, "The Washing of the Disciples' Feet in John 13:1–20," *ZNW* 61 (1970): 248–49.

[43] Marchadour, *Personnages*, 55.

is no indication that any of the disciples present (except Judas) are any wiser about this issue (13:28). The fact that "no exception to this ignorance is made for either the disciple whom Jesus loved or Peter [...] suggests that despite the exchange between Peter and the other disciple, the primary focus of the scene is on neither of them, but on Judas."[44] In other words, we should be careful not to draw too much from the characterisation of both Peter and the Beloved Disciple in this section. For instance, Gunther asserts that since Peter could only pose a "private question" to Jesus through the Beloved Disciple, it implies that "Peter's position at the Supper was one of lesser favor, honor and accessibility than that of the beloved disciple."[45] However, if the text does indicate that Peter had a lesser accessibility to Jesus, nothing is said regarding the lesser favor or honor. If it is likely that the implied author wished to stress the intimate relationship between Jesus and the Beloved Disciple,[46] it does not follow that he wished Peter's relationship to Jesus to contrast negatively with it.[47]

It is impossible to draw clear conclusions on the faith and understanding of Peter from this section of the narrative. Peter is, together with the other disciples, characterised as ignorant of the identity of the betrayer, but nothing is said explicitly regarding his faith and understanding. This is simply not the point of the passage.[48] If anything, once again, the identification of Judas as the Betrayer contrasts negatively with the other disciples, but this does not add anything to Peter's characterisation so far in the narrative.

5. *"Till you have denied me three times" (13:36–38)*

The third appearance of Peter in chapter 13 comes in the "Farewell Discourse" proper (13:31–16:33). Once more, after 13:6–9, Peter will be characterised by his spontaneity, and Jesus, who foretells Peter's denials, thus adds a new element to Peter's characterisation. Immediately prior to the mention of Peter, Jesus announced his departure to the Father "in a little while" (13:33), and gave the disciples "a new commandment" to love one another (13:34).

Peter does not respond to the love commandment, but simply to Jesus' upcoming departure that obviously troubles him. Most likely, Peter functions again as the spokesperson of the Twelve when he asks Jesus: "Lord, where are you going?" And yet, the ensuing dialogue is strictly between Jesus and Peter:

---

[44] Conway, *Men and Women*, 172.

[45] Gunther, "Relation," 127.

[46] *E.g.*, G. R. O'Day, "The Gospel of John," in *The New Interpreter's Bible IX* (Nashville, TN: Abingdon, 1995), 729.

[47] Likewise, *e.g.*, Marchadour, *Personnages*, 56, proposes that three modes of faithfulness are presented in this section: the Beloved Disciple is the perfect disciple, Peter is the reticent disciple, and Judas is the "antidisciple," but this compartmentalising is also unwarranted.

[48] Quast, *Figures*, 66–67, may be correct in his assessment: "It is precisely because the roles of Peter and the Beloved Disciple are foremost in the minds of the present day interpreters that explanations are offered on behalf of the evangelist."

"Peter alone bears the full weight of Jesus' prediction."[49] Jesus thus answers him: "where I am going, you [sg.] cannot follow me now, but you will follow me afterward" (13:36). Peter persists in his questioning, and reveals his lack of understanding regarding Jesus' unequivocal announcement. Peter considers himself not only able to follow Jesus, but also ready to follow him all the way to martyrdom if necessary: "I will lay down my life for you" (13:37). Peter, however, does not understand the implications of his words. In using the language of laying down one's life, he wrongly portrays himself as capable of the sort of love Jesus was to demonstrate for his disciples in his death (10:11, 17–18). Moreover, Peter has missed the distinction made by Jesus between "now" and "afterward" (13:36): "Not until Jesus' hour has been completed and his love demonstrated in death will Peter have the resources for living out Jesus' model (*cf.* 21:18–19)."[50] Peter "cannot" follow Jesus "now" (13:36) because Jesus' death is a necessary prerequisite to continual discipleship: "Peter must not outrun Jesus to the cross."[51] Such incompetence will also be exposed dramatically in the near future, as Jesus solemnly foretells Peter's upcoming denials (13:38), after having sarcastically questioned his misplaced confidence ("Will you lay down your life for me?"). In this context, it becomes evident that Peter's denials are "a natural consequence of his ignorance about the necessity of Jesus' death."[52]

With Quast, it is important at this point to mention that, though Peter is portrayed as lacking wisdom and understanding in his remarks, his characterisation up to Jesus' foretelling of the denial is not blatantly critical.[53] Peter's words, however ignorant, show his eagerness and commitment to follow the Lord, and cannot be doubted. Peter is obviously well intentioned in his dialogue with Jesus. Thus, his characterisation is different from that of Judas: Peter is never portrayed as being part of "the world" and he is still considered as a faithful disciple of Jesus.[54] Thus, if Peter will deny his Lord, implied readers are not

---

[49] Conway, *Men and Women*, 173. For Quast, *Figures*, 70, however, "Peter's attitude and actions here are to be taken as representative of the eager but ignorant commitment of the twelve who were yet to understand the dynamics of Jesus' forthcoming arrest and crucifixion."

[50] Lincoln, *John*, 388.

[51] D. Kim, *An Exegesis of Apostasy Embedded in John's Narrative of Peter and Judas Against the Synoptic Parallels*, SBEC 61 (Lewiston, NY/Queenston/Lampeter: Edwin Mellen, 2004), 109.

[52] Kim, *Apostasy*, 108.

[53] Quast, *Figures*, 69–70.

[54] Tolmie, *Farewell*, 202: "Although his behaviour is unacceptable, it does not imply the value of false discipleship or being part of the world (as in the case of Judas), but should be interpreted as expressing a negation of discipleship – a value that is distinguished from that of false discipleship or being part of the world by the fact that a relationship between Jesus and the disciple exists – a precondition that is absolutely vital for the existence of discipleship. Accordingly, the implied reader will view the character more sympathetically than Judas."

concerned about him abandoning or betraying Jesus like Judas. Indeed, Jesus promised him: "you will follow me later" (13:36).

Once more, the faith of Peter (however weak it is potentially), and his lack of understanding of Jesus' identity and work continue to run parallel to each other. Peter's authentic discipleship struggles to comprehend his Master, especially the necessity of his death, and what is expected of him as a disciple, but the narrator shows that Jesus is in total control over his discipleship.

6. *"Put your sword into its sheath" (18:10–11)*

Several chapters later, when the disciples are present with Jesus in the garden (18:1), Peter illustrates that he still has not understood Jesus' mission, even after the long Farewell Discourses (13:31–16:33). Peter is mentioned at the end of the scene, as Jesus is about to be arrested and taken away. Jesus was ready to be apprehended by the soldiers, and he asked that his disciples be let go for "of those you gave me I have lost no one" (18:9). But Peter refused to let it happen and so began to fight, cutting the high priest's servant's ear (18:10). The fight does not get very far, however, because Jesus swiftly stopped it, ordering Peter to put his sword back in his sheath and rebuking him: "shall I not drink the cup that the Father has given me?" (18:11).[55]

These two verses are significant for the unfolding of Peter's characterisation in the narrative.[56] First, it shows that Peter's prior willingness to die for Jesus (13:37) was real and honest, since he actually put it into action. More importantly, it shows that Peter still does not understand that Jesus *must* die. He is not ready to let go of his own understanding of what a Messiah ought to be and do, and so chooses to disobey Jesus and the Father: "Il choisit l'épée du sang versé plutôt que le calice du sang donné en obéissance à son Père."[57] Because of this, the contrast between Peter and Judas, another disciple present on the scene (18:2, 3, 5), is more ambiguous here than earlier in the narrative. Judas betrays his master by divulging where Jesus is to Jewish authorities, and so seeks his death. Peter, on the other hand, fights against Jesus' apprehension that would lead to his death. But these two opposed actions from the disciples are not as different as one might think. Indeed, they both desire to divert Jesus from the way leading to his Passion: "Peter is thwarting God's design as Judas is thwarting God's design."[58] Though their motivations are diametrically opposed, they

---

[55] Köstenberger, *John*, 509: "'Cup' serves here as a metaphor for death. In the OT, the expression refers primarily to 'God's cup of wrath,' which evildoers will have to drink. [...] This imagery may have been transferred to the righteous, guiltless one taking upon himself God's judgment by way of substitutionary suffering."

[56] *Pace* Becker, *Johannes*, 2:544, who claims that Peter's actions serve no other purpose than to introduce Jesus' acceptance of the Father's will.

[57] Marchadour, "Simon-Pierre," 190. See also Wiarda, *Peter*, 139.

[58] Moloney, *John*, 484.

refuse the path prepared for Jesus by the Father. Peter's loyalty and desire to protect Jesus is thus reprehensible because it is misguided and it stands between Jesus and his mission in the world.[59] As a whole, Peter's misunderstanding has grave consequences since it leads him to disobedience.

7. "And at once the rooster crowed" (18:15–18, 25–27)

The next passage in which Peter appears continues to draw on the consequences of Peter's inability to understand Jesus and brings to a dramatic conclusion Jesus' prediction about Peter's denials in 13:38. As Jesus is taken away to Annas' court to be interrogated (18:13), Peter follows Jesus from a distance with "another disciple."[60] It is because of this other disciple that Peter gains access to the court, for he "was known to the high priest" (18:15).[61] But as Peter was about to enter the court, the woman who guarded the door asked him: "You also are not [μή] one of this man's disciples, are you?" Peter answered by a lie, saying: "I am not" (18:17). Interestingly, this lie, "οὐκ εἰμί," which Peter will repeat in 18:25, is the exact reversal of Jesus' words, who revealed his identity in the garden declaring "ἐγώ εἰμί" (18:5, 8). As proposed by Lincoln, "Depicting Peter's denial in this fashion shows up the failure of his witness not only in contrast to that of Jesus in the surrounding narrative but also in contrast to John [...] at the beginning."[62] The narration of this event then briefly shifts focus from Peter to the officers (ὑπηρέται) and servants who had prepared a charcoal fire to

---

[59] Droge, "Peter," 311, goes too far in his indictment of Peter: "Moreover, when Peter's desperate act is interpreted in light of Jesus' statement 'If my kingdom was of this world, my subject would fight' (18:36), it becomes clear that the author of the Fourth Gospel has leveled a devastating indictment at Peter. That Peter *does* fight suggests, at a minimum, that he has a fundamental misunderstanding of Jesus and of the nature of his kingship. Worse still, Peter's action reveals that he is not a 'subject' of Jesus' heavenly kingdom [...]." Indeed, Jesus here only says that if his kingdom was of this world, he would order his disciples to fight, but it does not necessarily follow that if one disciple started to fight, his membership in the kingdom would be jeopardised! It is simply that this disciple has failed to grasp the nature of the Kingdom of which he is a member.

[60] Most probably, this disciple is none other than the "Beloved Disciple" (see *e.g.* Lincoln, *John*, 452–53). The section on the faith and understanding of the Beloved Disciple will come back to the issue of his identification.

[61] For Kim, *Apostasy*, 36, "John's mention of the other disciple's help in this passage may be intended to shed light on Peter's determination to follow Jesus even to the point of death as he alleges in 13:37." This proposition is, unfortunately, difficult to assess textually.

[62] Lincoln, *Truth*, 64. John twice said "I am not" when he was questioned three times about being the Messiah or Elijah (1:20, 21), just as Peter says "I am not" twice also responding to three questions. Obviously, John's answers were part of his "confessing" of Jesus, while Peter's are part of his "denying." *Pace* Quast, *Figures*, 87, for whom "Peter's reticence in entering the courtyard is not so much a refusal to be identified with Jesus as it is a fear of retribution for cutting off the ear of the guard," no textual element favours such a reading, while the insistence of the text in using the word μαθητής four times may indicate that discipleship is the issue at stake.

warm themselves up (18:18a). The ὑπηρέται have already been mentioned in this chapter (18:2), when they came out carrying torches to arrest Jesus (18:2). Thus, when the focus returns to Peter in 18:18b who was "with them" (μετ᾽ αὐτῶν) it is difficult not to think of Judas who was also "with them" earlier in the narrative (18:5).[63] What the implied author may have wished to communicate by this parallelism is more difficult to assess. For Moloney, "Peter is joining Judas, moving away from the light of the world toward the darkness."[64] Whether or not Moloney infers too much from this, it is true that for the first time in the Gospel, implied readers do indeed wonder where Peter stands in his discipleship.

Readers are left for several verses in the ambiguity of this situation, as the narrator now turns the focus on Jesus who is also being questioned about his disciples and about his teaching (18:19–24). When the narrator returns to Peter in 18:25, he first reminds readers where Peter had been left, and then reports a second set of questions from the people who were warming themselves up around the fire. The second question (18:25a) is practically word for word the same as the first one (18:18), and so is Peter's answer: "He denied it and said: 'I am not'" (19:25b). This repetition creates a frame around Jesus' response that his teaching would be found in those who have heard him (18:20, 21), and thus indicts Peter even more.[65] Upon a third question from a servant of the high priest who happened to be a relative of Malchus, the man whose ear Peter had cut off earlier (18:10), he denies having even been in the garden with Jesus (18:27a). The narrator finally concludes this section with a dramatic, though laconic, "and at once a rooster crowed" (18:27b).

Throughout Peter's interrogation, Peter never explicitly denies that Jesus is "the Christ, the Son of God" (20:31), but that he is one of Jesus' disciples.[66] This leads Kim to assert that Peter could therefore *not* be considered an apostate at this point.[67] Even more, Kim insists that Peter is here portrayed as an example to follow:

John seems to be more concerned with portraying Peter as a faithful disciple whose example its audience should follow. As Peter avoids denying Jesus with the words "I do not know him," so should John's audience. It seems that the author of John does not want Peter's threefold deni-

---

[63] Moloney, *John*, 487.

[64] Moloney, *John*, 487.

[65] Marchadour, "Simon-Pierre," 191. R. M. Fowler, *Let the Reader Understand: Reader-Response Criticism and the Gospel of Mark* (Minneapolis, MN: Fortress, 1991), 143–44, shows: "Intercalation is narrative sleight of hand, a crafty manipulation of the discourse level that creates the illusion that two episodes are taking place simultaneously." The simultaneousness of Jesus' and Peter's responses to questions thus creates a dramatic effect.

[66] Culpepper, *Anatomy*, 120.

[67] Kim, *Apostasy*, 46.

als to damage his theological construction of Peter's exemplary discipleship and this goal is fulfilled by its mild literary treatment of Peter's denial.[68]

Such a position, however, is untenable on a narrative level. Indeed, Jesus had predicted in 13:38 that Peter would deny *him* three times before the rooster crowed, and so it must be concluded that Peter's refusal to admit his discipleship amounts to a denial of Jesus himself.[69] Thus, "Jesus is on his way to his death and (at the time at least) Peter is no follower of his."[70]

In light of the importance of the discipleship motif in the Fourth Gospel, Peter's denial is a very serious indictment of his character.[71] His misunderstanding of Jesus' identity and mission has led him to such confusion of mind that he is unable to stand trial in faithfulness to his Lord. Though Jesus points to those who had heard him teach for favourable witness in the world, Peter fails miserably the test of faithfulness. This event thus highlights how unprepared Peter is for his role as witness at this point of the narrative.[72] His faith in Jesus, though one cannot assert that it is non-existent, is certainly not bearing fruit. Indeed, Peter denying his discipleship amounts to denying his belief in Jesus. What a contrast with his earlier statements (6:68–69, 13:7)! Even so, the rest of the narrative will show that Peter's denials do not cut him off definitively from fellowship with the other disciples and with Jesus.

8. "Simon Peter ... went into the tomb" (20:2–10)

Peter will be absent from the rest of Jesus' trial and crucifixion, unlike the Beloved Disciple, and the three women (19:25). Implied readers understand that, after his denials, Peter decided to "lie low," and keep away from Jesus and danger. On the first day of the week (20:1), however, Mary Magdalene goes to the tomb while it is still dark[73] and sees that the stone has been taken away from

---

[68] Kim, *Apostasy*, 49. Kim adds, explaining the differences between the Synoptic Gospels' rendering of Peter's crying after the rooster had crowed and the absence of such repentance in the fourth Gospel: "Peter does not deny the Lord directly and publicly [Kim insists that Peter's denials happened in private], so he has no reason to repent for this" (p. 59).

[69] Kim's conclusion (following Bultmann, *John*, 648) that "the rooster's crow does not have any literary role within John's theological description of the whole story of Peter's denial" is therefore nonsensical (Kim, *Apostasy*, 60). With Lincoln, *John*, 456, it is preferable to say that "Peter's remorse in reaction to the cock crowing is, of course, presupposed in what follows and reflected in 21:15–17."

[70] Culpepper, *Anatomy*, 120.

[71] A. H. Maynard, "The Role of Peter in the Fourth Gospel," *NTS* 30 (1984): 538. Likewise, Droge, "Peter," 311, speaks of Peter's denials as "his confession."

[72] Lincoln, *John*, 456.

[73] As often in the Fourth Gospel's narrative, the mention of darkness is probably intended to symbolise the realm of doubt and unbelief.

the tomb. Alarmed, she runs and goes to Peter and the Beloved Disciple to tell them that Jesus' body had been taken away from the tomb (20:2).[74]

After Peter's denial, it is at first surprising to find him as one of the recipients of Mary Magdalene's news. Even though Peter has denied Jesus, the narrator still characterises him as "the leading figure among the disciples."[75] Peter and the Beloved Disciple, after hearing the news, run toward the tomb, and though they were running together, the Beloved Disciple outran Peter and so reached the tomb first (20:4). In depicting the Beloved Disciple running faster, the implied author may well wish to symbolise his pre-eminence in his love for Jesus.[76] A contrast thus seems obvious between the Beloved Disciple and Peter: "Simon-Pierrre court aussi, son attachement pour le Seigneur résistant à ses infidélités, mais il court plus lourdement, encore encombré dans ses contradictions."[77]

When the Beloved Disciple arrived, he stopped at the entrance of the tomb and simply looked in (20:5). Peter, however, directly entered the tomb upon his late arrival, and from inside also witnessed the linen clothes lying there (20:6). Then the Beloved Disciple followed Peter inside and reacted as follows: "he saw and believed" (20:8).[78] Interestingly, nothing is said about Peter's reaction in this section, but this is certainly due to the implied author's desire to focus primarily on the Beloved Disciple's reaction. Thus, Brown is correct: "What John wishes to *emphasize* here is not the failure of Simon Peter to believe but the extraordinary sensitivity of the other disciple, stemming from the love of Jesus, that enables him to believe."[79] The following verse emphasises even more the contrast between the Beloved Disciple and Peter: "for as yet, they did not understand the Scripture, that he must rise from the dead" (20:9). Such a narratorial comment reminds implied readers of similar verses in 2:22 and 12:16, and in this context indicates that Peter has not yet reached this understanding of Jesus' resurrection based on Scripture, while the Beloved Disciple reached belief in the resurrection independently of Scripture.[80] The last verse of this section is somewhat anticlimactic, as the two disciples simply "went back to their homes" (20:10), not witnessing to what they had seen!

---

[74] As Lincoln, *John*, 489, mentions: "Apparently at this stage the sight of the stone having been removed from the tomb's entrance is enough to convince her that the body must no longer be there."

[75] Köstenberger, *John*, 562.

[76] Cf. Lincoln, *John*, 489; Quast, *Figures*, 111–13.

[77] Marchadour, "Simon-Pierre," 192.

[78] Thus, with Hoskyns, *Fourth Gospel*, 541: "his entrance is delayed in order that his faith may form the climax of the narrative." See Quast, *Figures*, 113–16, for other options regarding the depiction of the Beloved Disciple stopping and allowing Peter to enter first.

[79] Brown, *Eastertime*, 68, n.81.

[80] Lincoln, *John*, 491; Brown, *John*, 2:987; Witherington, *John*, 325.

In this section, implied readers discover that Peter is, even after his denials, still to be considered as a leading disciple of Jesus. Peter's faith is not mentioned in these verses, while his lack of understanding is once more emphasised. What the narrator insists upon, however, is that Peter, just like the Beloved Disciple, witnessed the fact that Jesus' clothes were still in the tomb. This depiction suggests that Jesus' body was not stolen, contrary to Mary Magdalene's first thought. With Quast, it may be that Peter's literary function in this section is "to verify the resurrection by serving as the best-known witness to the earliest evidences of the resurrection."[81] Peter's lack of understanding and belief in Jesus' resurrection could thus be assessed more positively than one would expect at first: "His witness can be regarded as an objective report of the actual physical situation. There was no anticipation or incipient faith to cloud his vision."[82] This scene is thus preparatory of Peter's future role as a witness. The fact remains, however, that Peter is lacking both understanding and faith in the resurrection at this point of the narrative.

9. "Feed my lambs" (21:2–22)

The last section under consideration is crucial for Peter's depiction in the narrative, as it brings a sense of closure to this character's struggles throughout the Fourth Gospel.[83] The section begins with the story of the miraculous catch of fish (21:1–14). On the shore of the sea of Tiberias, Jesus revealed himself for the third time after his resurrection (21:14) to the disciples Simon Peter, Thomas called the Twin, Nathanael of Cana in Galilee, the sons of Zebedee, and two others (21:1–2). In this scene, Peter appears once more as a leader of the disciples, as he is the one initiating the night of fishing (21:3). As the day was breaking in, Jesus appeared on the scene, but was not recognised at first by the disciples. It is only after he ordered them to cast their net on the other side of the boat, and the disciples caught a great amount of fish, that the Beloved Disciple recognises Jesus: "That disciple whom Jesus loved therefore said to Peter, 'it is the Lord!'" (21:7a). But if that disciple is the first to recognise Jesus, Peter extravagantly jumps into the water to reach Jesus (20:7b).[84] Readers are not told explicitly about Peter's belief, but his energetic response to the Beloved Disciple's identification of Jesus shows his excitement to be with Jesus again.

Once on land, "they saw a charcoal fire in place" (20:9), a setting obviously reminiscent of 18:18 which brings back to implied readers' mind the

---

[81] Quast, *Figures*, 117.

[82] Quast, *Figures*, 117.

[83] Marchadour, "Simon-Pierre," 192, sees in this section "une reconformation du programme annoncé par Jésus à Simon-Pierre in 1,42."

[84] The fact that the Beloved Disciple is once more first to reach a correct conclusion about Jesus is coherent with his portrayal in the narrative as having superior insight, and Peter's reaction also recalls events of chapter 20 (Moloney, *John*, 550).

unresolved issue of Peter's threefold denials.[85] In a theological reading of this chapter, Williams proposes that:

Peter must recognize himself as a betrayer: that is part of the past that makes him who he is. If he is to be called again, if he can again become a true apostle, the 'Peter' that he is in the purpose of Jesus rather than the Simon who runs back into the cosy obscurity of 'ordinary' life, his failure must be assimilated, lived through again and brought to good and not to destructive issue.[86]

Thus, at this point, if Peter is portrayed as an apostle, it is as a failed apostle. But before the disciples partake in the breakfast, Peter goes back to the boat to help haul the net full of 153 large fish (21:11), symbolically attesting to the completeness and unity of those drawn in by the disciples' mission.[87] Thus, with the other disciples, Peter is portrayed as a potential successful leader in the task Jesus gave them to draw people to him through their witness.[88] But if hope is alive, the matter of Peter's betrayals must still be addressed.

After the breakfast, as they were probably still standing around the charcoal fire, Jesus begins questioning Peter. The presence of the other disciples around the fire may here be significant because the following dialogue may thus serve as a *public* reinstatement of Peter, just as his denials were public.[89] Jesus in this section addresses Peter as "Simon, Son of John," his birth name.[90] Jesus then asks Peter: "do you love me more than these?" (21:15). As the great majority of scholars propose, what Jesus probably asks is whether Peter loves him more than the other disciples do, rather than whether he loves Jesus more than he loves the other disciples.[91] But Peter, in his answer, does not pick up on this comparison, and simply says: "Yes Lord, you know I love you." So Jesus charges him, saying: "Feed my lambs." As is well known, this question / answer / commission sequence will be repeated two other times (21:16, 17) with minor stylistic differences.[92] Upon the third question Peter is said to be

---

[85] Lincoln, *John*, 512.

[86] R. Williams, *Resurrection: Interpreting the Easter Gospel*, 2nd ed. (London: Darton, Longman & Todd, 2002), 28–29.

[87] Lincoln, *John*, 512–13.

[88] Okure, *Mission*, 220.

[89] Carson, *John*, 676: "Whatever potential for future service he had therefore depended not only on forgiveness from Jesus, but also on reinstatement amongst the disciples."

[90] This serves to reinforce the prior assertion in this section that the new name "Cephas" given by Jesus refers to the future role of the disciple. Before this role is assigned, however, Peter is asked three times whether he loves Jesus (Brown, *Eastertime*, 88–89).

[91] Peter had previously assured Jesus of his great love for him in his readiness to die for Jesus (13:37), and Jesus may be picking up on this.

[92] For instance, ἀγαπάω is used in the first two questions, and φιλέω in the third, while Peter only replies using φιλέω. This is probably simply due to Johannine vocabulary variation, as is commonly accepted today (though see *e.g.* Léon-Dufour, *Lecture*, 289–90 for a different position). Likewise, two verbs are used in the charge: βόσκω (21:15, 17) and ποιμαίνω (21:16). Moreover, the comparison between Peter's and the other disciples' love for Jesus is

grieved but still insists: "Lord, you know everything; you know that I love you" (21:17). Thus Peter reaffirms his love for Jesus, and after each of his answers, he is charged to feed or tend Jesus' lambs. Therefore, just as this triple question "Do you love me?" inevitably evokes Peter's threefold denials and puts these denials in the perspective of Peter's lack of love for Jesus, now Peter's confessed love for Jesus is equivalent to a professed belief in him as the "Christ, the Son of God" (20:31). As a result, Jesus reinstates him in his mission.[93]

Peter will need to demonstrate his love for and faith in Jesus by caring for his sheep as an "undershepherd", for Jesus remains "the good shepherd" (10:1–18, 26–8).[94] And, just as Jesus had previously answered to Peter's readiness to die for the Lord with a prediction of denials (13:38), the charge Jesus gives Peter as a response to Peter's love is now accompanied by a prediction about martyrdom (21:18). Peter will indeed lay down his life for Jesus, thus glorifying God (21:19). He will at last be coherent with his faith and love for Jesus and will not deny him any more in the face of danger and persecution. Resseguie rightly perceived that the type of death Peter would experience distinguishes the Peter characterised so far in the narrative from the new Peter:

> The self-willed Peter insisted on following Jesus on his own terms [...] By contrast, the new Peter follows the will of another: he loves the good shepherd and cares for his sheep (21:15–17), and gives his own life for the shepherd and his sheep (21:18–19).[95]

When Jesus concludes this exchange by saying "follow me" (21:19), one is reminded of Peter's earlier incomprehension about his incapacity to follow Jesus (13:37). Now that Jesus has died for his disciples, Peter is able to be the kind of disciple who follows Jesus even to his death.[96] Even more, 21:22 indicates that Peter "can only 'shepherd' Jesus' sheep by doing himself what is expected of the sheep of the good shepherd: *following* the Good Shepherd!"[97] This section has thus brought Peter's characterisation full circle, providing real closure to his narrative depiction.[98]

---

only present in the first question.

[93] For Conway, *Men and Women*, 176–77, if Peter is experiencing rehabilitation here, "it can only be in regard to his reputation enjoyed somewhere other than in the Fourth Gospel where, as we have seen, there is little evidence of an earlier good standing." For Conway, Peter only takes a "new dimension" in chapter 21, thus compensating for his earlier portrayal. But *contra* Conway, Peter's "good standing" has been affirmed from the beginning, and his reinstatement is necessary as his actions in Annas' court have brought important doubt about his discipleship in implied readers' minds.

[94] Lincoln, *John*, 518.

[95] Resseguie, *Strange*, 155.

[96] Lincoln, *John*, 519–20.

[97] D. F. Tolmie, "The (not so) Good Shepherd: The Use of Shepherd Imagery in the Characterisation of Peter in the Fourth Gospel," in *Imagery in the Gospel of John: Terms, Forms, Themes, and Theology of Johannine Figurative Language*, ed. by J. Frey, J. G. van der Watt, and R. Zimmermann, WUNT 200 (Tübingen: Mohr Siebeck, 2006), 367.

[98] As mentioned by Claussen, "John 21," 66: "According to the recency effect, Peter will

Yet, the new Peter is not perfect, and Jesus once more needs to rebuke him. As he wondered about the Beloved Disciple's destiny, Jesus promptly answered: "If it is my will that he remain until I come, what is it to you? You follow me!" (21:22). Carson puts it well: "The burden of Jesus' reply is tart: in brief, Peter is told that it is none of his business."[99] His business is to follow Jesus, as Jesus almost desperately seems to remind him. Jesus may have particular plans for the Beloved Disciple, and his ministry may not be the same as Peter's. Yet, Peter has been prepared, and now recommissioned by Jesus for a particular task of his own. It is on this task and on his own destiny as a follower of Jesus that he must concentrate.

Peter was not the first person to express belief in Jesus as the Messiah in the narrative, Andrew was (1:41). However, Peter is constantly portrayed in the Fourth Gospel as a leader of Jesus' disciples (6:68–69; 20:2; 21:3, 7, 11, 15–17), and from early on in the narrative, Peter's belief is expressed, first implicitly (1:42), then explicitly (6:68–69). While many disciples had fallen away and stopped following Jesus, Peter took the lead affirming the Twelve's willingness to remain with Jesus. Likewise, while one of the disciples was a "devil" (6:70–71), Peter and the other disciples were obviously faithful to Jesus. Up to 6:68–69, therefore, Peter has been portrayed in a positive and unambiguous light. While his understanding of Jesus is probably very low, his faith is real and, to a certain extent, exemplary.[100]

But with the scene of the footwashing (13:6–9), Peter expressly misunderstands Jesus' action. His faith is not questioned as he is obviously attached to Jesus whom he respects greatly, but Peter shows real limitations in his discipleship. His characterisation thus becomes much more ambiguous. Indeed, the following instances where Peter appears by name (before chapter 21) all reveal how his misunderstandings of the identity and actions of Jesus lead to dramatic consequences. His misunderstanding first leads him to commit foolishly to laying down his life for Jesus (13:37). Though Jesus predicts that his commitment will show itself to be rather weak (13:38), Peter nonetheless continues to understand Jesus as a kind of Messiah who will require his disciples to fight by the sword. Peter will put this understanding into effect during Jesus' arrest (18:10). He continues to be loyal to Jesus, but his loyalty is misplaced because Jesus must die, and he will die willingly (18:11). Such misunderstanding is most likely also the cause of Peter's denials of Jesus in 18:15–18, 25–27, which now call into question his very allegiance to Jesus as a disciple.[101] Finally, his misunderstanding will once more come to the fore in 20:1–10, where his witnessing of the empty tomb does not lead him to belief in the resurrection.

---

not be remembered as the one who betrays Jesus but rather as the one to whom the Lord entrusted his followers."

[99] Carson, *John*, 681.

[100] Quast, *Figures*, 163.

[101] *Contra* Quast, *Figures*, 164, and Kim, *Apostasy*, 29–67.

All in all, however, chapter 21 cannot be considered a complete reversal of Peter's character compared with the first 20 chapters of the story. Throughout the narrative, Peter's faith is never explicitly denied, but often shows itself to be lacking its proper fruits because it is accompanied by misunderstanding. Implied readers, between Peter's denials and his reinstatement by Jesus, are nonetheless left with real ambiguity in regard to understanding Peter's faith, for it is practically impossible to consider him either as a believer or as an unbeliever. The portrayal of his faith during these chapters does not allow neat categories to be applied to him, but it is exactly this ambiguity that is lifted in chapter 21, which "redeems" this character and clarifies his standing as a disciple. There, he will in effect receive Jesus' forgiveness, and in reaffirming his love for and faith in Jesus, he is commissioned to a leadership role in the early church. Finally, Peter is able to truly follow Jesus (21:19).[102] Even more, a death that is glorifying to God is predicted for him (21:18), thus highlighting his continued faithful discipleship to the end. In chapter 21, Peter's faith is not doubted, as it may have been earlier in the narrative. Implied readers receive the assurance of his fidelity to Jesus to the end

B. Judas

The Fourth Gospel gives relatively little information about Judas, and yet his characterisation is rich and dramatic. Judas appears in several sections of the narrative, and always in a negative light. Though he is clearly identified as one of "the Twelve," he is nonetheless called "a devil" (6:70) and "a thief" (12:6). Most famously, of course, Judas is the disciple who betrays Jesus (6:71; 12:4; 13:11, 21–30; 18:2–5), a betrayal that leads to Jesus' trial and crucifixion. As a whole, one might say that Judas is portrayed as a "figure of the night" (13:30).[103] This section will therefore attempt to understand the Fourth Gospel's perspective on Judas' faith and understanding (or, rather, unbelief and lack of understanding), drawing on the implied author's artful depiction of this character's several dimensions and of his role in the plot of Fourth Gospel. Since Judas is clearly portrayed as a disciple, albeit an errant one, it will be of interest for this study to notice how the implied author chose to contrast his characterisation with that of other disciples.

1. "One of you is a devil" (6:64, 70–71)

The final section of chapter 6 (6:60–71) builds on the preceding bread of life discourse.[104] But whereas in the discourse Jesus' conversation partners were

---

[102] For Bauckham, *Eyewitnesses*, 395–96, Peter represents throughout the Fourth Gospel a kind of discipleship that can be called "active service.".

[103] Collins, *These Things*, 30.

[104] "This saying," in 6:60 is a clear reference back to Jesus' discourse.

"the crowd" and "the Jews," this section focuses on the disciples: first a general group of Jesus-followers who ultimately abandon him (6:60–66), and second "the Twelve" who, through the representative confession of Peter, acknowledge that Jesus is "the Holy one of God" (6:67–71). Judas, in this section, is mentioned both in relation to the first group, though only implicitly, and as a member of "the Twelve," with Jesus singling him out in very strong terms.

In 6:64, Jesus mentions that some of his disciples do not believe. In other words, among his followers were some who were unable to receive and believe the words spoken by Jesus because his words were "spirit and life" (6:63).[105] In a narratorial aside, implied readers learn that "Jesus knew from the beginning who those were who did not believe, and who it was who would betray him." As Carson mentions, "Jesus was going toward his God appointed task with his eyes wide open,"[106] knowing perfectly well that one of his disciples was a traitor. Arguably, the first mention of the character of Judas is implicitly given at this point by the narrator, and it comes in the context of both Jesus and the narrator mentioning the paradox that some disciples are in fact unbelievers. The betrayer is therefore most naturally to be understood also as a non-believer,[107] and one whose understanding of Jesus and his words is "fleshy."[108]

The second mention of Judas comes also in this section of the narrative, but this time explicitly and in relation to "the Twelve." After Peter's confession of faith, Jesus addresses his band of close disciples as follows: "Did I not choose you, the Twelve? And yet, one of you is a devil" (6:70). This is an identification of Satan himself,[109] which indicates that the devil has been able to infiltrate even Jesus' closest followers.[110] As was already mentioned in our study of the faith and understanding of the group of Jesus' disciples, this mention of a devil among "the Twelve" does not necessarily reflect poorly on the group as a whole and does not need to induce suspicion of the entire group, for indeed, the devil is immediately identified personally by the narrator in 6:71.[111] There,

---

[105] Lincoln, *John*, 237–38: "Among would-be disciples of Jesus, there are those who are unable to come to proper belief because their merely natural categories of judgment have not been transformed."

[106] Carson, *John*, 302. This impression is reinforced in 6:70, where Jesus claims to have chosen "the Twelve," including the "devil" among them.

[107] Kim, *Apostasy*, 154: "What is interesting in 6:64 is John's juxtaposition of the theme of unbelief and the theme of betrayal. In this way John deliberately links the theme of unbelief with Judas' betrayal."

[108] Moloney, *John*, 228.

[109] The substantive διάβολός in the New Testament always refers to Satan, even though in common Greek it could also mean "slanderer" or "false accuser." Thus, one might say that Satan "so operates behind failing human beings that his malice becomes theirs. Jesus can discern the source, and labels it appropriately" (Carson, *John*, 304).

[110] Lincoln, *John*, 239.

[111] *Contra*, e.g., Conway, *Men and Women*, 169; and D. A. Carson, *Divine Sovereignty and Human Responsibility: Biblical Perspectives in Tension*, NFTL (Atlanta, GA: John Knox, 1981;

he explains that the "devil" of whom Jesus spoke was "Judas, the son of Simon Iscariot, for he, one of the Twelve, was going to betray him." The betrayer or unbeliever mentioned in 6:64 is thus now clearly identified, and starkly contrasts with Peter who professed faith in Jesus on behalf of "the Twelve."[112]

The motif of the betrayal strongly dominates Judas' characterisation in this section of the narrative. Yet, the implied author does not treat Judas solely as a "betrayer." If the author in 6:64, 71 already anticipates the betrayal that would in fact be effective only in 18:2, Judas' characterisation is not entirely stereotyped.[113] Paffenroth argues that "all attempt to understand him as a human character has dropped out, and he becomes merely an illustration of John's ideas about evil."[114] But this probably goes too far. Though Paffenroth is correct to state that Judas' betrayal dominates his characterisation, the narrator does take time to present Judas as a real human, a son,[115] and a member of "the Twelve," although, as will be argued below, his human features are not fully exploited by the implied author. Certainly, this character raises acute issues, for he is a man of flesh and blood chosen by Jesus himself to be part of his little troupe of followers, yet a devil who would later betray him. Interestingly, the text gives no indication that Judas himself was aware, at this point, of being a devil, a betrayer, or an unbeliever.[116] Only through Jesus' words, explained by the narrator's asides, do implied readers learn about Judas' unbelieving state and future treason.[117] In the next section, in potential accordance with Judas' characterisation as a "devil," implied readers learn that he was far from upright even prior to his betrayal, for he was a thief.

2. "He said this ... because he was a thief" (12:4–8)

If Judas remained silent in his first appearance in the narrative, he appears in this new section as a critic of Mary's anointing of the feet of Jesus with expensive ointment. In fact, it is the only time in the Fourth Gospel that Judas manifests a

---

reprint, Eugene, OR: Wipf and Stock, 2002), 130.

[112] As noted by Kim, *Apostasy*, 154–55, the link between Judas' betrayal and his unbelief is reinforced by his appellation as "a devil," for, in line with the Fourth Gospel and the New Testament as a whole, the themes of unbelief and of the devil are often connected (*e.g.*, Matt. 16:23; Lk. 22:31–32; Jn. 8:44; 1 Jn. 3:10).

[113] *Pace* Marchadour, *Personnages*, 187.

[114] K. Paffenroth, *Judas: Images of the Lost Disciple* (Louisville, KY: Westminster John Knox, 2001), 36.

[115] Koester, *Symbolism*, 73: "Since the Fourth Gospel accents the demonic elements in Judas' character, these references are important for perspective: Judas is a person with a human father whose name was Simon." Judas will be identified as "the son of Simon Iscariot" again in 13:2, 26.

[116] In 13:2, the narrator mentions that "the devil had already put into the heart of Judas Iscariot, Simon's son, to betray Jesus," but he does not specify when this actually happened.

[117] Interestingly, the disciples are not said to have questioned Jesus on the identity of this "devil" at this point. Such questioning will only come in 13:22.

personal reaction to an event by speaking. Or, to use Booth's terminology, it is the only instance of "showing," allowing implied readers to draw conclusions from Judas' action.[118] But before he even opens his mouth, he is introduced by the narrator as "Judas Iscariot, one of his disciples (he who was about to betray him)" (12:4). Once more, the paradox of a disciple about to betray his master is brought to the fore. Such an aside certainly colours the apparently unobjectionable reaction of Judas: "Why was this ointment not sold for three hundred denarii and given to the poor?" (12:5). From the implied author's perspective, however, such an introduction is perfectly legitimate since Judas' concern for the poor was hypocritical. From his question only, implied readers may have drawn the wrong conclusions about Judas' character. Thus, the narrator also adds that Judas was a "thief, and having charge of the moneybag he used to help himself to what was put into it" (12:6).

Here, it can be noted that this latter aside is consistent with the depiction of Judas in the Synoptic tradition, where it is made clear that his betraying of Jesus was motivated by money (Mk. 14:10–11; Matt. 26:14–16).[119] However, on a purely literary level, the narrative of the Fourth Gospel is unconcerned with any psychological or political motivations for Judas' betraying Jesus.[120] If he was guilty of stealing from the purse, money does not appear to have been a motivation for his betrayal in the narrative.[121] Rather, Judas is consistently portrayed as under the influence of the devil (13:2, 27), or, as we have seen, as "a devil" himself (6:70). As such, he is related to his father the devil, and his will is to do what his father desires, that is, to murder and to lie (*cf.* 8:44; 13:2).[122] Likewise, the label "thief" is employed elsewhere in the narrative to denote an opposition to Jesus and his fold (10:1, 8, 10), and here the term may well serve a similar function.[123] The implied author thus uses Judas to show how evil has cosmic dimensions (betraying Jesus, the Son of God), but also petty and trivial ones (lying about one's concern for the poor, stealing money from the purse).[124]

Most notably, as far as the present study is concerned, Judas' faith and understanding contrast strongly with that of Mary in this section.[125] Indeed, while Mary's exuberant devotion to Jesus displayed her acceptance of the necessity of

---

[118] Booth, *Fiction*, 3–9.

[119] See, *e.g.*, Lincoln, *John*, 338.

[120] Likewise, Judas will show no remorse after his betrayal, but will simply disappear from the story.

[121] L. Eslinger, "Judas Game: The Biology of Combat in the Gospel of John," *JSNT* 77 (2000): 51; R. E. Brown, *The Death of the Messiah, From Gethsemane to the Grave: A Commentary on the Passion Narratives in the Four Gospels*, 2 vols (New York, NY/London/Toronto/Sydney/Auckland: Doubleday, 1994), 2:1402.

[122] Culpepper, *Anatomy*, 124.

[123] Lincoln, *John*, 339.

[124] Paffenroth, *Judas*, 34.

[125] Lee, *Symbolic*, 190.

Jesus' death,[126] Judas' response is to be seen as "a complete lack of insight into what he has witnessed."[127] Even more, Judas, in complaining about Mary's action, reveals a form of apathy towards Jesus: he is simply not concerned about Jesus' upcoming death.[128] Jesus thus swiftly reprimands Judas (12:7–8). Mary had understood the urgency and brevity of the time left before Jesus' death and had responded appropriately by anointing Jesus' feet as a preparation for his burial.[129] Concerns for the poor are constantly valid (Deut. 15:11), but they pale in comparison to Jesus' approaching departure. Judas was thus wrong on both counts: he sought to mislead people about concerns for the poor that were, in any case, inappropriate at that point. It should be noted, finally, that it is only through the narratorial aside or inside view that implied readers learn about Judas' hypocrisy. Jesus only addresses Judas' misunderstanding.

3. *"You are clean, but not every one of you" (13:1–20)*

Before the feast of the Passover (13:1), Jesus had supper with his disciples, during which Judas will often be mentioned (13:2, 11, 18, 21–30, 31). First, Jesus interrupts the meal to wash his disciples' feet (13:5). But before proceeding with the story, the narrator mentions the presence of Judas, once more in very negative terms. He explains that the scene took place "during supper, when the devil had already put it into the heart of Judas Iscariot, Simon's son, to betray him" (13:2).[130] As Carson mentions, "John ensures that his readers grasp just how strongly this episode attests the loving character of Jesus. The disciples whose feet he was about to wash include Judas Iscariot, son of Simon, whose

---

[126] Bauckham and Hart, *At the Cross*, 17.

[127] Lincoln, *John*, 339. Lincoln further shows the irony of Judas' misunderstanding of the necessity of Jesus' death and his own upcoming role in bringing it about. As we have seen in an earlier part, Judas is certainly not alone in his lack of insight, as the other disciples themselves will lack such an understanding even after Jesus teaches them about it in the farewell discourse.

[128] Kim, *Apostasy*, 172–73. T. Thatcher, "Jesus, Judas, and Peter: Character by Contrast in the Fourth Gospel," *BSac* 153 (1996): 442, goes a step farther: "Judas sought to control both Jesus and Mary by forcing the Savior to rebuke her."

[129] For Lee, *Symbolic*, 219, Mary's prophetic action "functions as a faith confession."

[130] The Greek text is ambiguous as it simply says that the devil put betrayal "in his heart" (εἰς τὴν καρδίαν). Moreover, there are variants in regard to Judas between the genitive Ἰούδα (A D K Δ Θ Π *f*[1] 28 33 700 892 *Byz*) and the nominative Ἰούδας (p[66] ℵ B L W X Ψ 0124 2141 *al*). Since the latter could be translated as follows: "The devil had already put into the heart that Judas should betray Jesus," one wonders whose heart this is referring to. Several commentators have taken it to mean that the devil put the idea of betrayal into his own heart (so, *e.g.* Barrett, *John*, 439; Moloney, *John*, 378; E. Delebecque, *Évangile de Jean. Texte traduit et annoté*, CahRB 23 (Paris: Gabalda, 1987), 183), but this interpretation is unlikely for the genitive Ἰούδα is "the easier reading, which, if original, would not have been altered to a more difficult construction" (Metzger, *Textual Commentary*, 239). For detailed discussions, see Brown, *John*, 2:550.

treacherous plot had already been conceived."[131] Jesus already knew that Judas was a devil (6:70), and as will become clear, his plans to betray Jesus were also known by Jesus (vv. 11, 18). Yet, Jesus offers the gift of μέρος to him by washing his feet (implied in the narrative).[132]

In 13:2, Judas is portrayed as a human ("Judas Iscariot, Simon's son"), yet one strongly affected by the devil, so that his characterisation remains ambiguous. Judas' decision to betray Jesus finds its roots in the devil himself, and even though the betrayal was to be mediated by a human, his decision and action can properly be understood as satanic. Such understanding of the betrayal, however, cannot be seen as an excuse for Judas' behaviour.[133] On the contrary, in insisting on the link between Judas' decision and the devil's purposes, the implied author seeks to portray Judas as a human agent of the devil, and thus guilty of a terrible sin.[134] Jesus was nevertheless able to put Judas' decision into proper perspective (13:3), as Newbigin suggests:

> But Jesus, in the assuredness of his unbroken communion with the Father, knows that even the treachery of Judas can only further the Father's purpose of salvation for the world, knows that this purpose has been wholly committed into his hands, and knows that it is both the source of his coming into the world and the goal of his going from the world.[135]

After having washed his disciples' feet, and in conclusion to his conversation with Peter (13:6–9), Jesus says: "The one who has bathed does not need to wash, except his feet, but is completely clean. And you are clean, but not every one of you" (13:10). Jesus says this, as the narrator explains: "for he knew who was about to betray him; that was why he said: 'not all of you are clean'" (13:11). As was argued in the study of the faith and understanding of the group of the disciples in the Fourth Gospel, what has made the disciples "clean" in this section seems to be that they have already believed in Jesus, as he later makes clear in 15:3.[136] Logically, it follows that the betrayer Judas is an unbeliever. He has not believed in Jesus, in his words and in his deeds, and thus the values to which the footwashing pointed (namely, abiding with Jesus through the pattern of glory through humiliation that Jesus would exemplify at the cross) were irrelevant and of no effect on him.[137]

---

[131] Carson, *John*, 461.

[132] Chennattu, *Discipleship*, 98.

[133] So Carson, *John*, 462: "The idea, then, is not that Judas was not responsible, for a heart incited by Satan actually wills what the devil wills (Schlatter, p. 279); rather, the plot against Jesus, however mediated by wicked human beings, was nothing less then [*sic*] Satanic."

[134] *Contra* Paffenroth, *Judas*, 35 and Bultmann, *John*, 482 who tends to eliminate any human element in Judas' characterisation.

[135] L. Newbigin, *The Light Has Come: An Exposition of the Fourth Gospel* (Grand Rapids, MI/Edinburgh: Eerdmans/Handsel Press, 1982), 167.

[136] Lincoln, *John*, 370.

[137] H.-J. Klauck, *Judas, un disciple de Jésus. Exégèse et répercutions historiques*, trans. by J. Hoffmann, LD 212 (Paris: Cerf, 2006), 89. For Klauck, the fact that Judas did not resist Jesus'

Indeed, as Jesus continues to expound the meaning of the footwashing as an "example" for his disciples to follow, he once more refers (implicitly, but very clearly to implied readers) to Judas: "I am not speaking of all of you; I know whom I have chosen. But the Scripture will be fulfilled, 'He who ate my bread has lifted his heel against me'" (13:18). The Scripture in question is Ps. 41:9, which may be referring back to Gen. 3:15,[138] so that Judas could once more be identified with the devil in 13:18. Jesus thus warns his disciples beforehand of what is about to happen in 13:26–27 and in the ensuing actions of Judas against him, seeking to ground these events in salvation history, more precisely in the cosmic conflict between God and evil. Such a prediction is also meant to assist the faith of the disciples (13:19):

> The disciples are warned beforehand, so that the terrible manifestation of the work of Satan in the very heart of the Church will not destroy their faith, but – on the contrary – enable them to believe that Jesus is indeed the Lord, the one who alone can say "I AM."[139]

Thus, once again in 13:10, 18, Jesus makes a clear distinction between his true disciples, those who have believed in him, and the betrayer Judas (*cf.* 6:70). Jesus is very much aware of Judas' intention to betray him, he knows that he cannot count him as one of his true disciples. As a whole, Judas' actions are to be understood in the whole scheme of salvation history, but if Judas is acting as an enemy of God, God remains in control of the events at hand, as will be made clear in 13:21–30; 17:12; 18:1–11.

4. "What you are going to do, do it quickly" (13:21–30)

This section of the narrative marks an important development in the treatment of Judas as this character begins to put his plan into action. The figure of the betrayer is the centre of attention in this section; in fact, it opens with Jesus being "troubled in his spirit" and testifying: "Truly, truly, I say to you, one of you will betray me" (13:21). Jesus had already mentioned to the disciples that one of them was "a devil" (6:70), that not everyone was "clean" (13:11), and that one of them had "lifted his heel against him" (13:18), but so far, none of the disciples had questioned Jesus about these remarks. In 13:22, however, "the disciples looked at one another, uncertain of whom he spoke." Peter thus decided to ask Jesus, via the Beloved Disciple, to be more explicit. Jesus answered the Beloved Disciple: "It is he to whom I will give this morsel of bread when I have dipped it" (13:26a). Jesus then gave it to Judas Iscariot (13:26b), and "after he had taken the morsel, Satan entered into him" (13:27a).

This remark is at first surprising given the fact that Judas had already been called "a devil" (6:70) and that "the devil had already put into [his] heart to

---

footwashing only aggravates what is already said about him in the narrative.

[138] Kim, *Apostasy*, 187–88.

[139] Newbigin, *Fourth Gospel*, 172.

betray [Jesus]" (13:2). It is probable that the implied author sought to show that, as the devil had already been active in planting the intention to betray Jesus in Judas' heart, such intention had now settled in Judas' heart, so that "Judas can be depicted as having been taken over by Satan."[140] But such a "possession" happens at the most inappropriate of times, immediately after Jesus gives him a piece of bread, so that "the final gesture of affection precipitates the final surrender of Judas to the power of darkness."[141] As Jesus very certainly knew that Satan had now taken a complete hold of his disciple, he tells Judas: "What you are going to do, do quickly" (13:27b). The idea of betrayal is thus set in motion, and just as Judas' identification with evil is complete, he immediately goes out (13:30). Judas understands exactly what Jesus is telling him.[142] He has fully accepted his role of betrayer, and made the conscious decision to deliver Jesus to the authorities. Ironically, even in this most ignominious act of betrayal, Jesus remains in control of the situation, and Judas does what Jesus tells him to do.[143]

The other disciples, however, have yet to understand who the betrayer is (13:28–29), so that their being at a loss about his identity is an implicit indication that they thought Judas to be on a similar level of discipleship with them up that point. Judas had probably not given them any external indications about his lack of faith or evil intentions, but such a situation could not last long. Indeed, the concluding words of this section are fitting, and symbolically very meaningful: "and it was night" (13:30). For Lincoln, "His walking out into the night is a graphic portrayal of the state of affairs in which 'the light has come into the world, and the people loved darkness rather than light because their deeds

---

[140] Lincoln, *John*, 379.

[141] Newbigin, *Fourth Gospel*, 173. For D. F. Tolmie, "Jesus, Judas and a Morsel. Interpreting a Gesture in John 13,21–30," in *Miracles and Imagery in Luke and John. Festschrift Ulrich Busse*, ed. by J. Verheyden, G. Van Belle, and J. G. Van der Watt, BETL 218 (Leuven/Paris/Dudley, MA: Peeters, 2008), 123, the gesture should be interpreted as one of feeding, so as to underline Judas' treacherousness. For Brown, *John*, 2:578, Judas' acceptance of the morsel of bread without changing his plans is an indication that "he has chosen for Satan rather than for Jesus." For Kim, *Apostasy*, 190–91, "Satan enters Judas' mind only after Jesus gives bread to Judas, as if Satan moves at Jesus' signal" and "Jesus gives Judas a chance to reconsider his plan by dipping the bread and giving it to him."

[142] D. L. Bartlett, "John 13:21–30," *Int* 43 (1989): 394, remarks: "In one sense Judas comprehends the light all too well. In fact, Judas alone understands exactly what Jesus means when Jesus tells Judas to do what he must do quickly (13:27). Judas understands the light. Yet, he does not really comprehend the light, grasp the light with his heart and will, embrace the light. If he comprehended the light, how could he stumble out into the night, to betray the light and to work judgment on himself?"

[143] Lincoln, *John*, 380. Bartlett, "John 13:21–30," 393, recalls Jesus' earlier saying in 11:10: "But if any one walks in the night, he stumbles, because the light is not in him", and concludes: "Now we see (in the light of the Gospel) more clearly what happens to Judas. When Jesus sends him out into the night, Jesus sends him out to stumble, to lose his footing, to lose his way." For Resseguie, *Strange*, 166, Judas' passive stance is evident throughout the supper.

were evil' (3:19)."[144] Finally, Judas is acting out his evil intent, and his true self is about to be revealed for all to see (*cf.* 18:3).[145]

The separation of light from darkness within the group of disciples means that Jesus can now turn to his faithful disciples, who, far from being perfect (*cf.* 13:36–28), will nevertheless receive Jesus' farewell instructions as a preparation for their upcoming role of witnesses (chap. 14–17).[146]

5. *"Not one of them has been lost, except the son of destruction" (17:12)*

The following reference to Judas is set in the context of Jesus' farewell prayer (chap. 17), at the end of the farewell material (chap. 14–17). Jesus is praying for his disciples, whom the Father has given him (17:6) and who have come to believe in him (17:8), asking his Father to "keep them in your name [...] that they may be one, even as we are one" (17:11). But, parallel to several other references studied in chapter 2 of this study, Judas is once more singled out from among the band of Jesus' close followers: "While I was with them, I kept them in your name, which you have given me. I have guarded them, and not one of them has been lost except the son of destruction, that the Scripture may be fulfilled" (17:12).

Jesus' statement about his disciples is reminiscent of his earlier saying about the good shepherd (10:28). During his ministry, Jesus took good care of the disciples that were given him; he was faithful to the task assigned him by the Father (*cf.* 6:37–39). That none of them "perished" or "were lost" (17:12) means that they were kept in the realm of salvation by Jesus during his ministry.[147] But in excluding Judas (the obvious referent to the "son of destruction") from those whom he has successfully kept in the Father's name, Jesus shows that Judas, though he was a member of "the Twelve," was not, in fact *could not be*, a recipient of the same care. However, Jesus immediately exonerates himself of any guilt or failure in regard to Judas, since Judas was the "son of perdition" and since Scripture had to be fulfilled (*cf.* 13:18 and its citation of Ps. 41:9).[148] Thus, the "loss" of Judas was not due to any deficiency on the part of Jesus.[149]

---

[144] Lincoln, *John*, 380. See also Chennattu, *Discipleship*, 99: "The role of Judas in the story thus epitomizes the acceptance of darkness (σκοτία) and the total rejection of light (φῶς) and the covenant relationship of the fellowship (μέρος) offered to a disciple."

[145] The seriousness of this departure into the darkness is perceived by Culpepper, *Anatomy*, 124: "John has no story of Judas' death; it is enough that he has gone out into the darkness."

[146] Newbigin, *Fourth Gospel*, 174.

[147] As mentioned by Lincoln, *John*, 437, "There is a rich scriptural background of 'keeping' language for Yahweh's relation to Israel (cf. e.g., Gen 28.15; Ps. 121.7–8; Isa. 42.6; 49.8). Yahweh 'will keep Israel, as a shepherd a flock' (Jer. 31.10)."

[148] Another, though less likely possible reference is Ps. 109:1–20 (*cf.* Acts 1:20).

[149] Lincoln, *John*, 437. See also Carson, *John*, 563, for whom: "The only exception is Judas Iscariot, and this exception is merely apparent, since Jesus repeatedly indicates not only his awareness of the traitor's schemes, but that his choice of him was antedated by his awareness of what would take place (6:64, 70; 13:10–11, 18, 21–22)." Several scholars, however, insists

Jesus had already showed his sovereignty over Judas' upcoming actions when he predicted that Judas would betray him so that his disciples might believe in him (13:19). It follows that Judas' status as the "son of perdition" reflects both on his status and on his destiny.[150] As Paffenroth argues:

Judas was a devil all along, outside of Jesus' realm (though completely under his control). Jesus could not have lost any of his own, because those who are his own are impossible to lose and those who are not his own are impossible to gain because they are completely and utterly different, just as darkness cannot become light.[151]

6. *"Judas, who betrayed him, was standing with them" (18:1–5)*

Judas appears one last time in the Fourth Gospel, in the most dramatic of scenes, as he takes part in the arrest of Jesus. After the Farewell material (chap. 14–17), Jesus and his disciples went across the Kidron valley and entered into a garden (18:1). Judas knew this place,[152] since Jesus and the disciples often met there (18:2), and he therefore brought with him both "soldiers" and "some officers from the chief priests and Pharisees" in order to arrest Jesus.[153] One might say that Judas thus brought with him the representative of "the world" in the Fourth Gospel.[154] Even more, he brought with him co-representatives of "darkness," which is made clear by the narrator's mention that they had to hold "lanterns and torches and weapons" (18:3).[155] Judas has already left Jesus' inner circle, he has been identified with the devil, but in 18:3 he now visibly places himself on the side of Jesus' foes. The narrator later reiterates this very point: "Judas, who betrayed him, was standing with them" (18:5).[156] The prophecy of the upper room has thus been fulfilled (13:18–19). As it happened, the disciples were

---

that Judas represents a failure on the part of Jesus. For instance, Culpepper, *Anatomy*, 125, concludes his short study on Judas as follows: "His loss, therefore, is Jesus' failure (17:12); however true a son of perdition Judas may have been, Jesus was not able to make him clean (13:11) or alter his course by the gesture of love (13:26)." Likewise, see J. A. T. Robinson, *The Roots of a Radical* (New York, NY: Crossroad, 1981), 139–43, who concludes that Judas is Jesus' failure.

[150] Thus, the Fourth Gospel's characterisation of Judas is in line with this Gospel's emphases on divine sovereignty, Jesus' predictive knowledge, and the significance of human agency and actions.

[151] Paffenroth, *Judas*, 35.

[152] As mentioned by Kim, *Apostasy*, 202: "This remark echoes the chief's priests' orders that 'if anyone found out where Jesus was, he should report it so that they might arrest him' (11:57)."

[153] Here, it is striking that the implied author emphasises that the betrayer Judas had intimate knowledge of Jesus and the disciples' whereabouts because he used to be a member of Jesus' inner circle of followers. This remark in 18:2 no doubt serves to underline Judas' treason.

[154] Koester, *Symbolism*, 74.

[155] Newbigin, *Fourth Gospel*, 239: "Judas had gone out into the darkness (13:30). Now, he returns with the agents of the power of darkness, who must carry lanterns because they belong to the world of darkness (cf. Luke 22:53)."

[156] Koester, *Symbolism*, 74.

to believe that "I am he" (13:19), and three times during his arrest, Jesus will remind them that "I am he" (18:5, 6, 8).[157]

As Jesus was about to be arrested, however, his sovereignty over these events is once more underlined (18:4: "knowing all that would happen to him"). More, he gives the overall impression of being in total control of his own arrest: he is the one asking questions (18:4, 7) and giving orders (17:8) to the forces of darkness. Finally, he shows his faithful care for his true disciples in ordering the soldiers to let them go, thus once more showing that Judas was not to be counted amongst them (17:8). Interestingly, Judas' presence in the narrative stops here. No mention is made of potential guilt or further actions on his part. Judas seems to have fulfilled his role in the narrative. The Fourth Gospel, just as it has not been interested in the psychology of this character's actions up to this point, is not intent on narrating what happens to him next.

In the Fourth Gospel, implied readers learn about Judas mostly through comments made by Jesus and especially the narrator who often explains Jesus' words about Judas. Judas only speaks in 12:5, and there too an inside view from the narrator is needed to explain Judas' hypocritical question. Thus, on the only occasion when Judas speaks, he cannot be trusted. These inside views on a character are unusual in this narrative. Indeed, implied readers generally learn what individual characters such as Peter, Andrew, or Thomas think through their speaking, with one exception in 20:8 where the narrator tells that the Beloved Disciple "saw and believed." Thus, this particular focalisation on Judas contrasts with the characterisation of other individual disciples in the story, and has the effect of turning implied readers' sympathy against him. In fact, Judas is never given any positive assessment from the narrator.[158]

Through the narrative of the Fourth Gospel, Judas is presented both as a member of the inner circle of Jesus' disciples, "the Twelve," whom Jesus himself chose (6:70), and at the same time as a member of the broader circle of disciples who yield to unbelief in 6:66.[159] As the story unfolds, though implied readers know early on that Judas was the one who would betray Jesus (6:64; 71), Judas begins to be influenced by the devil (13:2, 27), and he proceeds to identify himself visibly with Jesus' adversaries, leaving the circle of Jesus' close disciples during supper (13:30), and standing in the garden with the soldiers who were to arrest Jesus (18:5). Clearly, therefore, as far as Judas' role in the plot of the Fourth Gospel is concerned, he is squarely taking part in the "complication," an obstacle that the protagonist Jesus must overcome for his commission to be carried out.[160]

---

[157] Schnackenburg, *John*, 3:223.

[158] As noted by Culpepper, *Anatomy*, 23, disciples as a group often receive such inside and retrospective views from the narrator (2:11, 17, 22; 4:27; 12:16; 13:28, 29; 20:9; 21:4).

[159] Koester, *Symbolism*, 74.

[160] Lincoln, *Truth*, 17: "The opposition is in fact involved in a counterplot within the plot, one that parodies the main plot [...]. The irony of the opposition's counterplot is that, in its

The implied author does not allow much ambiguity as far as the believing status of Judas is concerned. The narrator portrays him both as a disciple and a traitor, consistently placing these two features in contrast.[161] He is thus a particular kind of disciple, one that is a follower of Jesus only outwardly, and only for a time (until 13:30). Moreover, the constant contrasts between him and the other disciples in the narrative drive home this point quite clearly. In 6:70, Jesus speaks of his choice of "the Twelve," but immediately singles Judas as "a devil." In 13:10, Jesus addresses his disciples as "clean", yet qualifies that "not every one of you" is clean, referring to Judas. Likewise, in 17:12, Jesus explains that none of his disciples have been lost, except "the son of destruction". Finally, in contrast to the disciples standing behind Jesus in the garden (18:4), Judas is standing among those who came to arrest Jesus (18:5). Judas can thus never be considered a true or faithful disciple of Jesus. Even though, for the sake of the argument, Judas was already a member of Jesus' band of disciples in 2:11 when the disciples are said to have "believed" in Jesus, he cannot be understood to have lost his faith at some point in the story (a loss which in any case is never mentioned). What is more, though in the Fourth Gospel Judas is one of "the Twelve" and thus a member of the believing community, the narrator is at times able to mention such fellowship, yet to clearly (though implicitly) exclude Judas from it (*e.g.* 2:22; 12:16).[162]

As a whole, the narrator portrays Judas as a real human, yet also identifies him completely with the devil. He is the son of Simon Iscariot (*e.g.* 6:71), but one who carries out the devil's purposes and who can properly be called "a devil" (6:70). Such ambiguity in his humanness, coupled with Judas' role in the complication of the plot and his overall portrayal as a traitor, inclines implied readers to also consider him as holding a representative or symbolic role in the narrative, potentially standing for a particular response to Jesus. Judas would then be "the betrayer." Even more, as Culpepper argues, he could represent "*the disciple* who betrays Jesus, for John emphasises that judas was 'one of the Twelve' (6:71), one of his disciples (12:4; cf. 6:64, 70)."[163]

---

success in putting Jesus to death, it brings about the resolution to main plot." On the plot of the Fourth Gospel's narrative, see chapter 4 below.

[161] Thatcher, "Character," 439, speaks of the "paradox" of a disciple who was a traitor from the beginning.

[162] It should be noted, however, that these issues are left to the readers to reflect upon rather than being cleared up in the narrative.

[163] Culpepper, *Anatomy*, 125 (emphasis original). Koester, *Symbolism*, 32–39, argued that the *dramatis personae* in Greek tragedies were understood by audiences as "real people," but that they nevertheless functioned as "types" as well. Koester's assumption that the same is true in the Fourth Gospel could thus potentially be illustrated in the Fourth Gospel's characterisation of Judas. The issue of Johannine characters as mimetic and/or functional will be dealth with in chapter 4.

C. Thomas

Thomas is mentioned in four scenes in the Fourth Gospel (11:16; 14:5; 20:24–29; 21:2). In spite of this relatively small number of appearances he remains one of the most well-known characters in this Gospel, due mostly to his third appearance through which he has been dubbed for centuries as "Doubting Thomas."[164] Thomas, in many cultures influenced by Christianity, has become a model of scepticism, one who only believes what he sees or touches. Through the narrative of the Fourth Gospel, however, Thomas appears as a complex character, one who is obviously attached to his master, yet shows great ignorance and lack of understanding about him (11:16; 14:5). Most of all, if Thomas has remained famous for his 'doubt,' one should not lose sight of the fact that the author of the Fourth Gospel has reserved for him the clearest and most climactic confession of faith given by a disciple in the story: "My Lord and my God!" (20:28).[165]

In this section of the study, Thomas' appearances will be analysed, seeking to discern how his characterisation progresses through the Fourth Gospel, especially as this portrayal relates to faith and understanding. The result will potentially be able to challenge the appropriateness of his famous nickname.

1. "Let us go also, that we may die with him" (11:16)

Thomas first appears in the narrative in the context of Jesus wanting to go back to Judea in order to "awaken" his friend Lazarus who had just died (11:7, 11). He is introduced as "Thomas, called the Twin."[166] But Jesus' readiness to go is met with reluctance on the part of his disciples (11:8). For Jesus and his group of disciples, Judea was a dangerous place (8:59; 10:39), so that the disciples attempted to convince Jesus that travelling to Bethany was unnecessary (11:12). In the meantime, however, they showed themselves to be quite ridiculous, missing Jesus' metaphor about "sleeping" and "awakening," thus requiring Jesus to be blunt about what he means (11:14–15).

After Jesus' explanation, Thomas challenges his fellow disciples to follow Jesus: "Let us go also, that we may die with him" (11:16). Such a challenge to the other disciples is quite ambiguous. First, in his willingness to follow his master unto death, Thomas displays not only courage but also commitment

---

[164] See S. Harstine, "Un-Doubting Thomas: Recognition Scenes in the Ancient World," *PRSt* 33 (2006): 435, who mentions that this nickname has been recorded in prestigious dictionaries such as *The Oxford English Dictionary,* 2nd ed. (Oxford: Clarendon Press, 1989) or *The American Heritage Dictionary of the English Langage,* 4th ed. (Boston: Houghton Mifflin, 2000).

[165] Thus, the title given him in Marchadour, *Personnages*, 129–41: "Thomas, le disciple des extrêmes."

[166] The name 'Thomas' sounds more like a nickname than an actual name, according to Marchadour, *Personnages*, 131. Indeed, in Aramaic, Thomas means 'twin', which, in Greek is translated by Δίδυμος.

toward Jesus.[167] As such, this is an act of faith worth noting. However, his state-ment misses the mark in that it disregards what Jesus had just explained to the disciples. Thomas does not seem interested in Jesus being about to display his glory through the "awakening" of his friend. Likewise, he does not care about receiving the "further boost to the process of believing"[168] that Jesus intended for them. *Pace* Vignolo, therefore, it is unlikely that "devant leurs hésitations, il les [his fellow disciples] invite à une réponse immédiate, généreuse, qui semblerait épouser sans condition le point de vue de Jésus, s'engageant sur la parole donnée."[169] Thomas' mind has not been put to rest by Jesus' words of explanation. For him, going to Judea means nothing but death for them all.[170]

To implied readers of the narrative, Thomas' words are also comical, and this led one commentator to speak of them as a "false bravado."[171] Indeed, if Thomas shows great courage in being willing to go and die with Jesus, such courage will later shatter as Jesus is arrested and actually put to death.[172] Tho-mas will not explicitly deny being a disciple in the story (unlike Peter), but his absence during and after this fateful moment (apparently until 20:24) makes one suspect him of cowardice. Yet, the same implied readers also recognise an important element of Johannine irony in these words. For the first time in the Fourth Gospel, explicit mention is made of the death that lies ahead of Jesus,[173] and Thomas certainly spoke more than he knew in asserting that to follow Je-sus means to die with him.[174] Even more, Thomas is correct in that it is Jesus' actions in Bethany that would trigger off the events ultimately leading to his death and putting the disciples in death-facing situations (16:2; 21:18–19).[175] Through the characterisation of Thomas, the implied author requires implied

---

[167] *Pace, e.g.*, Köstenberger, *John*, 332, who rejects the idea that Thomas is courageous because he "represents the sober, realistic human mind" whose call in 11:16 must be seen as "sarcastic" rather than "sincere." But the two are not mutually exclusive. Why could Thomas not be both courageous *and* realistic?

[168] Lincoln, *John*, 321.

[169] R. Vignolo, *Personaggi del Quarto Vangelo, fidure della fede in San Giovanni* (Milan: Glossa, 1994), 56–57, quoted in Marchadour, *Personnages*, 132. See also the overly positive stance on Thomas' characterisation in Vignolo, *Personaggi*, 56–57. For him, Thomas displays "an incredible picture of faith," and constitutes "a model disciple."

[170] This led Moloney, *John*, 327, to write: "The reasons for the two decisions to go to Betha-ny, one from Jesus and the other from Thomas, are at cross-purposes. Misunderstanding inten-sifies among the disciples."

[171] Stibbe, "Tomb," 46.

[172] Stibbe, "Tomb," 46.

[173] Bultmann, *John*, 400: "For the first time the truth emerges that the disciples must accept for themselves the destiny that lies ahead of Jesus; the farewell discourses are to develop this theme, and the resigned submission is to give place to firm resolution. For the moment, it is but a blind devotion that is at stake [...]."

[174] So Carson, *John*, 410; Newbigin, *Fourth Gospel*, 141, who also mentions that Thomas' words "do not yet attain to the faith that this dying is the way of life."

[175] Lincoln, *John*, 322.

readers to think through his statement and draws them into his perspective on Jesus' work and discipleship.[176]

Therefore, Thomas' call to the disciples in 11:16 may be called a loyal resignation to die with Jesus, which contrasts positively with the other disciples' hesitations to follow Jesus. But such resignation does not sit well with Jesus' own intent for going to Bethany. He was "glad" for the sake of his disciples, knowing full well that this expedition would be beneficial to them (11:15). This, Thomas completely misunderstood, so that his overall attitude, despite his evident display of faith, is tainted negatively.

2. *"Lord, we do not know where you are going" (14:5)*

The second section in which the character of Thomas occurs is found within Jesus' farewell discourse. In this discourse, the disciples generally do not play a very active role, and when they are mentioned (*e.g.* 14:5, 8, 22; 16:17–18), it is because they need clarifications about Jesus' teaching.[177] Thomas' question in 14:5 serves this very purpose in the narrative. Jesus had just exhorted his disciples to believe in him since he was about to go back to the Father and would come again to take them to himself (14:1–3). He concluded in affirming: "And you know the way to where I am going" (14:4). But Thomas speaks up expressing the disciples' ignorance: "Lord, we do not know where you are going. How can we know the way?" (14:5), to which Jesus responds with a famous self-revelation making clear that his destination is the Father and that it is only through himself that the Father is accessible (14:6). More, the disciples' faith in and knowledge of Jesus means that they already know the Father and see him authentically (14:7).[178] However, the disciples failed to realise that in knowing Jesus they already knew the Father and the way to him.[179] The reason for their failure to grasp such important truth is most certainly that Thomas (and the other disciples with him) could only conceive of the goal and the way as "things within the world."[180] He was "looking for a literal road map, complete

---

[176] For an analysis of irony as revelatory mode, see O'Day, *Revelation*, 11–32 (esp. 31–32).

[177] Later, in 16:9, Jesus will even anticipate his disciples' question. Thus, for Marchadour, *Personnages*, 133: The disciples are "[…] placés là pour donner plus de vie à la parole de Jésus et anticiper les objections."

[178] On 14:7, we follow, *e.g.*, Moloney, *Glory*, 37, Barrett, *John*, 458–59, and Bultmann, *John*, 607, n.3, who make the choice to read this verse as a real condition, implying a promise (choosing the variants ἐγνώκατέ/γνώσεσθε over ἐγνώκειτέ/ἤδειτε: "If you have come to know me, you shall know my Father also") rather than a contrary-to-fact condition, implying a reproach (*e.g.* the ESV reading: "If you had known me [which, alas, you do not], you would have known my Father also"). See also Metzger, *Textual Commentary*, 207, who gives this reading a "C."

[179] Jesus will clarify such explanation further in the following question/answer in 14:8–11.

[180] Bultmann, *John*, 603. Or, as Carson, *John*, 490, proposes, in the "most crassly natural way."

with specific directions that would enable him to know how to get to where Jesus is going."[181]

Besides this blatant misunderstanding, there is a comical element in Thomas' dull-witted question. In his previous intervention in the narrative, Thomas had bluntly expressed his desire to follow Jesus and die with him (11:16), but he now honestly admits that he does not know where Jesus is going.[182] In all fairness to this character, it was clear to Thomas in 11:16 that Jesus was going to Judea; yet, in 14:5, the narrator uses Thomas once more to represent the disciples' ignorance regarding Jesus' destiny. Thomas had not come to terms with Jesus' departure as necessary to the accomplishment of the mission given him by the Father, and so failed to find coherence in the circumstances surrounding it.[183] Likewise, he failed to "see" that Jesus provided, in his person and his work, the sole access to the Father. Thomas' question is thus representative of great lacunae in the disciples' understanding of Christ's person (*i.e.*, Jesus as the Revealer of the Father) and work (*i.e.*, his upcoming departure). Yet, Jesus is convinced that "from now on, you do know him [the Father] and have seen him" (14:7). Thomas' misunderstanding, thus, is first and foremost a failure to grasp what he already has. If Jesus expresses the need for Thomas and the disciples to grow in knowledge and understanding in order to interpret the upcoming events appropriately, he does not question his and their believing status.

So far in the narrative, the two interventions in which this character speaks have been examples of Johannine misunderstanding. Thomas was portrayed in 11:16 as a disciple attached to Jesus, wanting to accompany him, but failing to understand that Jesus' goal in going to Bethany was first and foremost to display his glory for the benefit of his disciples. On a similar level, such failure to move beyond a "this-worldly" vision of Jesus leads him to miss the point of both Jesus' departure and destination. Yet, Thomas seeks explanations and clarifications from Jesus, which once more displays his attachment to his Master. Clearly, Jesus' destiny matters to Thomas, though he seems unable to grasp or accept what it will mean for Jesus himself.

3. *"My Lord and my God!" (20:24–29)*

In 20:24, implied readers learn that Thomas had been absent from the previous scene (20:19–23). Here, he is clearly identified as "one of the twelve" who "was not with them when Jesus came."[184] It is difficult to know what to

---

[181] Köstenberger, *John*, 428.

[182] So Vignolo, *Personaggi*, 59, remarks: "Il y a ici une charge d'ironie dramatique: celui précisément qui prétendait partager le même chemin et le même destin que Jésus (Jn. 11, 16), maintenant admet qu'en vérité il ne sait rien du chemin et du but vers lequel Jésus s'avance" (as quoted by Marchadour, *Personnages*, 134).

[183] Köstenberger, *John*, 428.

[184] Lincoln, *John*, 501–02, remarks that this reference to "them" in 20:24 may either be a

make of this absence. It could be that Thomas had not been back at all with the disciples since Jesus' arrest, or that, for a moment, he went out before Jesus miraculously entered the room. The choice is impossible to make for nothing in the text would warrant it. However, on a literary level, Thomas' absence can be explained retrospectively in terms of the consequences it produces, namely, a highly significant encounter between him and Jesus.[185] This makes sense as "biblical narrative often withholds pieces of expositions until the moment in the story when they are immediately relevant" and "narration in the biblical story is finally oriented toward dialogue."[186] The mention of Thomas' absence thus alerts implied readers that an important element of the story is at hand.

Before Thomas' dialogue with his master, however, a first dialogue must take place between him and the disciples who had been present in the previous scene. As Thomas now joins them, they witness to him about their encounter with the risen Jesus: "We have seen the Lord."[187] Thomas' legacy as a "sceptic" or "doubter" is based on his reply to them: "Unless I see in his hands the mark of the nails, and place my finger into the mark of the nails, and place my hands into his side, I will never believe" (20:25). Thus, as the witnessing ministry of the disciples has just begun, in obedience to Jesus' commissioning (20:21), it is met with the strong refusal to receive it, not least by a member of the Twelve! Thomas refuses to be dependent on the testimony of others in order to believe. Instead, he sets his own strict conditions for accepting such claims.[188]

It is unlikely that Thomas' categorical refusal to believe the disciples ("I will *never* believe") is intended "to expose the absurdity of what the disciples tell him."[189] His response does not indicate that, in his mind, Jesus' resurrection was impossible or absurd, but rather that certain prerequisites had to be met prior to his belief. Lee's proposal may thus be closer to the mark. For her, Thomas' demand is indicative of a positive desire to meet the risen Jesus in faith.[190] Yet, in

---

loose reference to the disciples or a narrower reference to the antecedent "the twelve." In this latter case, this could potentially indicate that Judas was present during the previous scene. However, Lincoln is correct to conclude that "the depiction of Thomas as one of the twelve is not necessarily meant to indicate which disciples were present at the earlier appearance."

[185] G. W. Most, *Doubting Thomas* (Cambridge, MA/London: Harvard University Press, 2005), 44.

[186] Alter, *Art*, 66. See also Lee, "Easter Faith," 43, for whom "absence is a favourite device of this narrator."

[187] Here, Most, *Doubting Thomas*, 45, fails to convince when he argues that it is "plausible, may even be preferable, to understand the disciples' words as an implicit reproach, almost as though they were gloating over the miracle that had been made available to them but denied to Thomas." Again, the stress of the narration is on the ensuing dialogue, not on what Thomas missed.

[188] See Most, *Doubting Thomas*, 47–50, for an interesting discussion of these conditions.

[189] *Pace* Ridderbos, *John*, 646–47. Along similar lines, see Bonney, *Doubting Thomas*, 159–60, who asserts that Thomas' reaction is a "sarcastic expression of unbelief."

[190] Lee, "Easter Faith," 43.

addition to this positive desire, implied readers inevitably perceive Thomas' demand for physical proofs negatively, not least because they lead to his unbelief. Though requiring such "hard" proofs seems perfectly legitimate,[191] it reveals a deep-rooted mistrust on the part of Thomas towards the disciples' testimony. Again, "Thomas' failure is not in misunderstanding the nature or even the possibility of the resurrection but in demanding a special, individual assurance of it: he wants a proof other than the testimony of the group of believers."[192] If implied readers are to "judge" Thomas, it is thus primarily for his mistrust of the testimony of the other disciples. Through his characterisation, the implied author wishes to communicate that it is essentially through the apostolic witness that one comes to believe in the risen Jesus. It is in and through such a community and its witness that the risen Jesus can be "seen" and "touched" because Jesus abides with them (14:20).[193] As a whole, Thomas' refusal to believe may be "une incrédulité qui ne demande qu'à se laisser confondre"[194] but it is a serious refusal since it relates to the testimony of the disciples.

The following verses, 20:26–29, are constructed in parallel fashion to 20:19–23: both accounts happen on the first day of the week,[195] in a room where the disciples are behind locked doors (20:19, 26). Jesus enters nonetheless and proclaims both times "Peace be with you" (20:19, 26), before showing his wounded body to the disciples (20:20, 27). To this manifestation, the disciples responded with gladness (20:20), while Thomas expressed his faith through a profound confession (20:28). Finally, both accounts end with Jesus commissioning his disciples (20:23, 29).[196] The one important difference between these accounts is that Thomas is absent in 20:19–23 and present in 20:26–29. Therefore, one is practically forced to conclude that the implied author wished to restage the previous scene for Thomas' benefit.[197] Moreover, as far as his characterisation is concerned, the presence of Thomas with the disciples in this section shows that this disciple, in line with his other statements studied above, is persistent. Though he refused to believe the disciples' testimony, he does

---

[191] As mentioned by Lincoln, *John*, 502: "After all, by asking to see Jesus' hands and side, he is requesting no more than was given to the other disciples in v. 20. […] Thomas' fault, therefore, cannot merely lie in his wish to see the risen Lord. Nor does it lie in his adding to the wish to see the wish to touch. This simply makes his desire more graphic."

[192] Williams, *Resurrection*, 94.

[193] See Williams, *Resurrection*, 91–98. Also, P. Prigent, *Heureux celui qui croit. Lecture de l'évangile de Jean* (Lyon: Olivétan, 2006), 298: "Le témoignage apostolique est le seul fondement possible de la foi: c'est le seul pont jeté entre Jésus et les générations ultérieures de croyants."

[194] F. Blanquart, *Le premier jour. Études sur Jean 20*, LD 146 (Paris: Cerf, 1991), 117.

[195] Carson, *John*, 657: "*A week later* is an idiomatic rendering of (lit.) 'After eight days'; the inclusive reckoning brings the action back to Sunday, one week after Easter."

[196] For our understanding of 20:29 as a commissioning of Thomas, see below.

[197] Lincoln, *John*, 502.

remain with them. To a certain extent, such presence underlines once more his openness and willingness to believe.[198]

As Jesus miraculously enters the room,[199] he greets the disciples ("Peace be with you")[200] and then addresses Thomas in particular. It is now clear why the narrator singled out Thomas in 20:24–25: a climactic dialogue with Jesus is about to begin, which must be read in its entirety in order to be understood properly. Jesus' first words to Thomas may give the false impression that he is favourably answering his challenge in 20:25, that he gives in to Thomas' 'ultimatum.'[201] Indeed, Jesus calls on Thomas to "Put your finger here, and see my hands; and put out your hand, and place it in my side" (20:27). But if Jesus' words resemble the disciple's prior demand, Jesus' purposes in coming into the locked room and talking to Thomas are more complex than his sole interest in showing Thomas that he is truly risen.[202] Jesus wanted to point out Thomas' inadmissible reluctance to believe the testimony of the disciples, since he himself was a member of this group. More, Jesus offers himself to Thomas to prepare him further for his own witnessing activity. If he is interested in Thomas' faith, it is because Thomas, as a disciple, is to be included in the group of those whose responsibility is to engage in a witnessing activity about Jesus. Indeed, Jesus has been training him and preparing him, together with the other disciples, throughout his earthly ministry. It is thus with this whole context in mind that implied readers understand Jesus' exhortation: "do not disbelieve but believe" (20:28).[203] This charge, on a literal level and taken out of the overall context of the Fourth Gospel, can easily be misunderstood. Indeed, if Thomas is "disbelieving," what is the object of his unbelief? More, what does it mean regarding his status as a disciple? Given the overall understanding we have gained regarding the believing status of the band of disciples in a prior chapter of this study, and given

---

[198] K. S. O'Brien, "Written That You May Believe: John 20 and Narrative Rhetoric," *CBQ* 67 (2005): 293–94.

[199] Interestingly, Jesus entering the room in 20:26 is described differently than his previous entrance in 20:19. In v. 19, the verb is the aorist tense (ἦλθεν), while in v. 26 it is in the present (ἔρχεται). Such tense change may be pertinent to the actualisation of this section, since, as will be argued below, Thomas is representative of those who have not seen and yet must believe (that is, the implied reader). See also 20:29.

[200] As mentioned by Blanquart, *Premier jour*, 126: "Les témoins discrédités deviennent par conséquent les témoins du dialogue qui va s'engager."

[201] *Contra* Carson, *John*, 657.

[202] Nor was it, in our opinion, intended to "shame" Thomas (so Ridderbos, *John*, 647).

[203] This exhortation is obviously highly relevant to the present study; but several New Testament translations can easily mislead us. For instance, the NIV, the NRSV, or the TNIV choose to use the verb "to doubt" in this verse (*e.g.* TNIV: "Stop doubting and believe"; see also *e.g.*, A. E. McGrath, *Doubting: Growing Through the Uncertainties of Faith*, 2nd ed. (Downers Grove, IL: InterVarsity Press, 2006), 53), but the term is not present here. Instead, Jesus is simply asking Thomas to change from being "unbelieving" (ἄπιστος) to being "believing" (πιστός).

the characterisation of Thomas up to that point in the narrative, it would be surprising if in this present section Thomas was now to be considered as outside
of the believing community.[204] It follows that what is implied in Jesus' charge
is not simply that Thomas must believe in the resurrection of the Lord, but also
that he must receive the testimony of his fellow disciples. Thomas is called to
trust their witness, and implicitly to become himself a witness.

Harstine, in an interesting essay on this section of the narrative, misses this
important element in his interpretation. Basing his understanding on different
recognition scenes from Homer and the use of the doublet πιστός/ἄπιστος in
the ancient world, he concludes that Thomas would not have been understood
as a sceptic or a doubter by ancient readers, but rather as a "loyal and faithful
servant, a servant who is waiting for a sign of recognition that only his true master can provide."[205] Harstine may well be correct about Thomas' anticipation,
or willingness to believe provided Jesus himself gives him a proof. Yet, given
the overall context of this narrative, an element of dissatisfaction is strongly
implied in Jesus' "Do not disbelieve but believe." This disapproval from Jesus
points to Thomas' failure to receive the disciples' testimony about Jesus' risen-
ness. Therefore, it is first and foremost his unbelief as an *attitude* toward the
disciples' witnessing activity that must change. And the reason why Jesus is so
adamant about this necessary change of attitude is because he will not remain in
the world, but is in the process of going back to his Father. Therefore, Thomas
is not simply called to rejoice in the return of his master, but fundamentally to
trust the testimony of the disciples and to take upon himself the responsibility
to take part in the witnessing activity of his fellow disciples. Thomas is himself
a member of this group, and as such the very testimony he is called to believe
in is that which he is called to proclaim. Jesus' charge is therefore to be understood firmly in the context of Thomas' preparation as a future witness.

As a result of Jesus' appearance and words, Thomas famously declares "My
Lord and my God" (20:28). Most commentators mention that the narrator does
not actually say that Thomas touched Jesus' body, but obviously, in this particular case, seeing Jesus is already believing.[206] It is because he recognized
the resurrected body of Jesus that Thomas was able to confess his faith in him.
The content of his confession corresponds to statements made by the narrator
earlier in the prologue (*e.g.* 1:1, 10, 14, 18) and by Jesus in a prior dialogue with

---

[204] *Pace* Bonney, *Doubting Thomas*, 168, who speaks of Thomas' "conversion." Harstine,
"Thomas," 447, asks: "Would this disciple characterized previously as loyal and faithful easily
exchange his fidelity for doubt and mistrust?" One could also note that Thomas' presence with
the disciples indicates, in spite of his reluctance to believe their testimony, that he still desires
to identify himself with them.

[205] Harstine, "Thomas," 447. Thus Harstine proposes: "Perhaps, 'Thomas the Loyal Twin' is
a more historically accurate moniker for this disciple" (p. 447).

[206] Ridderbos, *John*, 647; Köstenberger, *John*, 579; Witherington, *John*, 344; Moloney,
John, 537.

Thomas (14:6–7). Finally, "Thomas is able to make explicit the implications of Jesus' words."[207] Though other characters in the narrative had addressed Jesus as "Lord," it is the first time that one declares him to be "God."[208] Clearly, then, Thomas is now able to apply to Jesus what implied readers have known since the beginning of the narrative. This is the belief that characters in the story have struggled to attain, but with Jesus' latest appearance to the disciples, Thomas did attain it and joyfully proclaimed it.[209]

When Jesus comments on Thomas' confession, once more it is difficult not to consider it, at least partly, as a mild reproach: "Have you believed because you have seen me? Blessed are those who have not seen and yet have believed" (20:29). Beirne argues that "Thomas is gently chided with the lesson that, profound as it is, his personal faith is not more blessed than that of future believers who will require no such sign of Jesus' physical presence in order to believe."[210] More importantly, however, Jesus is once again implicitly referring to Thomas' failure to accept the disciples' testimony: Thomas should have been able to receive it without making seeing a precondition for faith. In turn, he is himself implicitly and quite ironically charged to take up his own witnessing activity about Jesus to "those who have not seen." This is not to say that Jesus is here somehow contrasting Thomas' faith with those who have not seen and yet have believed. Jesus' point is not to degrade the faith of those who "have seen" and to extol that of those "who have not seen."[211] Rather, this section warns implied readers not to imitate Thomas' unbelief prior to his seeing. In fact, "The readers of the Gospel are like Thomas in that they are not part of the group that saw the risen Jesus (20:19–23), but they are also like Thomas in that they received testimony about Jesus – the Gospel itself bears witness to him."[212] Their response must therefore also be one of continual belief (20:30–31), even as Jesus is physically absent. Consequently, in 20:29, as Jesus is implicitly sending Thomas out on a mission towards those who have not seen, he is also exhorting implied readers to receive the testimony of the disciples. If the intent of 20:19–23 was to give an account of Jesus commissioning his disciples, 20:24–29 restages

---

[207] Lincoln, *John*, 503.

[208] Koester, *Symbolism*, 72, remarks that: "By calling Jesus 'my Lord,' Thomas affirmed what the disciples had said after the resurrection, when they announced that they had seen 'the Lord"; and by calling Jesus 'my God,' he corroborated what he had heard at the last supper, when Jesus told him that in seeing Jesus he would see God."

[209] For Resseguie, *Strange*, 164: "The difference between Thomas and the authorities is that when the disciple is presented with overwhelming evidence to the contrary he confesses his faith, not his disbelief."

[210] Beirne, *Discipleship*, 205.

[211] So Beirne, *Discipleship*, 215, n.73, Koester, "Hearing," 346; and Lee, "Easter Faith," 47–48. *Pace*, *e.g.*, Bultmann, *John*, 687–96, who interprets the evangelist as downgrading resurrection faith based on sight in favour of a purely spiritual concept. Indeed, such an understanding would go directly against Jesus' words in 11:15 for instance.

[212] Koester, *Symbolism*, 72–73.

the prior scene not simply for Thomas' benefit, but first and foremost for the implied readers'.

4. *"By the sea of Tiberias" (21:1–2)*

Finally, Thomas is one of the seven disciples present for Jesus' final appearance by the sea of Tiberias (21:2). It is difficult to know exactly what to make of this: the disciples were just sent by Jesus to bear witness about him, but they are found fishing –unsuccessfully– instead. It was argued in chapter 2 that the narrator is setting up a very symbolic call to mission, after the two already given in chapter 20. Thus, this scene is not meant to reflect one way or the other on the disciples' faith, but rather to express *how* the disciples will be able to bring people into Jesus' fold: it is only in response to Jesus' directives that they are able to catch fish (21:6). Consequently, if Jesus is to draw people to himself (12:32), it is through the obedient ministry of his disciples.[213] Jesus remains the primary missionary, but the disciples are the means through which he accomplishes his work.[214] In including Thomas in this last call to mission, the narrator certainly wanted to emphasise that this disciple would indeed remain obedient to Jesus in his own witnessing ministry, and thus would be used by Jesus to bring people to believe in him.

Through this narrative analysis of Thomas' faith and understanding a character has been discovered who, not unlike Peter, is one who speaks his mind freely, expressing his desires, misunderstandings, and conditions. He consistently voices his thoughts, questions, and disagreements in such a way that commentators have described him as "sober" or "realistic."[215] But Thomas' questions and misunderstandings are expressed in the context of belief. He wishes to remain faithful to Jesus, but fails to grasp the mission of Jesus, his identity, and his destiny. As such, Thomas is a character with whom implied readers may easily identify, as they accompany him through misunderstanding towards a full confession of faith (20:29). Though Thomas may always be remembered as a doubter, this study has shown that 'doubting' is, at bottom, not the manner with which the implied author wished to characterise him *per se*. Thomas' unbelief in 20:24–29 regarding Jesus' risen-ness, though undoubtedly problematic, is treated as only secondary to his mistrust of the witnessing activity of his fellow disciples.[216] In failing to believe in the resurrection of Jesus, Thomas is chided precisely because he fails to believe the disciples' testimony. The irony, of course, is that, as a disciple, he is himself called to witness to those who "have not seen."

---

[213] Koester, *Symbolism*, 134–35.

[214] Okure, *Mission*, 219–26.

[215] Ridderbos, *John*, 393; Culpepper, *Anatomy*, 124.

[216] *Pace* Culpepper, *Anatomy*, 124: "Realist more than doubter, Thomas stands in for all who, like Mary Magdalene, embrace the earthly Jesus but have yet to recognize the risen Christ."

If Thomas is to be understood as representing a particular group, it is that of the later Christians who have not seen the Lord and yet are called to believe on the basis of others' testimony.[217] In his contradictions, his misunderstandings, and his reluctance to believe, Thomas' condition is similar to that of those who struggle to make sense of the narrative's presentation of Jesus. One may thus say with Simoens that Thomas is a "disciple en position précaire, il prend valeur typologique. À ce titre peut-il être notre 'jumeau' à tous!"[218]

D. The Beloved Disciple

The Beloved Disciple remains a mystery. Hypotheses about his identity have failed to reach a consensus and continue to divide scholars.[219] Yet, the present chapter is not an attempt to defend (or add) a proposal to this historical question. Its purpose is solely to discover how the faith and understanding of this disciple, as a character in a story, is portrayed throughout the narrative of the Fourth Gospel. From this standpoint, we will seek to draw literary conclusions on the status and literary function of that disciple. Conclusions of that order, without being entirely consensual, have enjoyed relative agreement,[220] though certain ambiguities, inherent to the literary portrayal of this disciple, necessarily remain. Reaching literary conclusions from insights gained through the study of this disciple's faith and understanding will thus hopefully bring fresh light and precision to the issues at hand.

Disagreements regarding historical and literary perspectives on the Beloved Disciple often reflect disagreements on smaller exegetical issues of particular sections. For instance, not everybody agrees on the amount of times this disciple is mentioned in the Fourth Gospel, and the answers exegetes give to these questions influence (and are influenced by) their overall perspectives on the Beloved Disciple. A most disputed reference in this regard is found in 1:35–40. There, John the Baptist directs two of his disciples to Jesus. One of these disciples is

---

[217] O'Brien, "John 20," 296

[218] Y. Simoens, *Selon Jean*, 3 vols, IET 17 (Bruxelles: Éditions de l'Institut d'Études Théologiques, 1997), 3:897–98.

[219] For a brief summary of opinions on the Beloved Disciple's historicity and/or role in the Fourth Gospel, see Conway, *Men and Women*, 177–79. More thorough is Charlesworth, *Beloved*.

[220] As mentioned by Culpepper, *Anatomy*, 121: "It is now generally agreed that the Beloved Disciple was a real historical person who has representative, paradigmatic, or symbolic significance in John." Common views are that the Beloved Disciple is representative of the ideal disciple or "the disciple par excellence" (so, *e.g.*, Lindars, *Gospel of John*, 457; R. F. Collins, "From John to the Beloved Disciple: An Essay on Johannine Characters," *Int* 49 (1995): 367), and that "It is above all through identification with the Beloved Disciple [...] that later Christians can know that they are 'beloved' as he was." (so B. Byrne, "The Faith of the Beloved Disciple and the Community in John 20," *JSNT* 23 (1985): 93–94).

identified as "Andrew, the brother of Peter" in 1:40, while the other disciple remains unnamed, leading several commentators to identify him as "John the son of Zebedee"[221] ("the sons of Zebedee" are later mentioned in 21:2). Bauckham recently argued for the identification of that character with the Beloved Disciples. For him, the vocabulary parallels between 1:35–40 and the end of chapter 21 where the Beloved Disciple is mentioned (*e.g.*, Greek verbs meaning "to turn," "to see," and "to remain" are used in 1:37, 38 and 21:20, 22, 23), together with the ideas that the Beloved Disciple is "the principal eyewitness behind the Gospel's narrative" and that his "witness encompasses the whole of his narrative", favour the view that the unnamed disciple of 1:35 is also the Beloved Disciple.[222] However, this proposal poses more questions than it answers, making it difficult to accept Bauckham's hypothesis whole-heartedly (which is not to say that such a hypothesis is necessarily wrong-headed). For example, why did the narrator leave this disciple unidentified if implied readers are meant to recognise the Beloved Disciple in him? Elsewhere, Bauckham proposes that once readers have encountered the Beloved Disciple in 13:23, they are able retrospectively to make the connection with an anonymous disciple at the beginning of Jesus' mission. His anonymity would then also be explained because he is here described as encountering Jesus for the first time, and could thus not be appropriately called "the Beloved Disciple."[223] But as mentioned by Lincoln, "It is by no means obvious that simply being unnamed makes a disciple a candidate for the role of the Beloved Disciple. After all, 21:2 mentions two unnamed disciples, only one of whom could be the Beloved Disciple"[224]

The earliest explicit mention of the Beloved Disciple is found in 13:23 under the epithet "the one whom he loved" (ὃν ἠγάπα).[225] Thus, the present study will not consider 1:35–40 as material directly relevant to the study of the Beloved Disciple in the narrative. Likewise, several interpreters contest that the "other disciple" mentioned in 18:15–16 is the Beloved Disciple.[226] Some, for

---

[221] Cf. Brown, *John*, 1:73.

[222] Bauckham, *Eyewitnesses*, 391–402.

[223] R. Bauckham, "The Beloved Disciple as Ideal Author," *JSNT* 49 (1993): 36.

[224] A. T. Lincoln, "The Beloved Disciple as Eyewitness and the Fourth Gospel as Witness," *JSNT* 85 (2002): 15, n.29

[225] In 19:26, the Beloved Disciple is also referred to as ὃν ἠγάπα, while 20:2 refers to him as ὃν ἐφίλει. As Bauckham, *Eyewitnesses*, 401–02, suggests, the fact that there is diversity in the way the "Beloved Disciple" is designated in the Fourth Gospel shows that "the disciple whom Jesus loved" is an epithet, not a title. For H. M. Jackson, "Ancient Self-Referential Conventions and Their Implications for the Authorship and Integrity of the Gospel of John " *JTS* 50 (1999): 31, this epithet is a self-designation adopted by the author of the Fourth Gospel to refer to himself in his own narrative (see the analysis of 21:20–25 below for another view on the authorship of the Gospel).

[226] See, *e.g.*, Gunther, "Relation," 147; Lindars, *Gospel of John*, 548. Some have proposed that this disciple's limited role (to enable Peter to enter into the high priest's courtyard) indicates that he should not be identified with the Beloved Disciple. For an overview of this discus-

instance, suggest that it is Judas Iscariot.[227] However, as mentioned by Conway, compared with 1:35–40 "the reference to ἄλλος μαθητής in 18:15–16 is more likely to be a reference to the Beloved Disciple."[228] Indeed, (*i*) it occurs in the context of Jesus' passion, together with the other, clear references to the Beloved Disciple; (*ii*) similarly to 13:23–26; 20:2–10; 21:7, this disciple is paired with Peter; (*iii*) the term ἄλλος μαθητής is later used to refer to the Beloved Disciple in 20:2 ("the other disciple, the one whom Jesus loved");[229] (*iv*) no other unnamed disciple has been mentioned in 13:21–26 and 19:26;[230] and, most convincingly (*v*) in the passion narrative, the Beloved Disciple is portrayed as the only disciple not to abandon Jesus (19:25–27), which is in line with his following Jesus into the courtyard.[231] Even though such identification is not beyond doubt and is highly contested, this section considers ἄλλος μαθητής in 18:15 as referring to the Beloved Disciple, and thus will treat this reference in the following analysis. The following sections of the Fourth Gospel's narrative (13:21–26; 19:25–27; 19:35–36; 20:1–10; 21:7; 21:20–24) will be the bases of the analysis of this character's faith and understanding, leading to proposals regarding the literary function of such a presentation.

1. "Reclining at the table close to Jesus" (13:21–26)

The Beloved Disciple appears for the first time in the narrative at this point, during the supper, as Jesus is "troubled in his spirit" and announces: "one of you will betray me" (13:21). The narrator then mentions that none of the present

---

sion, see Charlesworth, *Beloved*, 336–59.

[227] For proponents of this view since 1730, see F. Neirynck, "The 'Other Disciple' in Jn 18,15–16," *ETL* 51 (1975): 120, n.41. More recently this view has also been endorsed by Brodie, *John*, 529. For a rebuttal of this particular position, see R. A. Culpepper, *John, the Son of Zebedee: The Life of a Legend*, SPNT (Columbia, SC: University of South Carolina Press, 1994), 58.

[228] Conway, *Men and Women*, 179. However, Conway herself chooses to ignore this reference in her analysis of the Beloved Disciple, following Bultmann, *John*, 645, n.4. Bultmann argues that there is no basis for identifying this disciple as the Beloved Disciple since in this verse Peter and the Beloved Disciple do not appear as "rivals or as contrasted types."

[229] Though note that the article is missing in 18:15.

[230] As mentioned by Tovey, *Narrative*, 130, all other individual disciples are named in these chapters (13:26; 14:5, 8, 22; 18:2, 10, 15).

[231] So, Lincoln, *John*, 453. *Contra*, e.g., Barrett, *John*, 525; Haenchen, *John*, 2:167 who have proposed that this disciple's limited role (to enable Peter to enter into the high priest's courtyard) indicates that he should not be identified with the Beloved Disciple. However, Quast, *Figures*, 78, responded that "To argue against identifying the other disciple here in ch. 18 with the Beloved Disciple on the basis that it has little part to play in the actual story line only serves to strengthen the argument for the identification, since the Beloved Disciple does not do much in any narrative where he is found." Quast may also overstate his case, but, in any case Lincoln's argument is a reminder that one cannot limit this disciple's role in this section to his assisting Peter: he also follows Jesus.

disciples knew of whom Jesus spoke, and he introduces the Beloved Disciple in these terms: "ἦν ἀνακείμενος εἷς ἐκ τῶν μαθητῶν αὐτοῦ ἐν τῷ κόλπῳ τοῦ Ἰησοῦ, ὃν ἠγάπα ὁ Ἰησοῦς" (13:23). Thus, before the mention that Jesus loved him, implied readers learn of his position in relation to Jesus (literally "in the bosom of Jesus"), so that O'Day is certainly correct to note that "the anonymity of this disciple suggests that the Fourth Evangelist understands the significance of this disciple to rest in his relationship to Jesus, not in his own identity."[232] Indeed, beyond the physical proximity of this disciple to his master, which for some suggests a place of honour at the table,[233] this verse recalls an earlier description of Jesus, in the prologue, as "ὁ ὢν εἰς τὸν κόλπον τοῦ πατρὸς" (1:18). Since in 1:18, this expression referred to Jesus' relationship to his Father, it follows that the implied author infers from 13:23 that an analogous relationship exists between Jesus and his disciple.

What is the nature of this relationship? For Beasley-Murray, these two relationships are analogous with respect to the notion of revelation. Just as Jesus revealed his Father by virtue of his intimacy with his Father (1:18), so is the Beloved Disciple able to communicate what he witnessed on the basis of his intimacy with Jesus.[234] Conway is correct to note that this emphasis is dependent on a further description of the Beloved Disciple in 21:24–25 and that, as a character in the narrative, "whatever knowledge he may have had of Jesus, he does not communicate it to others."[235] For her, therefore, the point of the analogy is not revelation but "intimacy shared between the Father, Jesus, and the Beloved Disciple."[236] Yet, it is not necessary to separate so sharply these notions. Jesus' intimacy with his Father enabled him to reveal his Father in 1:18, so that the similar description of the Beloved Disciple in 13:23 already suggests his qualification to testify about Jesus.[237] This is indeed not explicit until 21:24 (or, as will be argued, 19:27, 35–37), but the ground for the Beloved Disciple's qualified witness is already set in 13:23: the Beloved Disciple has a close relationship to Jesus.

Once that disciple's intimacy with Jesus is mentioned, the narrator adds that he is "ὃν ἠγάπα ὁ Ἰησοῦς" (13:23). Rarely in the Fourth Gospel is an individual said to be loved by Jesus (see also the members of the Bethany family in 11:3, 5, 26), and in the context of the farewell discourse, this presentation is highly significant. Jesus is portrayed as "loving his own to the end" (13:1) and throughout this discourse, the close relationship between him and his followers is expressed in terms of mutual love (14:21; 15:9). Clearly, therefore, the

---

[232] O'Day, "John," 729.

[233] See the discussion in Quast, *Figures*, 59.

[234] So, *e.g.*, Beasley-Murray, *John*, 238; E. Cothenet, *La chaîne des témoins selon l'évangile de Jean: De Jean-Baptiste au disciple bien-aimé*, Lire la Bible 142 (Paris: Cerf, 2005), 127.

[235] Conway, *Men and Women*, 181.

[236] Conway, *Men and Women*, 181.

[237] Culpepper, *Anatomy*, 121.

Beloved Disciple is to be understood not only as intimate with Jesus, but also in a loving relationship with him. Though nothing is said in this section about the disciple's faith, a relationship of that sort strongly implies that he was also in a faithful relationship with Jesus. Even more, "this designation as the one whom Jesus loved means that when his authorship role is revealed in 21:24 readers will trust his insight and witness."[238]

Much has been written about the exchange that takes place after the introduction of the Beloved Disciple and the mention that the disciples (apparently including the Beloved Disciple) were troubled by Jesus' announcement (13:24–26). For many, the following scene signals the superiority of the Beloved Disciple over Peter, who is thus relegated to a subordinate status.[239] This is only secondarily relevant to the present study, so we will not enter fully into the debate.[240] Yet, the fact that Peter "motioned to him to ask Jesus of whom he was speaking" (13:24) only serves to reinforce the privileged position of the Beloved Disciple in regard to Jesus. Certainly, that he was able to ask Jesus "Lord, who is it?" may simply refer to his physical proximity to his master,[241] but this is also in line with later occurrences of the Beloved Disciple having greater perception than Peter (20:8; 21:7).[242] In this case, the Beloved Disciple is let in on the identity of the betrayer, while Peter and the other disciples remain in the dark (13:28–29). This, once more, underlines the particular intimate relationship between the Beloved Disciple and Jesus.[243]

Interestingly, the Beloved Disciple's knowledge of the identity of the Betrayer does not affect the action. He does not pass this newly gained information back to Peter, and he does not attempt to dissuade Judas.[244] Even more, the narrator's own comment in 13:28, after Jesus speaks to Judas, ignores the Beloved Disciple's role in this section of the narrative: "Now, no one at the

---

[238] Lincoln, *John*, 378.

[239] *E.g.*, Tolmie, *Farewell*, 199; Maynard, "Peter," 543–45.

[240] For an overview, see Blaine Jr., *Peter*, 69–74.

[241] Blaine Jr., *Peter*, 72: "Because Peter motions rather than whispers to BD, however, we get the impression his inability to question Jesus is logistical: he is not within speaking distance of either one of them. Simply put, he does not have a particularly good seat at the table."

[242] Conway, *Men and Women*, 182, proposes that "the beloved disciple appears to act as mediator between Peter and Jesus" but then rightly acknowledges that "nothing actually results from this mediation."

[243] In this sense, Quast's suggestion that "this text itself cannot be understood as introducing the Beloved Disciple as 'having a special knowledge of Jesus'" since he himself had to ask Jesus about his betrayer (*contra* D. J. Hawkin, "The Function of the Beloved Disciple Motif in the Johannine Redaction," *LTP* 33 (1977): 143) misses the point. The Beloved Disciple may very well have had to *gain* this special knowledge (the narrative explicitly states so), but it is because of his close proximity and intimacy with Jesus that he was *able* to receive such insight (see Quast, *Figures*, 143).

[244] On this phenomenon, see also 19:35 and 20:8. Lincoln, *John*, 378, thus rightly observes that "The account would proceed smoothly if taken up again in v. 26b" [without 13:23–26a].

table knew why he said this to him." As Pamment observes, it is as though the Beloved Disciple is "both present and absent" at the same time.[245] Of course, it does not follow that his role is insignificant in this section. We have already mentioned that the implied author, in presenting the Beloved Disciple's privileged intimacy with Jesus, suggested that this disciple was qualified to testify about Jesus. Now his privileged knowledge qualifies him as a key witness to the significance of the first in a series of decisive moments in the last part of Jesus' life, namely, that Jesus knew and had control over his own betrayal.

Thus, even though the Beloved Disciple appears for the first time in this section of the narrative, he is characterised from the start as having a unique relationship with Jesus. Implied readers are not told where this disciple comes from and whether or not he has been with Jesus from the beginning of his earthly ministry. Yet, as Jesus' ministry is coming to a dramatic end, this disciple is presented as surpassing the other disciples in terms of intimacy with, and knowledge of, Jesus. If such intimacy and knowledge do not impact the events of the narrative in 13:21–30, they do qualify him for a future witnessing activity (a responsibility which, as implied readers know from 21:24, he has taken upon himself as reflected in the writing down of this narrative). All in all, one may say that his role in this section is for the sake of the readers more than for the sake of the plot. Through this depiction, readers are encouraged to trust the validity and truth of his testimony.[246]

2. *"He entered with Jesus into the court of the high priest" (18:15–16)*

In line with the characterisation of the Beloved Disciple in his previous appearance, it is not surprising to find him again with Jesus, following (ἠκολούθει) and entering with him (συνεισῆλθην) into the high priest's courtyard (18:15). As remarked by Blaine, "In John's Gospel, συνεισέρχομαι denotes not only simultaneous movement but intimate association"[247] so that it may be inferred that the Beloved Disciple is not afraid to associate himself with Jesus. If this remark is correct, this disciple contrasts positively with Peter, who, in the upcoming scene of his threefold denial, will refuse to associate with Jesus (18:17, 25, 27). To carry this point a step further, several commentators mention that the Beloved Disciple remained in the high priest's courtyard and did not deny Jesus.[248] While nothing is said about this disciple remaining in (or leaving) the

---

[245] M. Pamment, "The Fourth Gospel's Beloved Disciple," *ExpTim* 94 (1983): 366. See also W. Kurz, "The Beloved Disciple and Implied Readers," *BTB* 19 (1989): 103, for whom "It is as though the Beloved Disciple joins the narrator and implied readers as omniscient observers outside the plot rather than being participant in the plot."

[246] Lincoln, *John*, 379.

[247] Blaine Jr., *Peter*, 93, n.39.

[248] *E.g.*, Culpepper, *Son of Zebedee*, 62; G. N. Stanton, *The Gospels and Jesus*, 2nd ed. (Oxford: Oxford University Press, 2002), 114.

courtyard, one naturally assumes that he stayed there for a while and that he witnessed both Jesus' trial and Peter's denials.[249]

In this scene, however, the focus is not so much on the Beloved Disciple as it is on Peter. It is *Peter* who is following Jesus, "and so did another disciple" (18:15). Contrary to his acolyte, the "other disciple" had no trouble entering the courtyard since "he was known to the high priest" (twice mentioned in 18:15, 16). As such, he was also able to assist Peter in entering, in intervening in his favour before the servant girl who kept watch of the door (18:16). Clearly, the Beloved Disciple had an active role in the process of giving Peter access into the courtyard, but it is unnecessary to search for a symbolic significance to this action. The Beloved Disciple seems to have been able to come and go in the high priest's courtyard, but this can hardly be considered to mean that the Beloved Disciple has "priority" over Peter.[250] Moreover, the text does not mention what exactly motivated the Beloved Disciple to go back and help Peter other than that Peter simply "stood outside at the door" (18:16), apparently forbidden to enter by the servant girl.[251]

In this section, therefore, the Beloved Disciple remains characterised as a close disciple of Jesus, willing to follow him even as Jesus is standing trial. The fact that he was willing to associate with Jesus, at least in entering the courtyard with him, marks his difference with Peter who thrice refused to acknowledge being one of his disciples. Truly, one should probably not carry this point, the contrast between Peter and the Beloved Disciple, too far since in this section of the narrative the narrator uses the Beloved Disciple mostly to explain how Peter entered the high priest's courtyard.[252] Yet, Zumstein's analysis is correct: "'L'autre disciple' agit dans le v. 16 comme dans le reste du récit de la Passion: il est le témoin silencieux qui accompagne Jésus sur le chemin de la Passion,

---

[249] Tovey, *Narrative*, 124–25, speaks of this aspect of the Beloved Disciple's characterisation as his "elusiveness" as the implied author makes this character fade from the scene only to reappear in the narrative at a later point.

[250] *Pace* Culpepper, *Son of Zebedee*, 62; and especially Haenchen, *John*, 2:173. As already mentioned, the lack of rivalry or contrasted types between the two disciples in this section is what led Bultmann to reject the identification of this "other disciple" with the "Beloved Disciple" (Bultmann, *John*, 645).

[251] R. T. Fortna, "Jesus and Peter in the High Priest's House: A Test Case for the Question of the Relation between Mark's and John's Gospels," *NTS* 24 (1978): 380, proposes that the Beloved Disciple noticed that Jesus was being mistreated in the hands of the High Priest and so came back to get Peter to intervene, but this is not warranted by the text.

[252] Thus, though P. S. Minear, "The Beloved Disciple in the Gospel of John: Some Clues and Conjectures," in *The Composition of John's Gospel: Selected Studies from Novum Testamentum*, ed. by D. E. Orton (Leiden: Brill, 1999), 199, correctly shows how the Beloved Disciple was willing, contrary to Peter, to accept "the charge of guilt by association," his constant comparison of the two disciples throughout the narrative (in favour of the Beloved Disciple), is certainly overstated.

sans pour autant se méprendre à son sujet ou l'abandonner."[253] As a faithful disciple, the credibility of the Beloved Disciple as a witness of this event is heightened further.[254]

3. *"Standing nearby" (19:25–27)*

In his next appearance (19:25–27), the narrator introduces this disciple for the second time as "the Beloved Disciple." In this very significant point in the passion narrative, he is standing by the cross, together with several women. The Beloved Disciple is the only male disciple to witness the event of the cross,[255] and as such takes precedence over other known male disciples (such as Peter) who are nowhere to be found. In contrast to these other male disciples, his presence at the cross implies that he has faithfully continued to follow Jesus throughout the trial proceedings.[256]

In 19:26a, the implied author chooses to concentrate on two important characters of the story: the mother of Jesus and the Beloved Disciple.[257] These two characters are similar in that they remain unnamed, and that the implied author chooses to speak of them with terms describing the nature of their relationship with Jesus: one is his mother (ἡ μήτηρ αὐτοῦ), the other the disciple he loves (τὸν μαθητὴν ὃν ἠγάπα).[258] Zumstein puts it well: "Le lien qui les unit à Jésus est celui de la proximité, plus encore de l'intimité. La scène qui va suivre se joue donc entre le Crucifié et ses intimes."[259] This interpretation is certainly in line with prior appearances of the Beloved Disciple in the narrative: he is that one disciple who is closest to Jesus and thus who is able to witness the most important events in the life and mission of Jesus.

Upon seeing his mother and disciple, Jesus utters these famous words: "Woman, behold, your son!" and then to the disciple: "Behold, your mother" (19:26b, 27a). Several scholars have interpreted the significance of this passage on a purely literal level, showing Jesus' concern as a son that his mother

---

[253] J. Zumstein, *L'évangile selon Saint Jean (13–21)*, CNTDs IVb (Genève: Labor et Fides, 2007), 210.

[254] Culpepper, *Son of Zebedee*, 62.

[255] Several authors highlight this characteristic, *e.g.*, Brown, Donfried, and Reumann, eds., *Peter*, 136; Minear, "Beloved Disciple," 119; Conway, *Men and Women*, 183.

[256] Tovey, *Narrative*, 130; Barrett, *John*, 552; and R. J. Cassidy, *Four Times Peter: Portrayals of Peter in the Four Gospels and at Philippi*, Interfaces (Collegeville, MN: Liturgical Press, 2007), 93.

[257] Thus, the three other women of 19:25 do not play any role in this section anymore. For Zumstein, *Jean (13–21)*, 248: "Il s'agit [...] de créer l'espace nécessaire à un dernier échange entre le Christ 'élevé' et ses proches. La dernière parole que le Crucifié a ainsi l'occasion d'adresser aux siens, revêt une importance exceptionnelle."

[258] So for M.-A. Chevallier, "La fondation de l'Eglise dans le quatrième Evangile: Jn 19, 25–30," *ETR* 58 (1953): 345: "On dirait aujourd'hui qu'ils ne possèdent pas d'autre identité que leur relation personnelle à Jésus."

[259] Zumstein, *Jean (13–21)*, 249.

is cared for after his death.[260] However, in a narrative so symbolically charged there is little doubt that elements of symbolism are also present in these verses, so that the theme of the 'family' (mother, son) is most certainly of overriding significance.[261] Nailed on the cross, Jesus sees these two persons he is about to leave and he expresses his will for them: "Au moment de mourir, le fils constitue la nouvelle famille."[262]

Several interpreters argue that since the Beloved Disciple is an exemplary disciple, Jesus is in fact calling his mother to become the mother of all believers.[263] Yet, in the text, Jesus does not do that. On the contrary, the fact that the Beloved Disciple takes Jesus' mother into his own home (19:27) implies that it is he who is given a specific role, not Jesus' mother.[264] Thus, Jesus' announcement brings about "a new fictive kinship" in which the Beloved Disciple somehow becomes Jesus' human successor as "son."[265] As such, he is to carry a similar role to that which Jesus held during his earthly ministry.[266] Yet, to understand what that particular role is for the Beloved Disciple, one must ask what symbolism is to be assigned to Jesus' mother as mother of the Beloved Disciple. Given the fact that Jesus' mother herself is portrayed as a faithful disciple in 19:25, as she stands by the cross, implied readers are led to recognise that she stands for other (or all) faithful disciples. If that is the case, the mother of Jesus is now put in the care of the Beloved Disciple, who, like Jesus, will instruct her and those she represents about authentic belief in Jesus:

> By taking care of the future through bringing the Beloved Disciple, as his successor, and his mother together as the new family of his followers, Jesus is seen as providing for the welfare of

---

[260] So *e.g.*, most of the Church Fathers, in addition to several illustrious modern commentators: Bernard, *John*, 2:633; Dodd, *Interpretation*, 428; Morris, *John*, 812; Bruce, *John*, 371–72.

[261] For an overview of the main symbolic interpretations, see Quast, *Figures*, 92–99.

[262] Zumstein, *Jean (13–21)*, 250. We may add, following Léon-Dufour: "Tout se passe comme si, les voyant côte à côte au pied de la croix, Jésus constatait la relation qui va les unir" (Léon-Dufour, *Lecture*, 4:141).

[263] So F. M. Braun, *Jean le théologien*, 3 vols, EBib (Paris: Gabalda, 1959–72), 3/2:108–15; and recently Moloney, *John*, 504; F. J. Moloney, *Mary: Woman and Mother* (Collegeville, MN: Liturgical Press, 1989), 31–50.

[264] Zumstein, *Jean (13–21)*, 250, following H. Schürmann, "Jesu lezte Weisung. Jo 19,26.27a," in *Ursprung und Gestalt: Erörterungen und Besinnungen zum Neuen Testament*, ed. by H. Schürmann (Düsseldorf: Patmos, 1970), 14–16.

[265] Lincoln, *John*, 476. In that sense, Jesus' announcement is "performative" (so Léon-Dufour, *Lecture*, 4:141).

[266] A fascinating note in Maccini, *Testimony*, 189, serves to reinforce this point. Maccini quotes an agraphon from 19:26–30 found in the *Codex evangelii Johannei Templariorum*: "He says to his mother, 'Don't cry. I am returning to my Father, and to eternal life. Look – your son! This man will take my place'. Then he says to his disciple, 'Look – your mother!' Then, bowing his head, he gave up his Spirit." (see R. J. Miller, ed., *The Complete Gospels: Annotated Scholars Version* (Sonoma, CA: Polebridge Press, 1992), 424).

believers by entrusting them to the one whose witness will ensure the true interpretation of the revelation he has proclaimed and embodied.[267]

This symbolic interpretation can be carried out a step further in taking into account 19:27b, where implied readers realise that Jesus' will was indeed accomplished when "from that hour, the disciple took her into his own home." Most likely, both "home" (εἰς τὰ ἴδια) and "from that hour" (ἀπ᾽ ἐκείνης τῆς ὥρας) are to be symbolically interpreted in relation to Jesus' announcement. This narrator's aside is unlikely to mean that the Beloved Disciple and the mother of Jesus left the scene at this very moment. Rather, the "hour" is to be understood as the reference to the elevation of Jesus on the cross. It is the hour of his glorification,[268] so that it is from that "hour" that the new family constituted by Jesus became effective. Understood symbolically, 19:27b does not simply describe the Beloved Disciple and the mother of Jesus as changing location, but as being in the "place" where the Beloved Disciple witnesses: "En prenant la mère de Jésus chez lui, le disciple bien-aimé lui permet de vivre dans l'espace de la révélation."[269] In entrusting the believing community to the care of the Beloved Disciple, Jesus puts them in a "place" where the true interpretation of the revelation would be provided for them.

In this section, the characterisation of the Beloved Disciple is developed so that his credibility as a witness of pivotal events in the ministry of Jesus finds new ground: Jesus symbolically charges him to be the one disciple whose testimony will represent the true interpretation of the revelation that Jesus himself embodied. Just as Jesus had promised that the Paraclete would be his successor (14:16, 26) he now entrusts the Beloved Disciple to be his human successor. There is little doubt that this role could only be given to him because he was considered a faithful disciple of Jesus, shown by his intimate presence with Jesus at the cross.[270] Again in this section, nothing is said about this disciple's understanding of what was being said and done (except that he obeyed Jesus' command in 19:27b and took his mother in his "home"). We may add that, so far in the narrative, his future quality as "witness" does not seem to depend on his proper understanding of what is taking place but on his presence and

---

[267] Lincoln, *John*, 477. See also Culpepper, *Anatomy*, 122, for whom: "Together, mother and son, they form the nucleus of a new community of faith."

[268] Lincoln, "Beloved Disciple," 13 is correct to remind that: "The use of the term 'hour' is not only highly significant but also very elastic in the narrative discourse." Indeed, in 12:27 and 13:1, implied readers discover that Jesus' "hour" has already arrived. Likewise, the prediction of 7:38–39 about rivers of living water flowing from Jesus' belly signals that this would happen at the time of Jesus' glorification. Thus, Lincoln concludes that "'From that hour' may well be meant to be taken as 'after Jesus' death and glorification'" (p. 13).

[269] So Zumstein, *Jean (13–21)*, 251.

[270] Bauckham, *Eyewitnesses*, 397, following S. van Tilborg, *Imaginative Love in John*, BibIntS 2 (Leiden: Brill, 1993), 246, writes: "The Beloved Disciple's special intimacy with Jesus is not just a privilege but an indication that Jesus expected a special role for him in the future" (*i.e.* with regard to his succession).

intimacy with Jesus at key points of the passion narratives. The implied author wishes to make clear that the Beloved Disciple's credibility is enhanced each time his presence by Jesus' side is mentioned, and even more as he receives this particular charge from Jesus.

4. *"His testimony is true" (19:35–36)*

In 19:31–34, the narrator recounts how, after Jesus had already died (19:30), "one of the soldiers pierced his side with a spear, and at once there came out blood and water" (19:34). This phenomenon has been interpreted differently, though elements of symbolism are necessarily at play. For some, the blood and the water make reference respectively to the sacraments of the Eucharist (6:53–56) and of Baptism (3:5, 8).[271] Yet, without denying sacramental overtones, it is probable that the basic level of reference of both "water" and "blood" is the theme of life. In 6:54, Jesus proclaimed "Whoever feeds on my flesh and drinks my blood has eternal life" and with 7:38–39, implied readers gather that the water that comes from Jesus' side signifies the life of the Spirit that comes from Jesus' glorification. The significance of blood and water flowing from Jesus' side is thus that his death provides life.[272]

The implied author has just recounted something of great value and significance in 19:34b. Thus, it is not surprising to find a narratorial intrusion into the narrative at this point. In 19:35, the narrator seeks to guarantee the veracity of what was witnessed: "He who saw it has borne witness – his testimony is true, and he knows that he is telling the truth – that you also may believe." But what is the identity of the one who "saw" (ἑωρακὼς) and "testified" (μεμαρτύρηκεν)? The text does not state it explicitly, maybe because the narrator does not wish to point to a particular person but to the importance of the testimony.[273] Yet, in this context (*cf.* 19:25–27) the most likely candidate remains the Beloved Disciple since he was present with Jesus at the cross. Moreover, later in 21:24 he is also described as a witness whose testimony is behind the present Gospel narrative.[274] Finally, this is in keeping with the Beloved Disciple's presence at key points of the Passion narrative.

---

[271] So *e.g.* Bultmann, *John*, 678; Haenchen, *John*, 2:563; Moloney, *John*, 505; Zumstein, *Jean (13–21)*, 258–59.

[272] So H.-J. Venetz, "Zeuge des Erhöhten. Exegetischer Beitrag zu Joh 19,31–37," *FZPhTh* 23 (1976): 354–55; Cothenet, *Témoins*, 132–33; Lincoln, *John*, 479.

[273] Zumstein, *Jean (13–21)*, 259.

[274] So *e.g.* Brown, *John*, 2:936; Léon-Dufour, *Lecture*, 4:165; *contra* P. S. Minear, "Diversity and Unity. A Johannine Case Study," in *Die Mitte des Neuen Testaments: Einheit und Vielfalt neutestamentlicher Theologie: Festschrift für Eduard Schweizer zum siebzigsten Geburtstag*, ed. by U. Luz and H. Weder (Göttingen: Vandenhoeck & Ruprecht, 1983), 162–63, for whom the most likely candidate is the soldier who pierced Jesus' side. See the discussion in Lincoln, "Beloved Disciple," 13.

His testimony is qualified in three ways. First, the narrator presents the Beloved Disciple as an eyewitness of events immediately following Jesus' death (the blood and water flowing from his side as a result of the soldier's piercing Jesus' side). Second, the truth of his testimony is sharply underlined: "his testimony is true and he knows that he is telling the truth."[275] Third, the narrator addresses readers directly (ὑμεῖς) for the first time in the narrative to express the goal of his reporting this testimony: "so that you may believe" (*cf.* 20:31). At one level, implied readers understand this verse as the narrator reporting events that the Beloved Disciple quite literally witnessed with his own eyes. Yet, on another level, they also bear in mind the broad metaphorical framework of the Fourth Gospel's narrative, the motif of a cosmic trial of the truth.[276] Then, both the 'eyewitness' and the 'truth' elements of the testimony of the Beloved Disciple in 19:35 can be understood as legal metaphors themselves.[277] The narrator aligns himself on the side of the positive judgement of life and wishes to draw implied readers to share his perspective on the life-giving nature of Jesus' death.[278] Since the testimony of the Beloved Disciple is true, implied readers can trust this witness and align themselves wholeheartedly on the side of life.

The next two verses (19:36–37) come to reinforce this perspective. For the narrator, the events that follow Jesus' death are the fulfilment of two scriptures: "For these things took place that the Scripture might be fulfilled" (19:36a). The first scripture quotation "Not one of his bones will be broken" (19:36b) refers to the fact that Jesus' legs did not need to be broken by Roman soldiers in order to quicken his death because he was already dead (19:32–33; *cf.* 19:18). The unbroken condition of Jesus' bones recalls that of the Passover sacrifice that brought about life (Ex. 12:46; Num 9:12). The second citation "They will look on him whom they have pierced" clearly comes from Zech. 12:10 and is used to refer to the soldier who pierced Jesus' side, with the ensuing water and blood flowing out (19:34). In the context of Zechariah, this citation occurs in a section about the death of the good shepherd. Later in that section, the prophet goes on to say: "On that day there shall be a fountain opened for the house of David and the inhabitants of Jerusalem, to clean them from sin and uncleanness" (Zech. 13:1). Thus, this Zechariah quotation was certainly also to emphasise that Jesus' death brought about new life through its cleansing from sin.[279]

---

[275] Barrett, *John*, 557–58, is correct to state that ἐκεῖνος οἶδεν in 19:35 refers to the witness himself.

[276] See Lincoln, *Truth*.

[277] Clearly, the Beloved Disciple is portrayed as an eyewitness of the blood and water, but his role as a witness within the metaphorical trial motif must take precedence over the literal "element of reporting of the past" strongly put forth by Bauckham, *Eyewitnesses*, 384–411. What seems to matter much more than the actual reporting of the event of the blood and water flowing from Jesus' side is the metaphorical significance it conveys to implied readers.

[278] Lincoln, *John*, 23.

[279] Lincoln, *John*, 482.

Moreover, this quotation may refer to something else in the events following Jesus' death. In addition to the reference to Jesus' side being pierced, implied readers wonder to whom "they will look on him" refers (19:37). Naturally, one may think first of the soldiers (and by extension Jesus' adversaries). Yet, the verb being used (ὄψονται) recalls what was said about the Beloved Disciple who "saw" (ἑωρακώς) Jesus being pierced (19:35). The narrator may therefore use this quotation to refer to the readers, calling them to "see" what the Beloved Disciple "saw" and thus to align themselves with the perspective of this true witness. Therefore, this second quotation may actually refer both to those whom the narrator addresses in 19:25 ("that you also may believe") and to the basis on which they are called to believe, that is, the significance of Jesus' side being pierced as interpreted by the Beloved Disciple.[280] In this rich section of the narrative, the Beloved Disciple is portrayed as putting in practice the role entrusted him by Jesus before he died (19:27). He is Jesus' human successor whose testimony represents the true interpretation of the revelation that Jesus himself embodied. As such, his testimony calls implied readers to believe and to align themselves with his perspective. Quite obviously, what can be said about the Beloved Disciple's faith and understanding in this section is exclusively reliant on the narrator's recounting his later perspective as an authorised and authoritative interpreter of events surrounding Jesus' Passion. Though the narrator does not explicitly say so, it appears that in order to interpret these events, the Beloved Disciple made use of Scripture, a phenomenon which recalls in the implied readers' mind the sections in which Scripture and memory are said to have been used by the disciples in order to understand words and actions of Jesus (2:17, 22; 12:16). As was concluded in our study of these passages in chapter 2, in the Fourth Gospel the past is foundational only retrospectively and must be interpreted in light of Easter. The use of memory (which is not mentioned *per se* in 19:35–37 but implied through the use of eyewitness terminology) both interprets Scripture and is structured by Scripture.[281] Therefore, it can be said that in this section the Beloved Disciple is portrayed, for the sake of the implied readers' faith, as a true witness, who, from a post-Easter perspective, testified about "these things" and exemplified the proper understanding of this key event of Jesus' earthly ministry.

5. "He saw and believed" (20:1–10)

In the next section in which the Beloved Disciple appears, he is once again portrayed as a character in the story. Mary informs Peter and the Beloved Disciple,[282]

---

[280] Zumstein, *Jean (13–21)*, 261.

[281] Zumstein, "Mémoire," 163.

[282] Here, the Beloved Disciple is described both as "the other disciple" (20:2a, 3, 4, 8) and as the "the one whom Jesus loved" (20:2b). Since the rest of this section speaks of him as simply "the other disciple," it is likely that the narrator wished to identify him expressly as

who appear together once more in this narrative (*cf.* 13:24; 18:15–16; 21:20), that the Lord has been removed from the tomb and that "we do not know where they have laid him" (20:2b). The two disciples thus go to the tomb, with the Beloved Disciple outrunning Peter and reaching the tomb before him (20:4). Again, one should probably not make too much of this "race."[283] As mentioned by Barrett, it is unwise to equate "fleetness of foot with apostolic preeminence"[284] for instance. In fact, Peter and the Beloved Disciple move past each other at various stages in the following verses. The Beloved Disciple, first at the tomb, stops at the entrance, peeks inside, but does not go in, contrary to Peter, who, upon reaching the tomb, goes immediately inside to witness the folded linen cloths lying there (20:6–7).[285] Then, the Beloved Disciple also goes in and the narrator reports that he "saw and believed" (20:8).[286] Through this phenomenon, the implied author may be using "a delaying tactic to build up the climax of this pericope, the Beloved Disciple's believing."[287]

It is the first time in the narrative that the faith of the Beloved Disciple is expressly mentioned. But what exactly did he believe, and on what basis? Again, it is unlikely that he only believed Mary Magdalene's earlier news that the body

---

"the Beloved Disciple" when he first appears on the scene (*Cf.* Mollat, *Études*, 141–42).

[283] For an overview of the many proposed significances of the Beloved Disciple outrunning Peter to the tomb, see Blaine Jr., *Peter*, 110–114. Throughout the centuries, the most popular explanation has been that the Beloved Disciples was propelled by superior love for Jesus (so Byrne, "Beloved," 86; Brown, *John*, 2:2007). Others focus on the status of the Beloved Disciple to explain this. For *e.g.* Mollat, *Études*, 143: "S'il a couru plus vite, s'il est arrivé le premier, c'est parce qu'il est 'le disciple que Jésus aimait.'" Similarly, Brodie, *John*, 561, asserts that this remark symbolically stresses the Beloved Disciple's superior discipleship. Others, as is well known, find in this section indications of a competition between Peter and the Beloved Disciple, who are in turn representative of a particular polemic in the early Church, but no one seems to agree on what polemic it is referring to (see Blaine Jr., *Peter*, 112–114, for an overview and evaluation of these proposals).

[284] Barrett, *John*, 563.

[285] As mentioned by Ridderbos, *John*, 632, Peter entering the tomb first and taking careful note of the situation is "of no less importance for the intent of the narrative" than the disciple arriving first at the tomb.

[286] See the structural analysis proposed by de la Potterie, "Foi pascale," 29–30, who considers that 20:8 and 20:29 form an *inclusio*. Though 20:8 necessarily evokes 20:29 "Blessed are those who have not seen and yet believe," the link between the two is difficult to assess. Is there a link between the faith of the Beloved Disciple and that of later generations who are blessed because they have not seen the risen Jesus? Apparently not, since the Beloved Disciple believed on the basis of 'seeing' (so Brown, *John*, 2:1005). Yet, following F. J. Moloney, "John 20: A Journey Completed," *ACR* 59 (1982): 426, and especially Byrne, "Beloved," 90: "The point is not that of 'not seeing and yet believing', but rather of 'not seeing *Jesus* and yet believing" (emphasis original).

[287] S. M. Schneiders, "The Face Veil: A Johannine Sign (John 20:1–10)," *BTB* 13 (1983): 95. Moreover, for Blaine Jr., *Peter*, 113, it accentuates the urgency of the situation and the enthusiasm of both disciples.

had been taken away from the tomb.[288] This would be rather anti-climactic,[289] and it would not adequately render the force of the expression "he saw and believed."[290] Even more, as mentioned by Mollat, such belief is excluded by the context: Mary had said that Jesus' body had been taken away, but the presence of linens in the tomb excludes this interpretation of Jesus' absence.[291] Rather, in keeping with the Beloved Disciple's role as a privileged interpreter, it is more plausible that he believed Jesus to be resurrected from the dead.[292] Just as the linen cloths (τὰ ὀθόνια) remind implied readers of those of Lazarus coming out of his tomb in 11:44, the state of the tomb can be said to be a 'sign' for the Beloved Disciple.[293] He is the first in the narrative to believe in Jesus' resurrection, and this character is the only one to reach Easter faith without a prior sight of Jesus' resurrected body.[294] This belief may be meant to contrast with Peter about whom nothing is said concerning potential belief, even though he too examined (θεωρεῖ) the linen cloths and the facecloth (20:6–7).[295]

Yet, the faith of the Beloved Disciple precedes an ambiguous narratorial comment by the narrator: "For as yet, they did not understand the Scripture, that he must rise from the dead" (20:9). How is it that the lack of understanding of the disciples is mentioned immediately after the faith of the Beloved Disciple has been noted? What argumentative coherence is to be found in this section of the narrative?[296] O'Day suggests that the force of this aside is to signal that the faith of the Beloved Disciple remains incomplete at this stage, since the disciples have not yet seen the resurrected Christ, since Jesus has not

---

[288] So Conway, *Men and Women*, 189–90.

[289] Lincoln, *John*, 490.

[290] *Cf.* C. Traets, *Voir Jésus et le Père en Lui selon l'Évangile de Saint Jean* (Rome: Libreria editrice dell'Università Gregoriana, 1967), 22–23.

[291] Mollat, *Études*, 144.

[292] So *e.g.* Brown, *John*, 2:987; Carson, *John*, 638–39; Witherington, *John*, 325; Köstenberger, *John*, 564; Lincoln, *John*, 491.

[293] *Cf.* Schneiders, "Face Veil," 95–97; Byrne, "Beloved," 88–89. For Zumstein, *Jean (13–21)*, 272, n.20, "Le jeu intertextuel est clair: enlever les bandelettes et le suaire est indice de vie, mais alors que Lazare doit être libéré par d'autres, c'est sans le soutien d'un acteur humain que le Christ Joh s'est libéré de la tombe."

[294] So Zumstein, *Jean (13–21)*, 272, titles this "une foi pascale achevée […] Il croit à la seule vue du tombeau vide, c'est-à-dire à la seule vue de la radicale absence du Christ. […] Il anticipe ainsi la foi qui sera célébrée par le Christ devant Thomas (v. 29), la foi qui croit sans voir."

[295] Though Bultmann, *John*, 684, proposes that Peter also came to believe, since his unbelief would have been mentioned by the narrator otherwise.

[296] A common explanation of this phenomenon comes from redaction criticism. For instance, Schnelle, *Antidocetic*, 16–17, argues that "In a tomb tradition that originally spoke only of Peter (v. 3a: ἐξῆλθεν [he set out]), the evangelist inserts within the framework of an extensive redactional editing (vv. 2, 3b [καὶ ὁ ἄλλος μαθητὴς (and the other disciple)] ... 4, 5b [οὐ μέντοι εἰσῆθεν (but he did not go in)], 6, 8, 10) the person of the Beloved Disciple as ὁ ἄλλος μαθητὴς ὃν ἐφίλει ὁ 'Ιησοῦς [the other disciple, the one whom Jesus loved]."

yet ascended to his Father, and since the Spirit has not yet been given.[297] The problem with this suggestion is that the faith of the Beloved Disciple is not in any way undermined in 20:8. Thus, with Zumstein, it is better to understand this narratorial comment as accentuating two notions: (*i*) it emphasises that the Beloved Disciple was able to believe without having to base his belief on the testimony of Scripture; (*ii*) it explains Peter's silence, who, without the Scripture, was unable to make sense of the empty tomb.[298]

Faith, in the Fourth Gospel, can be attained without a prior understanding of Scripture. This is also the conclusion we have reached in an earlier section on the faith and understanding of the disciples as a group in the Fourth Gospel. What is extraordinary about the Beloved Disciple, however, is that though he had not yet gained an understanding of the Scripture "that he must rise from the dead," he still believed in Jesus' resurrection simply by noting the absence of Jesus' body from the tomb. As the narratorial aside indicates, for him as well as for the other disciples, full scriptural understanding came later.[299] In line with 2:22 and 12:16, 20:9 thus implicitly portrays the Beloved Disciple as later remembering the event of the empty tomb and understanding its meaning on the basis of Scripture. This, however, is not to undermine the quality of insight the Beloved Disciple gained from seeing the empty tomb, but rather to highlight it.

It should be noted, finally, that the faith of the Beloved Disciple, in this section, does not lead to witness at the time the narrative recounts. Even more, it has no effect on other characters and does not impact the action: "Then the disciples went back to their home" (20:10). If our proposal is correct regarding the lack of scriptural understanding of the Beloved Disciple, it may explain his attitude in 20:10. The Beloved Disciple believed but did not yet know what to make of this belief, he had no basis on which to build a full understanding of the resurrection. Moreover, the conclusion of this section leaves open the question of whether or not Peter will come to believe in the resurrection.[300]

As a whole, it is interesting that after the Beloved Disciple, as the narrator, addressed the readers with his post-Easter understanding of two scriptures that make sense of the event recounted (19:35–37), he is now portrayed as a character in the story that has not yet attained a Scripture-based understanding of the

---

[297] O'Day, "John," 841.

[298] Zumstein, *Jean (13–21)*, 273. This is also the conclusion of Brown, *Eastertime*, 69. *Pace* J. P. Heil, *Blood and Water: The Death and Resurrection of Jesus in John 18–21*, CBQMS 27 (Washington, DC: Catholic Biblical Association of America, 1995), 125: "That the beloved disciple believed in the resurrection of Jesus before 'they,' that is, Peter, Mary, and those for whom she speaks (20:2), understood the scripture that he must rise from the dead (20:9), implies that he, as the ideal, beloved disciple, already understood the scriptural necessity for the resurrection of Jesus."

[299] See the conclusion of this study for developments on this notion in dialogue with Bultmann.

[300] Lincoln, *John*, 491.

resurrection. Yet, his faith in the resurrection is highlighted. The prior characterisation of the Beloved Disciple having an intimate and faithful relationship
with Jesus and as being present in key events of the Passion narrative (13:23;
18:15; 19:26–27) prepared implied readers not to be surprised when this disciple attains belief in the resurrection solely on the evidence of the empty tomb.
The Beloved Disciple is here characterised as a perceptive witness who has
spiritual insights into this most foundational event,[301] a quality that again qualifies him in the eyes of implied readers to truthfully witness about Jesus.

6. "It is the Lord!" (21:7)

In this section of the narrative, implied readers find the Beloved Disciple together with others by the sea of Tiberias, where Jesus would again reveal himself to them (21:7). Once more, the Beloved Disciple is portrayed as a character
in the story. Seven disciples were present by the sea of Tiberias: "Simon Peter,
Thomas (called the twin), Nathanael of Cana in Galilee, the sons of Zebedee,
and two others of this disciples" (21:2). It is probable that the Beloved Disciple
is one of these "two others of his disciples" since he is also unnamed in the rest
of the narrative and is identified clearly in 21:7.

Upon Peter's initiative, these seven disciples decide to go fishing, and that
night, they caught nothing (21:3).[302] In the early hours of the day, the narrator
lets readers know that Jesus was standing on the shore but that "the disciples
did not know that it was Jesus" (21:4). Jesus and the disciples then dialogued
about the result of their night of fishing, and a miraculous catch of fish ensued
(21:4–6). It is at this point that the Beloved Disciple tells Peter: "It is the Lord!"
(21:7a).[303] Although he too seems to have needed a sign to recognise Jesus, the
Beloved Disciple's insight into the identity of Jesus clearly contrasts with the
other disciples' ignorance, especially that of Peter (*cf.* 13:28).[304] As proposed by
Hooker, it is certainly the Beloved Disciple's intimacy with Jesus, as described
earlier in the Fourth Gospel, that made this discovery possible.[305] Moloney suggests that since Peter and the Beloved Disciple, after encountering the empty
tomb, simply went back to their homes (20:10), it is the first time that they see
the risen Lord. There, the Beloved Disciple had believed without seeing Jesus
so that "by bringing Jesus back into the lives of these disciples the author suggests that the Beloved Disciple no longer falls under the blessing of 20:29. He

---

[301] Bauckham, *Eyewitnesses*, 399.

[302] As mentioned by Lincoln, *John*, 511, this fishing metaphor points beyond itself to the
disciples' mission.

[303] For Moloney, *John*, 552: "The words of the Beloved Disciple must be given their full
post-Easter significance. He confesses his belief in the presence of Jesus as the risen Lord (*ho
kyrios estin*)."

[304] For Léon-Dufour, *Lecture*, 4:279, the implied author here shows once more "le disciple
supérieur à Pierre dans l'intelligence de Jésus."

[305] M. Hooker, *Endings: Invitations to Discipleship* (Peabody, MA: Hendrickson, 2003), 76.

believes in 21:7a because he sees Jesus."[306] Moloney's proposal can only be
correct on the basis of the (unlikely) possibility that these two disciples were
not present when Jesus appeared to his disciples in 20:19–29. Yet, the Beloved
Disciple is not described as believing because he sees Jesus, but because of the
miraculous catch of fish, that is, because Jesus revealed himself (21:1). Thus,
though it is possible that the implied author wished to make explicit that these
two disciples also encountered and witnessed the risen Jesus, his purpose was
not necessarily to show that the Beloved Disciple believed on account of seeing Jesus. Once more, it is his ability to perceive truth that is underlined in the
narrative.

It is the first time in the Fourth Gospel that the Beloved Disciple actually
speaks (here, to Peter) and that he has a real impact on the action of the narrative. As a result of the Beloved Disciple's declaration, Peter throws himself into
the water to join Jesus on the shore, followed by the other disciples on the boat
(21:7b–8). In this section, the characterisation of the Beloved Disciple is thus
developed so that, contrary to the sections studied above, the spiritual insight
gained by this disciple actually impacts the action and other characters. In sharing his insight with Peter, the character of the Beloved Disciple becomes both
witness and mediator.[307] Implied readers knew that, during the story time, the
Beloved Disciple was capable of special insights based on signs (20:8) and that
he later was able to bear true witness as expressed in this narrative (19:35–37).
In this section, implied readers discover that he had a witnessing activity even
within the story time, the ministry of Jesus as the author of the Fourth Gospel
recounts it. As a result, his qualification as a witness of truth is enhanced even
more in their eyes.

7. "If it is my will that he remain until I come back..." (21:20–25)

Jesus revealed himself for the third time after he was raised from the dead
(21:14), and he rehabilitated Peter (21:15–19). The following section is a conversation between Jesus and Peter about the Beloved Disciple (21:20–23). This
disciple thus appears for the last time in the narrative, through the eyes of Peter.
Interestingly, Jesus has just told Peter to "follow me" (21:19), so that the repetition of ἀκολουθεῖν once more introduces a comparison between Peter and the
Beloved Disciple: "Peter turned and saw the disciple whom Jesus loved following them" (21:20).[308] The disciple is thus described as a follower of Jesus to the
very end of the narrative, so that "la suivance à laquelle [Peter] est appelé deux
fois durant son entretien avec le Ressuscité (v. 19.22), est supposée réalisée
par le disciple bien-aimé."[309] Even more, the narrator recalls that disciple's role

---

[306] Moloney, *John*, 550.
[307] Conway, *Men and Women*, 154.
[308] Conway, *Men and Women*, 184.
[309] Zumstein, *Jean (13–21)*, 314.

in 13:23 ("reclining at the table close to him"). That both the first and last appearances of the Beloved Disciple mention his intimacy with Jesus, forming an
inclusio, is certainly not coincidental. The implied author intends to situate this
characteristic as central to the Beloved Disciple's portrayal in this narrative.[310]
As mentioned in the study of 13:21–26, it is this intimacy that qualifies the Beloved Disciple to bear true witness.

Seeing the Beloved Disciple behind them, Peter asks Jesus "Lord, what
about this man?" (21:21b) most certainly in an attempt to compare their fate.
"Will the Beloved Disciple also die as a martyr?" is in essence what Peter asks
Jesus.[311] Quite abruptly, yet enigmatically, Jesus answers: "If it is my will that
he remain until I come, what is it to you? Follow me!" (21:22). Jesus does not
have a particular prediction to make about the Beloved Disciple's fate, yet the
possibility of the Beloved Disciple's continual remaining until the *parousia* is
underlined. But through this saying, Jesus primarily desires that Peter focus on
his own discipleship and particular role, that of shepherding (21:15, 16, 17).[312]
As mentioned by many interpreters, Jesus' rebuke must also be taken as referring to the different kinds of ministry with which Peter and the Beloved Disciple are entrusted. While Peter is portrayed as a shepherd who will die a martyr
death, the Beloved Disciple is the one who abides with Jesus and is a true witness to the works and life of Jesus.[313] These roles need to be understood neither
in opposition to one another, nor of unequal value. Jesus himself emphasises
that these disciples are given these particular responsibilities in accordance
with his sovereign will (21:24).

In a narratorial aside, readers learn that these words of Jesus later triggered
an issue "among the brothers"[314] (21:23a). These words had been interpreted as
a prediction that the Beloved Disciple would not die. The narrator, therefore,
wishes to clarify Jesus' statement by mentioning what Jesus did not say ("yet
Jesus did not say to him that he was not to die"), and by restating Jesus' answer
to Peter (21:23b). At issue is the status of the Beloved Disciple. Indeed, this
aside suggests that the Beloved Disciple may have already died, so that the narrator emphasises that the importance of that disciple is not diminished by the

---

[310] Lindars, *Gospel of John*, 638.

[311] Blaine Jr., *Peter*, 176.

[312] Claussen, "John 21," 66, helpfully proposes that "Jesus' harsh response to Peter regarding the fate of the Beloved Disciple (21:21–22) clarifies that the recommissioning of the one is
not meant to dishonor the other."

[313] So *e.g.*, Quast, *Figures*, 153–156; Lincoln, *John*, 520–21; Chennattu, *Discipleship*, 176.
Recently, Bauckham, *Eyewitnesses*, 395, proposed: "[…] Peter and the Beloved Disciple represent two different kinds of discipleship: active service and perceptive witness. The story of
these two disciples, as it is told especially from ch. 13 to ch. 21, shows how each became qualified for these two different kinds of discipleship."

[314] The expression "among the brothers" suggests that it refers to members of the post-
paschal community (*cf.* Zumstein, *Jean (13–21)*, 314; Brown, *John*, 2:1110).

fact (or the manner[315]) of his death. Likewise, the credibility or reliability of Jesus' words is also at stake, so that the narrator emphasises the exact formulation of Jesus' declaration.[316] Jesus never denied the Beloved Disciple's death, but he affirmed that he held that disciple's destiny in his own hands: it is the Lord who would fix both the length and mode of presence of this disciple.[317]

The narrator's argument against this apparent 'rumour' (ὁ λόγος) does not stop there: what he says about the Beloved Disciple in 21:24 is intrinsically linked to 21:23.[318] According to 21:24, the author of the Fourth Gospel (ὁ γράψας ταῦτα) is none other than the Beloved Disciple. Thus, when the narrator uses the first person plural at the end of this verse to emphasise the veracity of the Beloved Disciple's testimony (καὶ οἴδαμεν ὅτι ἀληθὴς αὐτοῦ ἡ μαρτυρία ἐστίν), he distinguishes himself and those he represents (*cf.* 1:14) from the person responsible for the content of the narrative, that is, the Beloved Disciple. But as noticed by Zumstein, the verbs are conjugated in different tenses: the writing of the Gospel belongs to the past (aorist participle), while the affirmation of the narrator "we know" (οἴδαμεν), together with the activity of the witness (ὁ μαθητὴς ὁ μαρτυρῶν περὶ τούτων; ὅτι ἀληθὴς αὐτοῦ ἡ μαρτυρία ἐστίν), are present. This serves to reinforce the point that the hand responsible for the writing of the Gospel is deceased, while the activity of the Beloved Disciple as witness and the value of his testimony as true are continuous: they remain.[319] Thus, once implied readers relate 21:24 to Jesus' saying in 21:22, they understand that Jesus' declaration was indeed accurate. Though the Beloved Disciple has died, his testimony remains present until the *Parousia* through the written testimony that he left behind: "L'Écriture le fait vivre jusqu'à la fin."[320] Therefore, "The Beloved Disciple is being claimed as

---

[315] Several commentators suggest that, contrary to Peter, the Beloved Disciple died of natural causes (*e.g.*, S. Agourides, "Peter and John in the Fourth Gospel," in *Studia Evangelica IV: Papers Presented to the Third International Congress on New Testament Studies held at Christ Church, Oxford, 1965*, ed. by F. L. Cross (Berlin: Akademie-Verlag, 1968), 7; Lincoln, *John*, 521). In any case, "the overall effect of vv. 20–23 is to downplay any comparison between the deaths of the two disciples" (Quast, *Figures*, 155).

[316] Lincoln, *John*, 522.

[317] Zumstein, *Jean (13–21)*, 315.

[318] *Cf.* Zumstein, *Jean (13–21)*, 315; Barrett, *John*, 716; *pace* I. de la Potterie, "Le témoin qui demeure: le disciple que Jésus aimait," *Bib* 67 (1986): 349–50, who structures 21:20–25 in three parts: 21:20–21; 21:22–23; and 21:24–25.

[319] Zumstein, *Jean (13–21)*, 315, n.33.

[320] Zumstein, *Jean (13–21)*, 315. Together with Lincoln, *John*, 523, it is important to note that "γράψας, 'has written', is best taken loosely in the sense of having instigated or been responsible for the writing of the bulk of the narrative rather than actually having penned it" (see also *e.g.* Moloney, *John*, 561; Brown, *John*, 2:1123). For Bernard, *John*, 2:713, the aorist participial form of the verb (ὁ γράψας) could have a causative sense: "he had these things written."

the authority for the distinctive perspective that has shaped and pervaded the witness of the narrative."[321]

The narrative ends in 21:25 with a disclaimer of sorts, where the narrator expresses that this narrative is only a selection of interpreted events during Jesus' ministry. Implicitly, he is saying that the activity of the Beloved Disciple as witness far surpassed the selection found in the present narrative. We may paraphrase the narrator as follows: "Now there are also many other things in the life of Jesus about which the Beloved Disciple witnessed. Were all of the Beloved Disciple's authoritative testimonies about Jesus to be written, the world itself could not contain the books that would be written."

As a whole, this section provides an appropriate closure to the narrative as well as the portrayal of the Beloved Disciple. The writing down of the narrative and the testimony of the Beloved Disciple that it contains are true. As Jesus had implicitly expressed in 21:22, that disciple "remains" through the written testimony that composed the Fourth Gospel. Because he has followed Jesus faithfully and intimately, the Beloved Disciple is qualified to bear witness continuously about the truth and to call readers to align themselves with the truth (19:35, 20:30–31).

Throughout the so-called "Book of Glory" (from chap. 13 to chap. 21), the Beloved Disciple has been portrayed as having a close relationship with Jesus: he reclines next to Jesus at the table (13:23, 25) and has access to information regarding the identity of the betrayer (13:26), he follows Jesus into the courtyard (18:15) and remains with him during his crucifixion (19:26). Such proximity is of course emphasised by the epithet given him in the narrative: he is "the disciple Jesus loved," so that implied readers are consistently reminded that the two share real intimacy. These two characteristics (closeness, intimacy), strongly implying faith on the part of the Beloved Disciple, form the basis upon which is developed the idea that the Beloved Disciple is a qualified true witness of Jesus' life and works. Indeed, his intimacy with Jesus enabled this disciple to be portrayed not only as an eyewitness of key events of Jesus' earthly ministry (13:21–30; 19:25–27, 31–35; 20:2–8; 21:3–13), thus enhancing the credibility of his testimony, but also as being able to perceive spiritual truth (13:25–26; 20:8; 21:7). Such qualification and credibility are then enhanced dramatically when Jesus calls him to become his successor as "son", thus also providing for the welfare of his followers who will be the beneficiaries of the Beloved Disciple's witnessing ministry (19:26–27). This portrayal of the Beloved Disciple as a character in the narrative is, in turn, mirrored in several references to his post-paschal witnessing activity that the narrator qualifies as 'true' (19:35–37; 21:24). Clearly, therefore, the implied author wishes to authenticate the Beloved Disciple's testimony in portraying him as a character who is qualified to wit-

---

[321] Lincoln, *John*, 523.

ness about the truth, and who, in turn, can be trusted by implied readers who are called to put their faith in Jesus on the basis of his testimony (19:35; 20:30–31).

Yet, it was noted that, in one particular instance (20:9), the Beloved Disciple had not yet gained a full scriptural understanding of the resurrection. This, however, is not meant to undermine his perceptiveness or qualification as a witness. Rather, the Beloved Disciple is here portrayed as a character who, like the other disciples, needed after Jesus' glorification to remember events of Jesus' earthly ministry through the lense of Scripture to understand their significance and be able to communicate them. Thus, since the Fourth Gospel repeatedly makes use of Scripture to interpret events of Jesus' life (not least in 19:36–37), the qualification of the Beloved Disciple is actually enhanced: as the 'author' responsible for the content of the Fourth Gospel, he exemplifies for the sake of implied readers a true, post-Easter scriptural interpretation of the life and works of Jesus.

Culpepper noticed an important characteristic of the Beloved Disciple that has not been mentioned yet: the references to this disciple in the Fourth Gospel strongly suggest similarity of role between him and the Paraclete as described by Jesus (14:17, 26; 16:13–14). Like the Paraclete, the Beloved Disciple has made Jesus known to those who received his testimony. He has taught, reminded, and borne true witness about Jesus: "The Beloved Disciple is not the Paraclete but he has embodied the Paraclete for others and shaped their understanding of the work of the Holy Spirit in their midst."[322] Just as the Paraclete was to become Jesus' successor in the trial of the truth, so is the Beloved Disciple called to be Jesus' human successor who bears witness to the truth and calls people to align themselves on the side of the positive verdict of life.

The characterisation of the Beloved Disciple is overwhelmingly positive in the Fourth Gospel. This is particularly evidenced by the continual comparisons between him and Peter. The Beloved Disciple contrasts positively with Peter in that he remains faithful to Jesus (even during Jesus' trial and crucifixion), and in that he is given exemplary insights into spiritual truth (*e.g.*, he is the first to believe in the resurrection of Jesus and to recognise him by the sea of Tiberias). Thus, though some scholars remain unconvinced,[323] there are good reasons to affirm that the implied author has portrayed him as "the disciple par

---

[322] Culpepper, *Anatomy*, 123.

[323] *E.g.*, Bauckham, "Beloved Disciple," 36, for whom the Beloved Disciples is only superior to the other disciples in respect to the specific role given him by Jesus, namely, that of being a true witness about Jesus. One could then consider Peter to be superior to the Beloved Disciple in regard to his specific role as shepherd, a role that is not mentioned regarding the Beloved Disciple. Yet, since the Beloved Disciple always shows deep perception and faithful following of Jesus throughout the narrative, and since both Peter and him are disciples but both are not shepherds, it is difficult to see how his discipleship could be regarded in any way less than ideal!

excellence,"[324] "the ideal disciple,"[325] or even "the paradigm of discipleship."[326] Together with the elusive aspect of that disciple,[327] the fact that everything that is said about him serves his characterisation as an "ideal witness" gives credibility to Thatcher's proposition according to which the Beloved Disciple is a "legendary expansion of a real person who was a key player early in the Johannine tradition."[328]

E. Mary Magdalene

Several commentators have proposed that the character called 'Mary Magdalene' (Μαρία ἡ Μαγδαληνή) in the Fourth Gospel is none other than Mary of Bethany.[329] Such a proposal is attractive, since in this case, Mary would already have had a prominent role in the teaching of Jesus about the resurrection (Chap. 11). However, nothing in the text indicates such an identification between these two "Marys."[330] On the contrary, it would be surprising that the same woman would be called both "of Magdala" and "of Bethany" since these towns are respectively in Galilee and Judea.[331] Thus, most likely, Mary Magdalene appears for the first time in the narrative at the cross (19:25), together with other women and the Beloved Disciple. She then appears in two more scenes, in the following chapter (20:1–2, 11–18), thus concluding her role in the narrative. There is no doubt that the implied author of the Fourth Gospel, despite the relatively small length of narrative space she occupies, intended to give Mary a place of choice amongst the many minor characters of the narrative. Indeed, Mary is present at very strategic moments of the story: the cross and the garden of the empty tomb. Yet, with such a late appearance in the narrative, one might wonder why a section on the development of this character's faith and understanding in the narrative of the Fourth Gospel is necessary in this study. Moreover, one might question whether Mary Magdalene should be considered as one of Jesus' disciples.

---

[324] Collins, "Characters," 367.

[325] So *e.g.*, Conway, *Men and Women*, 178; Davies, *Rhetoric*, 341.

[326] *E.g.*, Culpepper, *Anatomy*, 121.

[327] Tovey, *Narrative*, 124–25.

[328] T. Thatcher, "The Legend of the Beloved Disciple," in *Jesus in Johannine Tradition*, ed. by R. T. Fortna and T. Thatcher (Louisville, KY: Westminster John Knox, 2001), 96. See also Lincoln, "Beloved Disciple," 18–19, for whom the Beloved Disciple's role in the narrative constitutes a "literary device." *Pace* Bauckham, *Eyewitnesses*, 386, for whom the portrayal of the Beloved Disciple as "eyewitness" must be understood as a serious claim to historiographic status.

[329] *E.g.*, Bernard, *John*, 2:657; B. Lindars, "The Composition of John 20," *NTS* 7 (1961): 143.

[330] As noted by E. L. Bode, *The First Easter Morning: The Gospel Accounts of the Women's Visit to the Tomb of Jesus*, AnBib 45 (Rome: Biblical Institute Press, 1970), 72.

[331] As F. Bovon, "Le privilège pascal de Marie-Madeleine," *NTS* 30 (1984): 50, remarks.

Traditionally, Jesus' disciples during his earthly ministry have been thought of as exclusively male characters, not least because of the importance of the twelve apostles in the Synoptic Tradition, whose lists do not mention any women (Matt. 10:1–4; Mk. 3:13–19; Lk. 6:12–16). However, as we have seen earlier, the implied author of the Fourth Gospel generally prefers to speak of Jesus' disciples as an unspecified group, so that "the Twelve" are only mentioned in passing in the narrative (6:67, 70, 71; 20:24), without giving any full list of their members. In fact, though these references are not necessarily insignificant, no clear literary function seems to be ascribed to this group in the narrative.[332] Most likely, "the Twelve" are thus distinct, though included, in the larger and unspecified group of Jesus' disciples. The presence of women in such an unspecified group of disciples, therefore, should not be thought surprising.[333] However, Setzer proposed that Mary is not understood as a disciple in the narrative.[334] Her argument is based on 21:14, where the narrator says: "This was now the third time that Jesus was revealed to the disciples after he was raised from the dead." Setzer correctly argues that the most likely candidates for these revelations are 20:26, 20:29, and 21:1, thus logically leaving Mary out of the group of the disciples since she actually was the first to encounter the risen Jesus in 20:11–18.[335] However, the narrator appears to underline Jesus' revelations to the disciples as a *group* in 21:14, which certainly explains why he only speaks of three such occurrences.

As for the rationale for treating a character appearing at such a late stage in the narrative, it will be shown that her character is narratologically pivotal as far as the themes of faith and understanding are concerned. Indeed, Mary appears both just before and just after Jesus' resurrection so that a focus on these two episodes may give insights into potential movement in her faith and understanding. In fact, together with the Beloved Disciple, Mary is the only disciple to proffer continuous witness between the cross and the resurrection of Jesus. As argued by Culpepper, the characterisation of Mary Magdalene deals with the relationship that believers in the story have with the pre–Easter and the post-Easter Jesus. Thus, the narrative function of Mary Magdalene may be

---

[332] On a historical level, however, the mention of "the Twelve" in the Fourth Gospel most likely betrays the author of the Fourth Gospel's use of traditional material, not least the Synoptic Gospels (see Lincoln, *John*, 26–39).

[333] After her study of the character of "Mary Magdalene as Disciple" (pp. 161–62, drawing similarities between the narrative of the first disciples of Jesus in 1:35–51 and Jesus' interaction with Mary in chap. 20), E. A. de Boer, *The Gospel of Mary: Beyond a Gnostic and a Biblical Mary Magdalene*, JSNTSup 260 (London/New York, NY: T. & T. Clark, 2004), 178, concludes that "In John, Mary Magdalene may perhaps be implied in the masculine plural of he [*sic.*] word disciples."

[334] C. Setzer, "Excellent Women: Female Witness to the Resurrection," *JBL* 116 (1997): 268.

[335] For Setzer, "Excellent," 268, this is indicative of "some discrepancy between Mary Magdalene's pivotal place as witness and her lack of status relative to the other disciples."

to teach implied readers how this character attained faith in the resurrection of Jesus and thus to express something about what faith in the risen Lord entails.[336]

1. "But standing by the cross ... Mary Magdalene." (19:25)

The presence of Mary Magdalene at the cross seems, at first, to lack significance. Nothing is said about her prior to this event in the narrative, and, in this particular section, nothing but her name is mentioned: while the other characters are presented in their relationship to someone else, Mary is not. Even more, Mary Magdalene is the last woman being introduced in the list, though the narrator may simply list them in order of degree of kinship to Jesus, not in order of importance.[337] She does not speak, and as a whole, this section (19:25–27) focuses on the new *familia Dei* that Jesus establishes before his death. Yet, it may be argued that the very fact of her presence in this section is more important than many scholars suppose, even though they intend to study her character in the narrative.[338] First, Mary Magdalene's presence contrasts positively with the disciples' absence, especially those who have been followers of Jesus from the very beginning (*e.g.*, Peter, Andrew). Contrary to those who have in cowardly fashion abandoned Jesus, she stands before the crucified Jesus. As such, she already expresses her faithfulness to him, so that in the narrative Mary Magdalene begins her journey of faith where others seem to have interrupted theirs.[339] Second, and most importantly, in being associated at the cross with the Mother of Jesus and the Beloved Disciple, she is portrayed as being a true friend of Jesus (15:15), a member of his fold who "follow Jesus, for they know his name" (10:5).[340] By her presence during this fateful event, she witnesses the reality of Jesus' death on the cross,[341] and she potentially incorporates the *familia Dei*, called to continue the work inaugurated by Jesus himself.[342]

---

[336] Culpepper, *Anatomy*, 143–44.

[337] M. Hengel, "Maria Magdalena und die Frauen als Zeugen," in *Abraham unser Vater: Juden und Christen im Gespräch über die Bibel. Festschrift für Otto Michel zum 60*, ed. by O. Betz, M. Hengel, and P. Schmidt, AGJU 5 (Leiden: Brill, 1963), 250.

[338] *E.g.*, Collins, *These Things*, 33: "She appears in two passages of the Fourth Gospel, John 20, 1–2 and 11–18." See also Koester, *Symbolism*, 68–70.

[339] So Lee, *Flesh*, 222.

[340] Marchadour, *Personnages*, 117–18.

[341] See *e.g.* P. A. Kerrigan, "Jn. 19,25–27 in Light of Johannine Theology and the Old Testament," *Anton* 35 (1960): 375. As mentioned by Léon-Dufour, *Lecture*, 4:137, the expression "the cross of Jesus" in 20:25 (where the mention of Jesus is redundant in this context) may thus indicate the historical and theological importance of the death of Jesus, "le mystère auquel ces êtres communient." For Bultmann, *John*, 672, "the evangelist is not interested in them as witnesses of the crucifixion; his interest centres on only one of them, the mother of Jesus." But then, it is unclear why the evangelist even mentions the other women. If the evangelist does focus primarily on the Mother of Jesus in this section (together with the Beloved Disciple), the mention of Mary Magdalene and the two other women (the mother of Jesus' sister and Mary the wife of Clopas) remains, even derivatively, symbolically significant. For the different arguments regarding the number of women present at the cross, see Maccini, *Testimony*, 185–86.

[342] S. Ruschmann, *Maria von Magdalena im Johannesevangelium. Jüngerin-Zeugin-Leb-*

Clearly, her first appearance in the narrative is worth noting. Even if her faith is not explicitly mentioned in this verse, her very presence at the cross assumes it. This point is also reinforced in light of Mary's later announcement in 20:2, 13, when, still unaware of Jesus' resurrection, she considered him "the Lord." In any case, though nothing of her understanding of what is taking place at the cross can be deduced from the text, her loyalty to Jesus is evident. Yet, this scene becomes truly significant when it is put in relation to Mary' later appearances in the narrative, that is, when she discovers the empty tomb, and when she meets and dialogues with the risen Jesus.[343]

2. "Mary Magdalene came to the tomb early" (20:1–2)

Chapter 20:1–18 is composed of two stories (20:1–10; 11–18) linked together by the presence of Mary Magdalene, first in vv. 1–2, then in vv. 11–18. Thus, not only does Mary remain with Jesus in death, but she also follows him to the tomb in the early morning. Indeed, she discovers the empty tomb and will be the first to see the risen Jesus. Such primacy should not go unnoticed,[344] and most certainly indicates that the implied author wishes to communicate, through her

---

ensbotin, NTAbh 40 (Münster: Aschendorff, 2002), 211, and Marchadour, *Personnages*, 117, strongly favour this argument, while Brodie, *John*, 548–49, adamantly rejects it. For him, Mary is not involved in the emergence of the new grouping, since "she just stood there" and as such, "[…] forms a contrast with the mother – as do the Jewish leaders who rejected Jesus' inscription (Schnackenburg, 3:278) – and the implication is that, in this gospel at least, she in some way represents those Jews who did not believe." This conclusion, however, in addition to being unwarranted by the text, does not make sense of Mary's presence *with* the other women and the Beloved Disciple. How could she represent unbelieving Jews while being at the same time associated with these other characters? While, we may not assert that Mary *de facto* incorporated the *familia Dei* through her presence at the cross, such presence can however only be seen positively.

[343] Marchadour, *Personnages*, 120. See also Mollat, *Études*, 136, for whom "cette concentration sur le personnage de Marie de Magdala concourt à dramatiser le récit."

[344] As Dodd, *Interpretation*, 440, does in passing over the women's significance in the post-resurrection scenes in the four Gospels. Neither should it be downplayed, as in Lagrange, *Jean*, 449, for whom Jesus' appearance to Mary is only preparatory for the appearances that are truly significant for the church, that is, appearances to male apostles. See also Barrett, *John*, 466, who asserts that chap. 20 intends to give the central place to the Beloved Disciple, thus reducing the significance of the Mary to almost nothing. *Contra* these positions, see *e.g.*, W. Thompson, *The Jesus Debate* (New York, NY: Paulist Press, 1985), 232: "The point is still secure: in the tradition, women are the first witnesses, regardless of any role that Peter may play or may have come to play in the Church." See also Bovon, "Privilège pascal," 51–52; E. Schüssler-Fiorenza, *In Memory of Her: A Feminist Theological Reconstruction of Christian Origins* (New York, NY: Crossroad, 1983), 304–05; Setzer, "Excellent," 259–72; G. O'Collins and D. Kendall, "Mary Magdalene as a Major Witness to Jesus' Resurrection," *TS* 48 (1987): 645; and Maccini, *Testimony*, 225–33.

characterisation, something of importance about Mary Magdalene's relationship to Jesus.[345]

"On the first day of the week," Mary arrives at the tomb while it was still
"dark." The implied author does not state Mary's motives for coming to the
tomb early,[346] giving a sense of vagueness to her characterisation and to the
scene he is about to depict.[347] However, the mentions of the "first day of the
week" and of the early morning darkness indicate that the upcoming scene is
highly meaningful. "The first day of the week" certainly sets the tone for understanding the scene as a new beginning.[348] The mention of the early morning
darkness is more difficult to assess. For de la Potterie, it indicates that the disciples (presently represented by Mary) were unprepared, "in a spiritual night,"
before the experience they were about to have of Jesus' resurrected body.[349]
However, it is unlikely that the early morning's darkness has the same symbolic force as the darkness of night in the Fourth Gospel. It has been argued
throughout the present study that the disciples have believed from very early
on in this narrative but that they had neither understood nor believed what Jesus said about his resurrection. It is probably in that sense that they can still
be considered in 'darkness.'[350] In any case, as Bouyer states, to mention the
darkness implicitly announces that light is coming![351] Thus, these two mentions
of "the first day of the week" and of darkness can be understood as temporal
indicators that an event of great importance is about to occur in the narrative.[352]

---

[345] For Lee, "Easter Faith," 41: "[…] the resurrection narrative begins with a 'beloved disciple' who has shown herself faithful, who has seen Jesus' life-giving glory in death and whose
fidelity has brought her to the tomb."

[346] Mollat, *Études*, 136–37: "Jean ne précise pas le but de sa venue au tombeau […] La scène
de Marie en larme à l'entrée du sépulcre autorise à dire, avec Loisy, qu'elle vient pour le visiter
et y pleurer."

[347] See J. Beaude, "De Marie de Magdala à la Madeleine, la formation d'une figure mystique," in *Variations johanniques*, ed. by B. Dominique, C. Coulot, and A. Lion, Parole présente
(Paris: Cerf/CERIT, 1989), 165, for whom the author "[…] ne fournit aucune lumière sur les
raisons et significations de sa présence personnelle et exclusive. Au contraire, si elles existent,
il les brouille et n'en propose en définitive aucune, il dispose plutôt chaque lecteur à s'en donner lui-même."

[348] *E.g.*, Blanquart, *Premier jour*, 19.

[349] de la Potterie, "Foi pascale," 31–32.

[350] F. J. Matera, "John 20:1–18," *Int* 43 (1989): 403: "The darkness, a Johannine image,
suggests the situation of Mary and every person who does not dwell in the light of resurrection
faith."

[351] L. Bouyer, *Le quatrième évangile. Introduction à l'évangile de Jean, traduction et commentaire*, BVC 6 (Tournai/Paris: Casterman/Maredsous, 1955), 230.

[352] Blanquart, *Premier jour*, 20. N. T. Wright, *The Resurrection of the Son of God. Christian
Origins and the Question of God, vol. 3* (Minneapolis, MN: Fortress, 2003), 666–67, proposes
that these two indicators are part of the frame formed by 1:1–18 and the whole of chapter 20. In
his understanding, the mentions of the 'first day' and of 'darkness' indicate that the whole story
of the Fourth Gospel is "about the new creation in Jesus," with Easter being the start of this new

As implied readers will soon gather, this "first day of the week" is also the day of Jesus' resurrection and that of the disciples' belief in his risen-ness.

In this context, Mary sees that "the stone had been taken away from the tomb" (20:1). Mary is thus the first witness of the empty tomb in the narrative, though the text only mentions that she saw the stone rolled away from the tomb. However, the next verse (20:2) clearly indicates that she drew from this sight that her Lord was absent from the tomb.[353] For the implied reader, the use of the passive ἠρμένον by the narrator potentially hints at the action of God.[354] Yet, Mary's first reaction is not to go into the tomb and consider the evidence. This she will do later (20:11), after having run to tell the news to Simon Peter and the other disciple. The narrator does not say what went through her mind as she ran toward the disciples, though it will appear that she clearly did not think of the resurrection.[355]

Her announcement is interesting: "They have taken the Lord out of the tomb, and we do not know where they have laid him." Mary's choice of pronouns is rather curious: who are "they", and why does she use the first person plural to speak of what *she* does not know? Several identities for *they* have been proposed, *e.g.* Joseph and Nicodemus, the Roman soldiers, grave robbers, and 'the Jews."[356] Most probably, however, the third person plural is here impersonal and equivalent to a passive, in a manner recalling Hebrew and Aramaic usage.[357] It is thus probably fruitless to ask who are the subjects of this verb. The sense of Mary's announcement is: "The Lord has been taken out of the tomb." The first person plural in Mary's announcement deserves more attention. For Maccini, it can be understood as (*i*) a Johannine idiom that is not a plural, (*ii*) an ancient mode of expression that is not a true plural, (*iii*) a true plural that reflects the presence of other women, and (*iv*) a link with or trace of the Synoptic

---

creation: "Reading chapter 20 in the light of the Prologue, we are thus to understand that Jesus' death and resurrection have together affected for the disciples the new birth which was spoken of in 1.13 and 3.1–13." However, Wright is not convincing as throughout the narrative, the 'light' is Jesus himself, and 'darkness' is contrasted with the light, thus primarily representing the absence of Jesus (*e.g.*, to walk in darkness is to walk without the light; 3:19; 8:12; 12:46). Thus, it is probable that the mention of 'darkness' in 20:1 refers to Jesus' absence, while 'the first day of the week' may indicate his imminent return. Clearly, as mentioned by Moloney, *John*, 518, darkness can also be associated with "unfaith" in the narrative, but in the present context, if there is lack of faith, it is simply faith in the resurrection of Jesus (not a total absence of belief in Jesus). With Maccini, *Testimony*, 208, it is thus better to link this 'darkness' with the ensuing narrative, *i.e.*, Mary's "inability to perceive the significance of the empty tomb."

[353] Mollat, *Études*, 138: "Marie de Magdala a-t-elle vu que le tombeau était vide? Jean ne le précise pas. Le verbe dont il se sert (*blepei*) signifierait plutôt qu'elle a aperçu seulement la Pierre mise de côté. Elle en a conclu à l'enlèvement du Seigneur."

[354] Mollat, *Études*, 138.

[355] Mollat, *Études*, 118.

[356] See discussion in P. S. Minear, "'We Don't Know Where...' John 20:2," *Int* 30 (1976): 126.

[357] So Barrett, *John*, 475, 562–63.

Tradition, sources, or Gospels, in which more than one woman goes to the tomb.[358] Leaving aside the historical explanations for this plural form,[359] Maccini's third hypothesis certainly gets close to the mark. Indeed, the representative value of the first person plural in the narrative of the Fourth Gospel probably continues to bear weight in this verse (*cf.* 1:14; 3:11; 4:22; 9:31), thus leaving implied readers a potential narratological explanation. But if this is so, Mary's declaration is indicative of the state of ignorance in which she, other women, and certainly also the disciples as a whole, find themselves before the risen Jesus reveals himself to them in the narrative. It is not the first time in the narrative that disciples and other characters use the verb οἴδαμεν in a representative manner (3:1, 11; 9:31). In particular, Mary's admission of ignorance is reminiscent of Thomas' "Lord, we do not know where you are going" in 14:5. Just as the disciples prior to the cross were ignorant of Jesus' destination to his Father, so Mary, confronted with Jesus' absence, represents the continuing ignorance on the part of the disciples.[360]

Thus, despite Jesus' explicit teaching, resurrection is, for her as for her fellow disciples, not an option that comes to mind. For de la Potterie, "Cette insistance de l'évangéliste sur l'ignorance des premiers témoins est frappante: il veut souligner leur impréparation totale à l'événement. Ils ne s'attendaient pas à la résurrection."[361] Yet, Mary's ignorance is counterbalanced by her use of the title τὸν κύριον to speak of Jesus. Though the narrator has already used such a title in 6:23 and 11:2, it is the first instance of its use by a character in the story (see also 20:16, 18, 20:28; 21:7).[362] For Conway, "These late appearances of ὁ κύριος may suggest that the use of this title is only appropriate after the resurrection"[363] in which case, Mary spoke more than she knew, giving implied readers a new hint at what characters of the story were about to experience as the risen Jesus revealed himself to them.

So far in the depiction of Mary's faith and understanding, what has often been noted regarding other disciples is also true of her characterisation. Though she was obviously attached to Jesus, being with him at the cross and visiting the tomb on "the first day of the week," she had yet to understand that Jesus could rise, and indeed already had risen. Her lack of knowledge concerning the location of Jesus' body is indicative of her lack of understanding and faith in

---

[358] Maccini, *Testimony*, 209.

[359] See Lincoln, *John*, 489, for the most likely.

[360] Conway, *Men and Women*, 187. For O'Day, "John," 840, "Mary understands herself to be expressing the puzzle of the empty tomb for all of Jesus' followers, not for herself alone."

[361] de la Potterie, "Foi pascale," 30.

[362] It should be noted that other characters have used the vocative κύριε as a respectful form of address (4:11, 15, 19, 49; 5:7; 6:34, 68; 9:38; 11:3, 12, 21, 27, 32, 34, 39; 13:6, 9, 25, 36, 37; 14:5, 8, 22; and even Mary Magdalene in 20:15, talking to the one she thought was the gardener).

[363] Conway, *Men and Women*, 187.

the risen-ness of Jesus. As such, she is representative of other believers in the narrative who have yet to believe in the resurrection. Her faith and theirs still needs to develop to include belief in the good news of Easter.[364]

3. *"I have seen the Lord!" (20:11–18)*

The third scene in which Mary Magdalene appears is obviously linked to the preceding two. In 20:11, we find Mary once again at the tomb, weeping, after Peter and the other disciple have left the scene (20:10). Thus, Mary shows persistence, going back to the tomb, apparently by herself.[365] Indeed, as mentioned by Conway, "Her reintroduction stands in contrast to the departure of the disciples in v. 10."[366] Moreover, if her weeping has been criticised by commentators,[367] it is difficult not to see in it her attachment to "the Lord" still missing from her sight. Mary is the only character weeping and mourning Jesus in the narrative (see also 20:11b, 13, 15). Though it certainly underlines her lack of understanding of the resurrection, it also reminds implied readers of previous words of Jesus: "You will be sorrowful, but your sorrow will be turned into joy" (16:20; see also 13:13b; 16:22), thus giving Mary representative significance as a disciple. In persisting in her search for Jesus, she will be rewarded and find joy.[368]

But Mary does not simply weep inactively, she also "stooped to look into the tomb" (20:11), just like the two disciples had done. Unlike the disciples, she sees "two angels in white, sitting where the body of Jesus had lain, one at the head and one at the feet" (20:12).[369] Upon being asked by the angels "woman, why are you weeping?" (20:13),[370] Mary repeats what she had told the disciples in 20:2, with the exception that her concern for the missing body becomes more personal: "They have taken away *my* Lord, and *I* do not know where they have laid him" (20:13). Though this shift from first person plural to first person singular may signify nothing more than Mary is answering personally a question asked *her* by the angels,[371] it might also serve to underscore Mary's personal misunderstanding and ignorance.[372] As such, she does not necessarily lose her

---

[364] Lee, "Easter Faith," 41.

[365] O'Brien, "John 20," 293.

[366] Conway, *Men and Women*, 192.

[367] *E.g.*, Brodie, *John*, 565.

[368] D. A. Lee, "Turning from Death to Life: A Biblical Reflection on Mary Magdalene (John 20:1–18)," *ER* 50 (1998): 113.

[369] For the significance of the presence and position of these two angels, see P. Simenel, "Les 2 anges de Jean 20/11–12," *ETR* 67 (1992): 71–76; Chennattu, *Discipleship*, 149–50.

[370] The force of this question is probably to imply that she should not weep but instead rejoice before the empty tomb. Though implied readers can understand the implications of their question, Mary was at present unable to do so.

[371] So Minear, "John 20:2," 128.

[372] de la Potterie, "Foi pascale," 33: "En 20:2, Marie était simplement messagère auprès des deux disciples; elle adoptait le point de vue de tout le groupe de frères ('nous'). Mais sa réponse

representative value, but another aspect of her characterisation is stressed. Even as angels question her, she remains oblivious to the significance of their presence, still unprepared to be challenged about her search for the location of Jesus' body.[373]

Upon answering the angels, Mary turns around (ἐστράφη εἰς τὰ ὀπίσω)[374] and sees Jesus, though she is unaware it is him (20:14).[375] Thus, still absorbed, one might even say "obsessed" by the location of Jesus' body, she fails to recognise the one she is looking for. In Mary's defence, it should be noted that in 21:4, the disciples who had already seen the resurrected Jesus did not recognise him when he appeared once more to them.[376] It is therefore Jesus who will initiate the process of Mary's recognition by posing two questions: "Woman, why are you weeping? Whom are you seeking?" (20:15). The first question is the same as that posed by the angels (20:13), and similar force should be attached to it. The second question, however, recalls Jesus' first words in the Gospel narrative (1:38). Mary does not exactly answer Jesus. Instead, thinking this man is none other than the gardener, she politely asks if *he* took the body (20:15)! The use of ironic misunderstandings is thus maximised by the implied author in this section. It is the third time Mary expresses her loss in similar fashion, with ignorance and incomprehension (20:2, 13, 15),[377] and this time, readers discover her motivation for wanting to find the body: to take him away (and, implicitly, put him back in the grave). Though Mary has turned toward Jesus, she continues to struggle awkwardly to find her Lord. Such misunderstanding is instructive as far as Mary's characterisation is concerned: by herself, Mary is not able to recognise Jesus and believe that he is resurrected. Only Jesus will, in revealing himself to her, enable her to access faith in the resurrection. This means that Mary's faith is a gift from Jesus.[378] Jesus, calling her by name (Μαριάμ, 20:16),

---

est nettement différente dans le second cas: C'est la *réaction personnelle* de Marie à l'enquête sur le tombeau vide qui est mise en avant, ainsi que son rapport personnel à Jésus."

[373] Lincoln, *John*, 492; Minear, "John 20:2," 129.

[374] Zumstein, *Jean (13–21)*, 277, explains well the significance of this expression: "Ce mouvement signale, tout d'abord, que Jésus n'est plus prisonnier du tombeau, mais qu'il apparaît dans un nouvel espace; il montre ensuite que Marie doit se détourner du tombeau qui est pour elle l'espace de la mort, si elle veut apercevoir Jésus."

[375] Lee, "Turning," 112–20, shows that the imagery of 'turning' is integral to the story of Mary Magdalene in John 20:1–18. After having turned towards pain and death, Mary Magdalene will ultimately turn towards the resurrected Jesus, starting in 20:14, though she is yet unaware of this.

[376] Thus, for Zumstein, *Jean (13–21)*, 306: "Le fait qu'à l'exemple de Marie de Magdala (cf. 20, 14), les anciens compagnons du Jésus terrestre ne reconnaissent pas leur maître, connote l'identité pascale du Christ: il est à la fois identique au Jésus terrestre et pourtant différent de lui."

[377] Resseguie, *Strange*, 145 correctly identifies an important contrast between Mary and the Beloved Disciple, who believed upon seeing the empty tomb: "Mary exegetes at a material level, while the beloved disciple exegetes at a spiritual level."

[378] Zumstein, *Jean (13–21)*, 278, 281.

graciously opens her eyes to his identity,[379] but also reminds implied readers
that Mary Magdalene should already be considered as belonging to the fold of
his disciples, that fold for whom Jesus laid down his life (10:1–18). Immediately, she "turns"[380] once more towards him, this time responding with the intimate
"Rabbouni", expressing both her love for him and a newfound understanding
of his teaching.[381] As argued by Lee, "Mary reveals herself as one of the flock,
responding in faith to the voice of the Good Shepherd (10:3); she enters the fold
of which he is the gate (10:7, 9)."[382] Mary, in the narrative of the Fourth Gospel,
is therefore first to see the risen Jesus. Even more, though the Beloved Disciple
was first to believe on account of the empty tomb (20:8), Mary has primacy
when it comes to belief in connection to actually seeing Jesus. The following
words of Jesus, "Do not cling to me, for I have not yet ascended to the Father"
(20:17a) indicate that a new form of relationship between him and Mary must
begin (and, through Mary, with the whole community of disciples).[383] Mary had
probably attempted to hold or touch[384] the Jesus of her old experience, but Jesus
implicitly reminds her of his earlier teaching: his return to life does not involve
a continuing physical presence with his disciples, but rather a presence through
the Spirit. After Jesus' glorification, the proper relationship with him is one of
mutual indwelling (*cf.* 14:19–20).[385] Instead of clinging to Jesus, Mary is commissioned by Jesus to become an active witness to his glorification: "But go to

---

[379] Lee, "Turning," 115, expresses this well: "Whatever else we say about Mary Magdalene's
search – her initiative, determination, persistence, longing – this story is, at a more fundamental level, about God's searching for her, God's call, God's commission to proclaim the Easter
message."

[380] This new "turn" is best explained by Bultmann, *John*, 686, n.5, for whom it "signifies
the sudden and lively movement towards him, as μή μου ἅπτου v.17 shows." Additionally, as
is explained by Lee, "Turning," 114, these successive "turns" may indicate that "at each point,
Mary moves closer and closer to what she seeks. Misunderstanding, in the end, leads her to
understanding." A similar interpretation to Lee's is given by Zumstein, *Jean (13–21)*, 279, n.15:
"[…] Marie Madeleine se détourne du tombeau qui signifie, pour elle, la réalité de la mort, pour
se diriger vers le vivant."

[381] So Lee, "Turning," 114; *contra* Bultmann, *John*, 686–87, for whom her use of such a
title shows that she still misunderstands Jesus, thinking that he simply "came back" from the
dead, still being the one she knew as "teacher;" and Brown, *John*, 2:1010, for whom this title
is reminiscent of its use by the disciples of John the Baptist in 1:38, thus being "characteristic
of the beginning of faith rather than of its culmination." These hypotheses are unlikely, for immediately following this recognition scene, Mary announces to the disciples "I have seen the
Lord" (20:18), infusing this address with new meaning (*cf.* 20:2, 13). Even more, in calling
Jesus Rabbouni, "Mary no longer speaks *about* Jesus or treats him as an *object*, a corpse; she
addresses him as a living *subject*" (Resseguie, *Strange*, 148).

[382] Lee, *Flesh*, 223.

[383] Chennattu, *Discipleship*, 148.

[384] Literally, μή μου ἅπτου means "stop touching me." See Brown, *John*, 2:992–94, for
several interpretations.

[385] Lincoln, *John*, 493; Chennattu, *Discipleship*, 152–53.

my brothers and say to them, I am ascending to my Father and your Father, to my God and your God" (20:17b). Mary is thus sent as a representative to Jesus' disciples referred to as his "brothers."[386] She is called to move beyond her own renewed relationship with Jesus to the community of believers, commissioned to declare what she has experienced, namely that Jesus' resurrection is part of his ascension to his Father. As a whole, therefore, Jesus, in resisting her physically clinging to him and commissioning her to be a witness, "acknowledges the readiness of her faith to be moved onto a whole new plane."[387] She becomes for the disciples, and for all future believers, the first witness to Jesus' bodily resurrection.[388]

In fact, when Mary Magdalene goes and announces to the disciples "I have seen the Lord – and that he had said these things to her" (20:18), she in essence proclaims her new faith in Jesus' resurrection and her renewed understanding of the person of Jesus. Indeed, Mary expresses once more (after 20:2) that Jesus is "the Lord," but this time a much greater understanding of this title is attached to it.[389] She accepted Jesus' teaching about their transformed relationship and obeyed his command to be a witness to her fellow disciples. For de la Potterie, this acceptance of Jesus' teaching is the last step that Mary had to make in her recognition of Jesus, and it is also the most important one, for it moves her beyond her attachment to what is tangible (the Jesus of her past), towards the future.[390] As Mary goes to Jesus' "brothers" to tell them her news, she now turns towards the community of believers, beginning the process of proclaiming Jesus' glorification and Lordship. For this reason, commentators have been correct to call her "the apostle to the apostles."[391]

---

[386] For many interpreters, Jesus reveals in this verse the new status of his disciples (*e.g.*, Chennattu, *Discipleship*, 154; O'Day, "John," 845; de Boer, *Gospel of Mary*, 174). But it is more likely that Jesus *confirms* to them that God is their Father and God.

[387] Beirne, *Discipleship*, 204.

[388] As O'Day, "John," 302, remarks: "Mary is the first Easter witness in both senses [...] She is first to see the risen Jesus, and the first to tell others what she has seen."

[389] So for Conway, *Men and Women*, 187: "Significantly, the context for Mary's two uses of ὁ κύριος reflect a progression of understanding on her part." See also Lincoln, *John*, 494, who mentions that "The two designations she uses for Jesus in this context – rabbouni and Lord – reflect Jesus' earlier affirmation in 13:13: 'You call me Teacher and Lord, and you speak rightly, for I am.'"

[390] de la Potterie, "Foi pascale," 35.

[391] Mary Magdalene was already refered as such in feminist writings of the 17th century, as demonstrated by M. Verbeelk-Verhelst, "Madeleine dans la littérature féministe du XVIIe siècle," *FoiVie* 90 (1991): 39. See also S. C. Barton, *Life Together: Family, Sexuality and Community in the New Testament and Today* (Edinburgh/New York, NY: T. & T. Clark, 2001), 160, who noticed that, for Paul in 1 Cor. 9:1, being able to say "I have seen the Lord" is an essential qualification for apostleship. These are precisely the words used by Mary in her announcement to the disciples in 20:18 (ἑώρακα τὸν κύριον), and the disciples will then use the same expression towards Thomas in 20:25 (ἑωράκαμεν τὸν κύριον).

The story of Mary Magdalene in the Fourth Gospel "represents the movement from grief and despair to hope and joy."[392] Mary, confronted with the death and absence of Jesus, experienced despair, but Jesus led her to faith in his resurrection, to a better understanding of his person, to a renewed relationship with him and finally to take on the task of witnessing about his resurrection. Such a 'movement,' though rapid as far as the story being narrated is concerned, was not made without struggles. Mary went through a series of misunderstandings, missing the significance of the empty tomb (20:1), the presence of the angels inside the tomb (20:12), the questions of both the angels and Jesus regarding her grief (20:13, 15), and the actual presence of Jesus whom she mistook for a gardener (20:14–15). Then, once she recognised Jesus, she still needed to realise that his presence was of a different order now that he had risen (20:17). Certainly, Mary did move closer and closer to what she sought in this whole process, showing great persistence in her search. Yet, it is Jesus' calling her by name which enabled her to move beyond misunderstanding to recognition, beyond despair to faith in his resurrection.

It should be noted, finally, that the Fourth Gospel does not depict the response of Jesus' "brothers" to Mary's testimony. This is not to deny the importance of her narrative function to pass on her knowledge about Jesus, but the lack of response from her fellow disciples potentially implies that the stress in Mary's characterisation is to be found first and foremost in her modelling the way from a relationship with the earthly Jesus to a renewed and spiritual relationship with "the Lord."[393] Mary's faith in Jesus is never questioned in her story, yet she needed to understand and believe that Jesus' glorification was necessary in order for the community of disciples to experience the mutual indwelling Jesus had previously talked about (14:19–20).

---

[392] Lee, "Turning," 117.
[393] de Boer, *Gospel of Mary*, 178.

Chapter 4

An Evaluation of the Disciples' Faith and Understanding in Narratological Perspective

The preceding two chapters of this study sought to analyse how the faith and understanding of the disciples developed throughout the narrative of the Fourth Gospel. Thoughout these chapters several narratological issues have been pinpointed, such as the manner with which implied readers are led to respond to the characterisation of the disciples, or the intriguing manner with which the implied author uses time in the narrative. Based on the findings of these two chapters, the present chapter will therefore first consider how the disciples' faith and understanding function within the plot of the Fourth Gospel, as well as within the rhetorical purpose of the narrative. These findings will lead to proposals regarding the relation between the disciples' faith and understanding and implied readers, that is, the rhetorical functions of the narrative presentation of the disciples' faith and understanding. Second, issues of temporality (narrative time) will be addressed, seeking to answer how one should understand the faith of the disciples prior to the events surrounding Jesus' glorification.

A. Of Disciples, Plot, and Purpose in the Fourth Gospel

1. The Place of the Disciples within the Plot of the Fourth Gospel

a. Plot Definition and Basic Plot Structures

What is a plot, and what is the role of the disciples' faith and understanding within the plot of the Fourth Gospel? Before answering these questions, a summary of different understandings of 'plot' and of the relationship between plot and characterisation is necessary. Indeed, definitions of the literary term 'plot' are legion. Perhaps the best-known definition is that proposed by Abrams, already quoted in the introduction: "The plot in a dramatic work is the structure of its actions, as these are ordered and rendered toward achieving particular emotional and artistic effects."[1] While many definitions of 'plot' emphasise

---

[1] Abrams, *Glossary*, 127.

movement[2] or causality[3] (following Aristotle), Abrams adds the important element of persuasion, which will be useful in the remainder of the present study.[4] As Culpepper proposes: "From these [elements of Abrams' definition] one may judge that the central features of 'plot' are the sequence, causality, unity, and effective power of a narrative."[5] Clearly, there is no such thing as a narrative without a plot. It is because of the plot that readers perceive that the series of events being related in a narrative are not accumulated in a disorderly fashion, but rather ordered with a purpose.

For Aristotle, Greek drama is structured in two parts: complication (nouement) and unravelling (dénouement). Nouement is everything happening from the beginning of the action to the turning point or climax, where good fortune turns into bad fortune or *vice versa*. The unravelling covers the moment of the climax up to the end, tracing the final transition of the hero to good or bad fortune. In this structure, the pivotal event is thus the climax.[6] Another similar way of setting out the basic aspects of a plot is according to the three-stage movement of commission, complication and resolution. In the first stage, the protagonist is given a commission or task to accomplish, but in the second stage, the protagonist faces obstacles (opposition) that need to be overcome if the commission is to be carried out. Finally, the opposition is resolved, so that the protagonist is able to fulfil his task, thus reaching the goal toward which the plot has been moving throughout the story.[7]

An author's choice of plot pattern depends on the emotional or artistic effects intended for his story.[8] For Frye, two common plot patterns in the New Testament are comedy (U-shaped plot) and tragedy (inverted U-shaped plot),

---

[2] For F. Kermode, *The Sense of an Ending: Studies in the Theory of Fiction* (New York, NY/London: Oxford University Press, 1967), 45: "The clock's *tick-tock* I take to be a model of what we call a plot, an organization that humanizes time by giving it form." Likewise, for R. Scholes and R. Kellogg, *The Nature of Narrative* (Oxford: Oxford University Press, 1966), 12, 207, 'plot' is basically "an outline of events" or "the dynamic, sequential element in narratives." Finally for P. Ricoeur, *Du texte à l'action. Essais d'herméneutique* (Paris: Seuil, 1986), 13–14, the plot is "un dynamisme intégrateur qui tire une histoire une et complète d'un divers d'incidents."

[3] Forster, *Aspects*, 86: "The plot is also a narrative of events, the emphasis falling on causality."

[4] See also P. Brooks, *Reading for the Plot* (Oxford: Clarendon, 1984), 13, for whom the plot is "the dynamic shaping force of the narrative discourse" (quoted by Lincoln, *Truth*, 17).

[5] Culpepper, *Anatomy*, 80.

[6] Aristotle, *The Poetics*, trans. by W. H. Fyfe, LCL (Cambridge, MA: Harvard University Press, 1953), chap. 18. For a more refined plot analysis based on Aristotle's proposal, see P. Larivaille, "L'analyse (morpho) logique du récit," *Poétique* 19 (1974): 287, who proposes "une séquence logique quinaire:" (1) Situation initiale (ou exposition); (2) Nouement; (3) Action transformatrice; (4) Dénouement; (5) Situation finale.

[7] This is one of the plot structures chosen by Lincoln, *Truth*, 17–19, 159–62, for the Fourth Gospel.

[8] Abrams, *Glossary*, 128.

so that the Bible is a series of disasters and restorations, ups and downs, from Genesis to Revelation.[9] As mentioned by Resseguie, "Generally speaking, it is also the plot of our own lives, which makes plot analysis more than an academic exercise."[10]

b. Plot and Characterisation

Chatman observed that "literary studies since Aristotle have based the analysis of plot macrostructures on the vicissitudes of the protagonist."[11] The centrality of characters, especially the protagonist, in a plot was already noticeable above, as we discussed plot definitions and plot structures. Indeed, so important are the characters in a plot that many theorists have debated the priority of one over the other. Many subordinate character to plot, following Aristotle's oft-quoted dictum that "the plot is the first principle and as it were the soul of tragedy: character comes second."[12] Others turn Aristotle on his head. According to Henry James for instance, character precedes plot in the creative process.[13] Today, there seems to be a consensus, however, that priority of plot or character is baseless and hermeneutically insignificant: "Character and plot are interdependent, and both are essential to narrative. [...] Where the interpretive emphasis falls depends largely on the varying interests of critics, readers, and authors."[14]

The interdependence of plot and character has given rise to many attempts to categorise plots. For instance, Crane classifies plots in three categories: plots of action (in which there is a change in the protagonist's situation), plots of character (in which there is a change in his moral character), and plots of thought (in which there is a change in his thoughts or feeling).[15] Similarly, Chatman proposed six plot-types:

In the realm of the fatal:
1. an unqualifiedly good hero fails: this is shockingly incomprehensible to us, since it violates probability;

---

[9] N. Frye, *The Great Code: The Bible in Literature* (New York, NY: Harcourt Brace Jovanovich, 1982), 169–71.

[10] Resseguie, *Narrative Criticism*, 204.

[11] Chatman, *Story*, 85.

[12] Aristotle, *Poetics*, 6:19.

[13] As used by J. A. Darr, *On Character Building: The Reader and the Rhetoric of Characterization in Luke–Acts*, LCBI (Louisville, KY: Westminster John Knox, 1992), 39.

[14] Darr, *Character Building*, 39. See also Chatman, *Story*, 113: "Stories only exist where both events and existents occur. There cannot be events without existents." On these issues, see discussion in Hochman, *Character*, 13–27; Phelan, *Reading People*; and Resseguie, *Narrative Criticism*, 197–98.

[15] *E.g.* R. S. Crane, "The Concept of Plot," in *Approaches to the Novel*, ed. by R. Scholes, Rev. ed. (San Francisco, CA: Chandler, 1966), 239 (cited by Culpepper, *Anatomy*, 81). Crane's system was later expanded into six types by N. Friedman, "Forms of the Plot," in *The Theory of the Novel*, ed. by P. Stevick (New York, NY: The Free Press, 1967), 157–62.

2. a villainous protagonist fails; about his downfall we feel smug satisfaction, since justice has been served;
3. a noble hero fails through miscalculation, which arouses our pity or fear;

In the realm of the fortunate:

4. a villainous protagonist succeeds; but this causes us to feel disgust, because it violates our sense of probability;
5. an unqualifiedly good hero succeeds, causing us to feel moral satisfaction;
6. a noble hero (like Orestes) miscalculates, but only temporarily, and his ultimate vindication is satisfying.[16]

Yet, these classifications are only helpful to a limited extent as far as the present study is concerned. If indeed characters are integrally related to the plot, and if one of their functions is to further the plot, it would be an error to reduce 'character' in a story to the protagonist. Since the present study is concerned with the manner in which characters other than the protagonist function in and further the plot (in which the protagonist is undoubtedly the central figure), the identity and role of these characters within the plot needs to be identified further. Harvey famously used three major categories of characters.[17] The *protagonist* is the most fully developed character in a narrative:

They are the vehicle by which all the most interesting questions are raised; they evoke our beliefs, sympathies, revulsions; they incarnate the moral vision of the world inherent in the total novel. In a sense, they are end-products; they are what the novel exists for, it exists to reveal them.[18]

On the opposite end of the spectrum come *background characters* who may "be allowed a moment of intensity and depth, but equally may be entirely anonymous, voices rather than individualized characters."[19] Between the protagonist and the background characters there are a wide variety of *intermediate figures*, such as the ficelle (under which category the Fourth Gospel's disciples would fall most naturally) who is:

… the character who while more fully delineated and individualized than any background character, exists in the novel to serve some function. Unlike the protagonist he is ultimately a means to an end rather than an end in himself.[20]

For Harvey, a ficelle functions in numerous ways within the plot. Though he may only "serve a purely mechanical role in the plot or act as chorus," Harvey

---

[16] Chatman, *Story*, 85.

[17] More recently, see also J.-L. Ska, *"Our Fathers Have Told Us." An Introduction to the Analysis of Hebrew Narratives*, SubBi 13 (Rome: Editrice Pontificio Istituto Biblico, 1990), 86–87, who proposes to classify characters according to their importance in the plot of a narrative: the protagonist, the foil, the agent (ficelle), and the crowd.

[18] Harvey, *Character*, 56.

[19] Harvey, *Character*, 56.

[20] Harvey, *Character*, 58.

emphasises how important his role may be since "in innumerable ways he may act as foil to the protagonist."[21]

Another very popular classification of characters in novels is one based on Greimas called actantial analysis ("le schéma actantiel").[22] Following the works of Russian formalist Propp and French structuralist Lévi-Strauss,[23] actantial analysis presupposes that all narratives, regardless of their surface level differences, have a common structure. For Greimas, characters in narratives can be grouped into six categories of 'actants,' distinguished in three pairs: Sender and Receiver, Subject and Object, Helper and Opponent.[24] According to this model, the Sender initiates the communication of an Object to the Receiver. The Subject is assigned it and must fulfil the role of communicating it to the Receiver, but on his way is either assisted by the Helper or must deal with obstacles in the form of the Opponent. Obviously, such an actantial model is not interested in the motivations, psychology, traits, or relationships between characters. Greimas' approach to characters is essentially functional, the characters in a narrative only having thematic roles to play or functions to fill. According to this model, characters are thus wholly subordinated to the plot.[25]

All in all, Harvey (followed by Booth[26]) and Greimas probably exaggerate the 'functional' aspects of characters in a narrative over against their potential 'mimetic' aspects. This longstanding debate concentrates on whether characters in literature are to be considered mere plot functionaries with certain commissions to fulfil within the narrative, or *personages*, that is, real beings with traits or even a personality.[27] Chatman argued that treating characters as mere plot functionaries was too limiting, and thus proposed an "open theory of character" that views characters as "autonomous beings" yet clearly to be interpreted within the bounds of the narrative.[28] Similarly, Hochman insists on "the full

---

[21] Harvey, *Character*, 63.

[22] A. J. Greimas, *Sémantique structurale. Recherche et méthode* (Paris: Larousse, 1966).

[23] *E.g.* V. Propp, *Morphologie du conte*, Collection Point (Paris: Seuil, 1970); C. Lévi-Strauss, *Anthropologie structurale* (Paris: Plon, 1958).

[24] Actants are "performers of transactions such as giving and taking, supporting or betraying." (Hochman, *Character*, 24). As such, they are not equivalent to characters of a story. Actants are wider categories that may be abstractions (*e.g.* liberty, peace) or collective characters (*e.g.* an army, a crowd). Moreover, an actant may be represented by different characters that all act in a definite way. In the actantial model, one character may simultaneously or successively assume different actantial functions.

[25] See analysis in C. Dionne, "Le point sur les théories de la gestion des personnages," in *Et vous, qui dites-vous que je suis? La gestion des personnages dans les récits bibliques*, ed. by P. Létourneau and M. Talbot, SBib 16 (Montréal/Paris: Médiaspaul, 2006), 16–17.

[26] Booth, *Fiction*, 102.

[27] The dichotomy is discussed in *e.g.* Chatman, *Story*, 111–19. For discussions of mimetic versus functional characters as this pertains to the Fourth Gospel's characters, see Conway, *Men and Women*, 50–58; and Culpepper, *Anatomy*, 101–02

[28] Chatman, *Story*, 119–26. For Chatman, while critics correctly resist speculations that overflow the bounds of the story or seek superfluous or overly concrete details, this does not

congruity between the way we perceive people in literature and the way we perceive them in life,"[29] yet argues that readers must strive to confer on characters in literature no more reality or verisimilitude than their texts legislate for them. In other words, while characters may appear to readers as 'real persons,' they only do so in relationship with other characters and only within the confines of the narrative structure. For Hochman: "If character is to be dealt with at all as an element in its own right, it must be dealt with as an aspect of the surface structure of the text, as one of the relatively complex and relatively independent interlocking elements that constitute the text."[30] Moreover, "The means of generating images of characters do not in themselves *constitute* character; they *signify* it. Character in itself does not exist unless it is retrieved from the text by our consciousness, together with everything else in the text."[31]

Thus, we may say that secondary characters such as *ficelles* in Harvey's classification, or those functioning as *Helper* in Greimas' actantial model, must be considered as more than mere plot functionaries. As Darr puts it, although characters are not "real people," readers still think about them as "persons."[32] Characterisation, within the field of narrative criticism, is interested in "the art and techniques by which an author fashions a convincing portrait of a person within a more or less unified piece of writing."[33] Thus, within a narrative, characters do 'exist' to serve specific plot functions, for instance in being portrayed as 'foils' or 'types of responses' to the protagonist, but they do not lose their impact as constructed persons. In the Fourth Gospel for instance, the disciples experience things tightly bound to narrative time, and so play an important role in making the story interesting.

---

mean that we should abstain from all speculation about what is constructed and communicated by the discourse.

[29] Hochman, *Character*, 44.

[30] Hochman, *Character*, 31.

[31] Hochman, *Character*, 32 (emphases original). See also, Bar-Efrat, *Narrative Art*, 48; Darr, *Character Building*, 46; A. Berlin, *Poetics of Interpretation of Biblical Narrative*, BLS 9 (Sheffield: Almond, 1983), 43; and especially discussion in M. M. Thompson, "'God's Voice You Have Never Heard, God's Form You Have Never Seen': The Characterization of God in the Gospel of John," *Semeia* 63 (1993): 178–85.

[32] Darr, *Character Building*, 47. Darr adds: "Characters are not just words (the sum of all the verbs in the text, as some structuralists claim) or textual functions, but rather, affective and realistic personal images generated by text and reader." See also R. Wilson, "The Bright Chimera: Character as a Literary Term," *CI* 7 (1979): 750, for whom "[…] characters are, for the purpose of critical reading, to be considered *as if* they were actual persons, and the emphasis on criticism […] is to discuss the response they engender in an intelligent reader" (quoted in Conway, *Men and Women*, 50, n.1).

[33] Culpepper, *Anatomy*, 107.

c. The Plot of the Fourth Gospel

How might this brief introduction to the literary concepts of plot and characterisation be applied to the study of disciples in the Fourth Gospel? Different
ways of understanding the Fourth Gospel's plot have been proposed. This section will focus on two significant proposals: those of Culpepper and Lincoln.
Culpepper implicitly bases the plot development of the Fourth Gospel on the
three-stage model of commission, complication and resolution. Jesus' task is to
reveal the Father by bearing witness to the truth and to take away the sin of the
world, and throughout the narrative, he receives intensified hostility towards
himself and his mission, which effectively dramatizes the radical differences
between those who believe and those who do not. Finally, resolution of the plot
is attained, paradoxically, as Jesus is put to death on the cross, which constitutes
the Fourth Gospel's *peripeteia*, the reversal of fortune. Thus, for Culpepper,
"Plot development in John [...] is a matter of how Jesus' identity comes to be
recognized and how it fails to be recognized."[34] According to this understanding of plot development, 1:11–12 can be regarded as a summary of the Gospel:
"He came to his own, but his own people did not receive him. But to all who
did receive him, who believed in his name, he gave the right to become children
of God." In a later essay, Culpepper emphasised the importance of *anagnoses*
(recognition scenes) throughout the narrative and their role in furthering the
plot of the Fourth Gospel: "The story unfolds in a series of recognition scenes,
until at the end the question is whether or not the reader has recognized in Jesus
the eternal Word."[35]

Lincoln uses two complementary models of plot development for the Fourth
Gospel. The first model is fairly basic and similar to that proposed by Culpepper, though Lincoln sets it resolutely within the overarching motif of a cosmic
trial between God and the world.[36] In the narrative, Jesus is commissioned by
the Father to be both witness and judge in the lawsuit. This two-fold task is
dramatically expressed in two different verses. In 18:37, at the end of the trial
narrative, Jesus expresses the witness aspect of his mission: "For this purpose
I was born and for this purpose I have come into the world – to bear witness
to the truth." In 9:39, he expresses his mission as judge of the trial as follows:
"For judgment I came into this world, that those who do not see may see, and
those who see may become blind." The complication is then the conflict be-

---

[34] Culpepper, *Anatomy*, 88.

[35] R. A. Culpepper, "The Plot of John's Story of Jesus," *Int* 49 (1995): 357. But for Resseguie, *Strange*, 170, this is a weakness in Culpepper's description of the Fourth Gospel's plot
since "*anagnorisis* is a plot *motif*; it is not the plot." A broader category is needed to explain
how the plot coheres. Following the description of Frye, *Code*, 169, he argues that the broader
model is comedy, that is, a plot with a U-shaped structure: a series of misfortunes and misunderstandings bring the action to a low point, but a twist brings the conclusion to a happy ending.

[36] Lincoln, *Truth*, 29–33, 159–62. See also his earlier A. T. Lincoln, "Trials, Plots and the
Narrative of the Fourth Gospel," *JSNT* 56 (1994): 12–14.

tween Jesus and the world (and its representatives) as Jesus takes up the role of being God's agent within the lawsuit. Such a complication takes the form of countertrials, in which accusations and charges are brought against him and judgement is ultimately passed on him as he is sentenced to die on a cross. Finally, Johannine irony is expressed dramatically in the resolution of the plot: "The resolution is achieved by the counterplot being taken up into the main plot or, in terms of our motif, by the countertrials unwittingly achieving the purpose of the overall lawsuit. The world's verdict on Jesus is what enables him to complete his commission as witness and judge (19:30)."[37] The second plot description chosen by Lincoln comes to complement the first one in focussing on the action in the narrative, but still within the overarching metaphor of the Fourth Gospel's cosmic trial motif. Using Greimas' actantial model, Lincoln shows that in the Fourth Gospel the Sender is God the Father, the Object is the trial constituted by Jesus' Mission, the Receiver is the world which is put on trial, and the Subject is Jesus who carries out his commission as witness and judge of the trial. Throughout the narrative, the Helper includes both the other witnesses in the trial (John the Baptist, God, Jesus' works, the Scripture, the Samaritan woman, and the crowd), together with those who are charged with being witnesses in the ongoing lawsuit following Jesus' departure (the disciples, the Paraclete, and the Beloved Disciple). The Opponent includes those who do not believe, such as the 'world' (in the Johannine negative sense of the word), 'the Jews,' Pilate, and the Devil.[38] Within such a plot description, it is therefore clear for Lincoln that characters are subordinated to the plot and that their function is primarily ideological, since "what is ultimately significant about them is whether they are witnesses to the truth or opponents of it, whether they receive the witness of Jesus or refuse it."[39]

d. The Disciples' Faith and Understanding within the Plot

Following this summary of our understanding of the plot of the Fourth Gospel, key elements of the interrelatedness of the characters of the disciples and the plot of the Fourth Gospel can now be proposed, naturally focusing on the disciples' characterisation in terms of their faith and understanding.

The plot developments of the Fourth Gospel proposed by Culpepper and Lincoln showed that the depiction of the disciples' reception of Jesus and wit-

---

[37] Lincoln, *Truth*, 30.

[38] Lincoln, *Truth*, 162–66. On page 164, Lincoln also presents a reversed version of his proposal, based on the counterplot of Jesus' trial rather than on the cosmic trial of God and the world.

[39] Lincoln, *Truth*, 166. Lincoln quickly nuances: "This does not, however, mean that all characters are merely embodiments of belief or unbelief, or plot functions. The narrative does display characters such as the Samaritan woman, the blind man, and Pilate as distinctive individuals and allows for development in their response to Jesus."

nessing activity about him serve to move the plot of the Fourth Gospel along.
From the very beginning, the disciples side with Jesus in the cosmic trial between God and the world. They receive his witness (or the witness of others
about him as in 1:35–36, 40–41, 44–45) and believe. This is precisely where
Culpepper's plot development analysis shows its limits. For him, each episode
of the narrative has essentially the same plot as the story as a whole: will the
characters recognise Jesus and receive eternal life?[40] Yet, although Culpepper
correctly stresses the importance of the varying responses to Jesus for the development of the plot,[41] the issue of belief or unbelief in the characterisation
of the disciples is settled from the very beginning of the narrative. As a result,
when the disciples reappear in the narrative, implied readers are not led to ask
whether or not these characters will recognize and believe in Jesus.[42] As was argued at length in the study of the disciples as a group and of several individual
disciples, their basic allegiance is never denied and nothing can "snatch them
out of [Jesus'] hand" (10:28).[43] Instead, once Jesus' disciples have received him
as "Messiah" (1:41), "Son of God," and "King of Israel" (1:49), once "they believed in him" (2:11), the narrative describes their struggles to understand and
follow him adequately. This is most dramatically depicted in the characterisation of Peter, whose misunderstandings of the person and mission of Jesus lead
him to deny being one of Jesus' disciples three times (18:15–18, 25–27). Yet,
despite these ambiguities, his faith in Jesus is never explicitly questioned, and
the narrative ends with Peter's reinstatement and commission. To use Lincoln's
terminology, being portrayed as believing in Jesus throughout the narrative, the
disciples necessarily fall on the side of the resolution of the basic plot structure,
and so *from the beginning*, rather than on the side of the complication. Likewise, in Greimas' model, the disciples fit within the category of Helper, not on
the side of Opponent. Therefore, the role of the disciples' portrayal within the
narrative of the Fourth Gospel must be found elsewhere than in Culpepper's
proposal.

   As was mentioned above, another way of looking at characterisation and
plot development is to focus on the interplay between the protagonist and secondary characters.[44] Intermediary characters often reveal something about the
protagonist, and this is particularly true of the Fourth Gospel's secondary characters.[45] Indeed, throughout the narrative, implied readers notice the effect of

---

[40] Culpepper, *Anatomy*, 89.

[41] See also Lincoln, *Truth*, 166–67.

[42] Culpepper's analysis remains adequate for all the secondary characters who meet Jesus
and quickly disappear from the narrative, such as the Samaritan woman, the Royal official or
the man born blind.

[43] In fact, even Judas' allegiance to darkness is made clear throughout his characterisation,
beginning in 6:70–71.

[44] So Darr, *Character Building*, 41–42.

[45] Culpepper, *Anatomy*, 104.

Jesus' self-revelation, so that each character tells the story of reception or rejection of Jesus. As a result, though there is no real change or development in the character of Jesus throughout the narrative, implied readers discover more of what his identity and mission entail as Jesus interacts with and reveals himself to other characters. For instance, our analysis of the disciples' faith and understanding throughout the Fourth Gospel has shown that the implied author used their limited understanding and, at times, blatant misunderstandings to communicate or clarify something about the work and mission of Jesus (*e.g.* 6:1–15; 9:2–4).

This description concurs with Marguerat and Bourquin, for whom in biblical literature characters other than the protagonist are non-autonomous in the sense that they exist only in their relationship with the central figure (God or Jesus).[46] However, though this may be generally correct, it does not comprehensively depict the Fourth Gospel's disciples in their relationship with Jesus. The sequential and cumulative effects of the characterisation of the disciples show that they are much more than 'foils' to the protagonist Jesus, that they in fact have a 'life' of their own. For instance, it becomes clear as the story unfolds that Jesus has set the disciples apart to become his human successors in the ensuing trial.[47] The function of the story of Thomas in 20:24–29 is clearly to indicate that Thomas should have believed his co-disciples' testimony about Jesus' resurrection because he is in a similar position to later Christians who are dependent on the witness of Jesus' disciples.[48] Thus, within the story time of the Fourth Gospel, the narrator not only tells the story of the protagonist Jesus, but also that of the disciples' faith, uncertainties, and development in preparation for their mission.[49] As such, the disciples are in one sense more important for readers than the protagonist Jesus, who, in many ways, is more "static"[50] than they are. Though implied readers are expected to share Jesus' evaluative point of view (together with that of the narrator), their situation is closer to that of the disciples and it is far easier for them to identify with Jesus' followers than with Jesus himself.

Considering the significance of the disciples within the narrative of the Fourth Gospel, it can legitimately be argued that Jesus and the disciples are the

---

[46] D. Marguerat and Y. Bourquin, *Pour lire les récits bibliques. Initiation à l'analyse narrative*, 3rd ed. (Paris/Genève: Cerf/Labor et Fides, 2004), 83. So also, Culpepper, *Anatomy*, 104.

[47] Early in the Fourth Gospel, the disciples already act as "witnesses" bringing others to faith (1:41–42, 45–46) so that "the pattern for the role of the disciples in bringing faith to others is therefore established at the very beginning" (Culpepper, *Anatomy*, 115–16).

[48] de Jonge, *Stranger*, 6.

[49] In that sense, the following remark by J. R. Donahue, *The Theology and Setting of Discipleship in the Gospel of Mark* (Milwaukee, WI: Marquette University Press, 1983), 2, could easily be applied to the Fourth Gospel as well. For Donahue, while "Mark has an obvious Christological thrust … the story of the disciples occupies a strong second position."

[50] Culpepper, *Anatomy*, 103.

characters of a story within the story, of a plot within the plot. Though the main plot of the narrative is concerned with Jesus' commission to be a witness and a judge in the cosmic trial between God and the world, a subplot can be discerned where a subsidiary aspect of Jesus' mission is to prepare a group of believers for a particular task, namely, the continuation of his mission within the ensuing cosmic trial between God and the world. The task that the disciples will have to accomplish, if Jesus successfully prepares them, is mentioned in the narrative as early as 4:38: "I sent you to reap that for which you did not labour. Others have laboured, and you have entered in their labour." Thus, as early as chapter 4 in the narrative, Jesus anticipates the final commission that the disciples will receive from him in 20:21–23, where Jesus declares: "as the Father has sent me, even so I am sending you" (*cf.* 14:12; 15:16–17, 26–27; 17:18). As was proposed in chapter 2 of this study, 9:4–5 may be the first time that Jesus implicitly teaches his disciples about their continuing task after his departure. Moreover, Jesus mentions that his Father would be glorified in the disciples' bearing fruit (15:8), which, as was also argued in chapter 2, refers to the disciples' witnessing ministry and conversions of those who would receive their witness. In their future mission, the disciples must therefore witness regarding the significance of Jesus' identity and ministry. In this regard, it is noteworthy that, if this future role is assigned to the core group of disciples in the narrative, the individual disciples who were studied in chapter 3 (excluding Judas), all present different facets of this future mission: Peter must be a shepherd who cares for the flock, Thomas' characterisation indicates that the witness of the disciples will have to be received by those who "have not seen," Mary Magdalene witnesses about Jesus' resurrection and portrays the new type of relationship one may experience with the resurrected Jesus, and the Beloved Disciple is the ideal witness on whose testimony is based the narrative of the Fourth Gospel.

The simple plot structure of commission, complication and resolution can be employed to show how Jesus was *commissioned* to prepare the disciples for their future ministry. As argued by Köstenberger, "the accomplishment of Jesus' mission involves his calling of others to follow him (cf. 1:37–43; 8:12; 10:4, 5, 27; 12:26; 21:19–23)."[51] Even more, a significant part of his task or commission is to provide a set of followers who will carry on his work, based on his decisive completion of that work. The text that comes the closest to an explicit commissioning statement is found in 6:38–39: "For I have come down from heaven, not to do my own will but the will of him who sent me. And this is the will of him who sent me, that I should lose nothing of all that he has given me, but raise it up on the last day." But Jesus' commission can also persuasively be reconstructed implicitly. Jesus mentions on several occasions that he *chose* his core group of disciples (6:70; 13:18; 15:19) and it is particularly noteworthy that Jesus, in 15:19, speaks of this choice in the context of his teaching about

---

[51] Köstenberger, *Missions*, 131.

the disciples' future ministry in the world (15:18–27). In this light it may also be significant that Jesus can announce his glorification – "Now the Son of man has been glorified" (13:31) – immediately after Judas has left the scene (13:31a) and shown his true colours by going off to betray him. Arguably, this signals that Jesus has now substantially completed his task of preserving his true followers (the core disciples minus Judas). Finally, Jesus' prayer in chapter 17 reflects on the completion of his mission and mentions that the keeping and protection of those whom God had given him for their remaining in the world was a significant aspect of his successful mission (17:6–26). Therefore, the disciples were clearly chosen and set apart for a purpose, namely, that of being sent into the world (17:18). Jesus was commissioned to prepare his disciples to play a significant role in his fruitful gathering activity (15:5, 8, 16; cf. 4:36; 14:12).[52]

As Jesus teaches and prepares his disciples, however, *complication* comes into sight since the disciples meet their own inadequacies as well as external opposition. First, as was shown at length in chapters 2 and 3, they continually struggle to understand Jesus and his mission. This struggle is of course part of their preparation, yet it necessarily questions their suitability for the task at hand, worrying, so to speak, the implied readers. Approaching the end of Jesus' earthly ministry, their unpreparedness for their role as witnesses is most clearly put to the fore as Jesus predicts that the disciples would be scattered and desert him (16:32). Moreover, as Jesus encounters unbelief in the narrative, so are the disciples confronted with this option. For instance, after "many of his disciples turned back and no longer walked with him" Jesus himself acknowledges that his core group of disciples, the Twelve, may be tempted to abandon him as well (6:66–67).[53] Finally, when Jesus announced "one of you will betray me," they all wondered of whom he spoke (13:21–22). Second, just as Jesus encountered growing opposition from "the Jews" throughout the narrative, sometimes the disciples were targeted also, though in a derivative way. The events following the blind man's healing (9:13–34) are particularly telling in this regard: the parents of the blind man "feared the Jews, for the Jews had already agreed that if anyone should confess Jesus to be Christ, he was to be put out of the synagogue" (9:22). In fact, "the Jews" accused the blind man of being one of Jesus'

---

[52] Köstenberger, *Missions*, 131–34, thus speaks of Jesus as a shepherd-teacher whose mission is both to call others to follow him and to gather fruit, especially after Jesus' life-giving death: "Jesus is addressed as 'teacher' (ῥαββί; in 20:16, ῥαββουνί; translated as διδάσκαλε in 1:38 and 20:16) in 1:38, 49; 3:2 (διδάσκαλος); 4:31; 6:25; [8:4: διδάσκαλε] 9:2; 11:8, 28 (διδάσκαλος); 13:3, 14 (διδάσκαλος) and 20:16. Jesus is presented as the good shepherd in chapter 10, where 'following' terminology is prominently used (cf. also 16:32). The fact that both Jesus' activity as a teacher and his (metaphoric) description as a shepherd are linked closely with 'following' terminology supports the claim that Jesus' role can be described as that of shepherd-teacher in the Fourth Gospel" (pp. 133–34, n. 330).

[53] As noticed by Brown, *John*, 1:297, the phrasing of Jesus' question μὴ καὶ ὑμεῖς θέλετε ὑπάγειν; ("Do you also want to go away as well?") implies a negative answer. Yet, the possibility for the disciples to go away is not negated.

disciples and so "cast him out" (9:28–34). As the narrator mentions several times, the opposition of "the Jews" created a climate of fear that spread among Jesus' followers (12:42–43; 19:38; 20:19). Therefore, already during the story time of the Fourth Gospel, Jesus' disciples grow aware that being known as such is to be in danger. At first, Jesus' close group of followers are not explicitly said to be targeted by such an opposition, yet that they are aware of the dangers of following Jesus becomes plain when they are portrayed as expecting death as a result of following Jesus (11:16; 13:37), or when they are said to be "in fear" (16:33). Moreover, when Jesus is arrested, he asks that his disciples be let go so that none of them would be lost (18:8–9), and when the High Priest questions Jesus, it is regarding "his disciples and his teaching" (18:19).[54] The emotional and tragic climax of the opposition toward the disciples is further suggested when Peter denies being one of Jesus' disciples, fearing what the "servant girl" could do to him (18:17, 25, 27).

Finally, the *resolution* of the subplot is triggered by the same elements that provided the resolution of the main plot, that is, the completion of Jesus' commission as witness and judge during his "hour" (*cf.* 2:4; 7:6, 8; 12:23, 27; 13:1, 31–32; 17:1). As Jesus hangs on a cross, he is able to say "it is finished" (19:30) so that implied readers understand that it is there that God is truly known and glorified. But interestingly, throughout the narrative, the narrator links the events surrounding Jesus' glorification with a turning point in the disciples' understanding of Jesus' identity and mission (2:22; 12:16; and implicitly 13:7).[55] Following Jesus' resurrection and his threefold revelation of himself to his disciples (20:19–23, 24–28; 21:1–23), the disciples remember events and sayings of Jesus, are able to interpret them correctly in light of Scripture, and thus understand their true significance. That Jesus' resurrection is pivotal in this regard is made explicit in the Beloved Disciple believing upon seeing the empty tomb, followed by the narratorial aside: "For as yet they did not understand the Scripture, that he must rise from the dead" (20:9). No doubt, the disciples' new-found understanding following Jesus' resurrection will be essential in their ministry of witnessing to the significance of Jesus' ministry and their proclamation of the truth in the world. Yet, as important as Jesus' resurrection may be to the resolution of the subplot, the accompanying gift of the Spirit is also necessary (20:22). Jesus had explained to his disciples that they would need the assistance of the Paraclete to guide them into all the truth and to take what is

---

[54] Léon-Dufour, *Lecture*, 4:45: "Devant le nombre croissant de ceux qui suivaient Jésus de Nazareth (11, 48), les pharisiens s'étaient inquiétés de voir prospérer une nouvelle secte (12, 19)." O'Day, "John," 809, argues further that this section is a "two-level drama" similar to that found in chapter 9, especially 9:27–28. For Zumstein, *Jean (13–21)*, 211, following O'Day: "La question posée [by Annas] concerne ainsi la doctrine chrétienne et ses adhérents. L'effet de transparence est indubitable. L'investigation menée par Hanne concerne aussi bien Jésus que les disciples des générations ultérieures."

[55] D. A. Carson, "Understanding Misunderstandings in the Fourth Gospel," *TynBul* 33 (1982): 82–86.

Jesus' and declare it to them (16:13–15; *cf.* 14:15–17, 25–26; 15:26–27). As chapter 21 shows, the disciples needed to undergo further boosts in the process of knowledge and understanding even after the resurrection and completion of Jesus' ministry, and for this purpose, it is the Paraclete who would take Jesus' place as teacher (14:26). As the mentions of the post-resurrection remembrances and understandings of the disciples show (2:22; 12:16), implied readers already know that the Paraclete's ministry has been successful. But the gift of the Spirit is not only necessary to resolve the inadequacies of the disciples – the complication of this subplot (mainly, the disciples' misunderstandings) – but also to resolve the external opposition of "the world." If the disciples are to be successful in their witnessing activity, the Paraclete is to assist them in convincing the world concerning "sin, righteousness, and judgment" (16:8).

The combination of the disciples' commission by Jesus and the gift of the Holy Spirit in 20:21–22, leading Jesus to proclaim "If you forgive the sins of anyone, they are forgiven; if you withhold forgiveness from anyone, it is withheld" (20:23), thus constitutes the resolution of this subplot.[56] For Köstenberger:

> The commissioning is the climax of the relationship the resurrected yet departing Jesus sustains with his disciples (cf. 1:18; 14:10–11; 15:15; chap. 17). Jesus has revealed the Father fully to them (cf. 15:15; 17:6–8). Now he can send them as the Father sent him, since they fully know Jesus as the one who was sent from the Father (cf. 17:6–8); cf. also 14:6–14). And this is the goal of their mission: that through them others may come to know Jesus (cf. 17:20; 20:29; cf. also 20:30–31).[57]

It is therefore with all their inadequacies, but equipped with their faith and newfound understanding of Jesus' identity and mission, and assisted by the Paraclete, that the disciples will be able to fulfil successfully their task. Indeed, the Fourth Gospel as a whole is a fruit of such a ministry (21:24).[58] Obviously, that this subplot has reached its resolution is not to say that the disciples would not struggle anymore. For instance, "the world" will continue to provide hostile opposition to the disciples' witness about Jesus after his departure to the Father. Indeed, Jesus spends a significant portion of his farewell discourse preparing them for such an eventuality (15:18–19; 16:1–3; 17:15), and the narrator later hints at Peter's future death as a martyr (21:19). Moreover, implied readers realise that at the very end of the narrative, the disciples are still faced with their own inadequacies. For instance, after Jesus' resurrection and his

---

[56] Zumstein, *Jean (13–21)*, 286, puts it well: "La finalité de ce don consiste dans l'accomplissement de la mission confiée aux disciples: donner la vie et la donner en plénitude."

[57] Köstenberger, *Missions*, 195–96.

[58] The description of the subplot based on the triptych of commission, complication, resolution can also serve as a basis to show how Greimas' actantial model can be applied to this subplot. The Sender is represented by God, the Object is the preparation for the witnessing ministry of the disciples, the Receiver is the disciples who must carry out Jesus' ministry, and the Subject is Jesus. During Jesus' ministry, "the world," represented primarily by "the Jews", together with the disciples' lack of understanding can be identified as the Opponent, while Jesus (during his earthly ministry) and the Paraclete (later) serve as Helper.

commissioning of the disciples (20:21–23), the disciples surprisingly go fishing instead of beginning to witness about Jesus (21:3), Peter is still concerned
with the Beloved Disciple's fate instead of worrying about his own ministry
(21:20–22), and a rumour spreads abroad among the "brothers" that the Beloved Disciple would not die (21:23).

Even though this proposal in relation to the subplot has not focused on it,
the faith of the disciples clearly serves as the necessary foundation upon which
Jesus was able to teach them so that they would grow in their understanding, be
prepared for their difficult task, and actually witness. In order to become true
witnesses in the ongoing lawsuit between God and the world, the disciples must
have believed and understood that the trial has already been won by Jesus on
the cross and that the case is now settled. Throughout Jesus' earthly ministry,
the failures, trials, denials, and lack of understanding of the disciples can thus
be understood as necessary steps preparing them for their future ministry, but
without their underlying faith, the story of their preparation for ministry could
not have come to a successful end.

2. The Rhetorical Functions of the Disciples' Faith and Understanding

Now that the place of the disciples' faith and understanding within the plot of
the Fourth Gospel has been detected, the next question that must be asked is:
to what purpose? Indeed, what may have been the implied author's rhetorical
intents in putting forth such a subplot in his narrative?

a. The Rhetorical Purpose of the Fourth Gospel

Before answering these questions more explicitly, an overall understanding of
the rhetorical purpose of the Fourth Gospel is necessary. The Fourth Gospel's
purpose has been puzzling to many modern exegetes.[59] As is often noticed,
it is ironic that the one Gospel which has an explicit statement of purpose
(20:30–31) is also the one for which there has been such little agreement within
scholarship as to its actual purpose. One stumbling stone has been the textual variant found for the verb πιστεύειν in 20:31. Following Metzger,[60] many
scholars have refused to choose one reading over the other and grammatical
research on this tense has often been inconclusive. In fact, many have taken the
position that it does not matter one way or the other since John does not use

---

[59] Obviously, space does not permit a full review of the different positions.

[60] The difficulty posed by the textual variant of 20:31 is put as follows by Metzger, *Textual
Commentary*, 219-20: "Both πιστεύητε and πιστεύσητε have notable early support. The aorist
tense, strictly interpreted, suggests that the Fourth Gospel was addressed to non-Christians so
that they might come to believe that Jesus is the Messiah; the present tense suggests that the aim
of the writer was to strengthen the faith of those who already believe ("that you may continue
to believe"). In view of this difficulty of choosing between the readings assessing the supposed
purpose of the evangelist (assuming that he used the tenses of the subjunctive strictly), the
Committee considered it preferable to represent both readings by enclosing σ within brackets."

tenses with precision.[61] It is against this attitude that Fee wrote an article that constitutes a notable exception.[62] Strongly objecting to Metzger's position, he advances the view that the present subjunctive πιστεύητε is in fact the better reading since it is the only one with notable early support (especially in the primary Egyptian witnesses). Moreover, on the basis of statistical data, he asserts that it makes more sense of the Greek and of patterns of transcription. For Fee, since the present subjunctive "presupposes a document intended for those who are already members of the believing community,"[63] it is likely that the author of the gospel addressed the gospel to Christians in order that "they may continue to believe," possibly to keep them from drifting away.[64] As a whole, Fee's research leaves a strong impression that the present subjunctive is to be preferred, but no scholar has been able to make a case beyond reasonable doubt.[65]

In addition to Fee's case, therefore, the question of the purpose of the Fourth Gospel must be settled on the basis of the Gospel as a whole or of its "implicit purpose."[66] And on such a basis, most scholars today propose that the Fourth Gospel intended to cause, arouse, or stir up the act of believing in *believers* rather than to evangelise non-believers.[67] Based on the opposition of "the Jews" to Jesus and his followers throughout the Fourth Gospel, literary analysts have tended to accept the historical claim that the particular situation of the Johannine community (real audience) was a difficult rupture with the Pharisaic synagogues.[68] For instance, Zumstein argues that the aim of the Fourth Gospel was to arouse belief in a Christological thesis that would enable believers who

---

[61] This is the view, for instance, of D. A. Carson, "The Purpose of the Fourth Gospel: John 20:31 Reconsidered," *JBL* 106 (1987): 640, though in a later essay, Carson agrees with Fee (D. A. Carson, "Syntactical and Text-Critical Observations on John 20:30–31: One More Round on the Purpose of the Fourth Gospel," *JBL* 124 (2005): 693–714). J. Frey, *Die johanneische Eschatologie. Vol. 2: Das Johanneische Zeitverständnis*, WUNT 110 (Tübingen: Mohr Siebeck, 1998), 152, strongly argues against the idea that the Fourth Gospel's author uses time indeterminately or without precision. On the contrary, his use of tenses has been carefully chosen and is relevant for interpretation.

[62] G. D. Fee, "On the Text and Meaning of John 20,20–31," in *The Four Gospels 1992: Festschrift Frans Neirynck*, ed. by F. Van Segbroeck et al., BETL 100 (Leuven: Leuven University Press, 1992), 3:2193–2205.

[63] Fee, "John 20,30–31," 3:2204–05.

[64] On this point, see criticisms of Fee's position in Witherington, *John*, 30–31.

[65] In the present narrative analysis of the Fourth Gospel's purpose, the question of the historical (real) setting and audience of the Fourth Gospel is set aside.

[66] R. Kysar, *The Fourth Evangelist and His Gospel: An Examination of Contemporary Scholarship* (Minneapolis, MN: Augsburg, 1975), 148.

[67] Lincoln, *John*, 87–88. For an overview of the different polemics in which some propose the Fourth Gospel may have been intended to take part, see S. Smalley, *John: Evangelist and Interpreter* (Carlisle: Paternoster, 1978), 125–36. See also Carson, "Purpose," for a view of the Gospel as evangelistic.

[68] Since the publication of Martyn's work in 1968, this has become the dominant position. For a revised version of this monograph, see J. L. Martyn, *History and Theology in the Fourth Gospel*, 3rd ed., NTL (Louisville, KY/London: Westminster John Knox, 2003).

were shaken by the rupture to find anew the pertinence of their faith.[69] To that end, the evangelist chose faith as the central theme of his gospel and organised his discourse according to this intention.[70] The evangelist sought to bring believers from an elementary belief to a structured and qualitatively different belief that consisted essentially of a better knowledge of Christ's identity, one that would transport believers to "un croire plus fondamental axé sur la haute christologie pensée dans ses ultimes conséquences."[71] Thus, Zumstein asserts elsewhere that:

> [...] toute la stratégie argumentative de l'évangile jouant sur la portée symbolique du language, sur l'ironie et le malentendu, suggère que les destinataires de l'évangile sont plutôt des 'insiders', à savoir les croyants eux-même des communautés joh appelés à un 'mieux croire.'[72]

For instance, the Prologue (1:1–18) opens the narrative as a reminder of the implied author and the implied readers' common faith, as the use of the first-person plurals indicate in such a confessional context (1:14, 16). From the very beginning of the Fourth Gospel, the implied author and his implied readership are therefore anchored in a common faith. The shared theological point-of-view proposed in the Prologue will enable implied readers to appreciate fully the ironies of the unfolding narrative and finally to see their point of view confirmed and reinforced.[73] For Zumstein: "Il convient alors d'envisager l'évangile comme la médiation qui essaie de *susciter le croire des croyants.*"[74]

---

[69] See Lincoln, *Truth*, 178–82. Though Lincoln believes that the implied readers of the Gospel are believers, he balances his judgment: "The narrative also leaves room for readers to enter its world at various points on its faith continuum – as those whose verdict needs more appropriate formulation, as those whose verdict needs to be reinforced, as those who have made their verdict and become witnesses, and as those who fall into more than one of these categories" (p. 180–81).

[70] J. Zumstein, "L'évangile johannique: une stratégie du croire," in *Miettes exégétiques*, MB 25 (Genève: Labor et Fides, 1991), 240.

[71] Zumstein, "Stratégie," 246.

[72] Zumstein, *Jean (13–21)*, 296.

[73] So Zumstein, *Apprentissage*, 50–52; R. Kieffer, "The Implied Reader in John's Gospel," in *New Readings in John: Literary and Theological Perspectives. Essays from the Scandinavian Conference on the Fourth Gospel in Aarhus 1997*, ed. by J. Nissen and S. Pedersen, JSNTSuppS 182 (Sheffield: Sheffield Academic Press, 1999), 51–53; and Culpepper, *Anatomy*, 233–34, who writes: "Finally, the gospel derives much of its power from the way it depicts its implied reader. The original readers no doubt felt that the narrator was speaking to them and taking into account the limitations of their understanding and the predispositions they brought to the narrative. At the same time, beliefs they held dear were reaffirmed and clarified so that they were drawn deeper into the faith to which they had committed themselves." Indeed, it may be added that throughout the narrative one gets the sense that the implied reader already has some knowledge of the story. For instance, 6:64, which claims that Jesus knew from the beginning who his betrayer was indicates that the audience is aware that a betrayal took place. Likewise, the reference to Jesus' resurrection in 2:22 indicates that the reader is assumed to know about, and probably believe in, Jesus' resurrection.

[74] Zumstein, "Stratégie," 243.

From this point on, one can define further the purpose of the Fourth Gospel by taking into account the overall metaphorical motif of the trial. If indeed the narrative presents the protagonist Jesus acting throughout his earthly ministry both as witness and judge in the cosmic trial between God and the world, and as preparing his believing disciples to carry on the task of witnessing about the truth in a hostile world, it follows that in wishing to reinforce the implied readers' faith and understanding, the implied author also implicitly sought to challenge them to become more effective in their own witnessing activity. Indeed, the implied readers are followers of Jesus who live after Jesus' glorification, so that they can naturally envisage themselves in the role assigned to the disciples after Jesus' departure. This phenomenon is also expressed through the use of the first-person plural at the end of the narrative: "and we know that his testimony is true" (21:24). As Lincoln shows, "The frame, [*i.e.*, constituted by 1:14, 16 and 21:24] both highlights the symbolic world of the narrative as that of God's lawsuit and, by its use of 'we' language, invites readers to share the perspective and values of such a world and then take these back into their own world."[75] In a similar way to the disciples, through the narrative implied readers are being prepared to become effective witnesses in their own world.

b. The Role of the Disciples' Misunderstandings within the Purpose

The implied author uses several literary devices in order to convey the proposed purpose of the Fourth Gospel through his characterisation of the disciples.[76] One technique that is particularly appropriate to consider in this study is the use of "misunderstandings," which raise the question: what is the effect of the disciples' misunderstandings upon the faith of the implied readers?

First, one must recognise that scholars have had difficulties agreeing on the Johannine concept of "misunderstanding" and thus on the instances in which it is present in the Fourth Gospel.[77] For Bultmann, misunderstandings occur in the Fourth Gospel when a character thinks that a concept or statement refers to earthly matters, while, in fact, it refers to heavenly matters.[78] Likewise, LeRoy, from his form critical analysis, understands the Johannine misunderstandings as pedagogical and catechetic concealed riddles that only the Johannine community could understand.[79] Yet, Vouga correctly questions the helpfulness of Bultmann and LeRoy's definitions since: "Jn n'utilise pas mécaniquement une

---

[75] Lincoln, *Truth*, 173.

[76] Zumstein, "Stratégie," 243–50, heavily depends on Culpepper to show how the Fourth Gospel's strategy to cause or re-tell the pertinence of faith is exercised through the Prologue, what Zumstein calls "l'herméneutique étagée" (the deepening of the faith of certain characters in a given episode, different techniques that serve the narration's implicit commentary), and the manner with which characters are portrayed.

[77] See a review of differing positions in Carson, "Misunderstandings," 60–67.

[78] Bultmann, *John*, 135, n.1.

[79] Leroy, *Rätsel und Missverständnis*, 1, 157–60.

'technique' applicable et appliquée de manière identique dans tous les textes."[80] Thus, it may not be necessary to speak of one particular misunderstanding "technique" or "device" used in the Fourth Gospel.[81] Rather, one may say that throughout the Fourth Gospel the implied author underlines, through numerous occasions, the misunderstanding inherent to humanity's encounter with the revelation of Jesus Christ.[82] With this in mind, Culpepper proposes the literary pattern of distinctive features of Johannine misunderstandings as follows:

(1) Jesus makes a statement which is ambiguous, metaphorical, or contains a double-entendre; (2) his dialogue partner responds either in terms of the literal meaning of Jesus' statement or by a question or protest which shows that he or she has missed the higher meaning of Jesus' words; (3) in most instances an explanation is then offered by Jesus or (less frequently) the narrator.[83]

The disciples are obviously not exempt from such encounters with Jesus, as a group (4:31–34; 11:11–16; 16:16–19, 29–33), as individuals (13:36–38) or as individuals representing the opinion of the group (14:4–6; 14:8–9). In fact, the implied author at times uses the phenomenon of the disciples' misunderstandings quite heavy-handedly, for instance as missing the common euphemism for death when Jesus speaks of Lazarus as having "fallen asleep" (11:11). This presentation gives the impression that the disciples are quite dense and dull-witted, which certainly indicates that the implied author used the disciples' misunderstandings with particular communicative intents that should not be missed. In that sense, the disciples' misunderstandings must be understood as "literary misunderstandings," as opposed to "daily life misunderstandings."[84] In daily life misunderstandings, two persons are normally taken into a vicious cycle that provokes a process of reciprocal misunderstandings, so that they are both on the same (mis)communicative level. But in literary misunderstandings, there are two different levels of communication and three "actors." On the first level of communication, that of the story being told, two characters (say, Jesus and the disciples) interact, and one of them misunderstands the other.[85] The second level of communication is that which takes place between the story being told and the intended readership. In the Fourth Gospel, though the victims of the misunderstandings often are the disciples, the readers are really the ones being targeted. The misunderstandings of the disciples have rhetorical

---

[80] Vouga, *Cadre*, 32–33. For Vouga, the whole of chapter 8 is in fact one long misunderstanding, just as Jesus' trial (18:1–19:30).

[81] Yet, we may agree with T. Thatcher, *The Riddles of Jesus in John: A Study in Tradition and Folklore*, SBLMS 53 (Atlanta, GA: Society of Biblical Literature, 2000), 189, for whom: "[…] it may be said that *FG's irony and misunderstandings are achieved primarily through the use of riddles and riddling sessions*" (emphasis original).

[82] Vouga, *Cadre*, 33.

[83] Culpepper, *Anatomy*, 152.

[84] This distinction is proposed by Dettwiler, "Compréhension," 375–76.

[85] It should be noted that Jesus, in the Fourth Gospel, never falls prey to misunderstandings. His role in this regard is primarily to provoke and eventually to solve misunderstandings.

intentions meant to produce certain desired effects on the readers. In fact, the narrator never mentions that the disciples are able to grasp Jesus' words once he replies to their misunderstandings, which further corroborates the view that such portrayals have rhetorical intentions.[86] And when the disciples do react to Jesus' words, they are shown to express further misunderstandings (11:16; 13:37; 14:8; 16:29–30). Yet, the study of the disciples' faith and understanding as a group in the narrative (chapter 2) noted that Jesus was able, even when his disciples' missed the point of his teaching, still to include them in his task (4:38; 6:10, 12; 9:4).

The effects of the disciples' misunderstandings on readers are, at first sight, quite obvious. First, they tend to remove doubts or misperceptions about key points of Johannine theology.[87] As such, they invite readers to be among those who truly understand. As far as the disciples' misunderstandings are concerned, these points of theology refer for the most part to the significance of Jesus' death/exaltation (4:33; 11:16; 13:36–39; 14:5; 16:17–18). The clearest example is found in 16:17–18 where the disciples are unable to understand that Jesus must die "in a little while," and that he will rise again from the dead (16:22). Their misunderstanding underscores the importance for readers not only to hold the right (Johannine) view on such matters, but also to understand them correctly. Moreover, in 16:29–33, the disciples confidently voice what they think is a proper understanding of Jesus (16:30) when Jesus casts doubt on what the disciples actually know and believe (16:31), reminding implied readers that knowledge and understanding of Jesus apart from his "hour" are necessarily imperfect.[88] Finally, in the Fourth Gospel, misunderstandings are twice explicitly linked with the disciples denying or abandoning Jesus (13:36–38; 16:29–33), so that they may serve as implicit reminders of the danger of misunderstanding. This is not to say that the implied readership struggles with the same misunderstandings as the disciples or other characters in the story. As Carson argues, albeit from a historical perspective, the misunderstandings experienced by the disciples during Jesus' earthly ministry cannot persist *in the same way* after the event of the death/resurrection/exaltation of Jesus, for this event is what was needed to explain the disciples' misunderstandings.[89] Thus,

---

[86] See Thatcher, *Riddles*, 191–93.

[87] Culpepper, *Anatomy*, 164–65.

[88] See the analysis of this particular misunderstanding in O'Day, *Revelation*, 104–09. See also, Ashton, *Understanding*, 397–98, who proposes a distinction that explains why the disciples were unable to understand sayings of Jesus ("riddles") such as that found at the end of chapter 16. For him, there is a clear and fundamental difference between two stages of revelation in the Fourth Gospel, one taking place during Jesus' lifetime, and one taking place after his death. The first stage is only "partial and obscure," while the second is "full and clear." While Jesus is the agent of revelation in the first stage, the second stage is assigned to the Spirit who "will take what is mine and explain it to you" (16:14).

[89] Carson, "Misunderstandings," 82–87. Carson adds: "[…] there can no longer be confusion over the meaning of the expressions or the basic nature of the truth-claims. Unbelief, yes,

implied readers must "hear" the message being communicated by the implied author through the depiction of the disciples' misunderstandings and recommit themselves to a proper understanding.

This remark leads to the second effect produced by the disciples' misunderstandings, which is to incite readers to distance themselves from the character of the disciples, giving them a sense of superiority about the disciples because they know or have understood something that the disciples have not. At times, misunderstandings may also make readers feel judgmental towards the disciples. For Culpepper, the most obvious function of the misunderstandings is thus "to enforce a marked distinction between 'insiders' and 'outsiders,' between those who understand Jesus and those who do not."[90] Indeed, some misunderstandings are at times so obvious that implied readers necessarily wonder how one can be so dull as to have missed the proper meaning of what Jesus was saying (*e.g.* 11:12). Yet, this is not always the case. For instance, when Jesus tells his disciples that he has "food to eat that you do not know about" (4:32), it is likely that even the most perceptive readers would miss what Jesus means until he explains it in 4:34 (and later in 6:27, 55). Upon reading this particular misunderstanding, implied readers do not feel as distant or judgmental towards the disciples as on other occasions. It may even be that they identify with the disciples in finding themselves on a similar level of misunderstanding.

On this basis, some scholars go further in their analyses of Johannine misunderstandings. For Dettwiler, the risk for readers would precisely be to find themselves feeling superior to the disciples, a position which, he argues, the implied author did not intend. For instance, Philip (on behalf of the disciples as a whole) voiced a particular misunderstanding regarding the relationship between the Father and Jesus: "Lord, show us the Father, and it is enough for us" (14:8). Dettwiler argues that such a misunderstanding expresses something of great value, that is, the deep human desire to enter into a direct and personal relationship with God, the source of life. Behind Philip's misunderstanding lies "un savoir implicite" or "une précompréhension" which implied readers are meant to receive and ponder before they are taken into the perspective that Jesus or the narrator propose on the topic at hand.[91] Yet, this is unlikely to be the implied

---

along with scepticism, rejection, doubt – but not this kind of confused misunderstanding. The cross and resurrection have polarized the debate" (p. 85).

[90] Culpepper, *Anatomy*, 164. Culpepper surprisingly speaks of those who misunderstand in the Fourth Gospel as having "rejected" Jesus. This is certainly not the case for the disciples. For Becker, *Johannes*, 1:135–36, one must make a distinction between "misunderstandings" and "non-understandings." Following Bultmann, Becker argues that "misunderstandings" happen when characters hold an "earthly" rather than "spiritual" understanding, so that misunderstandings are signs of unbelief. Therefore, for him the disciples in the Fourth Gospel do not properly misunderstand but simply show a lack of instruction that Jesus must make up (with the exception of 4:14, which, according to him, only proves the rule).

[91] Dettwiler, "Compréhension," 379–80; see also Moloney, *John*, 399, who links the spiritual search expressed by Philip with that of Moses in Ex. 33:18 (*cf.* also Ex. 24:9–11; Is. 6:1; 40:5).

author's intent. The Prologue (especially 1:14, 16) shows that implied readers are already "in the know," sharing the perspective of the implied author, so that throughout the narrative they have the advantage of a superior knowledge regarding the objects of the disciples' misunderstandings. Though at times they may find themselves also lacking understanding, coming dangerously close to that of the disciples, the literary function of the disciples' misunderstandings is primarily to *reinforce* or to *remind them* of their superior knowledge. Thus, if they find themselves on a similar level of understanding to that of the disciples, they receive the explanations of Jesus or the narrator and are reminded of and strengthened in the perspective they already hold, that of "insiders." Indeed, in the particular example given above by Dettwiler (14:8), this perspective is most obvious as the Prologue has already answered the disciples' misunderstanding: "No one has ever seen God; the only one God, who is at the Father's side, he has made him known" (1:18, *cf.* also 5:18; 8:19, 38; 10:30, 38).

Therefore, and in accordance with the overall rhetorical purpose of the Fourth Gospel, together with the analysis of the Gospel's subplot developed above, it can be concluded that through the particular use of the disciples' mis-understandings, implied readers are nurtured in their position as believers and thus prepared further for their witnessing ministry. The disciples' characteri-sation clearly plays a role in the disclosure of the implied author's rhetorical intents. The plotted depiction of their faith and lack of understanding during the preparation for their witnessing activity is meant to reassure and reinforce implied readers' faith so as to equip and challenge them to become effective witnesses to the truth of the trial between God and world.

Several scholars, noticing that the Fourth Gospel's disciples underwent a process of growth through the narrative (be that a process of growth in belief, in understanding, or both), conclude that discipleship, understood in Johannine terms, must therefore necessarily involve a continuing process of growth. This is most clearly expressed by Gloer:

Like the disciples in the Johannine narrative, we are called not once but in a continuing way to 'come and see,' to continue to seek a deeper and fuller understanding of who Jesus is. [...] The Johannine narrative makes it very clear that genuine discipleship involves a necessary and inev-itable progression of perception. It demonstrates that our confessions, no matter how orthodox, are in the final analysis always inadequate, and even as the disciples learned again and again the inadequacy of their understanding, so we must be open to learning the inadequacy of ours.[92]

This is fine, since "growth" was obviously part of the implied author's rhe-torical intent, but it does not follow that the Fourth Gospel is a general treatise encouraging the life-long growth of disciples simply on a cognitive level. More to the point, the implied author built the narrative to bring implied readers into

---

[92] Gloer, "Come and See," 289–90. For a similar statement, see Chennattu, "Becoming," 496: "We can reasonably conclude that discipleship is a process of becoming, a process of growth."

a renewed understanding of Jesus and his mission *in order to* empower them to take on the task of witnessing about the truth within their own world. Growth in understanding, maturity, and faith must lead to effective mission.[93] Moreover, there is a sense in which the content of the witness proposed by the Fourth Gospel does not lend itself to further challenges or additions by readers. Indeed, the Fourth Gospel offers itself as a definitive interpretation of the significance of Jesus and his mission: "and we know that his testimony is true" (21:24). This is not to say that there can be no other account of the life and significance of Jesus, as though the Paraclete's role in teaching everything (14:26) and leading into all the truth (16:13) was a once and for all activity fulfilled in the Beloved Disciple's testimony.[94] Yet, as far as the implied readers of the Fourth Gospel are concerned, it is first and foremost in *this* story that they will find the deeper and fuller understanding that can lead them to effective witness.[95] This is so because the Fourth Gospel is the testimony of the Beloved Disciple whom the Paraclete led into all the truth concerning the content of his testimony.

c. The Relation between the Disciples' Characterisation and Implied Readers: The State of the Research

After these proposals on the manner in which the faith and understanding of the disciples relate to the overall presentation of the discourse and purpose of the Fourth Gospel, this section of the study focuses on the exact relation between the presentation of the faith and understanding of the disciples and implied readers. If implied readers are to be reinforced and nurtured in their position as believers in order to be further prepared for their own witnessing ministry, how has the implied author of the Fourth Gospel constructed the characters of the disciples to achieve his purpose? What are the precise rhetorical functions of the implied author's specific presentation of the disciples' faith and understanding? In other words, how does the implied author persuade his implied readership to participate in the story of the disciples' faith and understanding in such a way that they would be appropriately reinforced and nurtured by it? Evidence as early as the third century indicates that Fourth Gospel characters, and disciples in particular, have been interpreted symbolically, as representing or referring to something beyond themselves (without necessarily denying that they were also historical figures). This is for instance the case with Origen, who

---

[93] Lincoln, *John*, 88: "The convictions about Jesus to which the evangelist had come were seen as essential for all believers if they were to bear effective witness."

[94] See discussion in Köstenberger, *Missions*, 150–53.

[95] See T. Thatcher, *Why John Wrote a Gospel? Jesus-Memory-History* (Louisville, KY: Westminster John Knox, 2006), 151: "Whatever else might be said about the elusive Johannine community, its prehistoric period ended at the moment the Fourth Gospel was published. After this critical moment, John and his allies could point to the Fourth Gospel and say, 'We are no longer talking about whether Jesus did X or Y; we are now talking about how to interpret what can be documented, what this book says he did.'"

understood the mother of Jesus as the mother of all believers.[96] Similar understandings of Johannine characters have persisted through the centuries,[97] so that
in the twentieth century, Bultmann famously proposed that Peter and the mother of Jesus were meant to represent Jewish Christendom, while the Beloved
Disciple represented Gentile Christendom.[98] Further, Rensberger argued, for
instance, that certain characters were not to be understood as historical figures
in the common sense: "Nicodemus and the blind man are 'historical' figures in
the gospel of John, not in the sense of their being figures from the past in whom
the gospel writer is interested, but as representatives of historical realities in the
experience of the Johannine community."[99]

Collins proposed a thorough analysis of the representativeness of Johannine
characters. Seeking what individual characters suggest about the background
and compositional history of the text, he handpicked fifteen of them in the narrative and argued that they had previously appeared in homiletic materials in
which they functioned as illustrative types.[100] For him, in their individuality,
these characters "appear to have been definitely type-cast by the evangelist so
that he might teach his readers about salvific faith and thereby enkindle and
confirm that faith within them."[101] For instance, Philip represents both the disciple who misunderstands and the Greek believer introducing others to Jesus,
Judas represents the world of Satan over against the world of the Father, Mary
Magdalene represents the believer who has faith in Jesus as the ascending one
but only because of the revelation of Jesus himself, Thomas represents the fact
that resurrection faith is faith in the divinity of Jesus, Peter is a representative
of the Twelve disciples of the common evangelical tradition, and the Beloved Disciple typifies the disciple of Jesus *par excellence* within the Johannine
tradition.[102]

More pertinent for the purposes of the present study, though it follows Collins closely, is Culpepper's pioneering literary critical analysis of characterisation in the Fourth Gospel.[103] Following contemporary literary analysts such as

---

[96] Origen, *Commentary on the Gospel according to John*, trans. by R. E. Heine, 10 vols,
The Fathers of the Church 81 (Washington, DC: Catholic University Press of America, 1989),
1.23; quoted in Conway, "Ambiguity," 326.

[97] Collins, *These Things*, 1–2, gives examples of such allegorical interpretations persisting
in the scholasticism of the Middle Ages.

[98] Bultmann, *John*, 484–85, 685.

[99] D. Rensberger, *Overcoming the World: Politics and Community in the Gospel of John*
(London: SPCK, 1989), 48.

[100] *Cf.* R. F. Collins, "The Representative Figures of the Fourth Gospel," *DRev* 94 (1976):
26–46, later reprinted in Collins, *These Things*, 1–45.

[101] Collins, *These Things*, 8.

[102] Collins, *These Things*, 23–25, 28–30, 33–45.

[103] Culpepper, *Anatomy*, 115–25, 145–48. Since Culpepper, several monographs and articles on aspects of Johannine characterization and studies of particular characters of the Fourth
Gospel have been written. In addition to the works reviewed in this section, see Quast, *Figures*;

Forster (the distinction between 'round' and 'flat' characters),[104] and especially Harvey,[105] Culpepper makes distinctions between the protagonist (Jesus), the intermediate characters (especially ficelles who often carry representative and symbolic values), and the background characters.[106] For him, since most characters in the story (except Jesus) are not developed in a 'full-blown' manner, "one is almost forced to consider the characters in terms of their commissions, plot functions, and representational value."[107] At the end of his chapter, Culpepper thus presents the two functions of characters other than Jesus in the narrative of the Fourth Gospel:

(1) to draw out various aspects of Jesus' character successively by providing a series of diverse individuals with whom Jesus can interact, and (2) to represent alternative responses to Jesus so that the reader can see their attendant misunderstandings and consequences.[108]

For Culpepper, when several otherwise different characters react in the same manner to the person of Jesus, a type of response is created. He proposes a continuum of seven types of responses to Jesus: rejection (*e.g.* "the Jews"), acceptance without open commitment (*e.g.* Nicodemus and Joseph of Arimathea), acceptance of Jesus as a worker of signs and wonders (*e.g.* those who believe in 2:23–25), belief in Jesus' words (*e.g.* the Samaritan woman), commitment in spite of misunderstanding (*e.g.* Nathanael, Thomas, Peter), paradigmatic discipleship (the Beloved Disciple), and defection (Judas).[109] For Culpepper, such characterisation is linked to the purpose of the implied author, for these types of responses "exemplify misunderstandings the reader may share and responses one may make to the depiction of Jesus in the Gospel."[110]

Although from yet another theoretical perspective, Koester also approaches Johannine characters as symbolic or representative figures.[111] Relying on an understanding of character portrayal in antiquity rather than on contemporary

Staley, "Stumbling," 55–80; J.-A. A. Brant, "Husband Hunting: Characterization and Narrative Art in the Gospel of John," *BibInt* 4 (1996): 205–23; S. Harstine, *Moses as a Character in the Fourth Gospel. A Study of Ancient Reading Techniques*, JSNTSup 229 (Sheffield: Sheffield Academic Press, 2002); Beirne, *Discipleship*; Marchardour, *Personnages*.

[104] Forster, *Aspects*, 67–78. Culpepper, *Anatomy*, 102–03, notes that most of the minor characters in the Fourth Gospel are 'flat characters,' the "personification of a single trait." Many, since Forster, have questioned the relevance of this distinction between round and flat characters. For instance, M. Bal, *Narratology. Introduction To the Theory of Narrative* (Toronto: University of Toronto Press, 1994), 116–17, refutes such a distinction since it is based first and foremost on psychological critirias. See also the discussion in Conway, *Men and Women*, 58–59.

[105] Harvey, *Character*, 58–67.
[106] Culpepper, *Anatomy*, 103–04.
[107] Culpepper, *Anatomy*, 102.
[108] Culpepper, *Anatomy*, 145.
[109] Culpepper, *Anatomy*, 146–48.
[110] Culpepper, *Anatomy*, 104.
[111] Koester, *Symbolism*, 33–77.

literary theory,[112] Koester shows that ancient audiences understood *dramatis personae* in Greek tragedies both as 'real people' and as 'types.'[113] The same, for him, holds true in the Fourth Gospel. Individual characters are presented as types with their various responses to Jesus serving as character indicators, but their representative roles do not negate their individuality or autonomy in the narrative. Rather, such roles develop their most distinctive traits.[114] For him, therefore, characters can function in more than one way in the Fourth Gospel. They respond to Jesus, and in doing so show different ways of relating to God, yet always falling on either side of the belief/unbelief divide: "When Jesus evokes positive and negative responses from people, he enables readers to see them not only as unique individuals and members of communities but as people who do or do not believe in Jesus and the God who sent him."[115] They are distinct individuals who may represent a group of people and disclose matters of significance to all people (they "typify a faith stance").[116] For instance, Koester shows that Mary Magdalene typifies the fact that disciples come to know Jesus on the basis of what they hear (in Mary Magdalene's case, Jesus calling her by name in 20:16) which enables them to make sense of what they see. As such, she represents later believers who would believe on the basis of what they hear rather than on seeing.[117] Likewise, Peter represents "all Christians" by the typical way in which he became a follower of Jesus (through the witness of a family member in 1:41), by his confession in 6:69, by Jesus' broad remark to him during the footwashing scene (13:10), but also by his failures that remain a disturbing possibility for all Christians threatened by persecution.[118] Thomas represents those who were not part of the group that saw the risen Christ and who have only received testimony about Jesus. Unlike Thomas, readers are invited to receive the Gospel's testimony without making seeing a precondition

---

[112] It can be noted that Culpepper's discussion is not without reference to ancient modes of characterisation (Culpepper, *Anatomy*, 103), but this is not his main approach.

[113] Koester, *Symbolism*, 37.

[114] Koester, *Symbolism*, 45.

[115] Koester, *Symbolism*, 76.

[116] Koester, *Symbolism*, 35. Similarly, Köstenberger, *Missions*, 160, proposes that in addition to having their historical and specific identities, individual disciples appear to fulfil representative roles in the Fourth Gospel: "As one surveys the Fourth Gospel, it appears that some duties are shown to pertain to every disciple of Jesus, such as the duty to obey Jesus and to love one's fellow-disciple, while other callings are specific to the individual disciple, such as certain kinds of witness, be it by pastoring or other forms of representing Jesus. This becomes apparent in the Fourth Evangelist's characterisation of individual disciples, especially Peter and the Beloved Disciple."

[117] Koester, *Symbolism*, 69.

[118] Koester, *Symbolism*, 71.

for faith.[119] Finally, though his betrayal was a singular act, Judas manifests the wider phenomenon of unbelief.[120]

Conway, both in her major work on gender and Johannine characterisation and especially in a more recent article, has questioned the legitimacy of restricting character analysis of John's Gospel to determining what each character represents.[121] She proposes that since the Fourth Gospel's characters are characters in their own right, they are not simply representative figures, but contribute to the Gospel's narrative in a multiplicity of ways. Likewise, against the 'clear-cut' alternative that a majority of analysts propose (*i.e.*, characters as either believers or unbelievers), Conway argues that the Fourth Gospel's characters "do more to complicate the clear choice between belief and unbelief than to illustrate it."[122] Though she agrees that in theory the traditional view of Johannine characterisation is plausible, she contends that the characters of the Fourth Gospel in fact "play a major role in undercutting the dualism of the Gospel."[123] Conway's arguments are persuasive, especially as she demonstrates that scholars too often disagree regarding the one trait that characters are supposed to represent or typify, or even regarding their status as believers or unbelievers.[124] Indeed, the present study itself has argued in favour of the early faith of the disciples contrary to other scholars (*e.g.* Moloney). In conclusion, Conway explains that while the world of the gospel is a starkly drawn world of contrasts – above and below, light and darkness – it is also a world filled with colourfully drawn characters that resist the gospel's binary categories: "If there is no clarity regarding these minor characters it is because they do not line up on either side of the belief/unbelief divide."[125] But such a conclusion raises the question of the Johannine rhetorical intent in presenting his characters in an ambiguous manner. Conway thus argues:

What I have come to conclude is that even in this dualistic Gospel, the construction of the characters gives implicit recognition of what actually constitutes a life of faith, whether in the

---

[119] Koester, *Symbolism*, 72–73.

[120] Koester, *Symbolism*, 74.

[121] Conway, *Men and Women*, 48; Conway, "Ambiguity," 324–41.

[122] Conway, "Ambiguity," 325. For an example of the way in which scholars tend to relate Johannine dualism to characterization, see the original study of Petersen, *Sociology of Light*, 80–109.

[123] Conway, "Ambiguity," 325.

[124] Conway, "Ambiguity," 328: "If these characters are so transparent, embodying only a single trait, one would expect that such traits could be readily discerned". On pages 330–39, Conway explains why different conclusions are normally reached by scholars by showing the ambiguities found in such characters as Nicodemus, Peter, Pilate, and women such as the Samaritan woman, Martha of Bethany, Mary of Bethany, Mary Magdalene, and finally the Beloved Disciple and the Mother of Jesus, in regard to 'faith.'

[125] Conway, "Ambiguity," 340. This conclusion is in direct opposition to Powell, *Narrative Criticism*, 54, for whom "Unlike some modern authors, our Gospel writers do not allow characters to hover ambiguously between these two poles [truth and untruth]."

first or twenty-first century. Here I am not speaking of the continuum of faith responses that Culpepper reads in the characters. Perhaps there is a continuum but it is found within individual characters, and as one moves through the narrative their positions seem always in motion.[126]

As a result, for Conway, while the dualism of the Fourth Gospel is undermined by the ambiguous manner in which characters are presented, the notion of faith is also transformed in the process, becoming "less stable, but no less productive" since the characters' resistance to be "flattened into a particular type warns against the temptation to flatten our own lives into an over-simplified, unambiguous posture."[127]

The cumulative effect of these works reveals that studies in the Fourth Gospel's characterisation have been fruitful, suggesting different ways in which its characters might play a role in communicating its intent. As evidenced by this brief overview, a debate is underway as scholars debate whether the Fourth Gospel's secondary characters such as the disciples should be treated as autonomous individuals, as strictly literary phenomena, or as a combination of both. Regarding this, Burnett has helpfully proposed that "it would seem wise to understand characterization, for any biblical text at least, on a continuum."[128] For him, if personages were for the most part flat and typical in ancient literature, they at times could also be read as developing and approaching individuality.[129] As a whole, one therefore wonders if literary analysts who emphasise the typical or representational aspects of characters in the Fourth Gospel (Culpepper) have not remained too dependent on form-critics (Bultmann, Collins) for their literary conclusions.[130] *Contra* this tendency, Conway proposed to consider further how the Fourth Gospel's characters develop and thus "seem always in motion."[131] Likewise, it has been this study's purpose to research how the faith and understanding of the Fourth Gospel disciples develop throughout the narrative. It was argued that Jesus was the protagonist of a plot within the plot, in which he was commissioned to train a group of believers to become his human successors in the ensuing trial. Throughout their training, the dis-

---

[126] Conway, "Ambiguity," 340.

[127] Conway, "Ambiguity," 341.

[128] F. W. Burnett, "Characterization and Reader Construction of Characters in the Gospels," *Semeia* 63 (1993): 15. See also Thompson, "God," 184: "It is impossible and unnecessary, then, to escape the view that characters are representational, in one respect or another, of 'real people.' Nevertheless, we can be profitably directed by the formalist cautions that the text itself is the primary shaping framework for understanding character."

[129] Burnett gives the example of Peter in the Gospel of Matthew (Burnett, "Characterization," 20–23).

[130] So Burnett, "Characterization," 9–10, who contends that "Biblical studies has inherited its emphasis upon the typical and the representative from the form-critics who, in turn, took over the emphasis on the typical from classicists." For him, "The typical and conventional were enhanced in the study of biblical characterization by the repression of the individual and the personal. The latter emphases in the Gospels were seen as later and legendary."

[131] Conway, "Ambiguity," 340.

ciples constantly struggled to understand and follow Jesus adequately. But if
the presentation of the disciples' faith and understanding is not exempt from
ambiguities, it must be stated once more that the implied author never explicitly
charges them with being in a state of unbelief.[132] Moreover, the development
and, at times, ambiguous characterisation of the disciples do not necessarily
cancel any typical or representative aspects on their part (as argued in chapter 3
regarding the characters of Judas and Thomas), but, as Conway showed, the
lack of consensus on such matters is at the very least disquieting.[133] Thus, based
on the conclusions reached throughout this study, it appears that research in the
area of the rhetorical functions of the presentation of the disciples' faith and
understanding could gain new insights by focusing on another, hopefully more
fruitful, direction.

d. A Way Forward: The Disciples as Figures for Identification

The conclusion proposed earlier regarding the rhetorical purpose of the Fourth
Gospel was that the implied author wished to lead his readers toward a better
rounded belief and understanding of Jesus and his mission so that, like the disciples, they may correspondingly take on the task of witnessing in their own
world. If such a conclusion is on the right track, it follows that a potentially
rewarding question to pose is the larger one of how the text invites readers to
participate in the narrative by identifying with the disciples, rather than simply
asking what the disciples and their response to Jesus may represent in the readers.[134] If the narrative is supposed to shape its readers, it is primarily because it
invites them to identify with some of its characters, especially the disciples. As
such, readers are bound closely to the text as narrative.

In recent years, Beck has made a significant contribution to the study of
Johannine characterisation in proposing that the anonymity of certain characters who receive important narrative space (*e.g.*, Jesus' mother, the Samaritan
woman, the lame man, the man born blind, the Beloved Disciple) enhances

---

[132] For instance, we argued that Thomas' unbelief in 20:24–29 regarding Jesus' risen-ness,
though undoubtedly problematic, was first and foremost a failure to trust in the witnessing activity of his fellow disciples. Moreover, it can be argued, together with Lee, "Easter Faith," 43,
and Blanquart, *Premier jour*, 117, that Thomas' demands for proof is indicative of a positive
desire to meet the risen Jesus in faith.

[133] At the very least, one might say that if indeed characters such as the disciples are meant
to be understood as 'types' or 'representatives,' today's readers must be very cautious, lest they
fall under Conway's judgment: "One is soon led to suspect that the proposed types are found
not so much in the text, as they are in individual interpretations of the text" (Conway, "Ambiguity," 328).

[134] This is not to deny that the disciples' response to Jesus in the narrative may in some way
represent certain stances in implied readers. In fact, it may be that readers identify with the
disciples because they are in some way representative of features in themselves.

their potential for readers' identification.[135] Thus, "their positive and consistent portrayal combines with their anonymity to facilitate the reader's entry into and involvement with the narrative world."[136] The most important of these anonymous characters is of course the Beloved Disciple since he presents the most complete paradigm of discipleship with which readers are supposed to identify. For Beck, this paradigm consists of an active faith response to Jesus' word, without the prerequisite of a 'sign' or any visible demonstration, that leads to witnessing to the power of Jesus' word and what it accomplishes.[137]

Unfortunately, Beck's stress on anonymity as a means of enticing readers to participate in the narrative leads him to overemphasise such a role.[138] More importantly, his analysis tends to belittle the significance of named characters for identification. Beck argues that "the responses of unnamed characters, culminating with the disciple Jesus loved, are offered by the Gospel as *the* model of appropriate response to Jesus."[139] Thus, the named characters with a degree of positive portrayal (*e.g.* John, Peter, Nathanael, Thomas, Mary Magdalene, Mary of Bethany, and Martha) remain inappropriate models for reader identification and imitation.[140] All in all, Beck considers that a degree of ambiguity in the portrayal of certain Fourth Gospel characters precludes them as models for identification. But this conclusion is unwarranted. Indeed, it appears that characters' potential for identification depends much more on the correspondence of their situation with that of implied readers and on the process they undergo in the narrative than on their positive and anonymous portrayal, though this certainly also plays a role to facilitate reader identification. Marguerat, for instance, puts it as follows: "La règle est simple: plus les personnages ressemblent à des êtres réels, c'est-à-dire plus leur vie coïncide avec celle (réelle ou fantasmée)

---

[135] Beck, *Discipleship*, 17–34: "When anonymity is consistently combined with indications of the character's narrative significance and positive portrayal, the identity distinction of the name is erased, creating a gap readers are invited to fill with their own identity. Identifying with the character may provide readers entry into the narrative world, confronting them with the circumstances and situations of the characters in the text" (p. 12). See also his prior D. R. Beck, "The Narrative Function of Anonymity in Fourth Gospel Characterization," *Semeia* 63 (1993): 143–58, with a critique by E. R. Thibeaux, "Reading Readers Reading Characters," *Semeia* 63 (1993): 220–24.

[136] Beck, *Discipleship*, 33.

[137] Beck, *Discipleship*, 137.

[138] For instance, Beck, *Discipleship*, 101–7, argues that the pericope of the adulterous woman (7:53–8:11) is only a partial fit to his proposed paradigm of appropriate response to Jesus because she shows no sign of a faith-response. Yet, he concludes that "The contrast with her accusers and the equivalence with which Jesus addresses her prompts readers to include her among the favourably portrayed respondents to Jesus' word, even though her response must be assumed since it is not explicit" (p. 137). The present study chose to pass over this section of the narrative on text critical grounds.

[139] Beck, *Discipleship*, 9 (emphasis added).

[140] Beck, *Discipleship*, 138–42.

du lecteur, plus ces personnages exerceront d'attrait sur le lecteur."[141] At this point, Conway's emphasis on the ambiguity of character portrayal in the Fourth Gospel must receive its due approval.

The characters that show signs of faith in the midst of their uncertainties and ambiguity still contribute in significant ways to the ministry and mission of Jesus. Indeed, perhaps they are more effective in and through their expression of a more rounded, more complex life of faith, than they might be from a place of flat and rigid certainty.[142]

It is *because* most disciples are not consistently portrayed positively that readers are led to identify with them and, in turn, to grow with them in faith and understanding. The implied author thus uses the resemblance between the disciples and the imperfect life of discipleship of his implied readership to nurture their faith and understanding.

How do implied readers identify with characters in the story? In the Fourth Gospel, implied readers can at times identify with the protagonist Jesus, for they share his evaluative point of view. Yet, since Jesus represents the perfect model of what implied readers would like to be (*e.g.* 13:12–17), and, more importantly, since he possesses traits that implied readers could never own (*e.g.* 20:29a), identification with him may be deemed "idealistic."[143] Further, since Jesus is portrayed as divine as well as human, there are aspects of his characterisation and mission with which readers cannot and should not identify. Clearly, in the narrative implied readers most easily identify with the disciples, for their situation is on the whole analogous to theirs: they too are disciples of Jesus, believing and being equipped to become effective witnesses.[144] This perspective nicely dovetails with Marguerat's theory of the process of identification with characters in Biblical literature.[145] For him, readers are called to a process of "refiguration,"[146] that is, the appropriation of the narrative's plot in order to graft it onto the plot of their own lives. Between these two plots, there is no simple replication, but "attirance, influence, sollicitation."[147] Readers must not simply adhere to characters, but are invited to take part, within their own world, in a process similar to that which characters are undergoing in the narra-

---

[141] Marguerat and Bourquin, *Lire*, 84.

[142] Conway, "Ambiguity," 340.

[143] See discussion in Powell, *Narrative Criticism*, 56–58.

[144] Moreover, since implied readers have come to empathise with Jesus, they share his sympathy for the disciples. See Powell, *Narrative Criticism*, 57: "As a general rule, the reader of a narrative will care the most about those characters for whom the protagonist cares the most."

[145] D. Marguerat, "L'exégèse biblique à l'heure du lecteur," in *La Bible en récits: L'exégèse biblique à l'heure du lecteur*, ed. by D. Marguerat, MdB 48 (Genève: Labor et Fides, 2003), 29–31. Marguerat, *inter alia*, agrees with Culpepper's typological analysis of Johannine characters (p. 29).

[146] "Refiguration," also called "mimesis III," comes after "préfiguration" and "configuration" in the theory developed by Ricoeur (*cf.* Ricoeur, *Temps et récit. Tome I*, 105–62).

[147] Marguerat, "Exégèse," 30.

tive. For instance, implied readers are not meant simply to identify with Mary Magdalene's feelings of despair and helplessness as she is confronted with the empty tomb (20:1–2, 11). Indeed, as believers, they already know that Jesus has risen from the dead. Yet, through Mary's lack of insight (20:1, 13, 15) and inadequate comprehension of Jesus' new kind of presence (20:17), they are led together with her to consider their understanding of and relationship with the person of Jesus in a renewed way, so that they too can go on and witness about Jesus' resurrection (20:18).[148] Arguably, what is true of the implied readers' mode of identification with Mary Magdalene is also true of their identification with the disciples as a group through the narrative. Implied readers identify with the disciples as the narrative recounts their preparation for ministry, so that their own faith can be reinforced and their understanding nourished. In that sense, de Jonge is correct to suggest that "the disciples' function in the argument is to provide a model of accepting Jesus' words and to be the link between the Jesus of the narrative and the reader after the narrative is finished (17:20; 20:23, 27; 21:15–17)."[149] For him, the model portrayed by the disciples is that of characters whose questions and misunderstandings "call for further instruction by Jesus, the true διδάσκαλος, or lead to new action by him,"[150] so that the term "model" must not be understood as implying that the disciples are excellent examples of specified qualities (such as faith and understanding).[151] Rather, the model they portray is meant to facilitate the process of reader's identification with them.

The notion of identification, therefore, must not be taken to mean that implied readers can be substituted for the disciples at all points in the narrative. To identify with characters is not equivalent to putting oneself under the skin of characters in the narrative, to feel what they feel for instance. Indeed, since the world of the narrative is different from that of readers, "le processus d'identification n'est pas une équation simple."[152] Rather, the process of iden-

---

[148] A similar process of identification is probably also intended in the instances where the disciples' lack of understanding of Jesus leads him to explain himself and to include the disciples further in his task (4:38; 6:10, 12; 9:4).

[149] de Jonge, *Stranger*, 15. Earlier, de Jonge explains what he means by "accepting Jesus' words": "True disciples listen, see, believe, overcome offence, remain with Jesus and follow him" (p. 14). He adds: "It is clear that the disciples, both in their acceptance and their misunderstanding of Jesus' word, are portrayed as models for future generations of believers" (p. 15).

[150] de Jonge, *Stranger*, 15.

[151] De Jonge's notion of "a model" could be (and has been) misunderstood. Indeed, this led Siker-Gieseler, "Disciples," 220–21, to retort to de Jonge's thesis that one must differentiate between *disciples* who are largely negative models for readers, while individual characters embodying *discipleship* (the Samaritan Woman, the Capernaum official, the man born blind, and Martha) "function to portray a more positive model for future generations of believers." However, as mentioned by Köstenberger, *Missions*, 150, n.29: "Certainly the concept of *discipleship* in the Fourth Gospel is also related to the Fourth Gospel's *disciples*."

[152] Marguerat, "Exégèse," 30.

tification with characters in a story allows for both attraction and repulsion, involvement and distancing in the relationship. The disciples exemplify a process of preparation for ministry, but as implied readers identify with them, they can have feelings of empathy, sympathy, and even antipathy towards them.[153] For instance, implied readers can certainly *empathise* with the disciples when Peter, speaking on behalf of the group, declares: "You have the words of eternal life, and we have believed, and come to know, that you are the Holy One of God" (6:68–69). They are in complete agreement with them and rejoice over such a confession on their part. However, they can only *sympathise* with the disciples as they question Jesus' willingness to go to Judea in 11:8: "Rabbi, the Jews were just seeking to stone you, and are you going there again?" Implied readers can understand the disciples' reluctance to let Jesus go to his death, yet they know that such a death is necessary and ultimately beneficial. Though they do not share the disciples' evaluative point of view, they are not led to judge them harshly or to disengage entirely from them. This, in fact, is the case for most of the instances of disciples' misunderstandings in the narrative. Finally, *antipathy* or disdain for the disciples is also produced in the narrative. The most obvious example is that of Judas, one of "the Twelve," whose hypocrisy and ultimate betrayal are in total opposition to the narrative's evaluative point of view on Jesus and his mission.[154] To a lesser extent, Peter's denials of Jesus (18:17, 25, 27) lead implied readers to evaluate his actions negatively and to distance themselves from him, though they certainly sympathise with his fear. From all this, the overwhelming sense is that the implied author of the Fourth Gospel partly relies on such a potential for identification to achieve his purpose. Since the situation of the implied readers, that of faithful followers of Jesus needing to be effective in their witnessing activity, is similar to that of the disciples in the narrative, it follows that the process of identifying with the disciples is necessary to the success of their mission. As Darr proposed regarding Lukan characters:

> The process of constructing character is neither neutral nor unidirectional. Even as we fashion *dramatis personae*, we are being positioned and maneuvered – indeed, shaped – by the rhetoric of the text. While building Luke's characters, the audience experiences a certain character building of its own![155]

---

[153] For discussions of these terms as they relate to identification, see *e.g.* Powell, *Narrative Criticism*, 56–58; Marguerat and Bourquin, *Lire*, 87–88.

[154] Thatcher, "Character," 439–40, shows that Judas is mostly characterised by "telling" so that his inner thoughts are displayed by the narrator. This contrasts with Peter, whose inner thoughts and motives are almost never revealed (except 20:9), so that implied readers are left to evaluate his actions with the telling asides. As Thatcher proposes: "Because observation is the normal means of determining the motives of individuals, this silence makes Peter a bit more 'real' to the audience than Judas" (p. 347). This potentially facilitates, for Peter and other faithful disciples, the process of identification by implied readers. On "telling" and "showing," see Booth, *Fiction*, 3–9.

[155] Darr, *Character Building*, 59.

This certainly applies to the Fourth Gospel's disciples as well. In constructing the characters of the disciples throughout the narrative, readers are being "built" by the text. As they identify with the characters of the disciples, they too are strengthened in their faith and understanding. It could therefore be argued that the implied author's emphasis on the faith and limited understanding of the disciples prior to Jesus' glorification is a rhetorical device used to enable readers to identify with key characters from the start of the narrative and not to see themselves as in a totally different situation until after the completion of Jesus' mission. Likewise, the early depiction of the disciples already acting as "witnesses" bringing others to faith (1:41–42, 45–46) may serve such a rhetorical function, so that the implied readers recognise in the disciples their own status as believers, their calling to become effective witnesses, and their potential lacunae in effectively fulfilling this calling. Like the disciples, readers too must move from belief to further understanding.

B. Temporality and the Disciples' Faith and Understanding

There are notorious problems associated with temporality (narrative time) in the Fourth Gospel.[156] The purpose of this section of the study is not to solve them, but rather to bring clarity to several issues of temporality surrounding the presentation of the disciples' faith and understanding in the Fourth Gospel, thus highlighting key difficulties of interpretation. The primary issue that this section will seek to clarify is how the instances of faith and understanding on the part of the disciples are meant to be understood prior to the resurrection of Jesus. To what extent, how, and for what purpose might the implied author's temporal perspective have affected his depiction of the pre-resurrection experience of the disciples? After a brief overview of scholarly theological and historical perspectives on the faith of the disciples in the Fourth Gospel, an attempt will be made to study this issue from the perspective of a literary critical analysis.

1. A Brief Overview of Theological and Historical Perspectives on the Faith and Understanding of the Disciples

The basis of much discussion about the faith and understanding of the disciples in the Fourth Gospel are often theological understandings and historical reconstructions of Johannine soteriology. Indeed, apart from rare exceptions,[157] the great majority of scholars agree that, in the Fourth Gospel, faith is the sole means of attaining salvation (*cf.* 1:12–13; 3:14–18, 35–36; 6:35, 39–40, 47; 7:37–39; 11:25–26; 20:31). But since scholars' soteriological findings are

---

[156] For an overview of such issues, see Culpepper, *Anatomy*, 51–75.

[157] *Cf.* Motyer, *Father*, 59: "Faith *on its own* carries no automatic promise of life at all" (*i.e.*, it must be supplemented by discipleship).

variegated, confusion can easily follow regarding the status of the faith and understanding of the disciples. For instance, Brown, representing the most common position, argues that in the Fourth Gospel "The life-giving factor is the Spirit (vi 63, vii 38–39), and that Spirit is given only after Jesus is lifted up to the Father (vii 39, xvi 7, xix 30, xx 22)." Thus, "the full faith in Jesus which brings life to men is possible only after the resurrection, when men confess him as Lord and God (xx 28). Only then do they understand what he means when he says, 'I AM' (viii 28)."[158] Brown does recognize that Jesus offers eternal life as a present opportunity during the course of his ministry (*e.g.* 3:15–16, 36; 6:40), but explains this paradox by stating that Jesus is actually talking to the post-resurrection believing audience of the Fourth Gospel.[159] Similarly, for Painter, it is only after the uplifting or glorification of the Son of Man which manifested the true glory of God in his love for the world, after the resurrection, and after the coming of the Paraclete, that authentic faith became possible through the effective judgment of the world by Jesus.[160] Before, people, including the disciples, were unable to believe because of the power of darkness that blinded their eyes (12:36b–43). However, when Jesus was lifted up, the power of evil was broken (12:31) and faith on a universal scale became possible.[161] Yet, the numerous references favouring the view that the disciples had a close and authentic faith relationship to Jesus necessitates Painter's ambiguous, if not contradictory, statement that "faulty perception led to their defection, but the *integrity* of their faith led to their reinstatement."[162] Thus, for him, although popular, partial, and

---

[158] Brown, *John*, 1:cxviii, 507. For similar views, see *e.g.* O. Cullmann, *Early Christian Worship*, trans. by A. S. Todd and J. B. Torrance (London: SCM, 1953), 40–47; G. M. Burge, *The Anointed Community: The Holy Spirit in the Johannine Tradition* (Grand Rapids: Eerdmans, 1987), 116–49; Dodd, *Interpretation*, 372; J. D. G. Dunn, *Baptism in the Holy Spirit: A Re-examination of the New Testament Teaching on the Gift of the Spirit in Relation to Pentecostalism Today* (Philadelphia: Westminster, 1970), 178–82; I. de la Potterie, "Parole et esprit dans S. Jean," in *L'Évangile de Jean: Sources, rédaction, théologie*, ed. by M. de Jonge, BETL 44 (Gembloux/Leuven: J. Duculot/Leuven University Press, 1975), 201: "La progression [of the theme of word and spirit] fondamentale consiste dans le passage du temps de Jésus au temps de l'Esprit. Dès le début, certes, il s'agit de la foi. Mais celle-ci ne devient la veritable foi chrétienne qu'à partir de la résurrection, sous l'action de l'Esprit."

[159] Brown, *John*, 1:cxviii. See also J. T. Forestell, *The Word of the Cross: Salvation as Revelation in the Fourth Gospel*, AnBib 57 (Rome: Biblical Institute Press, 1974), 19, 191–92: "The death of Jesus is the necessary condition for the communication of life to men. The historical events of the public ministry are seen as signs or types of the relationship which now prevails between Jesus and the believer on the one hand, and between Jesus and the world on the other. It is the glorified Jesus who speaks throughout the gospel and he addresses the readers of the gospel more than the disciples and the Jews of the public ministry" (p. 19).

[160] Painter, *Quest*, 414–15. See also J. Painter, "Eschatological Faith in the Gospel of John," in *Reconciliation and Hope: New Testament Essays on Atonement and Eschatology Presented to L. L. Morris on his 60th Birthday*, ed. by R. J. Banks (Exeter: Paternoster, 1974), 36–52.

[161] Painter, *Quest*, 391–411.

[162] Painter, *Quest*, 414 (emphasis added).

superficial faith is the only type of faith expressed during Jesus' ministry,[163] the cases where the belief of the disciples is presented in authentic terms simply "overshadow the development of the fullness of faith and are an assessment in retrospect which recognizes an integrity lacking in the superficial faith of the multitudes."[164] For Painter:

> Because the Gospel purports to be written testimony for this new situation, there is no distinction in terms between the professions of faith and the descriptions of authentic faith in Jesus' discourses. The record of his words and works, which were largely ineffective during his ministry, is offered as that which can provoke authentic faith (20:30f.).[165]

Over against these understandings, several scholars believe that, according to the Fourth Gospel, life was already fully available during Jesus' earthly ministry. Fortna, for instance, follows Bultmann's views on realised eschatology and understanding of the cross in the Fourth Gospel[166] to assert that Jesus' crucifixion did not accomplish salvation.[167] For him as for Bultmann, what rendered salvation available was solely the incarnation of the Messiah, recognized by faith.[168] Likewise, arguing against Thüsing who interprets all the images of life and salvation in the Fourth Gospel (water, bread, light, resurrection) as referring to realities not available prior to the coming of the Spirit and as reflecting the author's post-Easter's situation,[169] Loader argues that such distinctions of time are irrelevant because "soteriology [...] is essentially Christology."[170]

---

[163] Painter, *Quest*, 414: "From the narrative confessions it is clear that authentic faith was not a reality during Jesus' ministry." Particularly relevant to the present study, Painter notes that misunderstanding of Jesus' role and significance is a mark of superficial faith (pp. 411–12).

[164] Painter, *Quest*, 414.

[165] Painter, *Quest*, 415.

[166] See below (Chapter 5. Conclusion: Johannine Faith and Understanding) for an overview and analysis of Bultmann's understanding of these themes.

[167] R. T. Fortna, "From Christology to Soteriology: A Redactional-Critical Study of Salvation in the Fourth Gospel," *Int* 27 (1973): 37: "Yet nowhere, so far as one can tell, did the author consider Jesus' death as itself effective, accomplishing in any way man's salvation."

[168] Fortna, "From Christology," 44–45: "But it follows from his thoroughly Christological purpose, concentrating on the deeds of Jesus during his lifetime, that such salvation as the Messiah bestows at his coming is now present among men, whose only need is to receive it by faith."

[169] W. Thüsing, *Die Erhöhung und Verherrlichung Jesu im Johannesevangelium*, 3rd ed., NTAbh 21 (Münster: Aschendorff, 1979), 321–24. For Thüsing, the author of the Fourth Gospel had no interest in what might have been available before Jesus' glorification, and therefore no interest either in what might have been available to the disciples prior to Jesus' resurrection (putting the issue on a similar level as what might have been available to Old Testament saints). Similarly, for J. Blank, *Krisis: Untersuchungen zur johanneischen Christologie und Eschatologie* (Freiburg im Breisgau: Lambertus-Verlag, 1964), 141, the evangelist knew of no proclamation or message of Jesus independent of what the Church proclaimed (quoted in W. R. G. Loader, *The Christology of the Fourth Gospel: Structure and Issues*, BBET 23 (Frankfurt: Verlag Peter Lang, 1989), 129).

[170] Loader, *Christology*, 128–29.

Events other than the incarnation of the Word do not impact on the availability of salvation. For instance, Loader argues that what is added by the coming of the Spirit mentioned in 7:37–39 (a reference often used by those denying that salvation was available prior to the resurrection in the Fourth Gospel) is not life but rather deeper understanding and abundance.[171] Müller also affirms that eternal life was available during Jesus' earthly ministry, but approaches the issue from a different angle in distinguishing the presence of salvation both before and after Jesus' resurrection, and the different basis for salvation before and after Easter. Before Easter, there was a unique and unrepeatable situation during which eternal life was given in encounter and fellowship with the earthly Jesus; after Easter, salvation came on the basis of Jesus' atoning death.[172]

Finally, other scholars argue that in the Fourth Gospel, life was only partially available before Christ's glorification, but somehow more fully after Easter. For instance, Porsch proposes a two-stage model of salvation which follows his two-stage model of the gift of the Spirit. First, partial salvation based on beginning faith is offered to people in the form of Jesus' revelatory word during his ministry. Second, such faith is perfected or completed after Jesus' glorification and gift of the Spirit.[173] Turner's work provides another example of a staged model of salvation. For him, disciples were unable to come to authentic faith during Jesus' earthly ministry, as only "foretastes" or "experiences" of life were available for them.[174] Yet, such a life became fully available after Jesus' glorification through his death and resurrection: "This complete, the Spirit can now be given by Jesus. People are then able to come to true authentic faith; his Spirit-imbued revelation can now take full, deep and transforming hold on their lives."[175] More recently, Bennema proposed yet another position in a study on the role of belief in salvation.[176] He argues that the cross is constitutional to salvation[177] and that adequate faith (one that leads to salvation if it is continuous)

---

[171] Loader, *Christology*, 129–31.

[172] T. E. Müller, *Das Heilsgeschehen im Johannesevangelium: Eine exegetische Studie, zugleich der Versuch einer Antwort an Rudolf Bultmann* (Zürich/Frankfurt: Gotthelf-Verlag, 1961), 24–25, 32–33, 132, 138–39.

[173] F. Porsch, *Pneuma und Wort: Ein exegetischer Beitrag zur Pneumatologie des Johannesevangelium*, FTS 16 (Frankfurt: Knecht, 1974), 66–72, 144.

[174] M. Turner, *The Holy Spirit and Spiritual Gifts: In the New Testament Church and Today*, Rev. ed. (Peabody, MA: Hendrickson, 1998), 60–75.

[175] Turner, *Holy Spirit*, 75.

[176] C. Bennema, *The Power of Saving Wisdom: An Investigation of Spirit and Wisdom in Relation to the Soteriology of the Fourth Gospel*, WUNT 2/148 (Tübingen: Mohr Siebeck, 2002), 142–47. See also Bennema, "Giving," 195–213.

[177] *Cf.* Bennema, *Saving Wisdom*, 2–17. Authors often bring references such as 1:29; 6:51; 10:15; and 20:23 in defence of an objective atoning view of the cross. See G. L. Carey, "The Lamb of God and Atonement Theories," *TynBul* 32 (1981): 97–122; Köstenberger, *Missions*, 76–81; M. Turner, "Atonement and the Death of Jesus in John: Some Questions to Bultmann and Forestell," *EvQ* 62 (1990): 99–122.

is "constituted by a belief that sufficiently understands the true identity and mission (especially the significance of the cross) of the Father and Son and the nature of their relationship."[178] Yet, Bennema recognises the paradox that in the Fourth Gospel life seems available both only after the cross *and* in the person and revelatory teaching of Jesus, hence before the cross (1:4; 5:21–26; 11:25; 14:6). To further complicate the matter, he acknowledges that, though it is generally not the case, the disciples at times demonstrate a sufficient understanding (17:6–8), an adequate belief-response (6:68–69; 16:29–30), and therefore a life-giving relationship with Jesus (13:10; 15:3; 17:12) before the cross and the giving of the Spirit (20:22). Thus, he proposes that the disciples were in a unique situation: "Before the cross, the disciples were already in a life-giving relationship with Jesus, but this life was tied to the historical Jesus, who was soon going to leave them."[179] For Bennema, the cross, which made "widely and fully available the life within him," and the gift of the Spirit who "would sustain the disciples' relation with the glorified Jesus and the Father, and hence their salvation" solved the problem of Jesus' leaving the disciples.[180] Bennema's conclusion thus also represents a staged model of salvation similar to that of Turner and Porsch, but for him, it does not follow that the Fourth Gospel presents corresponding stages of faith (since adequate belief-responses were already possible before the cross).[181]

The reconstructions attempted by these scholars had to take into account instances where faith appears to be a reality during the pre-Easter ministry of Jesus, and thus had to reckon with the fact that the story as a sequence of events told in the narrative neither easily matches their theological and historical reconstructions of Johannine soteriology, nor their understanding of what constitutes true faith. The multiplicity of understandings proposed suggests that it might be fruitful to attempt to find greater clarity in these matters through a

---

[178] Bennema, *Saving Wisdom*, 142.

[179] Bennema, *Saving Wisdom*, 144.

[180] Bennema, *Saving Wisdom*, 144. Bennema clarifies: "Before the cross, the availability of life and the activity of the Spirit were limited and tied to the historical Jesus (cf. αὔτω γὰρ ἦν πνεῦμα in 7:39), but after Jesus' glorification, the life of the glorified Son and the Father would become fully available through the Spirit. Thus, it appears that the life of the Father and Son and the life-giving Spirit could already be adequately (though partially) *experienced* during Jesus' ministry, but could only be '*given*', i.e., more fully experienced, after Jesus' glorification" (p. 145).

[181] Bennema, *Saving Wisdom*, 212, also distinguishes between "life" and "salvation": "[...] salvation encompasses the gift of eternal life (as the divine life of the Father and Son in which the believer participates), but also denotes the liberation/removal from sin, change of father, etc. As a result, within Jesus' ministry a life-giving relationship with Jesus was already available, but not yet all its benefits." Furthermore, for Bennema, if the cross is climactic and constitutional for salvation, life was already available during Jesus' earthly ministry based on the Spirit's activity.

narrative analysis of the Fourth Gospel in general, and more specifically in the present case, through its treatment of narrative time.

2. Retrospection and the Merging of Time Perspectives

In the Fourth Gospel, the temporal perspective of the narrator is "retrospective."[182] The narrator tells the story of Jesus from the vantage point of a group of later followers of Jesus, as several confessional uses of "we" language indicate (*cf.* 1:14, 16; 21:24). Therefore, throughout the Fourth Gospel, it is the perspective of the Johannine community[183] that is implicitly presented as the correct interpretation of the events related in the narrative and of the person and ministry of Jesus.[184] But one cannot lose sight of the fact that it is also *for* this community that the Fourth Gospel is written (20:31). As mentioned by Schnelle:

> This means that there are two fundamental levels in the communication process sought by the evangelist: (1) the level internal to the text, which portrays the ongoing periods of the narration from the preexistence to the post-existence of Jesus Christ; (2) the level of the Johannine community, external to the text, for which John conceived his story of Jesus in order to lead them to the knowledge and understanding of the saving work of God in Jesus Christ. The interpreter must always keep both levels in mind, since John intends his story of Jesus for the community but at the same time binds the community to the story of Jesus.[185]

Thus, within the narrative time, that is, what Schnelle calls the "level internal to the text," are present both (*i*) the time of the story of Jesus and the disciples, and (*ii*) the time of the narrator and the implied readers.[186] But to complicate this matter further, in the Fourth Gospel the two perspectives are sometimes clearly distinguished, and sometimes creatively compressed.[187] A well-known example is 16:1–4, where Jesus announces to his disciples that a time would come when believers would be excommunicated from the synagogue. Yet, the story of the blind man (9:42) and the conclusion of the first part of the narrative (12:42), indicate that what Jesus in the Farewell discourse considered to be a future event

---

[182] Culpepper, *Anatomy*, 27–32. Resseguie, *Strange*, 8, prefers to speak of "posterior narration."

[183] In the present literary analysis, the term "community" refers to the implied audience, which, as was argued, is itself composed of believers. It does not, therefore, refer to historically reconstructed Johannine communities (*cf.* Brown, *Community*; Martyn, *History*; Ashton, *Understanding*, 166–74). For a critique of such historical reconstructions and proposals for letting insights gained by literary criticism be taken seriously by social-scientific and historical critics, see *e.g.* S. C. Barton, "Can We Identify the Gospel Audiences?," in *The Gospels for All Christians: Rethinking the Gospel Audiences*, ed. by R. Bauckham (Edinburgh: T. & T. Clark, 1998), 173–79, 189–94.

[184] Culpepper, *Anatomy*, 28: "By employing the device of a narrator who speaks retrospectively, the author shows that he is not attempting to record 'history' without interpreting it, for to do so would mean that the reader might miss its significance."

[185] U. Schnelle, "Recent Views on John's Gospel," *WW* 21 (2001): 355–56.

[186] This perspective thus approximates that of Brown as discussed in the preceding section.

[187] Lincoln, *Truth*, 20–21.

had already been narrated as integral to his own story. This creative merging of time perspectives in the Fourth Gospel is the work of the Beloved Disciple, the narrator of the story, aided by the Paraclete. Indeed, the way the retrospective temporal perspective of the narrator can be played on two levels, that of the earthly Jesus and the disciples, and that of the Beloved Disciple's community, is due to the Paraclete being the link between the witnessing activity of Jesus and that of his disciples: "[The Paraclete] will bring to remembrance what Jesus has said, not simply by reproducing his words but by unfolding their significance for the new situation in which the disciples find themselves."[188] More importantly, for Lincoln, "the perspectives can merge because, for the implied author, both the trial of Jesus and that of his followers are part of the overall lawsuit of God with the world."[189] These insights dovetail quite well with the analyses of the Gospel's subplot and of implied readers' identification with the disciples proposed above. As Lincoln further asserts: "[...] By involving its implied readers in the narrative, [the story] reinforces for them the right verdict they have made [*i.e.*, belief] and, if they are experiencing the costs of such verdict [*i.e.*, expulsions from the synagogue], gives them the resources of the perspective of the ongoing lawsuit so that they continue their own witness."[190]

It is important to note that this merging of temporal perspectives necessarily leads contemporary readers to consider to what extent the narrative depiction of the disciples' faith and understanding is affected by the present, historical situation of the implied author and its implied readership. What is at issue is how one must decide whether to interpret the disciples' portrayal in the narrative at face value or as reflecting a post-Easter state of affairs. As was hinted in chapter 2, the merging of time perspectives is evident in the confessions of the disciples early on in the narrative regarding Jesus as the Messiah (1:41), the one written about in the Mosaic Law and in the prophets (1:45), the Son of God, and the King of Israel (1:49), since they seem to reflect the implied author's post-resurrection belief and understanding of Jesus.[191] But should readers understand that the disciples historically believed in Jesus as a result of Jesus manifesting his glory in 2:1–11 or does such an account simply reflect the belief of the post-Easter disciples and community who beheld Jesus' glory manifested

---

[188] Lincoln, *John*, 397. On the Spirit/Paraclete as agent to the remembering of the disciples, see L. W. Hurtado, "Remembering and Revelation: The Historic and Glorified Jesus in the Gospel of John," in *Israel's God and Rebecca's Children, Christology and Community in Early Judaism and Christianity: Essays in Honor of Larry W. Hurtado and Alan F. Segal*, ed. by D. B. Capes, A. D. DeConick, and H. K. Bond (Waco, TX: Baylor University Press, 2008), 207–12.

[189] Lincoln, *Truth*, 34.

[190] Lincoln, *Truth*, 35.

[191] Painter, "Faith," 49, presents possible alternative interpretations (regarding 1:49): "The working of the confession is capable of being understood at two levels: in terms of the Messiah of Jewish expectation or in terms of the unique, incarnate, Son of God of Johannine understanding." And, as he puts it in a note (n.2): "Understood in terms of Johannine irony the words 'Rabbi, you are the Son of God...' express awareness of the incarnation, that the unique Son of God is to be known in a man, a mere Rabbi."

during "the hour" (2:4), *i.e.* events surrounding his death and resurrection?[192] In other words, for contemporary readers, the difficulty is to distinguish questions about the historical disciples and questions about the disciples in the Fourth Gospel's narrative. Or, to put it another way, what is the relationship of the 'story world' of the Johannine narrative's disciples to the 'real world' of the life of the historical disciples?[193]

This move from a narrative to a historical level is certainly influenced by the historical consciousness of present day readers. Moreover, such a move is not the primary interest of this study. Yet, it must be said that the narrative itself raises such historical questions, for the narrative of the Fourth Gospel is "history-like."[194] In the next section, another aspect of the narrator's retrospective point of view will be highlighted, since the narrator will be shown to uphold a clear distinction between the pre- and post-resurrection experience of the disciples.

3. Retrospection and Order

According to Estes, interpreters should not consider the whole Gospel narrative as organised using absolute chronology. For him:

> As a pre-modern Gospel writer, the Fourth Evangelist clearly understood a relatively linear chronology. [...] However, it is anachronistic to expect that the Fourth Evangelist would be able (or constrained) to construct his narrative account against an absolute timeframe as would a modern historian.[195]

For Estes, the Fourth Evangelist chose a relative or "dimensional" temporal configuration,[196] which may explain "the perceived disjuncted nature of the text"[197] in the Fourth Gospel. Thus, Estes argues that the Fourth Gospel is more

---

[192] On this section, Brown, *John*, 1:101, puts the issue as follows: "[...] for John the true glory of Jesus is revealed only in 'the hour.' Since vii 39 states clearly that during the ministry Jesus had not yet been glorified, we are to think of vs. 11 either as referring to a partial manifestation of glory, or as being part of the capsulizing of the training of the disciples where their whole career, including their sight of the glory of the resurrected Jesus, is foreshadowed."

[193] Tovey, *Narrative*, 36, asks this very question, but about Jesus.

[194] For a discussion of the relation of narrative analysis to historical analysis, see *e.g.* Ashton, *Understanding*, 425–34; Lincoln, *Truth*, 354–97. As mentioned by Lincoln (p. 380), recognizing that this narrative is history-like is not yet to determine whether "this history-likeness is the result of accurate reporting, is a mix of historical tradition and fictional elements for the sake of making theological points, or is simply a piece of fiction aiming for verisimilitude." Thus, Tovey, *Narrative*, 267–68, is correct to assert that "a narrative-critical approach to the Gospel does not necessarily nor inevitably require the bracketing out of historical questions." Indeed, for Tovey, "it is the Gospel's nature as a theological display text which pushes it into the border region between history and fiction" (p. 268).

[195] D. Estes, *The Temporal Mechanics of the Fourth Gospel: A Theory of Hermeneutical Relativity in the Gospel of John*, BibIntS 92 (Leiden/Boston, MA: Brill, 2008), 135–36.

[196] See Estes, *Temporal*, 74–76, 90–91, for overviews of this concept.

[197] Estes, *Temporal*, 136.

episodic than linear in its overall narrative temporality. Though it is arranged in a coherent and intentional manner, as underscored by the use of cross-references and anachronies,[198] temporal markers or connectives (*e.g.*, μετὰ ταῦτα, τῇ ἐπαύριον, καὶ τῇ ἡμέρα τῇ τρίτη, καὶ ἐγγὺς ἦν τὸ πάσχα) are dependent on the context and can be used to denote a non-linear chronology. For instance, Estes strongly argues that the recurrent mentions of the festivals (*e.g.*, "the feast" in 4:45) are not necessarily chronological but rather thematic markers used to signal thematic shifts that segment the narrative.[199] So for Estes: "the block universe of narrative created by the Fourth Evangelist is not absolute in nature, but in fact composed of multiple dimensions of discrete narrative scenes juxtaposed in the Fourth Evangelist's grand miscellany of temporality."[200] Tovey, likewise, recognises the dimensional temporal configuration of the narrative, with large pieces of material (*e.g.* the prologue, the farewell discourses) appearing to remove the Fourth Gospel from the category of narrative. Yet, he is more resolute than Estes to not lose track of the chronological aspect of the narrative:

> [...] while not entirely free of the episodic character of the Synoptic narratives, the Fourth Gospel shows a more integrated and developed narrative form. [...] The frequent use of temporal markers [...] and connectives such as μετὰ ταῦτα, and the use of flashforward and flashback, give the narrative a chronological and thematic unity.[201]

Therefore, though the Fourth Gospel's narrative gives a strong sense of chronology and order, this is not to say that all the particulars of the narrative necessarily fit neatly within a chronological frame. With this in mind, the Fourth Gospel's narrative is certainly to be understood as both thematically and chronologically organised.[202]

That being said, one particularly relevant aspect of the presentation of the disciples does highlight chronology in the Fourth Gospel. Indeed, the disciples are clearly portrayed as believers already during the earthly ministry of Jesus but as reaching a proper understanding of his person and mission only after his glorification. This is most apparent in the use of anachronies in the narrative. Genette, in his seminal monograph *Figure III*, devotes an important section to order as a narrative category, providing a way to analyse methodologically the temporal movement and sequence of a given narrative.[203] Genette's taxonomical

---

[198] Estes, *Temporal*, 146.

[199] Estes, *Temporal*, 151. Consequently, Estes denies that the Fourth Evangelist meant to present the earthly ministry of Jesus as lasting two and an half years.

[200] Estes, *Temporal*, 162–63.

[201] Tovey, *Narrative*, 34.

[202] Thus, though to some extent it may be said that this perspective relativises the importance of studying characters as they are portrayed sequentially in the narrative, it is far from eliminating its pertinence altogether.

[203] Genette, *Figure III*, 77–121.

theory of the temporal ordering of narratives falls within two broad categories that have been labelled "synchronie" and "anachronie."[204] For him:

Étudier l'ordre temporel d'un récit, c'est confronter l'ordre de disposition des événements ou segments temporels dans le discours narratif à l'ordre de succession de ces mêmes événements ou segments temporels dans l'histoire, en tant qu'il est explicitement indiqué par le récit lui-même, ou qu'on peut l'inférer de tel ou tel indice indirect.[205]

For Genette, "anachronies" must be split into the categories of "analepse" and "prolepse," terms that Genette prefers to "rétrospection" and "anticipation" because they have fewer psychological connotations.[206] On the one hand, analepsis, commonly called "flashback," happens when a narrative discourse re-orders the story by jumping back to an earlier point in the story. On the other hand, prolepsis, commonly called "flash forward," designates the re-ordering of a given story by jumping forward to a later event. Analepsis or prolepsis may refer to events occurring within the construct of the narrative (they are thus internal analepsis or prolepsis), or to events outside of the narrative proper (external analepsis or prolepsis). Finally, Genette identifies "mixed forms" of analepses or prolepses, events beginning either prior to the narrative and continuing into it or beginning during the narrative and continuing beyond it.[207]

Genette's categories remain helpful for the purpose of the present work since two important references to the disciples' faith and understanding are found in external prolepses, referring to events as past even though they are to happen in the future of the disciples, outside of the narrative proper:

2:22   When therefore he was raised from the dead, the disciples remembered that he had said this, and they believed the Scripture and the word that Jesus had spoken.

12:16 His disciples did not understand this at first, but when Jesus was glorified, then they remembered that these things had been written about him and had been done to him.

---

[204] See also Marguerat and Bourquin, *Lire*, 114: "Un récit synchrome se calque sur la chronologie de l'histoire racontée (commençant par le début et terminant par la fin). L'anachronie surgit dès le moment où le récit fait un bond, soit en arrière (vers le passé), soit en avant (vers le futur)."

[205] Genette, *Figure III*, 78–79.

[206] Genette, *Figure III*, 82.

[207] Genette, *Figure III*, 91. Culpepper relies heavily on Genette in a section on "order" in his *Anatomy of the Fourth Gospel*, and he attempts to refine Genette's theory by adding categories that better reflect the temporal field of the Fourth Gospel (Culpepper, *Anatomy*, 51–75). For instance, Culpepper speaks of "historical" and "pre-historical" analepses, recalling respectively events happening in the history of Israel and those occurring in the Godhead in "the indefinable past of the incarnate logos" (p. 57). Likewise, he speaks of "historical" and "eschatological" prolepses, referring to events occurring among the disciples and later believers for the former and to the "end time" for the latter (p. 64). Yet, Culpepper is also forced to admit that the Fourth Gospel often resists precise temporal categorisations. Likewise, Genette, *Figure III*, 79, had himself acknowledged that it was not always possible to reconstitute order in a narrative.

The potential significance of these prolepses[208] is that they cast doubt on the disciples' faith and understanding during the pre-Easter ministry of Jesus, since the disciples had not yet "believed the Scripture and the word that Jesus had spoken" (2:22), and since they had not yet understood Jesus and the Scripture (12:16). Clearly, these references purport that at least several events and sayings of the life of the earthly Jesus, but maybe also his whole life and ministry, could only make sense to the disciples in light of Easter.[209] As mentioned by Hurtado:

> Although GJohn can rightly be characterized as programmatically presenting the earthly ministry of Jesus in light of what believers subsequently came to perceive as his full significance, the author also actually underscores the comparatively limited grasp of Jesus' person that characterized the time of his ministry.[210]

As was argued at length, it does not follow that faith and understanding were altogether absent prior to Easter.[211] On the contrary, they are affirmed at many points in the story, not only through general pronouncements about belief (*e.g.* 5:21–26; 11:25), but also through actual instances of it (*e.g.* 1:41, 45, 49; 2:11; 6:66–69). Thus, through these prolepses, the implied author intends to distinguish the disciples' pre- and post-Easter understandings and insights into the significance of Jesus' identity and ministry in order to demonstrate that Jesus' resurrection produced the decisive growth for them. Because of such a pivotal event, the disciples, now assisted by the Paraclete (14:26; 16:14), were able to

---

[208] Zumstein, "Mémoire," 162, and Zumstein, "Relecture," 174–76, speaks of these as "prolepses de la mémoire," and adds 20:9 to the list. In our opinion, however, this reference is simply reporting a state of affair, though implicitly, one may argue that it points forward to the time when the disciples would understand the Scripture that Jesus must rise from the dead.

[209] So for U. Schnelle, *Das Evangelium nach Johannes*, THKNT 4 (Leipzig: Evangelische Verlagsanstalt, 1998), 21: "The *post-Easter retrospective* is for John equally a theological program and a narrative perspective; it makes it possible for the fourth evangelist to transform theological insights into narrated history." And "The understanding and the unfolding of the Christ-event are carried out as Spirit-wrought post-Easter anamnesis (cf. John 2.17, 22; 12.16; 13.7; 20:9)" (Both quotations and their translations are from P. Stuhlmacher, "Spiritual Remembering: John 14.26," in *The Holy Spirit and Christian Origins. Essays in Honor of James D. G. Dunn*, ed. by G. N. Stanton, B. W. Longenecker, and S. C. Barton (Grand Rapids, MI/ Cambridge: Eerdmans, 2004), 60–61, emphases original).

[210] Hurtado, "Remembering," 200.

[211] Though written from a historical perspective, the following comment by Dunn also makes much sense of the Fourth Gospel's presentation of the faith of the disciples: "I am asserting that the teaching and events of Jesus' ministry did not suddenly become significant in the light of Easter – much more significant, no doubt, as various markers in the Gospels indicate [*e.g.* Mark 9:9; John 2:22], but not significant for the first time. The suggestion that the remembered Jesus was wholly insignificant, unfascinating and unintriguing, having no real impact prior to his death and resurrection, is simply incredible. Peter and others did not first become disciples on Easter day. There was already a response of faith, already a bond of trust, inspired by what they first and subsequently heard and saw Jesus say and do" (J. D. G. Dunn, *Christianity in the Making, volume 1: Jesus Remembered* (Grand Rapids, MI/Cambridge: Eerdmans, 2003), 132).

understand the true significance of Jesus' ministry through the use of memory and Scripture. Post-resurrection and Spirit-led retrospection enabled them to gain new insights into the life of Jesus and thus to believe in a fresh way.[212] They, for instance, remembered the events of the Temple in 2:13–16 and were able to make sense of them through the use of Ps. 69.[213] Likewise, they realised that in 2:19 Jesus was speaking figuratively of the temple of his body that would be destroyed in death but raised up after three days, and so they believed Scripture and Jesus' words.

But what may be the implied author's rhetorical purpose in inserting these prolepses within his narrative? These may arguably be interpreted as pointers to the resolution of the subplot studied above. By indicating how and when the future event will take place, the implied author assists implied readers in their need to comprehend and envisage its resolution.[214] Thus, just as implied readers are led to understand that God's purpose will be accomplished through Jesus' death,[215] they likewise understand that the events surrounding his glorification, especially the resurrection, will provide part of the subplot's resolution. But as Davies proposes, the reference to two times of the disciples "serves to encourage belief in the reader."[216] Indeed, these historical prolepses flash forward to the time when the disciples would react positively to the story in grasping the significance of Jesus' true identity and ministry. Their newfound understanding of the glorification was necessary to their becoming faithful witnesses of the truth at stake in the trial, as it is reflected in the testimony of the Beloved Disciple in the Fourth Gospel. Thus, through the process of identification with the disciples, implied readers are, in turn, encouraged in their belief. Since the prolepses underline the importance of correctly understanding the significance of Jesus' glorification to become effective witnesses, implied readers recognise that they too are being reinforced in their own belief and understanding and thus prepared to become effective witnesses in the ongoing trial. They, like the disciples, must positively react to the story of Jesus by grasping afresh the significance of Jesus' glorification even before it happens in the story proper.

At this point, however, a note of caution must be re-emphasised. The decisive growth in understanding that the implied author upholds regarding the

---

[212] Hurtado, "Remembering," 199, also adds 14:25–26; 16:7, 12, 25 as instances of contrast between the pre- and post-resurrection understanding of the disciples.

[213] See Hays, "Reading," 224.

[214] Marguerat and Bourquin, *Lire*, 166.

[215] This is particularly significant in the allusions to the "hour" interspersed through the narrative, especially in chapters 1–12 (2:4; 7:30; 8:20; 12:27). Through these allusions, the reader is led to anticipate the coming of the "hour" of Jesus: "'The hour' directs the reader forward from the events of chaps. 1–12 to another point in time. This metaphor provides the fourth evangelist with the means of representing in narrative form the dramatic overlay of story time (the events of the Passion) with narrative time (the progress of the 'hour')" (O'Day, "Narrative Time," 158).

[216] Davies, *Rhetoric*, 62.

disciples of Jesus in the narrative is not one that has or still needs to occur in his implied readership. In this sense, the story of the disciples is not, it cannot be, the story of the implied readers read back into the narrative. Indeed, implied readers are *already* in agreement with the ideological perspective of the narrator, so that through the process of identification with the disciples, they are simply called to *recommit* themselves to a proper understanding of the significance of Jesus' life and ministry, but not to go through a similar decisive growth in understanding of the events surrounding Jesus' glorification. As a result, it is not the case that the faith and understanding of the disciples *necessarily* and *always* represent a post-Easter state of affairs that is integrated, or read back, into the story of the pre-Easter Jesus and his disciples.

Of course, proposing that the implied author was able to and, in fact, did distinguish between two times of the disciples is not to say anything about whether or how he maintains such a distinction throughout the narrative. The difficulty is that, despite the "hour," the post-Easter retrospective perspective of the narrator necessarily governs the presentation of the disciples in the Fourth Gospel both before and after "the hour." But in noticing that a merging of time perspective *and* a clear distinction between the pre- and post-Easter understanding of the disciples are present in the narrative, it can safely be said that the post-resurrection retrospective perspective of the implied author does not influence his portrayal of the disciples *uniformly*. As a result, the real questions are how these two phenomena can be present in the same narrative, and what coherence is to be assigned to the story of the disciples.

4. Literary and Theological Functions of Time in the Fourth Gospel

To answer these questions, an understanding of the literary and theological functions of 'time' put forth in the Fourth Gospel may be of assistance. As will be seen, research in this area has been productive and gives potential leads to better grasp the ambiguous manner in which the implied author retrospectively portrayed the disciples. For centuries, the unique sense of time in this narrative has been the centre of much speculation and confusion. Research in this domain has focused attention on the farewell narrative (chapters 13–17) because in these chapters the steady flow of time overflows its boundaries. Past, present, and future are mingled together with no apparent distinction. For instance, Jesus announces his departure to his disciples in 13:33: "Little children, yet a little while I am with you," but in his prayer he speaks as one who has already left them behind: "While I was with them" (17:12). Similarly, Jesus is able to announce his imminent departure from the world by saying, "In a little while, the world will no longer see me" (14:19), but also, seemingly prematurely, to state: "And I am no longer in the world" (17:11). Jesus also refers to his death as a coming conflict with "the ruler of this world" (14:30), but soon thereafter heralds his success in the conflict as a past event: "But take heart, I have overcome the world" (16:33). Later, Jesus begins his prayer by asking his Father to "glorify your son" (17:1), but he has already insisted earlier in 13:31 that "Now the Son of Man has been glorified" (13:31).[217]

This led Culpepper to propose that, "in the Farewell Discourse, Jesus speaks proleptically of the life situation of the fictional narrator."[218] But, for O'Day, the fact that Jesus often uses past and present tenses to refer to his victory or his departure indicates that in these chapters the future is not the subject of a simple prolepsis. For instance, she argues that "John 16:33 is more than (or other than) proleptic because it does not anticipate or look ahead to the moment of Jesus' victory. Instead, it announces that *this* is the moment of victory. It does not bring the narrative present into the future, but brings the future into the narrative present."[219] Ironically, one could argue that O'Day describes what proper "prolepsis" does: it brings the future into the present, it is a flash forward that affects the present. But beyond the issue of one's definition of literary terms, the purpose of this literary phenomenon is well put by O'Day:

> By placing the promises and words of assurance before the Passion narrative, not after, the fourth evangelist emphasizes that these words are part of the present reality for the disciples rather than part of some distant future [...] In this way, not only is the disciples' present changed, but their future is also transformed. The voice of the risen Jesus offers them new categories with which to meet their future, categories that promise that the victory over the world is already available, at any given moment.[220]

In the narrative, it is all too clear that the disciples were not, at the time, able to understand and use these new categories. However, implied readers also re-

---

[217] These examples have been emphasised by G. L. Parsenios, "'No Longer in the World' (John 17:11): The Transformation of the Tragic in the Fourth Gospel," *HTR* 98 (2005): 1–21, as he seeks to study time in the farewell narratives within the context of ancient literature. He puts it well, as he states: "It is as though two discourses have been blended together, one that Jesus delivers around the table on the night of his betrayal, and one that he delivers from the realm of the Father after the Ascension. Jesus is alternately here and there, before and after, above and below" (p. 3). For an analysis of these phenomena, see also Frey, *Eschatologie 2*, 130–46, 247–52. For him, the post-Easter community is here represented by the group of pre-Easter disciples whom Jesus addresses in his discourses. It is thus the community's situation, mainly the problem of the absence of Jesus and the delay of the parousia, which is primarily addressed in chapters 13–17. On this, this also J. Zumstein, "Le passé transfiguré: l'histoire sub specie aeternitatis selon Jean 17," in *Histoire et herméneutique. Mélanges offerts à Gottfried Hammann*, ed. by M. Rose, Histoire et Société 45 (Genève: Labor et Fides, 2002), 431–40.

[218] Culpepper, *Anatomy*, 37 (though Culpepper also shows that Jesus speaks both prospectively and retrospectively about his death and resurrection in the Farewell Prayer).

[219] O'Day, "Narrative Time," 162. O'Day adds: "This is different from speaking of the overlap between the future envisioned by Jesus and the present experience of Johannine community (Culpepper:37). A temporal link is established between the narrative and the reader's experience, but it is established by changing the shape of the narrative present, not simply by using the future tense to point to the reader's present."

[220] O'Day, "Narrative Time," 164.

ceive Jesus' words of assurance, so that they are reminded of the presence of Jesus' victory at any given moment.

Interestingly, a similar phenomenon is also present earlier in the narrative. For instance, in chapters 1–12, Jesus or the narrator mention several times that Jesus' "hour has not yet come" (2:4; 7:30 or 8:20) so that it can be read as a chronological device pointing to and thus underlining the importance of this upcoming event. Then, in 12:23, 27; 13:1; 17:1, the time of Jesus' hour is introduced into the narrative as having come. Yet, in addition to this coherent sequence of events, Jesus twice speaks of an "hour" which is already, *now*, present in his ministry (4:23; 5:25). It follows that, for the implied author, the hour of Jesus' upcoming death is theologically significant for the whole of the narrative, even for the events occurring before the "hour" proper.[221] Just as Jesus could, in the farewell narrative, bring his future victory to bear on the present of the disciples, here his "hour" is also brought to bear on the present of his ministry and his encounter with characters in the story.

To explain how readers are to make sense of such phenomena, Kieffer argues that, though the implied author remains interested in temporal causality and chronology, in the Fourth Gospel chronology is relativised in light of a superior perspective:

Toutes ces indications chronologiques situent la vie de Jésus dans une perspective théologique: le temps pendant lequel Jésus est apparu aux hommes est minime par rapport au temps infini qui a précédé ou qui suivra. Jésus lui-même est maître du temps, et son heure le fait revenir à la gloire qu'il a toujours eue auprès du Père et qui ne connaîtra pas de fin.[222]

Along similar lines, Davies proposes that the Fourth Gospel's implied author sets chronology within the confines of eternity, *i.e.*, a dimension outside of time:

The story of Jesus' ministry is set within a very general presentation of human history from its beginning (1.3–13), but this presentation is structured by a concern not just with history but with eternity. The Gospel begins in eternity (1.1–2) and the reader is repeatedly reminded of the eternal dimension in the discourses within the story.[223]

---

[221] For R. Kieffer, *Le monde symbolique de Saint Jean*, LD 137 (Paris: Cerf, 1989), 30: "L'instant de la mort a une dimension théologique qui éclaire toute la vie publique de Jésus." (Pages 11–33 of Kieffer's monograph are entitled "L'espace et le temps dans l'évangile de Jean" and were previously published in R. Kieffer, "L'espace et le temps dans l'évangile de Jean," *NTS* 31 (1985): 393–409).

[222] Kieffer, *Symbolique*, 30–31. Later, Kieffer rightly cautions: "Pour rendre justice à cet évangile éminemment spirituel, il faut prendre au sérieux justement ses indications géographiques et chronologiques, car elles participent de la nature du 'signe' *(sèmeion)* et sont le point de départ obligé de la réflexion johannique elle-même."

[223] Davies, *Rhetoric*, 44–45. Similarly, Frey, *Eschatologie 2*, 267–68, shows how Jesus is presented in the narrative both chronologically and as the representative of God's ever present being. This perspective is different from that found in an interesting yet ultimately unconvincing study by Gourgues, in which he argues that in the Fourth Gospel the evangelist presents Jesus' ministry according to a double temporality (the real and the symbolic) that he superimposes throughout the narrative. For Gourgues, though in the narrative Jesus' ministry is presented

For her, this is because "the story which the Fourth Gospel tells [...] is intended to illuminate the eternal dimension of God's creative purpose for his world."[224] Thus, if we grant the usefulness of this account, the implied author would not have needed to treat chronology and temporal causality in a systematic and completely coherent manner.[225] Using chronology as a subset of 'eternity,' a dimension outside of time or history, he would not be interested in giving precise historical data on the moment of the availability of faith and life in the Fourth Gospel, for instance. In other words, the implied author would be less interested in conveying to his readers certain historical 'facts' (however he may have understood this concept) than to persuade them of the theological significance of these events, giving him the impetus to creatively tell a story that underlined the perpetual relevance of the person and work of Jesus for Jesus' disciples during his ministry as for the implied readers.[226]

Yet, as interesting as these proposals may be, does the Fourth Gospel actually work with a concept of "eternity" such as that proposed by Davies and, implicitly, by Kieffer? In his recent monograph, Estes challenges incorrect assumptions (mostly inherited from the Enlightenment) about temporality applied to Biblical narratives.[227] He then surveys the temporal mechanics of the Fourth Gospel in light of modern physics, positing an innovative approach that applies the temporality of the Theory of Relativity to the study of time in the Fourth Gospel. For him, time in narrative, thus in the Fourth Gospel, is "finite," "dimensional" (see the section on order above), "deterministic," "warped," and "restrictive."[228] Most relevant to the question at hand is the first of these categories.

For Estes, time in the Fourth Gospel is "finite" in that "the time of both text and world is a finite time."[229] In any narrative, "creation and narrative are forever temporally bounded by a beginning and an end."[230] Since the Fourth Gospel's narrative proceeds from the point of creation (ἡ ἀρχῇ), it provides a temporal key to the Gospel, setting it firmly in the finite universe.[231] 1:1 talks of "in the beginning," not "in eternity," despite Davies' attempt to understand

---

as occurring during a three year period, it is also symbolically presented as one working day, progressively going from sunrise to sunset (M. Gourgues, "Superposition du temps symbolique et du temps réel dans l'évangile de Jean," in *Raconter, interpréter, annoncer. Parcours de Nouveau Testament. Mélanges offerts à Daniel Marguerat pour son 60ème anniversaire*, ed. by E. Steffek and Y. Bourquin, MB 47 (Genève: Labor et Fides, 2003), 171–82).

[224] Davies, *Rhetoric*, 45.

[225] Davies, *Rhetoric*, 66.

[226] See Bennema, *Saving Wisdom*, 15–17, for a concise and balanced view on this topic.

[227] See Estes, *Temporal*, 251–54, for a brief summary of his conclusions.

[228] See especially Estes, *Temporal*, 31–97.

[229] Estes, *Temporal*, 129.

[230] Estes, *Temporal*, 129.

[231] Estes, *Temporal*, 114..

this expression metaphorically.[232] Likewise, the epilogue provides a temporal closure, leaving the reader "with a new hope for the future of creation."[233] Thus, such a conception goes against the interpretations that underline the primeval/ eternal time before and after creation as a framework for understanding the Fourth Gospel's temporality.[234] Moreover, though it is acceptable to speak of a transcendent divine realm in the Fourth Gospel (*e.g.*, 17:11) and of Jesus' pre-existence (*e.g.*, 17:5[235]), it is questionable whether the implied author considered this dimension as outside of time, and especially as affecting the narrative's temporality. There does not appear to be any clear evidence for such an understanding in this Gospel. Jesus is portrayed as pre-existent and he is identified ontologically with the Father through the use of the ἐγώ εἰμι formula,[236] but nowhere is it clear that their divine status somehow relativises the narrative's chronology.[237]

This conception of the Fourth Gospel's narrative as firmly set in "finite" time means that the issues surrounding the temporal conception of Jesus' "hour," whether in the farewell discourses or in chapters 1–12, must be elucidated from an angle other than the often proposed eternal framework of the narrative.

5. Realised Eschatology and the Disciples' Faith and Understanding

Germane to the literary and theological aspects of time in the Fourth Gospel is the concept of realised eschatology. The following section will therefore suggest that Johannine eschatology could provide a key to uphold the theological significance of Jesus' "hour" for the whole narrative without altogether sacrificing temporal causality and chronology. In other words, it could explain how the disciples can be portrayed in the narrative as believing and having life before Jesus' glorification. Unfortunately, space does not permit a comprehensive

---

[232] Davies, *Rhetoric*, 44. As argued by Estes, *Temporal*, 113, in 1:1–2 "The Fourth Evangelist was not trying to paint an idyllic picture of eternity but offer a lucid snapshop of creation – one of which the uncreated λόγος is present and active."

[233] Estes, *Temporal*, 129.

[234] So *e.g.* Davies, *Rhetoric*, 44–45; D. F. Tolmie, "The Characterization of God in the Fourth Gospel," *JSNT* 69 (1998): 62; Schnelle, *Johannes*, 31. One may add that, as is well known, in the Fourth Gospel eternal life is "the life of the age to come," rather than a timeless life (so Ashton, *Understanding*, 214–20; M. M. Thompson, "Eternal Life in the Gospel of John," *ExAud* 5 (1989): 46–50.

[235] Additionally, J. D. G. Dunn, *Christology in the Making: An Inquiry into the Origins of the Doctrine of the Incarnation*, 2nd ed. (London: SCM, 1989), 56, mentions 6:38; 8:23, 38, 42; 10:36; 16:28 as indications of Jesus pre-existence.

[236] Ball, *I am*, 276–79.

[237] *Contra* Frey, *Eschatologie 2*, 151–52, who argues that ἐγώ εἰμι is indicative of the Fourth Gospel's assertion of Jesus' timeless essence, Estes, *Temporal*, 105, proposes that "in one respect, the Johannine λόγος is foundational, existing outside of spacetime as the transcendental signified; the λόγος is unbounded by time. Yet the temporally infinite λόγος exists – and to a certain degree is captured – within a finite, bounded narrative world."

account of Johannine eschatology.[238] However, this section will investigate whether such eschatology could be of assistance to clarify the status of the disciples, especially during Jesus' earthly ministry.

Several significant statements underline realised eschatology in the Fourth Gospel (*e.g.* 3:16–21, 36; 4:23; 5:24–25; 6:47, 54; 8:51; 11:23–27). For Beasley-Murray, "Truly, truly, I say to you, whoever hears my words and believes him who sent me has eternal life. He does not come to judgement but has passed from death to life" (5:24) is "the strongest affirmation of realized eschatology applied to the believer in the NT."[239] For Bultmann, as is well-known, the evangelist responsible for the greater part of the text as it now stands no longer expected any apocalyptic future events beyond God's decisive offer in Jesus.[240] Thus, the emphasis on realised eschatology in the Fourth Gospel is such that Bultmann attributes any reference to a future eschatology (*e.g.*, 5:28–29; 6:39–40, 44, 54; 12:48) to a later redactor.[241] There is no doubt that, in the Fourth Gospel, the emphasis is on present eschatology, but many since Bultmann have shown that futuristic elements also play an important role in this Gospel's eschatology.[242]

In 5:25, for instance, the hour that is coming, when "the dead will hear the voice of the Son of God," has in fact already entered the present, it is "now here" (καὶ νῦν ἐστιν). Here the "dead" must be understood as the spiritually dead who "hear" (believe) Jesus and thus receive life.[243] Yet, immediately following this statement, Jesus points exclusively to the future when he claims

---

[238] For a recent survey of discussion on Johannine's eschatology, also serving as a summary of his conclusions, see J. Frey, "Eschatology in the Johannine Circle," in *Theology and Christology in the Fourth Gospel*, ed. by G. Van Belle, J. G. van der Watt, and P. J. Maritz, BETL 184 (Leuven: Leuven University Press/Peeters, 2005), 47–82. For an actual full-blown proposal regarding Johannine eschatology, see his three volume work in J. Frey, *Die johanneische Eschatologie. Vol. 1: Ihre Probleme im Spiegel der Forschung seit Reimarus*, WUNT 96 (Tübingen: Mohr Siebeck, 1997); Frey, *Eschatologie 2;* and J. Frey, *Die johanneische Eschatologie. Vol. 3: Die eschatologische Verkündigung in den johanneischen Texten*, WUNT 117 (Tübingen: Mohr Siebeck, 2000).

[239] Beasley-Murray, *John*, 76.

[240] Bultmann, *John*, 128: "The completion of the eschatological event is not to be awaited at some time in the future; it is taking place even now in the life and destiny of Jesus." Bultmann was followed by a majority of interpreters in the 20th century, especially in German scholarship. For an extended overview of Bultmann's eschatology, see Frey, *Eschatologie 1*, 85–157.

[241] de Jonge, "Eschatology," 482, comments sharply: "The theory advanced by Bultmann and his followers is remarkable. The evangelist is thought to correct current Christian expectation, but even in Johannine circles his views were eventually not followed."

[242] *E.g.* de Jonge, "Eschatology," 481–87; Ashton, *Understanding*, 223–26; and especially Frey, *Eschatologie 2*, 269–83. A notable exception to this understanding of present eschatology as dominant in the Fourth Gospel is C. C. Caragounis, "The Kingdom of God in John and the Synoptics: Realized or Potential Eschatology?," in *John and the Synoptics*, ed. by A. Denaux, BETL 101 (Leuven: Leuven University Press, 1992), 473–80, on which, see below.

[243] See *e.g.* Lincoln, *John*, 204.

that the physically dead will hear the Son and come out of their tombs either to "the resurrection of life" or to "the resurrection of judgment" (5:28–29). If life has entered the present, life also awaits the final verdict which "functions as the full and visible exhibition of the present verdict."[244] As several references make clear, in the Fourth Gospel the verdict of life or condemnation depends on one's response to the Son, and such a verdict is experienced already in this life (3:16–19, 36; 5:24; 11:25–26). But does this apply to Jesus' disciples in the story of Jesus' earthly ministry, or is it necessary to distinguish pre- and post-resurrection times in this regard as well? If life has entered the present, had it also entered the present of Jesus' earthly disciples? Caragounis interestingly challenges the very basis of this question by arguing that if the Fourth Gospel presents eternal life as being attained only through faith (3:36; 5:24; 6:47; 6:54), such a presentation is not meant to highlight the present possession of life for believers over against a future possession of it. In fact, for Caragounis, eternal life is always future in the Fourth Gospel.[245] For him, the point of 5:24 and the other "eternal life" sayings is to "stress the decisiveness of faith rather than the present as against the future."[246] For Caragounis:

According to the view taken here *the Eschaton, eternal life, and judgment, which are essentially future events, are potentially 'present' in Jesus during his ministry, since they are bound up with his destiny, and they are spoken of as 'present' realities only in principle inasmuch as the predetermined hour of Jesus, which is to actually initiate them, is irrevocable and imminent.* Hence it would seem that a more accurate description of John's standpoint [...] is not Realized but rather *Potential Eschatology.*[247]

Yet, if Caragounis' emphasis on the "decisiveness of faith" is certainly correct, Jesus does speak of the *possibility* of faith and therefore of life "now" rather than only later. Caragounis argues that certain Greek verbs such as ἔρκομαι (so in 5:25) "naturally denote an imperfective or ongoing action and consequently suggest the future completion of an event,"[248] but the present tense in 5:25, coupled with "καὶ νῦν ἐστιν," compels interpreters to understand it as an instance of Johannine realised eschatology, that is, not simply potential or imminent eschatology.[249]

---

[244] Lincoln, *John*, 205.

[245] Caragounis, "Kingdom," 477–78.

[246] Caragounis, "Kingdom," 477.

[247] Caragounis, "Kingdom," 480 (italics original). See also C. C. Caragounis, "The Kingdom of God: Common and Distinct Elements Between John and the Synoptics," in *Jesus in Johannine Tradition*, ed. by R. T. Fortna and T. Thatcher (Louisville, KY/London/Leiden: Westminster John Knox, 2001), 133: "It is the nexus between present faith – the decisive factor for one's eschatological destiny – and the future character of the Eschaton that brings future and present together in Jesus."

[248] Caragounis, "Kingdom of God," 132.

[249] So Frey, *Eschatologie 2*, 2–5.

Moreover, Caragounis may have overlooked an important aspect of Johannine eschatology, where realised eschatology is presented first and foremost on the basis of Christology. De Jonge is correct to assert that "John's eschatology with its special stress on the present effects of the Son's mission to the world is the corollary of his radical Christology."[250] Similarly, Frey argues that "the accentuation of the present eschatology is a consequence of the Christological convictions of the author (and his community)."[251] Indeed, in the Fourth Gospel, Jesus is presented as having "life in himself"[252] so that he can grant life to others (5:26–27).[253] Arguably, this very idea explains the presence, *now*, of resurrection life for believers such as it is expressed in 5:25. Likewise, according to 3:35–36, those who believe in God's Son have eternal life because the Father has given all things into his Son's hand.[254] In 6:63, the words that Jesus has spoken are "Spirit and life,"[255] and elsewhere Jesus refers to his revelatory ministry as obedience to his Father's commandment, which, in turn, is eternal life (12:49–50).[256] Therefore, since Jesus' presence and revelatory ministry are at issue in the references given above, it follows that those presented as having heard his words and having believed in him during his earthly ministry are to be considered as *already* benefiting from such a life-giving presence.[257]

But the question remains: how far did the post-resurrection retrospective perspective of the implied author impact the narrative presentation of the disciples? Is it simply the case that, as Caragounis admits, "along with the literary *Sitz im Leben*, [the author] may have allowed the post-resurrection time

---

[250] de Jonge, "Eschatology," 484.

[251] Frey, "Eschatology," 75–76.

[252] For Carson, *John*, 257, the verse relates to the "eternal generation of the Son," but clearly, it also expresses that Jesus, like God, is able to grant life to others.

[253] Beasley-Murray, *John*, 77; G. E. Ladd, *A Theology of the New Testament*, 2nd ed. (Grand Rapids, MI: Eerdmans, 1993), 341. Indeed, it is because of this and the other ideas expressed in 5:25–27 (that Jesus raises the spiritually dead and exercises judgment) that Jesus calls "the Jews" to "not marvel" (5:28). If Jesus had not somehow challenged the traditional Jewish understanding of eschatology in proclaiming that these things were taking place through his own activity as the Son, then why would "the Jews" be tempted to marvel? So Frey, "Eschatology," 78: "Jesus' most offending claim was that he has the authority to give life and pass sentence even in the present."

[254] For Köstenberger, *John*, 140, "Similar to 'see/enter the kingdom' and 'practice the truth,' 'see life' is a typical Jewish expression meaning 'experience or enjoy life.'"

[255] Moloney, *John*, 228, puts it well: "What matters is the life-giving power of the Spirit, made available to the disciples in and through the revelation of God in and through the word of Jesus."

[256] Throughout the Fourth Gospel, Jesus is presented as the Father's unique revelation (3:15–16; 5:36–38; 6:29, 35, 40; 7:38; 8:19, 24, 42, 45–46).

[257] So for Schnackenburg, *John*, 1:569: "Every substantial element of the Christian doctrine of salvation is preserved, even the future 'resurrection to life' after death (5:29; 6:39f.); but all the emphasis is on the present possession of the life and strength which is imparted and constantly sustained by the divine envoy and bringer of divine life (5:26)."

perspective to influence his expression speaking of events that in the former *Sitz im Leben* were future, but now had been realized?"[258] Frey's grammatical analysis of the Fourth Gospel's use of mode and tense brings much clarity on this matter. For him, the common idea that time is insignificant for the Fourth Gospel's evangelist is incorrect and indeed misinterprets the complexities of Johannine temporal relationships. Key to Frey's argument is that the Fourth Gospel's author uses tenses in order to express the community's understanding of its place in salvation history.[259] For instance, one particular way in which the Fourth Evangelist expresses the view of a post-Easter community regarding Jesus' work and significance is by employing the perfect tense, which unites aspects of the aorist and present tenses (thus referring to the present results of past actions), with greater frequency as compared to other New Testament authors.[260] Moreover, Frey argues that the evangelist melds the experience of the later community into the story of the life of Jesus because the evangelist views Jesus' life and work in terms of the post-Easter kerygma.[261] Thus, the use of double meanings for words such as "temple" (Jn. 2:19) or "lift up" (Jn. 3:14, 8:28; 12:32, 34) reflects the later community's understanding of Jesus' status and work. For Frey, this melding of temporal horizons is most pronounced in John 13–17 where the evangelist directly addresses the contemporary community through the words of Jesus,[262] and where the perfect tense is employed with high frequency.[263]

Yet, Frey shows that while the temporal horizons are melded in the Fourth Gospel, they are not abolished. Indeed, the Fourth Gospel maintains a strong contrast between present and future, thus providing a clear distinction between the time of Jesus' life and ministry and that of the author and the author's audience.[264] For Frey, the Paraclete provides understanding of the significance of Jesus' work only to the post-Easter community, and it is as a Spirit-enlightened writer that the evangelist portrays the earthly life of Jesus.[265] Therefore, Frey insists that, even with the melding of the temporal horizons, eschatological expectation is not sacrificed in the Fourth Gospel.[266] Rather, the evangelist preserves both the historic and eschatological perspectives in dynamic tension. For instance, and most relevant to this study, Frey notes that the phrase, "the hour is coming and now is" (5:25) reflects both the situations of the Johannine Jesus *and* the Johannine community, and should thus be read on two levels. For

---

[258] Caragounis, "Kingdom," 480. See also Brown, *John*, 1:CXVIII.
[259] Frey, *Eschatologie 2*, 38–146.
[260] Frey, *Eschatologie 2*, 97.
[261] Frey, *Eschatologie 2*, 247–68.
[262] Frey, *Eschatologie 2*, 250–52.
[263] See Frey's chart in Frey, *Eschatologie 2*, 233.
[264] Frey, *Eschatologie 2*, 147–51, 221–27.
[265] Frey, *Eschatologie 2*, 223–27.
[266] Frey, *Eschatologie 2*, 269–83.

the earthly Jesus, the words, "the hour comes," refer to the post-Easter community, while the phrase, "now is" indicates his own time. For the community, the "now is," refers to its own experience, while, "the hour comes," points to its eschatological hope.[267] Thus, the evangelist uses Jesus' words both to predict the formation of the Christian community and to hold the eschatological hope of that community in tension between the "already" and the "not yet."

Consequently, though the emphasis on realised eschatology may have been meant primarily to encourage or comfort implied readers in their own trials,[268] its weight is not to be erased or ignored as far as the narrative portrayal of Jesus' earthly disciples is concerned. As argued by Frey, in the Fourth Gospel, the time marked by the νῦν is both the narrated time of Jesus' earthly ministry and that of the narrator.[269] Thus, as the disciples were able to hear his words and believe in him, so the implied author clearly portrays them as having life in the "now" of Jesus' earthly ministry.

6. Conclusion

The overall narrative depiction of the disciples is that of believers who stood in a living relationship with Jesus even before his glorification, but who also experienced significant growth from the resurrection on. The implied author, no doubt, felt much freedom in telling his story from the post-resurrection vantage point of the Johannine community. As a result, chronology is not always respected in the Fourth Gospel, and, more importantly, the implied author often speaks of the disciples in terms that could only make sense with reference to post-resurrection disciples, thus creatively compressing the pre- and post-resurrection temporal horizons. Yet, if the post-resurrection perspective affects the presentation of the disciples' faith and understanding in the narrative, it was argued above that its impact is not so wide-ranging as to tell their story in terms solely appropriate to the post-resurrection period. Indeed, the implied author made a point of distinguishing between the two times of the pre- and post-Easter disciples, and between the earthly life of Jesus and that of the Johannine community. The implied author felt a particular freedom to let his post-resurrection vantage point influence his portrayal of the disciples, depicting the disciples as believing and having life based on the very presence of Jesus in the world. According to the implied author's post-resurrection perspective, the earthly Jesus had "life in himself" and "the words of eternal life" (6:68), so that he could call disciples, who, upon hearing his voice, believed and were made partakers of Jesus' own divine life.

---

[267] Frey, *Eschatologie 2*, 282–83.
[268] So Frey, "Eschatology," 80: "[…] the Gospel has to comfort them not only by emphasizing the present gift of life but also by the promise of future resurrection and of a definite state of communion with Jesus (Jn 12,2f.; 17,24)."
[269] Frey, *Eschatologie 2*, 282–83.

As has been amply argued throughout, to make a case for the Fourth Gospel's presentation of the disciples as believers standing in a relationship with Jesus that involves life is not to say that these disciples arrived at a well-rounded understanding of Jesus and his saving work before his resurrection. Such an understanding, as is made clear by the prolepses found in 2:22 and 12:16, only came later, after Jesus' resurrection and the sending of the Paraclete. But what the Fourth Gospel's realised eschatology stresses is the reality of faith and life during Jesus' earthly ministry, based on Jesus' very presence. It follows, as far as the story of the disciples is concerned, that the difference made by Jesus' glorification is not the sudden emergence of adequate faith leading to life for the disciples.[270] On the basis of our entire argument so far, Jesus' glorification (including the giving of the Paraclete) essentially functions as the pivotal moment after which the disciples gained a deeper perception of the person and work of Jesus. In turn, it is their renewed understanding, together with their underlying faith and the assistance of the Spirit, which enabled them to become true and effective witnesses to the significance of Jesus' life and works in the world. In the subplot in which the disciples are being prepared by Jesus for their future ministry, Jesus' glorification functions as that which triggers the resolution. It is once he is glorified that he can commission his disciples (20:19–23). In turn, as Jesus' glorification provides the key to unlock the disciples' potential and decisively equips them for their task of witnessing in the world, implied readers realise that they too must grasp afresh the significance of this event to be reinforced in their own faith and understanding, and in their responsibility to witness in a renewed manner. The ways in which the implied author uses time in the farewell material and in which he uses the theme of the "hour" throughout the narrative corroborate this point. Since the hour of Jesus' upcoming death is theologically significant for the whole of the narrative, and for the disciples in particular, implied readers progressively come to the realisation that they too are meant to be renewed in their understanding of its meaning for their own lives of faithful service to Christ.

The implied author's use of narrative time coheres with the study's earlier conclusions regarding the rhetorical functions of the disciples' characterisation. In order for the disciples to play their role as figures for identification, they had to be portrayed as showing clear resemblance to their post-resurrection counterparts, *i.e.* the implied readers. The implied author chose to depict this resemblance by emphasising, during Jesus' earthly ministry, the twin phenomena of the disciples' faith and life *and* their potential and need for growth in understanding the significance of Jesus' glorification. Moreover, by collapsing time perspectives in his story telling, the continuity of experience between the disciples and the implied readers is stressed by the implied author, thus making it a crucial part of the narrative's rhetorical strategy. Clearly, the implied au-

---

[270] *Pace, e.g.* Brown, *John*, 1:cxviii; Painter, "Faith," 36–52.

thor's theological and rhetorical intentions weigh heavily in his portrayal of the story of Jesus and the disciples. But though his post-resurrection retrospective perspective pervades the entire narrative, it was also important to the implied author that his implied readership be reinforced in its own perspective based on the accomplished ministry of Jesus, that is, both his mission to be witness and judge in the cosmic trial and his preparation of the disciples. It could therefore be proposed that it is to these ends that the implied author chose both to merge time perspectives and to clearly distinguish the pre- and post-Easter situations of Jesus and his disciples.

Overall, these two phenomena are presented in dynamic tension in the narrative. At times, the implied author highlights one over the other, but both are present throughout, arguably because both were necessary to the accomplishment of the rhetorical purposes of the narrative.

Chapter 5

Conclusion: Johannine Faith and Understanding

On the basis of chapters 2 and 3, the discussion in chapter 4 proposed a way to consider the Fourth Gospel's rhetorical strategy regarding the faith and understanding of the disciples, thus attempting to answer the three key questions posed in the introduction of this study:

– How does the implied author's evaluative point of view shape the presentation of the disciples' faith and understanding in the Fourth Gospel's narrative?
– How does the presentation of the disciples' faith and understanding function rhetorically within the narrative of the Fourth Gospel?
– How does the implied author's temporal perspective shape the presentation of the disciples' faith and understanding?

But as the study comes to a close, it is necessary to ask what impact these literary explorations may have on focused theological considerations. More to the point, what does the presentation of the disciples' faith and understanding in the Fourth Gospel purport to teach implied readers about what faith is in relation to understanding? Obviously, the Johannine concepts of faith and understanding, and the relationship between the two, are topics too large to be dealt with adequately in the concluding part of a narrative analysis. Thus, this conclusion will only offer the beginnings of one possible literary-theological conversation on the Johannine faith and understanding motifs. Certainly, this move to theological investigation from a literary one may be deemed problematic to those for whom theologically oriented matters are irrelevant to or incompatible with a focus on the narrative aspects of a text. Yet, it can be argued that it is not to move to an entirely different dimension. In short, there are continuities whereby, for instance, ideological or evaluative points of views are in some ways functionally equivalent to the implied author's theological perspective. Moreover, temporal point of view is not unrelated to theology, as has previously been insinuated regarding the implied author's eschatology.

One way to initiate this literary-theological conversation is to dialogue with Johannine theologians. And when it comes to Johannine theology, Bultmann's epoch-making *The Gospel of John: A Commentary* and *Theology of the New*

Testament cannot be ignored and naturally come to mind as dialogue partners.[1] Though many today would disagree with much of his thought, Bultmann remains a scholar to be reckoned with as a watershed in Johannine scholarship. It is little surprise that in these volumes Bultmann addressed at length several issues related to this study and has had a major impact on subsequent discussions on the topic. But since Bultmann, Johannine scholarship has paid greater attention to the Fourth Gospel's narrative character (both the Gospel as narrative and the Gospel as fitting within the broader Biblical story of God and humanity). For Smith, Bultmann's lack of attention to narrative

> [...] results from his appropriation of an existentialist perspective. But it is just that perspective that has made Bultmann's exegesis so interesting, for one cannot discuss exegesis with Bultmann without entertaining theological issues. Certainly, that is what Bultmann himself intended.[2]

In turn, to revisit Bultmann's proposals having in mind the perspective of narrative analysis, such as that suggested so far, could potentially advance both theological and literary studies on the Fourth Gospel. Thus, the following pages propose to discuss the theological issue of faith's relationship to understanding by relating the narrative analysis proposals of this study to Bultmann's mostly exegetical work on the Fourth Gospel. In the background to this conversation will be the following question: what difference would it have made, if any, to Bultmann's agenda and his discussion of faith if he had been able to start with a narrative investigation such as that proposed above, ask questions about evaluative and temporal point of view, and pay attention to the rhetoric of the Gospel?

As has been amply argued, in the Fourth Gospel's narrative the disciples believed in Jesus upon encountering him in the early days of his ministry. They met him, were confronted by his presence, works, and words, and they believed in him (2:11). Of course, their initial faith was not unrelated to a certain

---

[1] Bultmann, *John*; R. Bultmann, *Theology of the New Testament*, trans. by K. Grobel, 2 vols (New York, NY: Scribner, 1951, 1955). In particular, Bultmann devotes an entire chapter to the concept of faith in his *Theology of the New Testament* dividing it into two headings: "Faith as the Hearing of the Word," and "Faith as Eschatological Existence" (Bultmann, *Theology*, 2:70–92). A testimony to Bultmann's deep influence on Johannine research is found in Ashton, *Understanding*, 3–117, where history of Johannine research is divided into three sections: "Before Bultmann," "Bultmann," and "After Bultmann."

[2] D. M. Smith, "Johannine Studies since Bultmann," *WW* 21 (2001): 351. It should be noted that Bultmann strongly rejected the charge that he is translating the kerygma into an alien philosophical framework, that is, Heidegger's existentialism. Bultmann actually argued that Heidegger's philosophy had "all by itself" discovered the New Testament message about the human condition: "Philosophy all by itself already sees what the New Testament says" (see S. M. Ogden, *Christ Without Myth: A Study Based on the Theology of Rudolf Bultmann* (New York, NY: Harper & Brothers, 1961), 69). Bultmann was also capable of distancing himself from Heidegger, as has been showed by *e.g.* G. D. Chryssides, "Bultmann's Criticisms of Heidegger," *Sophia* 24 (1985): 28–35.

understanding. From early on, the disciples were able to state their faith in propositional terms such as "we have found the Messiah" (1:41), "we have found him of whom Moses in the Law and also the prophets wrote" (1:45), or "you have the words of eternal life" (6:69), which indicates that they are presented as having already attained a degree of understanding of Jesus' person and role in the world. Indeed, they came to believe in Jesus after hearing testimonies about his identity (1:35, 41, 45). Yet, foundational to their faith was much more than an adequate intellectual or propositional understanding of Jesus, even though, to some extent, that also was necessary. Rather, it is an *encounter* with his presence, his word, and his works that led their whole selves to turn towards him in discipleship. Clearly, therefore, as far as the implied author's ideological perspective on faith and understanding is concerned, faith in Jesus cannot exist without (at least some) understanding.

At first sight, this basic picture of the disciples' coming to faith seems to largely concur with Bultmann's view of what faith is in Johannine terms. For him, faith proceeds from genuine hearing and/or seeing (5:24; 5:37; 8:38) and *is* hearing and seeing in their fullest sense, that is, not mere physical perception.[3] *Contra* some of his critics (*e.g.* Karl Barth), faith for Bultmann is not simply a decision in which the individual freely authenticates his or her own existence, for no person is in control of his or her existence. For Bultmann, faith "is not an achievement, but a gift,"[4] a movement in which human beings turn away from themselves and towards God in obedience.[5] In that sense, Bultmann speaks of faith as "self-understanding," that is, the act of faith in which one's very being is constituted and determined through an encounter with Jesus.[6] In faith, the world is called to surrender the understanding it has had of itself and to let itself be reached by a new paradigm (all the while not falling into a du-

---

[3] For him, since Jesus, his word, and his works are identical (*i.e.* they are "revelation"), his words and works can also be the object of faith (5:47; 10:38). This explains why the expressions "believe in him" and "believe him" are identical in the Fourth Gospel. Thus, one cannot first believe or trust *in* Jesus without believing him (and *vice-versa*): "one can do neither without both." (Bultmann, *Theology*, 2:71). On verbal constructions of πιστεύειν, see also Morris, *John*, 298; Painter, "Faith," 38–40; Hawthorne, "Faith," 117–26. For Gaffney, "Believing and Knowing," 228–31, the two constructions "believe in" plus the accusative and "believe" plus the dative diverge in their objects. Jesus is the object of the former, while 'testimonies' or 'signs' leading to a belief (in Jesus) that is ulterior and terminal are the objects of the latter. This view of faith as proceeding in stages of development is also that of *e.g.* Huby, "Connaissance," 385–421; Decourtray, "foi," 561–76.

[4] R. Bultmann, *Faith and Understanding*, trans. by L. P. Smith (New York, NY: Harper & Row, 1969), 245.

[5] Bultmann, *Theology*, 1:319. On this, see also D. Gallagher, "The Obedience of Faith: Barth, Bultmann, and *Dei Verbum*," *JCTR* 10 (2006): 39–63.

[6] For an excellent explanation and rebuttal of scholars' misconceptions about the Bultmannian concept of "self-understanding," see B. Myers, "Faith as Self-Understanding: Towards a Post-Barthian Appreciation of Rudolf Bultmann," *IJST* 10 (2008): 21–35.

alistic worldview).[7] Faith is *desecularisation*,[8] a transition into eschatological existence: judgment lies behind believers, they already have life.[9] But interestingly, for Bultmann, this does not happen on the level of consciousness.[10] Faith is an act of the whole person. As Myers explains:

> Once faith has been understood this way, we will have put behind us all superficial debates about whether faith is 'seated' in the intellect or in the will, or whether faith involves assent to specific propositional content. If faith is a movement of the whole person, then it is pointless to ask whether faith arises in any particular 'location' within the self, just as it is pointless to ask whether faith consists in an objective set of beliefs which stands over against the self. For faith is nothing other than the acting self, borne up by the divine address and transfigured in response to that address. And just so, faith clearly involves specific content and knowledge, even though it is never reducible to propositional content. Indeed, all attempts to reduce faith to *any* isolated factor must be resisted, since such attempts contradict the very nature of faith as an active movement of the whole self in response to God.[11]

To better grasp Bultmann's understanding of faith, it should be noted that, for him, faith is genuine insofar as it is *knowing* faith.[12] In the Fourth Gospel, faith and knowledge do not differ in their substance, nor is one subordinate to the other (except in the exceptional case of 8:30–32, but here faith is not genuine) so that the two terms are used interchangeably (17:8, 21–23), and have the same objects.[13] Knowledge is therefore a structural element of faith, but this knowing has neither an intellectual dimension nor a mystical one, it is not the comprehension of the meaning of particular content.[14] Rather, "it is an exis-

---

[7] See R. Bultmann, "πιστεύω," in *Theological Dictionary of the New Testament*, ed. G. Kittel and G. Friedrich (Grand Rapids, MI: Eerdmans, 1964–76), 223–25.

[8] Bultmann, "πιστεύω," 225: "Faith is an act of desecularisation in the sense that it overcomes the offence and banishes all the autonomous power of man. Positively it is a grasping of the revelation which comes in the Word."

[9] Bultmann, *Theology*, 2:78.

[10] Bultmann, *Faith*, 319.

[11] Myers, "Faith," 34–35. See also Marchadour, *Personnages*, 183: "Alors que, dans les synoptiques, la foi est souvent liée à une situation particulière et à une intervention de Jésus, chez Jean la foi est un engagement personnel qui touche en profondeur le disciple, le destabilise, le déçoit parfois, mais aussi le transfigure." For an example of the tendency criticised by Myers, see *e.g.*, Huby, "Connaissance," 385–403.

[12] Bultmann, *Theology*, 2:73–74.

[13] Bultmann, "πιστεύω," 227. This equation between believing and knowing is nuanced in Gaffney, "Believing and Knowing," 239–40, but his definitions of the two terms are far removed from those of Bultmann. For Gaffney, to believe is "the idea, namely, of accepting testimonies, of freely submitting to the moral force of a certain kind of religious evidence," while knowing "is a kind of discernment of signs, a quality of insight into the transcendental reference of various symbolisms, ambiguities, and veiled allusions."

[14] Kysar, *Maverick*, 90–92, disagrees with Bultmann's argument regarding knowledge as the structural quality of believing. Yet he also goes on to argue that the Fourth Gospel uses knowing as a synonym for believing. For him, "knowing refers to a relationship" as in the Hebrew Bible sense.

tential knowing, not to be tested by objective observation and investigating scrutiny but by reality."[15]

Bearing in mind this study's conclusions on the emergence of faith in the disciples as well as Bultmann's particular understanding of faith, it is interesting to ponder the significance of "misunderstanding" in the Fourth Gospel, and its relationship with faith. If indeed faith involves specific content and a degree of understanding (without being reduced to this), how is one to understand theologically the misunderstandings of believers such as the disciples? This study has argued that, although the disciples are portrayed as believers from early on in the narrative, they are also portrayed as lacking understanding, and, at times, as blatantly misunderstanding Jesus and his work. On a narrative critical level, faith and misunderstandings are therefore not antithetical, even though the presentation of the disciples' misunderstandings were first and foremost part of the implied author's rhetorical intention to nurture and reinforce the faith and understanding of his implied readership.

Yet, Bultmann's existential understanding of faith leads him to present misunderstandings as occurring in the context of *unbelief* in the Fourth Gospel. According to him, misunderstandings are common responses to the coming of the Son, to Jesus' ambiguous activity (miracles, deeds, words) as Revealer. His activity is not understood because it is a disturbance to what is familiar to the world, and as such cannot be conceived in the category of worldly thought. Simply put, misunderstandings find expression in the offence or attack of the assertion: "the word became flesh" (1:14).[16] Even though Jesus speaks openly all along, his activity as Revealer remains a riddle to the world. For Bultmann, this is so because:

Men do not *know* God; for knowing God does not mean to have ideas (perhaps) correct ideas about him. To know him is to see him as really made manifest, and that means to recognize him as Creator, to submit one's self to be determined by him. Those who are 'of the world' certainly know much that is 'right'; but it all turns to their mouths as falsity, to a lie, because they do not understand that it is limited. [...] So it is understandable that, when confronted by revelation, they become untrue even to their own law in which they take pride (7.49f.). Their obedience is manifestly not genuine.[17]

---

[15] Bultmann, *Faith*, 182. Bultmann was careful to distinguish the Fourth Gospel's teaching from that of the Gnostics, for whom faith and knowledge should be distinguished as two stages: "In the Christian Church, there are not two classes of people, as there were among the Gnostics who distinguished between the '*pistics*' (men of faith) and '*gnostics*' (men of knowledge). Faith is not the acceptance of a dogma upon which there follows a disclosure of items of esoteric knowledge or a mystic vision. No, faith is everything. Knowledge cannot cut loose from faith and soar on out beyond it; faith, however, also contains knowledge – faith itself knows" (see Bultmann, *Theology*, 2:74, emphasis added. See also, Bultmann, *John*, 494–95).

[16] Bultmann, *Theology*, 2:41.

[17] Bultmann, *Faith*, 168. Thus, as explained by Painter, for Bultmann "the question why more men, or all men, do not believe can only be answered by saying that, in order to bring grace, the revelation must also bring offence, because the word of grace is qualitatively other

Clearly, Bultmann's model did not allow faith and misunderstanding to co-exist. But if misunderstandings are linked essentially to unbelief, to being offended by God's revelation in Jesus, Jesus' disciples either did not have faith in the Fourth Gospel, or they did not truly misunderstand. Bultmann chooses the former option. According to him, authentic Christian knowledge could only occur in the future for the Fourth Gospel's disciples – thus downplaying their presentation as believers in the narrative. Even though, for Bultmann, nothing new is added to Jesus' incarnation by his glorification, it brings about "the special experience or knowledge which the believer gains in light of the cross."[18]

Such an exegetical move on Bultmann's part is surprising, since, as is well-known, Bultmann strongly favoured a strict realised eschatology in his interpretation of the Fourth Gospel.[19] For Bultmann, eschatology begins with the incarnation: Jesus' having come is the revelation and the offence of the divine in the world.[20] In this sense Jesus is the eschatological salvation-bringer. His coming is the eschatological event and constitutes a unity with his departure.[21] In fact, his departure or exaltation not only belongs to the whole as its culmination but is that which makes the whole what it is: both revelation and offence.[22]

---

than this world of darkness. […] Those who are committed to this world can only be judged by the word of grace." (J. Painter, *Theology as Hermeneutics: Rudolf Bultmann's Interpretation of the History of Jesus*, HTIBS (Sheffield: Sheffield Academic Press, 1987), 210).

[18] Bultmann, *John*, 128, n.2, 467–68; Bultmann, *Faith*, 174. Bultmann is ambiguous on the possibility of faith and salvation during Jesus' earthly ministry according to the Fourth Gospel, which led to disagreements in the interpretations of his work. For instance, Loader argues that Bultmann thought that eternal life was already available before Easter (Loader, *Christology*, 13–16), but Bennema correctly challenged him because, for Bultmann, "the believer's eschatological existence can only be facilitated by a genuine faith-relationship with the *exalted* Jesus (through the Spirit), which would only be possible after Jesus' death and resurrection" (Bennema, *Saving Wisdom*, 13, n.65, emphasis original). Bennema argues his case from Bultmann, *John*, 467, 619–20, 691 and Bultmann, *Theology*, 2:43, 85.

[19] For post-Bultmann views of Johannine eschatology, see E. Käsemann, *The Testament of Jesus: A Study of the Gospel of John in the Light of Chapter 17*, trans. by G. Krodel (London: SCM, 1968), 16–17; and R. T. Fortna, *The Fourth Gospel and its Predecessors: From Narrative Source to Present Gospel* (Edinburgh: T. & T. Clark, 1989), 289–91, who expound the view according to which the Fourth Gospel presents a purely realised eschatology. See also the debate on this issue between Caragounis, "Kingdom," 473–80 and de Jonge, "Eschatology," 481–87. For a thorough analysis of Johannine eschatology, strongly arguing against a Bultmannian strictly realised eschatology, see Frey, *Eschatologie 1–3*.

[20] See Bultmann, *Faith*, 165–83 (his chapter entitled "The Eschatology of the Fourth Gospel").

[21] This perspective contrasts with other canonical theological presentations of these events: "There is not a word in John of the idea that not until the resurrection and exaltation after his death was Jesus made Lord of all cosmic and demonic powers (*cf.* for example, Phil 2:11; Eph. 1:20ff; I Pet. 3:21f.; Phil. 2:1). For the Father did not delay the gift of life-creating power to him until the resurrection but gave it to him from the outset: 'he has granted the Son also to have life in himself' (5:26)" (Bultmann, *Theology*, 2:56).

[22] Bultmann, *Theology*, 2:48.

Thus, for Bultmann, in the Fourth Gospel the death of Jesus has no pre-eminent importance for salvation and is therefore better understood as "completion" and "release from commission."[23] In the same way, it is not an event whose catastrophic nature could be removed only by his subsequent resurrection. Since in the Fourth Gospel Jesus' death is already his "exaltation," his resurrection cannot be an event of special significance.[24] Therefore, though for Bultmann the traditional salvation events (the cross, the resurrection, the exaltation) do play a theological role in the Fourth Gospel,[25] what matters most is the one single event: the Revelation of God's reality (ἀλήθεια) in the earthly activity of Jesus, and faith as "overcoming of the offence,"[26] that is, "the victory that Jesus wins when faith arises in man by the overcoming of the offence that Jesus is to him."[27]

With such an eschatology, one might therefore have expected Bultmann to acknowledge that the disciples truly believed as a result of their encounter with Jesus as Revealer in the Fourth Gospel. Yet, though in the Fourth Gospel Jesus calls the believer into life "now" (5:25; 11:25), for Bultmann, this "now" is distinguished by the proclamation of Jesus "having come,"[28] that is, a proclamation that can only be made after the coming of the Spirit. In other words, this realised eschatology applies only to the Christology and not to the human response. This is so because, for Bultmann, the Spirit is "the power within the Church which brings forth both knowledge and the proclamation of the Word."[29] Interestingly, Bultmann argues that nothing new is given with the Spirit in terms of knowledge: the Spirit only *reminds* believers what Christ has already said (14:26), he only *repeats* what he has heard (16:13, 14). Yet, since the Spirit teaches in a new setting and under a new light, whatever Jesus taught becomes clear for the first time in its true meaning. The Spirit gives knowledge

---

[23] Bultmann, *Theology*, 2:52. This means that the death of Jesus as an atonement for sin has no place in the Fourth Gospel: "His life-work as a whole is sacrifice-an idea well expressed in the description of Jesus as he 'whom the Father consecrated and sent into the world' (10:36)" (p. 55). So for Bultmann, release from sin in the Fourth Gospel comes from the revelation of Jesus, the truth mediated by his word. Whoever accepts Jesus' testimony is clean.

[24] Reading Bultmann, one may wonder how the resurrection actually functions. His answer is as follows: "It is not surprising that the evangelist narrates some *Easter-stories* (following the tradition). The question is, what do they mean to him? [...] The resurrection appearances just like the miracles of Jesus are reckoned among his 'signs.' They symbolize the fulfilment of the prediction of 16:22: 'So you have sorrow now, but I will see you again and your heart will rejoice' (*cf.* 16:16). So far as they are actual occurrences – and the evangelist need not have doubted their reality – they resemble the miracles in that ultimately they are not indispensable; in fact there ought to be no need for them, but they were granted as a concession to man's weakness" (Bultmann, *Theology*, 2:56).

[25] See a critique of Bultmann's understanding in Turner, "Atonement," 99–122.

[26] Bultmann, *Theology*, 2:58.

[27] Bultmann, *Theology*, 2:57.

[28] Bultmann, *Faith*, 174.

[29] Bultmann, *Theology*, 2:88.

that finds expression in the proclamation and preaching of the disciples so that
the eschatological occurrence which took place in Jesus' coming and going is
to continue to take place in preaching.[30]

Manifestly, such an understanding does not sit well with the narrative presentation of the faith and understanding of the disciples suggested in this study.
One may therefore question whether Bultmann would have come to similar
conclusions had he taken into account both the intricate impact of the implied
author's post-resurrection temporal perspective on the narrative and the Gospel's rhetorical purpose. Indeed, it can be argued that both Bultmann's appropriation of an existentialist perspective and his lack of attention to literary
markers directed him to an interpretation of faith's relationship to understanding that is foreign to the Johannine thought-world.

Interestingly, the conclusions of this study are actually not far off Bultmann's
own reconstruction of Johannine eschatology: both emphasise the fact that the
Son had "life in himself" already during his earthly ministry. Yet, other factors
have led Bultmann on a different path, and thus to different conclusions on the
relationship between faith and understanding. To begin with, as this study indicated, the Johannine "now" (5:25) is *both* that of the disciples in the story and
that of the Johannine community. The implied author's story of the disciples'
faith and life is shaped by an eschatology according to which the Son had "life
in himself" (5:26) so that those who put their faith in him during his earthly
ministry, even though their faith was lacking full understanding, were made to
partake in his life. In that sense, it may be said that Bultmann has introduced
a historical distinction, in regard to the disciples' response to Jesus, between
Jesus' coming and the Spirit's coming in a way that distorts the Fourth Gospel's
narrative presentation. From a narrative analysis perspective, the disciples are
in a faith and life relationship with the earthly Jesus already before the events
surrounding his glorification.

Moreover, the manner with which Bultmann presses the incompatibility of
faith and misunderstandings seems to have deeply impacted his conclusions
on the emergence of faith in the disciples. While for Bultmann faith and misunderstanding are antithetical, this study has argued that they went hand in
hand in the characterisation of the disciples. But this is because, unlike what
Bultmann's existential approach to "misunderstanding" allows for, the full understanding of the disciples is first and foremost *scriptural* understanding in
the Fourth Gospel. After the events surrounding Jesus' glorification, memory
and Scripture led them, aided by the Spirit, to a fuller realisation of the significance of Jesus' words and ministry, and thus to believe in a fresh way (2:19,
23; 12:16; 20:9). In that sense, their post-resurrection faith was also nurtured
by their new-found scriptural understanding. But as important as it was, this

---

[30] Bultmann, *Theology*, 2:90: "This continuing eschatological occurrence is the Spirit's
activity in preaching."

step towards deeper understanding did not disqualify their faith prior to these events. Moreover, their misunderstandings (unlike that of Jesus' opponents – *e.g.* 8:31–59) are not presented as rejections of Jesus' revelation, but as struggles to truly understand him (*e.g.* 4:31–34; 11:11–16; 13:36–38; 14:4–6, 8–9; 16:16–19, 29–33). Though they bring to the fore the disciples' lacunae, they are *learners'* lacunae, and so cannot be set on a similar plane as the rejections of Jesus' opponents. The disciples' misunderstandings are the reactions of believers to the revelation of God in Jesus, while the misunderstandings of Jesus' opponents stem from their unbelief. Thus, Bultmann's tendency to consider all the Johannine characters' misunderstandings to be one technique applied uniformly by the Fourth Gospel's author shows its limits. Clearly, according to the Fourth Gospel, misunderstandings do not always denote man's tendency to reject God's revelation, but may actually represent faith's desire to understand.[31]

Moreover, this study's investigation of the place of the disciples within the subplot of the narrative led to the realisation that, though the resurrection and the gift of the Spirit provided the disciples with a much deeper understanding of Jesus' person and ministry (2:22; 12:16), such newfound understanding was first and foremost to qualify them for their ministry as witnesses. In the Fourth Gospel, the disciples are dependent upon Jesus' glorification, not for their faith and life but for the success of their mission.[32] The disciples' mission is multifaceted in the Fourth Gospel. Jesus trained them so that they would be prepared to adequately call their contemporaries to believe in Jesus as the Christ, the Son of God. As such, they were to let Jesus, through his word, encounter and move people to believe in him, redefining them as people of the light instead of people of the darkness (3:18–21). Equipped by their faith and newfound understanding, the disciples would both call to faith in Jesus and clarify potential misunderstandings in their listeners. But another aspect of the witnessing ministry undertaken by the disciples is represented by the Fourth Gospel itself. As a whole, this Gospel is an attempt by the evangelist to declare once more to those who have already believed in Jesus the significance of his person and work.

---

[31] In his discussion of the faith of the crowds and of the disciples in the Fourth Gospel, Faux, *Foi*, 217, correctly shows that, contrary to the Gospel of Mark, the Fourth Gospel does not have a dialectical view of the disciples' faith ("I believe, help my unbelief" – Mk. 9:24) but that the *attitude* of people towards Jesus reveals what is in their hearts. It follows that the faith of the disciples does not need to be viewed as false because of their latent lack of understanding in the narrative. For Faux: "'Tu as les paroles de la vie éternelle' exprime la vraie foi des disciples, encore imparfaite dans son énoncé, mais véritable et définitive dans sa démarche, car elle est l'œuvre du Père: 'Personne ne peut venir à moi si cela ne lui est donné par le Père' (6.65). Rien, pas même la crise de la passion, ne pourra l'ébranler; au contraire cette foi des disciples leur permettra de franchir avec Jésus le cap de l'heure, et d'entamer avec lui le retour vers le Père au-delà du jugement (*krisis*) où s'arrête la foi des foules" (pp. 215–16).

[32] It should be noted that Bultmann insisted that, far from being self-centred or individualistic, Johannine faith involved not only the love of one's neighbour (the community of faith), but also bore a wider responsibility for the world (Bultmann, *Theology*, 2:50–51).

The evangelist sought to strengthen their faith and their understanding of Jesus, encouraging them to continually let Christ redefine their whole selves. For, as a deepening of their understanding of the significance of Christ's identity and ministry occurs, they too would adequately be prepared to take on the task of witnessing in their own world.

Thus, the Fourth Gospel's intent is to nurture the faith and understanding of *believers* through its presentation of the person and work of Christ, and through a process of identification with the disciples who are themselves being prepared for their witnessing ministry. It follows that, even for post-glorification believers, while faith and understanding are present, growth and deepening of both faith and understanding can also occur. Though the implied author realises that his implied readers' understanding is much deeper than that of the disciples in the story (indeed, it was argued that believers' misunderstandings could not occur in the same way after Jesus' resurrection, for it provided what was necessary to clarify the disciples' misunderstandings), they too were to benefit from a story exposing afresh the significance of Jesus' life and work in order to be equipped to witness in their own world.

As a whole, therefore, the Fourth Gospel presupposes that faith may arise and continue to exist without a full intellectual understanding of Jesus and his revelation, yet also that faith remains the necessary foundation upon which understanding can flourish.[33] Such formulations resembles the Old Testament pattern found for instance in LXX Is. 7:9: "ἐὰν μὴ πιστεύεσητε, οὐδὲ μὴ συνῆτε" ("if you do not believe you will not understand"), as well as later similar formulations.[34] In Johannine perspective, understanding is obviously not opposed to faith (as though faith was independent of understanding), but faith may exist even when understanding is lacking (though it can never be altogether absent). Faith is foundational for the Christian life in ways that understanding cannot be, though one cannot be present without the other. Faith, not understanding, is what is necessary to be made a partaker of eternal life: "but these things are written so that you may believe that Jesus is the Christ, the Son of God, and that by believing you may have life in his name" (20:31). This is what the disciples believed from the very beginning of the narrative, turning their whole

---

[33] So Koester, *Theology*, 172, argues: "For John, faith is the context in which understanding develops."

[34] For instance, Anselm famously taught "credo ut intelligam" ("I believe so that I may understand) (see M.-F. Berrouard, *Oeuvres de Saint Augustin 72: Homélies sur l'Evangile de Saint Jean XVII–XXXIII*, BA (Paris: Desclée de Brouwer, 1977), 596–613 and R. W. L. Moberly, "How Can We Know the Truth? A Study of John 7:14–18," in *The Art of Reading Scripture*, ed. by E. F. Davis and R. B. Hays (Grand Rapids, MI/Cambridge: Eerdmans, 2003), 243–45). Likewise, Augustine declared: "Intellegere vis? Crede." ("Do you want to understand? Believe"). For an overview and interaction with this theme in early Christian literature, see P. Helm, *Faith and Understanding*, Reason and Religion (Edinburgh: Edinburgh University Press, 1997), 53.

selves towards Christ as is made explicit by their confessions of faith and further physical following of Jesus. Yet, they had to grow in the understanding of what these propositions really meant in order to be prepared to take on the task given them by Jesus.

Bibliography

Abrams, M. H. *A Glossary of Literary Terms.* 3rd ed. New York, NY: Holt, Rinehart and Winston, Inc., 1971.

Adkinson, R. L. "An Examination of the Concept of Believing in the Gospel of John." Unpublished Ph.D. Thesis. New Orleans, LA: New Orleans Baptist Theological Seminary, 1990.

Agourides, S. "Peter and John in the Fourth Gospel." In *Studia Evangelica IV: Papers Presented to the Third International Congress on New Testament Studies held at Christ Church, Oxford, 1965,* edited by F. L. Cross, pp. 3–7. Berlin: Akademie-Verlag, 1968.

Aletti, J.-N. *L'art de raconter Jésus Christ.* Parole de Dieu. Paris: Seuil, 1989.

Alter, R. *The Art of Biblical Narrative.* New York, NY: Basic Books, 1981.

Aristotle. *The Poetics.* Translated by W. H. Fyfe. LCL. Cambridge, MA: Harvard University Press, 1953.

Ashton, J. *Understanding the Fourth Gospel.* Oxford: Oxford University Press, 1993.

Bal, M. *Narratology. Introduction To the Theory of Narrative.* Toronto: University of Toronto Press, 1994.

Ball, D. M. *'I Am' in John's Gospel. Literary Function, Background and Theological Implications.* JSNTSup 124. Sheffield: Sheffield Academic Press, 1996.

Bar-Efrat, S. *Narrative Art in the Bible.* BLS 17. Sheffield: Almond, 1989.

Baron, M. "La progression des confessions de foi dans les dialogues de Saint Jean." *BVC* 82 (1968): 32–44.

Barrett, C. K. *The Gospel according to St. John: An Introduction with Commentary and Notes on the Greek Text.* 2nd ed. Philadelphia, PA: Westminster, 1978.

Bartlett, D. L. "John 13:21–30." *Int* 43 (1989): 393–97.

Barton, S. C. "Can We Identify the Gospel Audiences?" In *The Gospels for All Christians: Rethinking the Gospel Audiences,* edited by R. Bauckham, pp. 173–94. Edinburgh: T. & T. Clark, 1998.

–. *Life Together: Family, Sexuality and Community in the New Testament and Today.* Edinburgh/New York, NY: T. & T. Clark, 2001.

Barus, A. "The Faith Motif in John's Gospel: A Narrative Approach." Unpublished Ph.D. Thesis. Aberdeen: University of Aberdeen, 2000.

Bauckham, R. "The Beloved Disciple as Ideal Author." *JSNT* 49 (1993): 21–44.

–. "John for Readers of Mark." In *The Gospels for All Christians: Rethinking the Gospel Audiences,* edited by R. Bauckham, pp. 147–71. Edinburgh/Grand Rapids, MI: T. & T. Clark/ Eerdmans, 1998.

–. *Jesus and the Eyewitnesses: The Gospels as Eyewitness Testimony.* Grand Rapids, MI/Cambridge: Eerdmans, 2006.

Bauckham, R., and T. A. Hart. *At the Cross: Meditations on People Who Were There.* Downers Grove, IL: InterVarsity Press, 1999.

Bauer, W., F. W. Danker, W. F. Arndt, and F. W. Gingrich. *Greek-English Lexicon of the New Testament and Other Early Christian Literature.* 3rd ed. Chicago: University of Chicago Press, 2000.

Beasley-Murray, G. R. *John.* WBC 36. Waco, TX: Word, 1987.

Beaude, J. "De Marie de Magdala à la Madeleine, la formation d'une figure mystique." In *Variations johanniques,* edited by B. Dominique, C. Coulot and A. Lion, pp. 157–73. Parole présente. Paris: Cerf/CERIT, 1989.

Beck, D. R. "The Narrative Function of Anonymity in Fourth Gospel Characterization." *Semeia* 63 (1993): 143–58.

–. *The Discipleship Paradigm: Readers and Anonymous Characters in the Fourth Gospel.* BibIntS 27. Leiden/New York, NY: Brill, 1997.

Becker, J. *Das Evangelium nach Johannes.* 2 vols. ÖTBK 4/1–2. Gütersloh/Würzburg: Gerd Mohn/Echter Verlag, 1979, 1981.

Beirne, M. M. *Women and Men in the Fourth Gospel. A Genuine Discipleship of Equals.* JSNTSup 242. Sheffield: Sheffield Academic Press, 2003.

Bennema, C. *Encountering Jesus: Character Studies in the Gospel of John.* Milton Keynes/Colorado Springs, CO/Hyderabad: Paternoster, 2009.

–. "The Giving of the Spirit in John's Gospel – a New Proposal?" *EvQ* 74 (2002): 195–213.

–. *The Power of Saving Wisdom: An Investigation of Spirit and Wisdom in Relation to the Soteriology of the Fourth Gospel.* WUNT 2/148. Tübingen: Mohr Siebeck, 2002.

Berlin, A. *Poetics of Interpretation of Biblical Narrative.* BLS 9. Sheffield: Almond, 1983.

Bernard, J. H. *A Critical and Exegetical Commentary on the Gospel according to St. John.* 2 vols. ICC. Edinburgh: T. & T. Clark, 1953.

Berrouard, M.-F. *Oeuvres de Saint Augustin 72: Homélies sur l'Evangile de Saint Jean XVII–XXXIII.* BA. Paris: Desclée de Brouwer, 1977.

Bienaimé, G. "L'annonce des fleuves d'eau vive en Jean 7, 37–39." *RTL* 21 (1990): 281–310.

Bittner, W. J. *Jesu Zeichen im Johannesevangelium: Die Messias-Erkenntnis im Johannesevangelium vor ihrem jüdischen Hintergrund.* WUNT 2/26. Tübingen: Mohr Siebeck, 1987.

Blaine Jr., B. B. *Peter in the Gospel of John: The Making of an Authentic Disciple.* AcaBib 27. Atlanta, GA: SBL, 2007.

Blanchard, Y.-M. *Des signes pour croire? Une lecture de l'évangile de Jean.* Lire la Bible 106. Paris: Cerf, 1995.

Blank, J. *Krisis: Untersuchungen zur johanneischen Christologie und Eschatologie.* Freiburg im Breisgau: Lambertus-Verlag, 1964.

Blanquart, F. *Le premier jour. Études sur Jean 20.* LD 146. Paris: Cerf, 1991.

Bode, E. L. *The First Easter Morning: The Gospel Accounts of the Women's Visit to the Tomb of Jesus.* AnBib 45. Rome: Biblical Institute Press, 1970.

Boismard, M.-É. *Du baptême à Cana (Jean 1:19–2:11).* LD 18. Paris: Cerf, 1956.

–. "Rapport entre foi et miracles dans l'évangile de Jean." *ETL* 58 (1982): 357–64.

Bonney, W. *Caused To Believe: The Doubting Thomas Story at the Climax of John's Christological Narrative.* BibIntS 62. Leiden/Boston, MA: Brill, 2002.

Bonningues, M. *La foi dans l'évangile de saint Jean.* Paris/Bruxelles: Office Général du Livre/La pensée catholique, 1955.

Booth, W. C. *The Rhetoric of Fiction.* 2nd ed. Chicago, IL: University of Chicago Press, 1983.

–. *The Company We Keep: An Ethics of Fiction.* Berkeley, CA/Los Angeles, CA/London: University of California Press, 1988.

Bouyer, L. *Le quatrième évangile. Introduction à l'évangile de Jean, traduction et commentaire.* BVC 6. Tournai/Paris: Casterman/Maredsous, 1955.

Bovon, F. "Le privilège pascal de Marie-Madeleine." *NTS* 30 (1984): 50–62.

Brant, J.-A. A. "Husband Hunting: Characterization and Narrative Art in the Gospel of John." *BibInt* 4 (1996): 205–23.

Braun, F. M. *La mère des fidèles: esssai de théologie johannique.* CAR. Tournai: Casterman, 1953.

–. *Jean le théologien.* 3 vols. EBib. Paris: Gabalda, 1959–72.

Brodie, T. L. *The Gospel according to John: A Literary and Theological Commentary.* Oxford/
New York, NY: Oxford University Press, 1993.

Brooks, P. *Reading for the Plot.* Oxford: Clarendon, 1984.

Brown, C., ed. *The New International Dictionary of New Testament Theology.* Grand Rapids,
MI: Zondervan, 1976.

Brown, R. E. "The Paraclete in the Fourth Gospel." *NTS* 13 (1966–67): 113–32.

–. *The Gospel according to John.* 2 vols. AB 29 & 29a. Garden City, NY: Doubleday, 1966,
1970.

–. *The Community of the Beloved Disciple: The Life, Loves, and Hates of an Individual Church
in the New Testament.* New York, NY/Mahwah, NJ: Paulist Press, 1979.

–. *A Risen Christ in Eastertime: Essays on the Gospel Narratives of the Resurrection.* Collegeville, MN: The Liturgical Press, 1990.

–. *The Death of the Messiah, From Gethsemane to the Grave: A Commentary on the Passion
Narratives in the Four Gospels.* 2 vols. New York, NY/London/Toronto/Sydney/Auckland:
Doubleday, 1994.

Brown, R. E., K. P. Donfried, and J. H. P. Reumann, eds. *Peter in the New Testament: A Collaborative Assessment by Protestant and Roman Catholic Scholars.* Minneapolis, MN:
Augsburg, 1973.

Bruce, F. F. *The Gospel of John. Introduction, Exposition and Notes.* Grand Rapids, MI: Eerdmans, 1983.

Bultmann, R. *Theology of the New Testament.* 2 vols. Translated by K. Grobel. New York, NY:
Scribner, 1951, 1955.

–. "πιστεύω." In *Theological Dictionary of the New Testament,* G. Kittel and G. Friedrich,
eds. 10 vols. Translated by G. Bromiley, 174–228. Grand Rapids, MI: Eerdmans, 1964–76.

–. *Faith and Understanding.* Translated by L. P. Smith. New York, NY: Harper & Row, 1969.

–. *The Gospel of John: A Commentary.* Translated by G. R. Beasley-Murray. Oxford: Blackwell, 1971.

Burge, G. M. *The Anointed Community: The Holy Spirit in the Johannine Tradition.* Grand
Rapids: Eerdmans, 1987.

Burnett, F. W. "Characterization and Reader Construction of Characters in the Gospels." *Semeia* 63 (1993): 3–28.

Byrne, B. "The Faith of the Beloved Disciple and the Community in John 20." *JSNT* 23 (1985):
83–97.

Caragounis, C. C. "The Kingdom of God in John and the Synoptics: Realized or Potential
Eschatology?" In *John and the Synoptics,* edited by A. Denaux, pp. 473–80. BETL 101.
Leuven: Leuven University Press, 1992.

–. "The Kingdom of God: Common and Distinct Elements Between John and the Synoptics."
In *Jesus in Johannine Tradition,* edited by R. T. Fortna and T. Thatcher, pp. 125–34. Louisville, KY/London/Leiden: Westminster John Knox, 2001.

Carey, G. L. "The Lamb of God and Atonement Theories." *TynBul* 32 (1981): 97–122.

Carson, D. A. *Divine Sovereignty and Human Responsibility: Biblical Perspectives in Tension.*
NFTL. Atlanta, GA: John Knox, 1981. Reprint, Eugene, OR: Wipf and Stock, 2002.

–. "Understanding Misunderstandings in the Fourth Gospel." *TynBul* 33 (1982): 49–91.

–. "The Purpose of the Fourth Gospel: John 20:31 Reconsidered." *JBL* 106 (1987): 639–51.

–. *The Gospel according to John.* PNTC. Leicester/Grand Rapids, MI: Apollos/Eerdmans,
1991.

–. "Syntactical and Text-Critical Observations on John 20:30–31: One More Round on the
Purpose of the Fourth Gospel." *JBL* 124 (2005): 693–714.

Carter, W. "The Prologue and John's Gospel: Function, Symbol and Definitive Word." *JSNT*
39 (1990): 35–58.

Cassidy, R. J. *Four Times Peter: Portrayals of Peter in the Four Gospels and at Philippi.* Interfaces. Collegeville, MN: Liturgical Press, 2007.

Charlesworth, J. H. *The Beloved Disciple: Whose Witness Validates the Gospel of John.* Valley Forge, PA: Trinity, 1995.

Chatman, S. *Story and Discourse: Narrative Structure in Fiction and Film.* Ithaca/London: Cornell University Press, 1978.

Chennattu, R. M. "On Becoming Disciples (John 1:35–51): Insights from the Fourth Gospel." *Sal* 63 (2001): 467–98.

–. *Johannine Discipleship as a Covenant Relationship.* Peabody, MA: Hendrickson, 2006.

Chevallier, M.-A. "La fondation de l'Eglise dans le quatrième Evangile: Jn 19, 25–30." *ETR* 58 (1953): 343–53.

Chryssides, G. D. "Bultmann's Criticisms of Heidegger." *Sophia* 24 (1985): 28–35.

Claussen, C. "The Role of John 21: Discipleship in Retrospect and Redefinition." In *New Currents in John: A Global Perspective*, edited by F. Lozada Jr. and T. Thatcher, pp. 55–68. SBLRBS 54. Atlanta, GA: SBL, 2006.

Collins, R. F. "The Representative Figures of the Fourth Gospel." *DRev* 94 (1976): 26–46.

–. *These Things Have Been Written: Studies on the Fourth Gospel.* LThPM 2. Louvain/Grand Rapids, MI: Peeters/Eerdmans, 1990.

–. "From John to the Beloved Disciple: An Essay on Johannine Characters." *Int* 49 (1995): 359–69.

Coloe, M. L. "Welcome into the Household of God: the Footwashing in John 13." *CBQ* 66 (2004): 400–15.

Colson, J. *L'énigme du disciple que Jésus aimait.* Paris: Beauchesne, 1969.

Conway, C. M. *Men and Women in the Fourth Gospel. Gender and Johannine Characterization.* SBLDS 167. Atlanta, GA: SBL, 1999.

–. "Speaking Through Ambiguity: Minor Characters in the Fourth Gospel." *BibInt* 10 (2002): 324–41.

Cortés, J. B. "Yet Another Look at John 7:37–38." *CBQ* 29 (1967): 75–86.

Cothenet, E. *La chaîne des témoins selon l'évangile de Jean: De Jean-Baptiste au disciple bien-aimé.* Lire la Bible 142. Paris: Cerf, 2005.

Cotterell, F. P. "The Nicodemus Conversation: A Fresh Appraisal." *ExpTim* 96 (1985): 237–42.

Crane, R. S. "The Concept of Plot." In *Approaches to the Novel*, edited by R. Scholes, Rev. ed., pp. 233–43. San Francisco, CA: Chandler, 1966.

Crossan, J. D. "It Is Written: A Structuralist Analysis of John 6." *Semeia* 26 (1983).

Cullmann, O. *Saint Pierre. Disciple - Apôtre - Martyr.* Bibliothèque Théologique. Neuchatel/ Paris: Delachaux & Niestlé, 1952.

–. *Early Christian Worship.* Translated by A. S. Todd and J. B. Torrance. London: SCM, 1953.

Culpepper, R. A. *Anatomy of the Fourth Gospel: A Study in Literary Design.* Philadelphia, PA: Fortress, 1983.

–. "The Johannine Hypodeigma: A Reading of John 13." *Semeia* 53 (1991): 133–52.

–. *John, the Son of Zebedee: The Life of a Legend.* SPNT. Columbia, SC: University of South Carolina Press, 1994.

–. "The Plot of John's Story of Jesus." *Int* 49 (1995): 347–58.

Culpepper, R. A., and F. F. Segovia, eds. *The Fourth Gospel from a Literary Perspective.* Semeia 51. Atlanta, GA: Scholars Press, 1991.

Cuvillier, É. "La figure des disciples en Jean 4." *NTS* 42 (1996): 245–59.

–. "La femme samaritaine et les disciples de Jésus. Histoires de rencontres et de malentendus. Une lecture de l'évangile de Jean 4,1–43." *Hok* 88 (2005): 62–75.

Darr, J. A. *On Character Building: The Reader and the Rhetoric of Characterization in Luke–Acts.* LCBI. Louisville, KY: Westminster John Knox, 1992.

Davies, M. *Rhetoric and Reference in the Fourth Gospel.* JSNTSup 69. Sheffield: Sheffield Academic Press, 1992.

de Boer, E. A. *The Gospel of Mary: Beyond a Gnostic and a Biblical Mary Magdalene.* JSNT-Sup 260. London/New York, NY: T. & T. Clark, 2004.

de Jonge, M. *Jesus, Stranger from Heaven and Son of God: Jesus Christ and the Christians in Johannine Perspective.* Translated by J. E. Steely. SBLSBS 11. Missoula, MT: Scholars Press, 1977.

–. "The Radical Eschatology of the Fourth Gospel and the Eschatology of the Synoptics: Some Suggestions." In *John and the Synoptics*, edited by A. Denaux, pp. 481–87. BETL 101. Leuven: Leuven University Press, 1992.

de la Potterie, I. "Parole et esprit dans S. Jean." In *L'Évangile de Jean: Sources, rédaction, théologie*, edited by M. de Jonge, BETL 44. Gembloux/Leuven: J. Duculot/Leuven University Press, 1975.

–. *La vérité dans Saint Jean.* 2 vols. AnBib 73–74. Rome: Biblical Institute Press, 1977.

–. "Genèse de la foi pascale d'après Jn. 20." *NTS* 30 (1984): 26–49.

–. *La passion de Jésus selon l'évangile de Jean.* Lire la Bible 73. Paris: Cerf, 1986.

–. "Le témoin qui demeure: le disciple que Jésus aimait." *Bib* 67 (1986): 343–59.

de Villier, J. L. "The Shepherd and his Flock." *Neot* 2 (1968).

Decourtray, A. "La conception johannique de la foi." *NRTh* 81 (1959): 561–76.

Delebecque, E. *Évangile de Jean. Texte traduit et annoté.* CahRB 23. Paris: Gabalda, 1987.

Destro, A., and M. Pesce. "Kinship, Discipleship, and Movement: An Anthropological Study of John's Gospel." *BibInt* 3 (1995): 266–84.

Dettwiler, A. *Die Gegenwart des Erhöhten. Eine exegetische Studie zu den johanneischen Abschiedsreden (Joh 13,31–16,33) unter besonderer Berücksichtigung ihres Relecture-Charakters.* FRLANT 169. Göttingen: Vandenhoeck & Ruprecht, 1995.

–. "Fragile compréhension. L'herméneutique de l'usage johannique du malentendu." *RTP* 131 (1999): 371–384.

Devillers, L. *La saga de Siloé. Jésus et la fête des Tentes (Jean 7,1–10,21).* Lire la Bible 143. Paris: Cerf, 2005.

Dewey, K. E. "Paroimiai in the Gospel of John." *Semeia* 17 (1980): 81–99.

Dionne, C. "Le point sur les théories de la gestion des personnages." In *Et vous, qui dites-vous que je suis? La gestion des personnages dans les récits bibliques*, edited by P. Létourneau and M. Talbot, pp. 11–51. SBib 16. Montréal/Paris: Médiaspaul, 2006.

Docherty, T. *Reading (Absent) Character: Towards a Theory of Characterization in Fiction.* Oxford: Clarendon, 1983.

Dodd, C. H. *The Interpretation of the Fourth Gospel.* Cambridge: Cambridge University Press, 1953.

Domeris, W. R. "The Confession of Peter according to John 6:69." *TynBul* 44 (1993): 157–67.

Donahue, J. R. *The Theology and Setting of Discipleship in the Gospel of Mark.* Milwaukee, WI: Marquette University Press, 1983.

Droge, A. J. "The Status of Peter in the Fourth Gospel: A Note on John 18:10–11." *JBL* 109 (1990): 307–11.

du Rand, J. A. "Narratological Perspectives on John 13:1–38." *HvTSt* 46 (1990): 367–89.

–. "Perspectives on Johannine Discipleship according to the Farewell Discourse." *Neot* 25 (1991): 311–25.

Duke, P. D. *Irony in the Fourth Gospel.* Atlanta: John Knox, 1985.

Dunn, J. D. G. *Baptism in the Holy Spirit: A Re-examination of the New Testament Teaching on the Gift of the Spirit in Relation to Pentecostalism Today.* Philadelphia: Westminster, 1970.

–. "The Washing of the Disciples' Feet in John 13:1–20." *ZNW* 61 (1970): 247–52.

–. *Christology in the Making: An Inquiry into the Origins of the Doctrine of the Incarnation.* 2nd ed. London: SCM, 1989.

–. *Christianity in the Making, volume 1: Jesus Remembered*. Grand Rapids, MI/Cambridge: Eerdmans, 2003.

Edwards, R. B. "The Christological Basis of the Johannine Footwashing." In *Jesus of Nazareth: Lord and Christ. Essays on the Historical Jesus and New Testament Christology*, edited by J. B. Green and M. Turner, pp. 367–83. Grand Rapids, MI/Carlisle: Eerdmans/Paternoster, 1994.

Eslinger, L. "Judas Game: The Biology of Combat in the Gospel of John." *JSNT* 77 (2000): 45–73.

Estes, D. *The Temporal Mechanics of the Fourth Gospel: A Theory of Hermeneutical Relativity in the Gospel of John*. BibIntS 92. Leiden/Boston, MA: Brill, 2008.

Evans, C. A. "Jesus' Action in the Temple: Cleansing or Portent of Destruction?" *CBQ* 51 (1989): 237–70.

Farelly, N. "John 2:23–25: What Kind of Faith Is This?" *Presb* 30 (2004): 37–45.

Faux, J.-M. *La foi du Nouveau Testament*. Bruxelles: Institut d'Études Théologiques, 1977.

Fee, G. D. "On the Text and Meaning of John 20,20–31." In *The Four Gospels 1992: Festschrift Frans Neirynck*, edited by F. Van Segbroeck, C. Tuckett, G. Van Belle and J. Verheyden, 3 vols., pp. 3:2193–2205. BETL 100. Leuven: Leuven University Press, 1992.

Fehribach, A. *The Women in the Life of the Bridegroom: A Feminist Historical-Literary Analysis of the Female Characters in the Fourth Gospel*. Collegeville, MN: Liturgical Press, 1998.

Forestell, J. T. *The Word of the Cross: Salvation as Revelation in the Fourth Gospel*. AnBib 57. Rome: Biblical Institute Press, 1974.

Forster, E. M. *Aspects of the Novel*. San Diego, CA/New York, NY/London: Harcourt, Inc., 1955.

Fortna, R. T. "From Christology to Soteriology: A Redactional-Critical Study of Salvation in the Fourth Gospel." *Int* 27 (1973): 31–47.

–. "Jesus and Peter in the High Priest's House: A Test Case for the Question of the Relation between Mark's and John's Gospels." *NTS* 24 (1978): 371–83.

–. *The Fourth Gospel and its Predecessors: From Narrative Source to Present Gospel*. Edinburgh: T. & T. Clark, 1989.

Fowler, R. M. *Let the Reader Understand: Reader-Response Criticism and the Gospel of Mark*. Minneapolis, MN: Fortress, 1991.

Frey, J. *Die johanneische Eschatologie. Vol. 1: Ihre Probleme im Spiegel der Forschung seit Reimarus*. WUNT 96. Tübingen: Mohr Siebeck, 1997.

–. *Die johanneische Eschatologie. Vol. 2: Das Johanneische Zeitverständnis*. WUNT 110. Tübingen: Mohr Siebeck, 1998.

–. *Die johanneische Eschatologie. Vol. 3: Die eschatologische Verkündigung in den johanneischen Texten*. WUNT 117. Tübingen: Mohr Siebeck, 2000.

–. "Eschatology in the Johannine Circle." In *Theology and Christology in the Fourth Gospel*, edited by G. Van Belle, J. G. van der Watt and P. J. Maritz, pp. 47–82. BETL 184. Leuven: Leuven University Press/Peeters, 2005.

Friedman, N. "Forms of the Plot." In *The Theory of the Novel*, edited by P. Stevick, pp. 145–66. New York, NY: The Free Press, 1967.

Frye, N. *The Great Code: The Bible in Literature*. New York, NY: Harcourt Brace Jovanovich, 1982.

Gaffney, J. "Believing and Knowing in the Fourth Gospel." *TS* 26 (1965): 215–41.

Gallagher, D. "The Obedience of Faith: Barth, Bultmann, and *Dei Verbum*." *JCTR* 10 (2006): 39–63.

Genette, G. *Figures III. Poétique*. Paris: Seuil, 1972.

–. *Nouveaux discours du récit*. Paris: Seuil, 1983.

Giblin. "Suggestion, Negative Response, and Positive Action in St. John's Portrayal of Jesus (John 2:1–11; 4:46–56; 7:2–14; 11:1–44)." *NTS* 26 (1980): 197–211.

Gloer, W. H. "'Come and See': Disciples and Discipleship in the Fourth Gospel." In *Perspectives on John: Methods and Interpretation in the Fourth Gospel*, edited by R. B. Sloan and M. C. Parsons, pp. 269–301. NABPRSSS. Lewiston, NY/Queenston/Lampeter: Edwin Mellen, 1993.

Gourgues, M. "Superposition du temps symbolique et du temps réel dans l'évangile de Jean." In *Raconter, interpréter, annoncer. Parcours de Nouveau Testament. Mélanges offerts à Daniel Marguerat pour son 60ème anniversaire*, edited by E. Steffek and Y. Bourquin, pp. 171–82. MB 47. Genève: Labor et Fides, 2003.

Greimas, A. J. *Sémantique structurale. Recherche et méthode*. Paris: Larousse, 1966.

Grelot, P. "L'interprétation pénitentielle du lavement des pieds." In *L'homme devant Dieu: Mélanges offerts au Père Henri de Lubac*, edited, 2 vols., pp. 1:75–91. Théologie 56. Paris: Aubier, 1963.

Grundmann, W. "Verständnis und Bewegung des Glaubens im Johannes-Evangelium." *KD* 6 (1960): 131–54.

Gunther, J. J. "The Relation of the Beloved Disciple to the Twelve." *TZ* 37/3 (1981): 129–48.

Haenchen, E. *A Commentary on the Gospel of John*. 2 vols. Translated by R. W. Funk. Hermeneia. Philadelphia, PA: Fortress, 1984.

Hakola, R. "A Character Resurrected: Lazarus in the Fourth Gospel and Afterwards." In *Characterization in the Gospels. Reconceiving Narrative Criticism*, edited by D. Rhoads and K. Syreeni, pp. 223–63. JSNTSuppS 184. Sheffield: Sheffield Academic Press, 1999.

Hallbäck, G. "The Gospel of John as Literature." In *New Readings in John: Literary and Theological Perspectives. Essays from the Scandinavian Conference on the Fourth Gospel in Aarhus 1997*, edited by J. Nissen and S. Pedersen, pp. 31–46. JSNTSuppS 182. Sheffield: Sheffield Academic Press, 1999.

Harstine, S. *Moses as a Character in the Fourth Gospel. A Study of Ancient Reading Techniques*. JSNTSup 229. Sheffield: Sheffield Academic Press, 2002.

–. "Un-Doubting Thomas: Recognition Scenes in the Ancient World." *PRSt* 33 (2006): 435–47.

Harvey, W. J. *Character and the Novel*. Ithaca, NY: Cornell University Press, 1965.

Hawkin, D. J. "The Function of the Beloved Disciple Motif in the Johannine Redaction." *LTP* 33 (1977): 135–50.

Hawthorne, G. F. "The Concept of Faith in the Fourth Gospel." *BSac* 116 (1959): 117–126.

Hays, R. B. "Reading Scripture in Light of the Resurrection." In *The Art of Reading Scripture*, edited by E. F. Davis and R. B. Hays, pp. 216–38. Grand Rapids, MI/Cambridge: Eerdmans, 2003.

Heil, J. P. *Jesus Walking on the Sea: Meaning and Gospel Functions of Matt. 14:22–33; Mark 6:45–52 and John 6:15b–21*. AnBib 87. Rome: Biblical Institute Press, 1981.

–. *Blood and Water: The Death and Resurrection of Jesus in John 18–21*. CBQMS 27. Washington, DC: Catholic Biblical Association of America, 1995.

Helm, P. *Faith and Understanding*. Reason and Religion. Edinburgh: Edinburgh University Press, 1997.

Henderson, S. W. *Christology and Discipleship in the Gospel of Mark*. SNTSMS 135. Cambridge: Cambridge University Press, 2006.

Hengel, M. "Maria Magdalena und die Frauen als Zeugen." In *Abraham unser Vater: Juden und Christen im Gespräch über die Bibel. Festschrift für Otto Michel zum 60*, edited by O. Betz, M. Hengel and P. Schmidt, pp. 243–56. AGJU 5. Leiden: Brill, 1963.

Hillmer, M. R. "They Believed in Him: Discipleship in the Johannine Tradition." In *Patterns of Discipleship in the New Testament*, edited by R. N. Longenecker, pp. 77–97. McMNTS. Grand Rapids, MI: Eerdmans, 1996.

Hochman, B. *Character in Literature*. Ithaca, NY/London: Cornell University Press, 1985.

Hodges, Z. C. "Problem Passages in the Gospel of John. Part 2: Untrustworthy Believers – John 2:23–25." *BSac* 135 (1978): 139–52.

Holleran, J. W. "Seeing the Light. A Narrative Reading of John 9; Part I: Background and Presuppositions." *ETL* 69 (1993): 5–26.

Hooker, M. *Endings: Invitations to Discipleship.* Peabody, MA: Hendrickson, 2003.

Hopkins, A. D. "A Narratological Approach to the Development of Faith in the Gospel of John." Unpublished Ph.D. Thesis. Louisville, KY: Southern Baptist Theological Seminary, 1992.

Hoskins, P. M. *Jesus as the Fulfillment of the Temple in the Gospel of John.* PBM. Milton Keynes/Waynesboro, GA: Paternoster, 2006.

Hoskyns, E. C. *The Fourth Gospel.* Rev. ed. London: Faber and Faber, 1947.

Howard, J. M. "The Significance of Minor Characters in the Gospel of John." *BSac* 163 (2006): 63–78.

Huby, J. "De la connaissance de foi dans Saint Jean." *RSR* 21 (1931): 385–421.

Hurtado, L. W. "Remembering and Revelation: The Historic and Glorified Jesus in the Gospel of John." In *Israel's God and Rebecca's Children, Christology and Community in Early Judaism and Christianity: Essays in Honor of Larry W. Hurtado and Alan F. Segal,* edited by D. B. Capes, A. D. DeConick and H. K. Bond, pp. 195–213. Waco, TX: Baylor University Press, 2008.

Hylen, S. E. *Imperfect Believers: Ambiguous Characters in the Gospel of John.* Louisville, KY: Westminster John Know, 2009.

Ibuki, Y. "'Viele glaubten an ihn' – Auseinandersetzung mit dem Glauben im Johannesevangelium." *AJBI* 9 (1983): 128–83.

Iser, W. *The Implied Reader: Patterns of Communication in Prose Fiction from Bunyan to Beckett.* Baltimore, MD: Johns Hopkins University Press, 1974.

–. *The Act of Reading: A Theory of Aesthetic Response.* Baltimore, MD: Johns Hopkins University Press, 1978.

Jackson, H. M. "Ancient Self-Referential Conventions and Their Implications for the Authorship and Integrity of the Gospel of John " *JTS* 50 (1999): 1–34.

Jeremias, J. "Die Berufung des Nathanael." *Angelos* 3 (1928): 2–5.

Joubert, H. L. N. "'The Holy One of God' (John 6:69)." *Neot* 2 (1968): 57–69.

Käsemann, E. *The Testament of Jesus: A Study of the Gospel of John in the Light of Chapter 17.* Translated by G. Krodel. London: SCM, 1968.

Kelber, W. H. "The Birth of a Beginning." *Semeia* 52 (1990): 121–44.

Kermode, F. *The Sense of an Ending: Studies in the Theory of Fiction.* New York, NY/London: Oxford University Press, 1967.

Kerrigan, P. A. "Jn. 19,25–27 in Light of Johannine Theology and the Old Testament." *Anton* 35 (1960): 369–416.

Kieffer, R. "L'espace et le temps dans l'évangile de Jean." *NTS* 31 (1985): 393–409.

–. *Le monde symbolique de Saint Jean.* LD 137. Paris: Cerf, 1989.

–. "The Implied Reader in John's Gospel." In *New Readings in John: Literary and Theological Perspectives. Essays from the Scandinavian Conference on the Fourth Gospel in Aarhus 1997,* edited by J. Nissen and S. Pedersen, pp. 47–65. JSNTSuppS 182. Sheffield: Sheffield Academic Press, 1999.

Kim, D. *An Exegesis of Apostasy Embedded in John's Narrative of Peter and Judas Against the Synoptic Parallels.* SBEC 61. Lewiston, NY/Queenston/Lampeter: Edwin Mellen, 2004.

Kingsbury, J. D. *Matthew as Story.* Philadelphia, PA: Fortress, 1986.

Klauck, H.-J. *Judas, un disciple de Jésus. Exégèse et répercutions historiques.* Translated by J. Hoffmann. LD 212. Paris: Cerf, 2006.

Koester, C. R. "Hearing, Seeing, and Believing in the Gospel of John." *Bib* 70/3 (1989): 327–48.

–. *Symbolism in the Fourth Gospel: Meaning, Mystery, Community.* 2nd ed. Minneapolis: Fortress, 2003.

–. *The Word of Life: A Theology of John's Gospel.* Grand Rapids, MI: Eerdmans, 2008.

Köstenberger, A. J. "The 'Greater Works' of the Believer According to John 14:12." *Did* 6 (1995): 36–45.

–. *The Missions of Jesus and the Disciples according to the Fourth Gospel: With Implications for the Fourth Gospel's Purpose and the Mission of the Contemporary Church.* Grand Rapids, MI: Eerdmans, 1998.

–. *John.* BECNT. Grand Rapids, MI: Baker Academic, 2004.

Kreitzer, L. J. "The Temple Incident of John 2:13–25: A Preview of What Is to Come." In *Understanding, Studying and Reading. New Testament Essays in Honour of John Ashton*, edited by C. Rowland and C. H. T. Fletcher-Louis, pp. 93–101. JSNTSuppS 153. Sheffield: Sheffield Academic Press, 1998.

Kurz, W. "The Beloved Disciple and Implied Readers." *BTB* 19 (1989): 100–107.

Kysar, R. *The Fourth Evangelist and His Gospel: An Examination of Contemporary Scholarship.* Minneapolis, MN: Augsburg, 1975.

–. *John, The Maverick Gospel.* Rev. ed. Louisville, KY: Westminster John Knox, 1993.

–. "The Dismantling of Decisional Faith: A Reading of John 6:25–71." In *Critical Reading of John 6*, edited by R. A. Culpepper, pp. 161–81. BibIntS 22. Leiden/New York, NY/Köln: Brill, 1997.

Ladd, G. E. *A Theology of the New Testament.* 2nd ed. Grand Rapids, MI: Eerdmans, 1993.

Lagrange, M.-J. *Évangile selon Saint Jean.* EBib. Paris: Gabalda, 1925.

Larivaille, P. "L'analyse (morpho) logique du récit." *Poétique* 19 (1974): 368–88.

Lee, D. A. *The Symbolic Narratives of the Fourth Gospel: The Interplay of Form and Meaning.* JSNTSup 95. Sheffield: Sheffield Academic Press, 1994.

–. "Partnership in Easter Faith: The Role of Mary Magdalene and Thomas in John 20." *JSNT* 58 (1995): 37–49.

–. "Abiding in the Fourth Gospel: A Case Study in Feminist Biblical Theology." *Pac* 10 (1997): 123–36.

–. "Turning from Death to Life: A Biblical Reflection on Mary Magdalene (John 20:1–18)." *ER* 50 (1998): 112–20.

–. *Flesh and Glory: Symbolism, Gender, and Theology in the Gospel of John.* New York, NY: Crossroad, 2002.

Lenglet, A. "Jésus de passage parmi les Samaritains. Jn. 4/4–42." *Bib* 66 (1985): 493–503.

Léon-Dufour, X. "Les miracles de Jésus selon Jean." In *Les miracles de Jésus selon le Nouveau Testament*, edited by X. Léon-Dufour, pp. 269–86. Paris: Seuil, 1977.

–. *Lecture de l'évangile selon Jean.* 4 vols. Paris: Seuil, 1988–1996.

Leroy, H. *Rätsel und Missverständnis; ein Beitrag zur Formgeschichte des Johannesevangeliums.* BBB 30. Bonn: P. Hanstein, 1968.

Létourneau, P., and M. Talbot, eds. *Et vous, qui dites-vous que je suis? La gestion des personnages dans les récits bibliques.* SBib 16. Montréal/Paris: Médiaspaul, 2006.

Lévi-Strauss, C. *Anthropologie structurale.* Paris: Plon, 1958.

Lightfoot, R. H. *St. John's Gospel: A Commentary.* Oxford: Oxford University Press, 1963.

Lincoln, A. T. "Trials, Plots and the Narrative of the Fourth Gospel." *JSNT* 56 (1994): 3–30.

–. "'I am the Resurrection and the Life': The Resurrection Message of the Fourth Gospel." In *Life in the Face of Death. The Resurrection Message of the New Testament*, edited by R. N. Longenecker, pp. 122–44. McMNTS. Grand Rapids, MI/Cambridge: Eerdmans, 1998.

–. *Truth on Trial: The Lawsuit Motif in the Fourth Gospel.* Peabody, MA: Hendrickson, 2000.

–. "The Beloved Disciple as Eyewitness and the Fourth Gospel as Witness." *JSNT* 85 (2002): 3–26.

–. *The Gospel according to Saint John.* BNTC 4. Peabody, MA/London: Hendrickson/Continuum, 2005.

–. "The Lazarus Story: A Literary Perspective." In *The Gospel of John and Christian Theology*, edited by R. Bauckham and C. Mosser, pp. 211–32. Grand Rapids, MI/Cambridge: Eerdmans, 2008.

Lindars, B. "The Composition of John 20." *NTS* 7 (1961): 142–47.

–. *The Gospel of John*. NCB. Grand Rapids, MI: Eerdmans, 1981.

Loader, W. R. G. *The Christology of the Fourth Gospel: Structure and Issues*. BBET 23. Frankfurt: Verlag Peter Lang, 1989.

–. "John 1:50–51 and the 'Greater Things' of Johannine Christology." In *Anfänge der Christologie: Festschrift für Ferdinand Hahn zum 65. Geburtstag*, edited by C. Breytenbach and H. Paulsen, pp. 255–74. Göttingen: Vandenhoeck & Ruprecht, 1991.

Lohse, E. "Miracles in the Fourth Gospel." In *What About the New Testament?*, edited by M. Hooker and C. Hickling, pp. 64–75. London: SCM, 1975.

Maccini, R. G. *Her Testimony Is True. Women as Witnesses according to John*. JSNTSup 125. Sheffield: Sheffield Academic Press, 1996.

Malbon, E. S. "Texts and Contexts: Interpreting the Disciples in Mark." *Semeia* 62 (1993): 81–102.

Malbon, E. S., and A. Berlin, eds. *Characterization in Biblical Literature*. Semeia 63. Atlanta, GA: Scholars Press, 1993.

Marchadour, A. "La figure de Simon-Pierre dans l'évangile de Jean." In *Raconter, interpréter, annoncer. Parcours de Nouveau Testament. Mélanges offerts à Daniel Marguerat pour son 60° anniversaire*, edited by E. Steffek and Y. Bourquin, pp. 183–94. MdB 47. Genève: Labor et Fides, 2003.

–. *Les personnages dans l'évangile de Jean: miroir pour une christologie narrative*. Lire la Bible 139. Paris: Cerf, 2004.

Marguerat, D. "L'exégèse biblique à l'heure du lecteur." In *La Bible en récits: L'exégèse biblique à l'heure du lecteur*, edited by D. Marguerat, pp. 13–40. MdB 48. Genève: Labor et Fides, 2003.

Marguerat, D., and Y. Bourquin. *Pour lire les récits bibliques. Initiation à l'analyse narrative*. 3rd ed. Paris/Genève: Cerf/Labor et Fides, 2004.

Marshall, I. H. *New Testament Theology: Many Witnesses, One Witness*. Downers Grove, IL/ Nottingham: InterVarsity Press/Apollos, 2004.

Martyn, J. L. *History and Theology in the Fourth Gospel*. 3rd ed. NTL. Louisville, KY/London: Westminster John Knox, 2003.

Matera, F. J. "John 20:1–18." *Int* 43 (1989): 402–06.

Matson, M. A. "The Temple Incident: An Integral Element in the Fourth Gospel's Narrative." In *Jesus in Johannine Tradition*, edited by R. T. Fortna and T. Thatcher, pp. 145–53. Louisville, KY: Westminster John Knox, 2001.

Maynard, A. H. "The Role of Peter in the Fourth Gospel." *NTS* 30 (1984): 531–48.

McGrath, A. E. *Doubting: Growing Through the Uncertainties of Faith*. 2nd ed. Downers Grove, IL: InterVarsity Press, 2006.

McHugh, J. *The Mother of Jesus in the New Testament*. London: Darton, Longman & Todd, 1975.

Mead, A. H. "The βασιλικὸς in John 4.46–53." *JSNT* 23 (1985): 69–72.

Metzger, B. M. *A Textual Commentary on the Greek New Testament*. 2nd ed. Stuttgart: Deutsche Bibelgesellschaft/United Bible Societies, 1994.

Miller, R. J., ed. *The Complete Gospels: Annotated Scholars Version*. Sonoma, CA: Polebridge Press, 1992.

Minear, P. S. "'We Don't Know Where...' John 20:2." *Int* 30 (1976): 125–39.

–. "Diversity and Unity. A Johannine Case Study." In *Die Mitte des Neuen Testaments: Einheit und Vielfalt neutestamentlicher Theologie: Festschrift für Eduard Schweizer zum siebzigsten*

Geburtstag, edited by U. Luz and H. Weder, pp. 162–75. Göttingen: Vandenhoeck & Ruprecht, 1983.

–. "The Beloved Disciple in the Gospel of John: Some Clues and Conjectures." In *The Composition of John's Gospel: Selected Studies from Novum Testamentum*, edited by D. E. Orton, pp. 85–98. Leiden: Brill, 1999.

Mlakuzhyil, G. *The Christocentric Literary Structure of the Fourth Gospel.* AnBib 117. Rome: Editrice Pontificio Istituto Biblico, 1987.

Moberly, R. W. L. "How Can We Know the Truth? A Study of John 7:14–18." In *The Art of Reading Scripture*, edited by E. F. Davis and R. B. Hays, pp. 239–57. Grand Rapids, MI/Cambridge: Eerdmans, 2003.

Mollat, D. *Études johanniques.* PdD 19. Paris: Seuil, 1979.

Moloney, F. J. "From Cana to Cana (Jn. 2:1–4:54) and the Fourth Evangelist's Concept of Correct (and Incorrect) Faith." *Sal* 40 (1978): 817–43.

–. "John 20: A Journey Completed." *ACR* 59 (1982): 417–32.

–. *Mary: Woman and Mother.* Collegeville, MN: Liturgical Press, 1989.

–. "A Sacramental Reading of John 13:1–38." *CBQ* 53 (1991): 237–56.

–. *Belief in the Word: Reading the Fourth Gospel, John 1–4.* Minneapolis, MN: Fortress, 1993.

–. "The Faith of Martha and Mary. A Narrative Approach to John 11,17–40." *Bib* 75 (1994): 471–93.

–. *Glory not Dishonor: Reading John 13–21.* Minneapolis, MN: Fortress, 1998.

–. *The Gospel of John.* SP 4. Collegeville, MN: Liturgical Press, 1998.

–. "Can Everyone be Wrong? A Reading of John 11.1–12.8." *NTS* 49 (2003): 505–27.

Moore, S. D. *Literary Criticism and the Gospels: The Theoretical Challenge.* New Haven, CT: Yale University Press, 1989.

Morgen, M. *Afin que le monde soit sauvé. Jésus révèle sa mission de salut dans l'évangile de Jean.* LD 154. Paris: Cerf, 1993.

Morris, L. *The Gospel according to John.* Rev. ed. NICNT. Grand Rapids, MI: Eerdmans, 1995.

–. *Reflections on the Gospel of John.* Peabody, MA: Hendrickson, 2000.

Most, G. W. *Doubting Thomas.* Cambridge, MA/London: Harvard University Press, 2005.

Motyer, S. *Your Father the Devil? A New Approach to John and 'the Jews'.* PBM. Carlisle: Paternoster, 1997.

Moule, C. F. D. "A Note on 'Under the Fig Tree' in John 1:48, 50." *JTS* 5 (1954): 210–11.

Müller, T. E. *Das Heilsgeschehen im Johannesevangelium: Eine exegetische Studie, zugleich der Versuch einer Antwort an Rudolf Bultmann.* Zürich/Frankfurt: Gotthelf-Verlag, 1961.

Myers, B. "Faith as Self-Understanding: Towards a Post-Barthian Appreciation of Rudolf Bultmann." *IJST* 10 (2008): 21–35.

Neirynck, F. "The 'Other Disciple' in Jn 18,15–16." *ETL* 51 (1975): 113–41.

–. "The Anonymous Disciple in John 1." *ETL* 66 (1990): 5–37.

Newbigin, L. *The Light Has Come: An Exposition of the Fourth Gospel.* Grand Rapids, MI/Edinburgh: Eerdmans/Handsel Press, 1982.

Neyrey, J. H. "The Jacob Allusions in John 1:51." *CBQ* 44 (1982): 586–605.

–. "Jesus the Judge: Forensic Process in John 8,21–59." *Bib* 68 (1987): 520–35.

Nicol, W. *The Sēmeia in the Fourth Gospel: Tradition and Redaction.* NovTSup 32. Leiden: Brill, 1972.

Nielsen, H. K. "John's Understanding of the Death of Jesus." In *New Readings in John: Literary and Theological Perspectives. Essays from the Scandinavian Conference on the Fourth Gospel in Aarhus 1997*, edited by J. Nissen and S. Pedersen, pp. 232–54. JSNTSuppS 182. Sheffield: Sheffield Academic Press, 1999.

O'Brien, K. S. "Written That You May Believe: John 20 and Narrative Rhetoric." *CBQ* 67 (2005): 284–302.

O'Collins, G., and D. Kendall. "Mary Magdalene as a Major Witness to Jesus' Resurrection." *TS* 48 (1987): 631–46.

O'Day, G. R. *Revelation in the Fourth Gospel: Narrative Mode and Theological Claim.* Philadelphia, PA: Fortress, 1986.

–. "'I Have Overcome the World' (John 16:33): Narrative Time in John 13–17." *Semeia* 53 (1991): 153–66.

–. "The Gospel of John." In *The New Interpreter's Bible IX*, edited, pp. 493–865. Nashville, TN: Abingdon, 1995.

Ogden, S. M. *Christ Without Myth: A Study Based on the Theology of Rudolf Bultmann.* New York, NY: Harper & Brothers, 1961.

Okure, T. *The Johannine Approach to Mission: A Contextual Study of John 4:1–42.* WUNT 2/31. Tübingen: Mohr Siebeck, 1988.

Origen. *Commentary on the Gospel according to John.* 10 vols. Translated by R. E. Heine. The Fathers of the Church 81. Washington, DC: Catholic University Press of America, 1989.

Paffenroth, K. *Judas: Images of the Lost Disciple.* Louisville, KY: Westminster John Knox, 2001.

Painter, J. "Eschatological Faith in the Gospel of John." In *Reconciliation and Hope: New Testament Essays on Atonement and Eschatology Presented to L. L. Morris on his 60th Birthday*, edited by R. J. Banks, pp. 36–52. Exeter: Paternoster, 1974.

–. *Theology as Hermeneutics: Rudolf Bultmann's Interpretation of the History of Jesus.* HTIBS. Sheffield: Sheffield Academic Press, 1987.

–. "Tradition and Interpretation in John 6." *NTS* 35 (1989).

–. *The Quest for the Messiah: The History, Literature and Theology of the Johannine Community.* 2nd ed. Nashville, TN: Abingdon, 1993.

Pamment, M. "The Fourth Gospel's Beloved Disciple." *ExpTim* 94 (1983): 363–67.

Pancaro, S. *The Law in the Fourth Gospel: The Torah and the Gospel, Moses and Jesus, Judaism and Christianity according to John.* NovTSup 42. Leiden: Brill, 1975.

Parsenios, G. L. "'No Longer in the World' (John 17:11): The Transformation of the Tragic in the Fourth Gospel." *HTR* 98 (2005): 1–21.

Parsons, M. C. "Reading a Beginning/Beginning a Reading: Tracing Literary Theory on Narrative Openings." *Semeia* 52 (1990): 11–31.

Pazdan, M. M. "Nicodemus and the Samaritan Woman: Contrasting Models of Discipleship." *BTB* 17 (1987): 145–48.

Perkins, P. *Peter: Apostle of the Whole Church.* SPNT. Columbia, SC: University of South Carolina Press, 1994.

Perry, M. "Literary Dynamics: How the Order of a Text Creates Its Meanings." *PT* 1 (1979): 35–64.

Petersen, N. R. *Literary Criticism for New Testament Critics.* Philadelphia, PA: Fortress, 1978.

–. *The Gospel of John and the Sociology of Light. Language and Characterization in the Fourth Gospel.* Valley Forge, PA: Trinity Press International, 1993.

Phelan, J. *Reading People, Reading Plots: Character, Progression, and the Interpretation of Narrative.* Chicago, IL/London: University of Chicago Press, 1989.

Pollard, T. E. "The Raising of Lazarus (John XI)." In *SE 6 (TU 112)*, edited by E. A. Livingston. Berlin: Akademie Verlag, 1973.

Porsch, F. *Pneuma und Wort: Ein exegetischer Beitrag zur Pneumatologie des Johannesevangelium.* FTS 16. Frankfurt: Knecht, 1974.

Porter, S. E. *Verbal Aspects in the Greek of the New Testament, with Reference to Tense and Mood.* SBG 1. Bern: Peter Lang, 1989.

–. "Can Traditional Exegesis Enlighten Literary Analysis of the Fourth Gospel? An Examination of the Old Testament Fulfilment Motif and the Passover Theme." In *The Gospels and the Scripture of Israel*, edited by C. A. Evans and W. R. Stegner, pp. 396–428. JSNTSup 104. Sheffield: Sheffield Academic Press, 1994.

Powell, M. A. *What Is Narrative Criticism?* GNTS. Minneapolis, MN: Fortress, 1990.

Prigent, P. *Heureux celui qui croit. Lecture de l'évangile de Jean.* Lyon: Olivétan, 2006.

Propp, V. *Morphologie du conte.* Collection Point. Paris: Seuil, 1970.

Pryor, J. W. "Jesus and Israel in the Fourth Gospel-John 1.11." *NovT* 32 (1990): 201–18.

Quast, K. *Peter and the Beloved Disciple: Figures for a Community in Crisis.* JSNTSup 32. Sheffield: Sheffield Academic Press, 1989.

Rensberger, D. *Overcoming the World: Politics and Community in the Gospel of John.* London: SPCK, 1989.

Resseguie, J. L. *The Strange Gospel: Narrative Design and Point of View in John.* BibIntS 56. Leiden/Boston, MA: Brill, 2001.

–. *Narrative Criticism of the New Testament: An Introduction.* Grand Rapids, MI: Baker Academic, 2005.

Rhoads, D., and D. Michie. *Mark as Story: An Introduction to the Narrative of a Gospel.* Philadelphia, PA: Fortress, 1982.

Rhoads, D., and K. Syreeni, eds. *Characterization in the Gospels: Reconceiving Narrative Criticism.* JSNTSup 184. Sheffield: Sheffield Academic Press, 1999.

Ricoeur, P. *Interpretation Theory: Discourse and the Surplus of Meaning.* Fort Worth, TX: Texas Christian University Press, 1976.

–. *Temps et récit. Tome I: L'intrigue et le récit historique.* Points-Essais. Paris: Seuil, 1983.

–. *Temps et récit. Tome II: La configuration dans le récit de fiction.* Points-Essais. Paris: Seuil, 1984.

–. *Temps et récit. Tome III: Le temps raconté.* Points-Essais. Paris: Seuil, 1985.

–. *Du texte à l'action. Essais d'herméneutique.* Paris: Seuil, 1986.

Ridderbos, H. N. *The Gospel of John: A Theological Commentary.* Translated by J. Vriend. Grand Rapids, MI: Eerdmans, 1997.

Robinson, J. A. T. *The Roots of a Radical.* New York, NY: Crossroad, 1981.

Ruschmann, S. *Maria von Magdalena im Johannesevangelium. Jüngerin-Zeugin-Lebensbotin.* NTAbh 40. Münster: Aschendorff, 2002.

Sanders, E. P. *Jesus and Judaism.* London/Philadelphia, PA: SCM/Fortress, 1985.

Schenke, L. "Johannine Schism and the 'Twelve' (John 6:60–71)." In *Critical Readings of John 6*, edited by R. A. Culpepper, pp. 205–19. BibIntS 22. Leiden/New York, NY/Köln: Brill, 1997.

Schlatter, A. *Der Glaube in Neuen Testament.* Stuttgart: Calwer Verlag, 1927.

Schnackenburg, R. *The Gospel according to John.* 3 vols. Translated by K. Smyth. HTKNT IV/1–3. London/New York, NY: Burns & Oates/Crossroad, 1968–1982.

Schneiders, S. M. "The Face Veil: A Johannine Sign (John 20:1–10)." *BTB* 13 (1983): 94–97.

–. *Written That You May Believe: Encountering Jesus in the Fourth Gospel.* 2nd ed. New York, NY: Crossroad, 2003.

Schnelle, U. *Antidocetic Christology in the Gospel of John: An Investigation of the Place of the Fourth Gospel in the Johannine School.* Minneapolis, MN: Fortress, 1992.

–. *Das Evangelium nach Johannes.* THKNT 4. Leipzig: Evangelische Verlagsanstalt, 1998.

–. "Recent Views on John's Gospel." *WW* 21 (2001): 352–59.

Scholes, R., and R. Kellogg. *The Nature of Narrative.* Oxford: Oxford University Press, 1966.

Scholtissek, K. *In Ihm Sein und Bleiben: Die Sprache des Immanenz in den johanneischen Schriften.* HBS 21. Freiburg: Herder, 1999.

Schürmann, H. "Jesu lezte Weisung. Jo 19,26.27a." In *Ursprung und Gestalt: Erörterungen und Besinnungen zum Neuen Testament*, edited by H. Schürmann, pp. 13–28. Düsseldorf: Patmos, 1970.

Schüssler-Fiorenza, E. *In Memory of Her: A Feminist Theological Reconstruction of Christian Origins.* New York, NY: Crossroad, 1983.

Segovia, F. F. "'Peace I Leave with You; My Peace I Give to You': Discipleship in the Fourth Gospel." In *Discipleship in the New Testament*, edited by F. F. Segovia, pp. 76–104. Philadelphia, PA: Fortress, 1985.

–. *The Farewell of the Word: The Johannine Call to Abide.* Minneapolis, MN: Fortress, 1991.

–. "The Final Farewell of Jesus: A Reading in John 20:30–21:25." *Semeia* 53 (1991): 167–90.

–. "The Journey(s) of the Word: A Reading of the Plot of the Fourth Gospel." *Semeia* 53 (1991): 23–54.

Setzer, C. "Excellent Women: Female Witness to the Resurrection." *JBL* 116 (1997): 259–72.

Sevrin, J.-M. "Le commencement du quatrième évangile: prologue et prélude." In *La Bible en récit. L'exégèse biblique à l'heure du lecteur*, edited by D. Marguerat, pp. 340–49. MB 48. Genève: Labor et Fides, 2003.

Siker–Gieseler, J. S. "Disciples and Discipleship in the Fourth Gospel: A Canonical Approach." *StudBibT* 10 (1980): 199–227.

Simenel, P. "Les 2 anges de Jean 20/11–12." *ETR* 67 (1992): 71–76.

Simoens, Y. *La gloire d'aimer: Structures stylistiques et interprétatives dans le discours de la Cène (Jean 13–17).* AnBib 90. Rome: Biblical Institute Press, 1981.

–. *Selon Jean.* 3 vols. IET 17. Bruxelles: Éditions de l'Institut d'Études Théologiques, 1997.

Ska, J.-L. *"Our Fathers Have Told Us." An Introduction to the Analysis of Hebrew Narratives.* SubBi 13. Rome: Editrice Pontificio Istituto Biblico, 1990.

Smalley, S. *John: Evangelist and Interpreter.* Carlisle: Paternoster, 1978.

Smith, D. M. "Johannine Studies since Bultmann." *WW* 21 (2001): 343–51.

Sproston, W. E. "'Is not this Jesus, the Son of Joseph…?' (John 6.42). Johannine Christology as a Challenge to Faith." *JSNT* 24 (1985): 77–97.

Staley, J. L. *The Print's First Kiss: A Rhetorical Investigation on the Implied Reader in the Fourth Gospel.* SBLDS 82. Atlanta, GA: Scholars Press, 1988.

–. "Stumbling in the Dark, Reaching for the Light: Reading Characters in John 5 and 9." *Semeia* 53 (1991): 55–80.

Stanton, G. N. *The Gospels and Jesus.* 2nd ed. Oxford: Oxford University Press, 2002.

Stibbe, M. W. G. *John as Storyteller: Narrative Criticism and the Fourth Gospel.* Cambridge/ New York: Cambridge University Press, 1992.

–. *John.* RNBC. Sheffield: JSOT Press, 1993.

–. *The Gospel of John as Literature: An Anthology of Twentieth-Century Perspectives.* NTTS 17. Leiden/New York: Brill, 1993.

–. "A Tomb with a View: John 11.1–44 in Narrative-Critical Perspective." *NTS* 40 (1994): 38–54.

Stuhlmacher, P. "Spiritual Remembering: John 14.26." In *The Holy Spirit and Christian Origins. Essays in Honor of James D. G. Dunn*, edited by G. N. Stanton, B. W. Longenecker and S. C. Barton, pp. 55–68. Grand Rapids, MI/Cambridge: Eerdmans, 2004.

Swetnam, J. "The Meaning of πεπιστευκότας in John 8,31." *Bib* 61 (1980): 106–109.

Szymanek, E. "Glaube und Unglaube im Evangelium des hl. Johannes." *ColT* 46 (1976): 97–121.

Tannehill, R. C. *The Narrative-Unity of Luke–Acts: A Literary Interpretation.* 2 vols. Foundations and Facets. Philadelphia, PA: Fortress, 1986–90.

–. "Beginning to Study 'How Gospels Begin'." *Semeia* 52 (1990): 185–92.

Tenney, M. C. "Topics from the Gospel of John. Part IV: The Growth of Belief." *BSac* 132 (1975).

Thatcher, T. "Jesus, Judas, and Peter: Character by Contrast in the Fourth Gospel." *BSac* 153 (1996): 435–48.

–. *The Riddles of Jesus in John: A Study in Tradition and Folklore.* SBLMS 53. Atlanta, GA: Society of Biblical Literature, 2000.

–. "The Legend of the Beloved Disciple." In *Jesus in Johannine Tradition*, edited by R. T. Fortna and T. Thatcher, pp. 91–99. Louisville, KY: Westminster John Knox, 2001.

–. *Why John Wrote a Gospel? Jesus-Memory-History.* Louisville, KY: Westminster John Knox, 2006.

Thatcher, T., and S. D. Moore, eds. *Anatomies of Narrative Criticism: The Past, Present, and Future of the Fourth Gospel as Literature.* SBLRBS 55. Atlanta, GA: Society of Biblical Literature, 2008.

Thibeaux, E. R. "Reading Readers Reading Characters." *Semeia* 63 (1993): 215–27.

Thomas, J. C. *Footwashing in John 13 and the Johannine Community.* JSNTSup 61. Sheffield: Sheffield Academic Press, 1991.

Thompson, M. M. *The Humanity of Jesus in the Fourth Gospel.* Philadelphia, PA: Fortress, 1988.

–. "Eternal Life in the Gospel of John." *ExAud* 5 (1989): 35–55.

–. "'God's Voice You Have Never Heard, God's Form You Have Never Seen': The Characterization of God in the Gospel of John." *Semeia* 63 (1993): 177–204.

–. "'His Own Received Him Not': Jesus Washes the Feet of His Disciples." In *The Art of Reading Scripture*, edited by E. F. Davis and R. B. Hays, pp. 258–73. Grand Rapids, MI/ Cambridge: Eerdmans, 2003.

–. "The Breath of Life: John 20:22–23 Once More." In *The Holy Spirit and Christian Origins. Essays in Honor of James D. G. Dunn*, edited by G. N. Stanton, B. W. Longenecker and S. C. Barton, pp. 69–78. Grand Rapids, MI/Cambridge: Eerdmans, 2004.

Thompson, W. *The Jesus Debate.* New York, NY: Paulist Press, 1985.

Thüsing, W. *Die Erhöhung und Verherrlichung Jesu im Johannesevangelium.* 3rd ed. NTAbh 21. Münster: Aschendorff, 1979.

Tolmie, D. F. *Jesus' Farewell To the Disciples: John 13:1–17:26 in Narratological Perspective.* BibIntS 12. Leiden/New York, NY/Köln: Brill, 1995.

–. "The Characterization of God in the Fourth Gospel." *JSNT* 69 (1998): 57–75.

–. "The (not so) Good Shepherd: The Use of Shepherd Imagery in the Characterisation of Peter in the Fourth Gospel." In *Imagery in the Gospel of John: Terms, Forms, Themes, and Theology of Johannine Figurative Language*, edited by J. Frey, J. G. van der Watt and R. Zimmermann, pp. 353–67. WUNT 200. Tübingen: Mohr Siebeck, 2006.

–. "Jesus, Judas and a Morsel. Interpreting a Gesture in John 13,21–30." In *Miracles and Imagery in Luke and John. Festschrift Ulrich Busse*, edited by J. Verheyden, G. Van Belle and J. G. Van der Watt, pp. 105–24. BETL 218. Leuven/Paris/Dudley, MA: Peeters, 2008.

Tovey, D. *Narrative Art and Act in the Fourth Gospel.* JSNTSup 151. Sheffield: Sheffield Academic Press, 1997.

Traets, C. *Voir Jésus et le Père en Lui selon l'Évangile de Saint Jean.* Rome: Libreria editrice dell'Università Gregoriana, 1967.

Turner, M. "Atonement and the Death of Jesus in John: Some Questions to Bultmann and Forestell." *EvQ* 62 (1990): 99–122.

–. *The Holy Spirit and Spiritual Gifts: In the New Testament Church and Today.* Rev. ed. Peabody, MA: Hendrickson, 1998.

Twelftree, G. H. *Jesus the Miracle Worker: A Historical and Theological Study.* Downers Grove, IL: InterVarsity Press, 1999.

van der Merve, D. G. "Towards a Theological Understanding of Johannine Discipleship." *Neot* 31 (1997): 339–59.

van Tilborg, S. *Imaginative Love in John.* BibIntS 2. Leiden: Brill, 1993.

Vanhoye, A. "Notre foi, oeuvre divine, d'après le quatrième évangile." *NRTh* 86 (1964): 337–54.

Vellanickal, M. "Discipleship according to the Gospel of John." *Jeev* 10 (1980): 131–47.

Venetz, H.-J. "Zeuge des Erhöhten. Exegetischer Beitrag zu Joh 19,31–37." *FZPhTh* 23 (1976): 81–111.

Verbeelk-Verhelst, M. "Madeleine dans la littérature féministe du XVIIe siècle." *FoiVie* 90 (1991): 33–42.

Vignolo, R. *Personaggi del Quarto Vangelo, fidure della fede in San Giovanni.* Milan: Glossa, 1994.

von Wahlde, U. C. "The Witnesses to Jesus in John 5:31–40 and Belief in the Fourth Gospel." *CBQ* 43 (1981): 385–404.

–. "Literary Structure and Theological Argument in Three Discourses with the Jews in the Fourth Gospel." *JBL* 103 (1984): 575–84.

Vouga, F. *Le cadre historique et l'intention théologique de Jean.* BeauR 3. Paris: Beauchesne, 1977.

Walter, L. "Foi et incrédulité selon Saint Jean." Thèse de doctorat. Paris: Institut Catholique de Paris, 1975.

–. *L'incroyance des croyants selon saint Jean.* Lire la Bible 43. Paris: Cerf, 1976.

Wead, D. *The Literary Devices in John's Gospel.* Basel: Friedrich Reinhardt Kommissionsverlag, 1970.

Westcott, B. F. *The Gospel according to St. John. The Authorized Version with Introduction and Notes.* Grand Rapids, MI: Eerdmans, 1981.

Wiarda, T. *Peter in the Gospels: Pattern, Personality, and Relationship.* WUNT 2/127. Tübingen: Mohr Siebeck, 2000.

Williams, R. *Resurrection: Interpreting the Easter Gospel.* 2nd ed. London: Darton, Longman & Todd, 2002.

Wilson, R. "The Bright Chimera: Character as a Literary Term." *CI* 7 (1979): 725–49.

Winbery, C. L. "Abiding in Christ: The Concept of Discipleship in John." *TTE* 38 (1988): 104–20.

Witherington, B. *John's Wisdom: A Commentary on the Fourth Gospel.* Louisville, KY: Westminster John Knox, 1995.

Witkamp, L. T. "Some Specific Johannine Features in John 6.1–21." *JSNT* 40 (1990): 43–59.

Wright, N. T. *The Resurrection of the Son of God. Christian Origins and the Question of God,* vol. 3. Minneapolis, MN: Fortress, 2003.

Wuellner, W. "Putting Life Back into the Lazarus Story and its Reading: The Narrative Rhetoric of John 11 as the Narration of Faith." *Semeia* 53 (1991): 113–32.

Zerwick, M. *Biblical Greek Illustrated by Examples.* Rome: Pontificii Instituti Biblici, 1963.

Zumstein, J. "L'évangile johannique: une stratégie du croire." In *Miettes exégétiques*, edited, pp. 237–52. MB 25. Genève: Labor et Fides, 1991.

–. "Mémoire et relecture pascale dans l'évangile selon Jean." In *La mémoire et le temps. Mélanges offerts à Pierre Bonnard*, edited by S. Amsler, P. Bonnard, D. Marguerat and J. Zumstein, pp. 153–70. MB 23. Genève: Labor et Fides, 1991.

–. *Miettes exégétiques.* MdB 25. Genève: Labor et Fides, 1991.

–. *L'apprentissage de la foi. À la découverte de l'évangile de Jean et de ses lecteurs.* Poliez-le-Grand: Moulin, 1993.

–. "Le processus de relecture dans la littérature johannique." *ETR* 73 (1998): 161–176.

–. "Foi et vie éternelle selon Jean." In *Résurrection: L'après-mort dans le monde ancien et le Nouveau Testament*, edited by O. Mainville and D. Marguerat, pp. 215–35. MB 45. Genève: Labor et Fides, 2001.

–. "Le passé transfiguré: l'histoire sub specie aeternitatis selon Jean 17." In *Histoire et herméneutique. Mélanges offerts à Gottfried Hammann*, edited by M. Rose, pp. 431–40. Histoire et Société 45. Genève: Labor et Fides, 2002.

–. "L'adieu de Jésus aux siens. Une lecture intertextuelle de Jean 13–17." In *Raconter, interpréter, annoncer. Parcours de Nouveau Testament. Mélanges offerts à Daniel Marguerat pour son 60e anniversaire*, edited by E. Steffek and Y. Bourquin, pp. 207–22. MB 47. Genève: Labor et Fides, 2003.

–. *L'évangile selon Saint Jean (13–21)*. CNTDs IVb. Genève: Labor et Fides, 2007.

Index of Sources

Index of Authors

Index of Subjects

Wissenschaftliche Untersuchungen zum Neuen Testament
Alphabetical Index of the First and Second Series

Bennema, Cornelis: The Power of Saving Wisdom. 2002. *Vol. II/148.*

Bergman, Jan: see *Kieffer, René*

Bergmeier, Roland: Das Gesetz im Römerbrief und andere Studien zum Neuen Testament. 2000. *Vol. 121.*

Bernett, Monika: Der Kaiserkult in Judäa unter den Herodiern und Römern. 2007. *Vol. 203.*

Betz, Otto: Jesus, der Messias Israels. 1987. *Vol. 42.*

– Jesus, der Herr der Kirche. 1990. *Vol. 52.*

Beyschlag, Karlmann: Simon Magus und die christliche Gnosis. 1974. *Vol. 16.*

Bieringer, Reimund: see *Koester, Craig.*

Bittner, Wolfgang J.: Jesu Zeichen im Johannesevangelium. 1987. *Vol. II/26.*

Bjerkelund, Carl J.: Tauta Egeneto. 1987. *Vol. 40.*

Blackburn, Barry Lee: Theios Aner and the Markan Miracle Traditions. 1991. *Vol. II/40.*

Blanton IV, Thomas R.: Constructing a New Covenant. 2007. *Vol. II/233.*

Bock, Darrell L.: Blasphemy and Exaltation in Judaism and the Final Examination of Jesus. 1998. *Vol. II/106.*

– and *Robert L. Webb* (Ed.): Key Events in the Life of the Historical Jesus. 2009. *Vol. 247.*

Bockmuehl, Markus: The Remembered Peter. 2010. *Vol. 262.*

– Revelation and Mystery in Ancient Judaism and Pauline Christianity. 1990. *Vol. II/36.*

Bøe, Sverre: Cross-Bearing in Luke. 2010. *Vol. II/278.*

– Gog and Magog. 2001. *Vol. II/135.*

Böhlig, Alexander: Gnosis und Synkretismus. Vol. 1 1989. *Vol. 47* – Vol. 2 1989. *Vol. 48.*

Böhm, Martina: Samarien und die Samaritai bei Lukas. 1999. *Vol. II/111.*

Börstinghaus, Jens: Sturmfahrt und Schiffbruch. 2010. *Vol. II/274.*

Böttrich, Christfried: Weltweisheit – Menschheitsethik – Urkult. 1992. *Vol. II/50.*

– and *Herzer, Jens* (Ed.): Josephus und das Neue Testament. 2007. *Vol. 209.*

Bolyki, János: Jesu Tischgemeinschaften. 1997. *Vol. II/96.*

Bosman, Philip: Conscience in Philo and Paul. 2003. *Vol. II/166.*

Bovon, François: New Testament and Christian Apocrypha. 2009. *Vol. 237.*

– Studies in Early Christianity. 2003. *Vol. 161.*

Brändl, Martin: Der Agon bei Paulus. 2006. *Vol. II/222.*

Braun, Heike: Geschichte des Gottesvolkes und christliche Identität. 2010. *Vol. II/279.*

Breytenbach, Cilliers: see *Frey, Jörg.*

Brocke, Christoph vom: Thessaloniki – Stadt des Kassander und Gemeinde des Paulus. 2001. *Vol. II/125.*

Brunson, Andrew: Psalm 118 in the Gospel of John. 2003. *Vol. II/158.*

Büchli, Jörg: Der Poimandres – ein paganisiertes Evangelium. 1987. *Vol. II/27.*

Bühner, Jan A.: Der Gesandte und sein Weg im 4. Evangelium. 1977. *Vol. II/2.*

Burchard, Christoph: Untersuchungen zu Joseph und Aseneth. 1965. *Vol. 8.*

– Studien zur Theologie, Sprache und Umwelt des Neuen Testaments. Ed. by D. Sänger. 1998. *Vol. 107.*

Burnett, Richard: Karl Barth's Theological Exegesis. 2001. *Vol. II/145.*

Byron, John: Slavery Metaphors in Early Judaism and Pauline Christianity. 2003. *Vol. II/162.*

Byrskog, Samuel: Story as History – History as Story. 2000. *Vol. 123.*

Cancik, Hubert (Ed.): Markus-Philologie. 1984. *Vol. 33.*

Capes, David B.: Old Testament Yaweh Texts in Paul's Christology. 1992. *Vol. II/47.*

Caragounis, Chrys C.: The Development of Greek and the New Testament. 2004. *Vol. 167.*

– The Son of Man. 1986. *Vol. 38.*

– see *Fridrichsen, Anton.*

Carleton Paget, James: The Epistle of Barnabas. 1994. *Vol. II/64.*

– Jews, Christians and Jewish Christians in Antiquity. 2010. *Vol. 251.*

Carson, D.A., O'Brien, Peter T. and *Mark Seifrid* (Ed.): Justification and Variegated Nomism.
Vol. 1: The Complexities of Second Temple Judaism. 2001. *Vol. II/140.*
Vol. 2: The Paradoxes of Paul. 2004. *Vol. II/181.*

Chae, Young Sam: Jesus as the Eschatological Davidic Shepherd. 2006. *Vol. II/216.*

Chapman, David W.: Ancient Jewish and Christian Perceptions of Crucifixion. 2008. *Vol. II/244.*

Chester, Andrew: Messiah and Exaltation. 2007. *Vol. 207.*

Chibici-Revneanu, Nicole: Die Herrlichkeit des Verherrlichten. 2007. *Vol. II/231.*

Ciampa, Roy E.: The Presence and Function of Scripture in Galatians 1 and 2. 1998. *Vol. II/102.*

Classen, Carl Joachim: Rhetorical Criticsm of the New Testament. 2000. *Vol. 128.*

Colpe, Carsten: Griechen – Byzantiner – Semiten – Muslime. 2008. *Vol. 221.*

– Iranier – Aramäer – Hebräer – Hellenen. 2003. *Vol. 154.*

Cook, John G.: Roman Attitudes Towards the Christians. 2010. *Vol. 261.*

Coote, Robert B. (Ed.): see *Weissenrieder, Annette.*

Coppins, Wayne: The Interpretation of Freedom in the Letters of Paul. 2009. *Vol. II/261.*

Crump, David: Jesus the Intercessor. 1992. *Vol. II/49.*

Dahl, Nils Alstrup: Studies in Ephesians. 2000. *Vol. 131.*

Daise, Michael A.: Feasts in John. 2007. *Vol. II/229.*

Deines, Roland: Die Gerechtigkeit der Tora im Reich des Messias. 2004. *Vol. 177.*

– Jüdische Steingefäße und pharisäische Frömmigkeit. 1993. *Vol. II/52.*

– Die Pharisäer. 1997. *Vol. 101.*

Deines, Roland and Karl-Wilhelm Niebuhr (Ed.): Philo und das Neue Testament. 2004. *Vol. 172.*

Dennis, John A.: Jesus' Death and the Gathering of True Israel. 2006. *Vol. 217.*

Dettwiler, Andreas and Jean Zumstein (Ed.): Kreuzestheologie im Neuen Testament. 2002. *Vol. 151.*

Dickson, John P.: Mission-Commitment in Ancient Judaism and in the Pauline Communities. 2003. *Vol. II/159.*

Dietzfelbinger, Christian: Der Abschied des Kommenden. 1997. *Vol. 95.*

Dimitrov, Ivan Z., James D.G. Dunn, Ulrich Luz and Karl-Wilhelm Niebuhr (Ed.): Das Alte Testament als christliche Bibel in orthodoxer und westlicher Sicht. 2004. *Vol. 174.*

Dobbeler, Axel von: Glaube als Teilhabe. 1987. *Vol. II/22.*

Docherty, Susan E.: The Use of the Old Testament in Hebrews. 2009. *Vol. II/260.*

Downs, David J.: The Offering of the Gentiles. 2008. *Vol. II/248.*

Dryden, J. de Waal: Theology and Ethics in 1 Peter. 2006. *Vol. II/209.*

Dübbers, Michael: Christologie und Existenz im Kolosserbrief. 2005. *Vol. II/191.*

Dunn, James D.G.: The New Perspective on Paul. 2005. *Vol. 185.*

Dunn , James D.G. (Ed.): Jews and Christians. 1992. *Vol. 66.*

– Paul and the Mosaic Law. 1996. *Vol. 89.*

– see *Dimitrov, Ivan Z.*

–, Hans Klein, Ulrich Luz, and Vasile Mihoc (Ed.): Auslegung der Bibel in orthodoxer und westlicher Perspektive. 2000. *Vol. 130.*

Ebel, Eva: Die Attraktivität früher christlicher Gemeinden. 2004. *Vol. II/178.*

Ebertz, Michael N.: Das Charisma des Gekreuzigten. 1987. *Vol. 45.*

Eckstein, Hans-Joachim: Der Begriff Syneidesis bei Paulus. 1983. *Vol. II/10.*

– Verheißung und Gesetz. 1996. *Vol. 86.*

Ego, Beate: Im Himmel wie auf Erden. 1989. *Vol. II/34.*

Ego, Beate, Armin Lange and Peter Pilhofer (Ed.): Gemeinde ohne Tempel – Community without Temple. 1999. *Vol. 118.*

– and Helmut Merkel (Ed.): Religiöses Lernen in der biblischen, frühjüdischen und frühchristlichen Überlieferung. 2005. *Vol. 180.*

Eisele, Wilfried: Welcher Thomas? 2010. *Vol. 259.*

Eisen, Ute E.: see *Paulsen, Henning.*

Elledge, C.D.: Life after Death in Early Judaism. 2006. *Vol. II/208.*

Ellis, E. Earle: Prophecy and Hermeneutic in Early Christianity. 1978. *Vol. 18.*

– The Old Testament in Early Christianity. 1991. *Vol. 54.*

Elmer, Ian J.: Paul, Jerusalem and the Judaisers. 2009. *Vol. II/258.*

Endo, Masanobu: Creation and Christology. 2002. *Vol. 149.*

Ennulat, Andreas: Die 'Minor Agreements'. 1994. *Vol. II/62.*

Ensor, Peter W.: Jesus and His 'Works'. 1996. *Vol. II/85.*

Eskola, Timo: Messiah and the Throne. 2001. *Vol. II/142.*

– Theodicy and Predestination in Pauline Soteriology. 1998. *Vol. II/100.*

Farelly, Nicolas: The Disciples in the Fourth Gospel. 2010. *Vol. II/290.*

Fatehi, Mehrdad: The Spirit's Relation to the Risen Lord in Paul. 2000. *Vol. II/128.*

Feldmeier, Reinhard: Die Krisis des Gottessohnes. 1987. *Vol. II/21.*

– Die Christen als Fremde. 1992. *Vol. 64.*

Feldmeier, Reinhard and Ulrich Heckel (Ed.): Die Heiden. 1994. *Vol. 70.*

Finnern, Sönke: Narratologie und biblische Exegese. 2010. *Vol. II/285.*

Fletcher-Louis, Crispin H.T.: Luke-Acts: Angels, Christology and Soteriology. 1997. *Vol. II/94.*

Förster, Niclas: Marcus Magus. 1999. *Vol. 114.*

Forbes, Christopher Brian: Prophecy and Inspired Speech in Early Christianity and its Hellenistic Environment. 1995. *Vol. II/75.*

Fornberg, Tord: see *Fridrichsen, Anton.*

Fossum, Jarl E.: The Name of God and the Angel of the Lord. 1985. *Vol. 36.*

Foster, Paul: Community, Law and Mission in Matthew's Gospel. *Vol. II/177.*

Fotopoulos, John: Food Offered to Idols in Roman Corinth. 2003. *Vol. II/151.*

Frank, Nicole: Der Kolosserbrief im Kontext des paulinischen Erbes. 2009. *Vol. II/271.*

Frenschkowski, Marco: Offenbarung und Epiphanie. Vol. 1 1995. *Vol. II/79* – Vol. 2 1997. *Vol. II/80.*

Frey, Jörg: Eugen Drewermann und die biblische Exegese. 1995. *Vol. II/71.*

– Die johanneische Eschatologie. Vol. I. 1997. *Vol. 96.* – Vol. II. 1998. *Vol. 110.* – Vol. III. 2000. *Vol. 117.*

Frey, Jörg and *Cilliers Breytenbach* (Ed.): Aufgabe und Durchführung einer Theologie des Neuen Testaments. 2007. *Vol. 205.*

– *Jens Herzer, Martina Janßen* and *Clare K. Rothschild* (Ed.): Pseudepigraphie und Verfasserfiktion in frühchristlichen Briefen. 2009. *Vol. 246.*

– *Stefan Krauter* and *Hermann Lichtenberger* (Ed.): Heil und Geschichte. 2009. *Vol. 248.*

– and *Udo Schnelle (Ed.):* Kontexte des Johannesevangeliums. 2004. *Vol. 175.*

– and *Jens Schröter* (Ed.): Deutungen des Todes Jesu im Neuen Testament. 2005. *Vol. 181.*

– Jesus in apokryphen Evangelienüberlieferungen. 2010. *Vol. 254.*

–, *Jan G. van der Watt,* and *Ruben Zimmermann* (Ed.): Imagery in the Gospel of John. 2006. *Vol. 200.*

Freyne, Sean: Galilee and Gospel. 2000. *Vol. 125.*

Fridrichsen, Anton: Exegetical Writings. Edited by C.C. Caragounis and T. Fornberg. 1994. *Vol. 76.*

Gadenz, Pablo T.: Called from the Jews and from the Gentiles. 2009. *Vol. II/267.*

Gäbel, Georg: Die Kulttheologie des Hebräerbriefes. 2006. *Vol. II/212.*

Gäckle, Volker: Die Starken und die Schwachen in Korinth und in Rom. 2005. *Vol. 200.*

Garlington, Don B.: 'The Obedience of Faith'. 1991. *Vol. II/38.*

– Faith, Obedience, and Perseverance. 1994. *Vol. 79.*

Garnet, Paul: Salvation and Atonement in the Qumran Scrolls. 1977. *Vol. II/3.*

Gemünden, Petra von (Ed.): see *Weissenrieder, Annette.*

Gese, Michael: Das Vermächtnis des Apostels. 1997. *Vol. II/99.*

Gheorghita, Radu: The Role of the Septuagint in Hebrews. 2003. *Vol. II/160.*

Gordley, Matthew E.: The Colossian Hymn in Context. 2007. *Vol. II/228.*

Gräbe, Petrus J.: The Power of God in Paul's Letters. 2000, ²2008. *Vol. II/123.*

Gräßer, Erich: Der Alte Bund im Neuen. 1985. *Vol. 35.*

– Forschungen zur Apostelgeschichte. 2001. *Vol. 137.*

Grappe, Christian (Ed.): Le Repas de Dieu / Das Mahl Gottes. 2004. *Vol. 169.*

Gray, Timothy C.: The Temple in the Gospel of Mark. 2008. *Vol. II/242.*

Green, Joel B.: The Death of Jesus. 1988. *Vol. II/33.*

Gregg, Brian Han: The Historical Jesus and the Final Judgment Sayings in Q. 2005. *Vol. II/207.*

Gregory, Andrew: The Reception of Luke and Acts in the Period before Irenaeus. 2003. *Vol. II/169.*

Grindheim, Sigurd: The Crux of Election. 2005. *Vol. II/202.*

Gundry, Robert H.: The Old is Better. 2005. *Vol. 178.*

Gundry Volf, Judith M.: Paul and Perseverance. 1990. *Vol. II/37.*

Häußer, Detlef: Christusbekenntnis und Jesusüberlieferung bei Paulus. 2006. *Vol. 210.*

Hafemann, Scott J.: Suffering and the Spirit. 1986. *Vol. II/19.*

– Paul, Moses, and the History of Israel. 1995. *Vol. 81.*

Hahn, Ferdinand: Studien zum Neuen Testament.

Vol. I: Grundsatzfragen, Jesusforschung, Evangelien. 2006. *Vol. 191.*

Vol. II: Bekenntnisbildung und Theologie in urchristlicher Zeit. 2006. *Vol. 192.*

Hahn, Johannes (Ed.): Zerstörungen des Jerusalemer Tempels. 2002. *Vol. 147.*

Hamid-Khani, Saeed: Relevation and Concealment of Christ. 2000. *Vol. II/120.*

Hannah, Darrel D.: Michael and Christ. 1999. *Vol. II/109.*

Hardin, Justin K.: Galatians and the Imperial Cult? 2007. *Vol. II /237.*

Harrison; James R.: Paul's Language of Grace in Its Graeco-Roman Context. 2003. *Vol. II/172.*

Hartman, Lars: Text-Centered New Testament Studies. Ed. von D. Hellholm. 1997. *Vol. 102.*

Hartog, Paul: Polycarp and the New Testament. 2001. *Vol. II/134.*

Hays, Christopher M.: Luke's Wealth Ethics. 2010. *Vol. 275.*

Heckel, Theo K.: Der Innere Mensch. 1993. *Vol. II/53.*

– Vom Evangelium des Markus zum vier-
gestaltigen Evangelium. 1999. *Vol. 120.*
Heckel, Ulrich: Kraft in Schwachheit. 1993.
Vol. II/56.
– Der Segen im Neuen Testament. 2002.
Vol. 150.
– see *Feldmeier, Reinhard.*
– see *Hengel, Martin.*
Heemstra, Marius: The Fiscus Judaicus and the
Parting of the Ways. 2010. *Vol. II/277.*
Heiligenthal, Roman: Werke als Zeichen. 1983.
Vol. II/9.
Heininger, Bernhard: Die Inkulturation des
Christentums. 2010. *Vol. 255.*
Heliso, Desta: Pistis and the Righteous One.
2007. *Vol. II/235.*
Hellholm, D.: see *Hartman, Lars.*
Hemer, Colin J.: The Book of Acts in the Setting
of Hellenistic History. 1989. *Vol. 49.*
Hengel, Martin: Jesus und die Evangelien.
Kleine Schriften V. 2007. *Vol. 211.*
– Die johanneische Frage. 1993. *Vol. 67.*
– Judaica et Hellenistica. Kleine Schriften I.
1996. *Vol. 90.*
– Judaica, Hellenistica et Christiana. Kleine
Schriften II. 1999. *Vol. 109.*
– Judentum und Hellenismus. 1969, ³1988.
Vol. 10.
– Paulus und Jakobus. Kleine Schriften III.
2002. *Vol. 141.*
– Studien zur Christologie. Kleine Schriften
IV. 2006. *Vol. 201.*
– Studien zum Urchristentum. Kleine Schrif-
ten VI. 2008. *Vol. 234.*
– Theologische, historische und biographische
Skizzen. Kleine Schriften VII. 2010.
Vol. 253.
– and *Anna Maria Schwemer:* Paulus zwi-
schen Damaskus und Antiochien. 1998.
Vol. 108.
– Der messianische Anspruch Jesu und die
Anfänge der Christologie. 2001. *Vol. 138.*
– Die vier Evangelien und das eine Evange-
lium von Jesus Christus. 2008. *Vol. 224.*
Hengel, Martin and *Ulrich Heckel* (Ed.): Paulus
und das antike Judentum. 1991. *Vol. 58.*
– and *Hermut Löhr* (Ed.): Schriftauslegung
im antiken Judentum und im Urchristentum.
1994. *Vol. 73.*
– and *Anna Maria Schwemer* (Ed.): Königs-
herrschaft Gottes und himmlischer Kult.
1991. *Vol. 55.*
– Die Septuaginta. 1994. *Vol. 72.*
–, *Siegfried Mittmann* and *Anna Maria
Schwemer* (Ed.): La Cité de Dieu / Die Stadt
Gottes. 2000. *Vol. 129.*

Hentschel, Anni: Diakonia im Neuen Testament.
2007. *Vol. 226.*
Hernández Jr., Juan: Scribal Habits and Theo-
logical Influence in the Apocalypse. 2006.
Vol. II/218.
Herrenbrück, Fritz: Jesus und die Zöllner. 1990.
Vol. II/41.
Herzer, Jens: Paulus oder Petrus? 1998.
Vol. 103.
– see *Böttrich, Christfried.*
– see *Frey, Jörg.*
Hill, Charles E.: From the Lost Teaching of
Polycarp. 2005. *Vol. 186.*
Hoegen-Rohls, Christina: Der nachösterliche
Johannes. 1996. *Vol. II/84.*
Hoffmann, Matthias Reinhard: The Destroyer
and the Lamb. 2005. *Vol. II/203.*
Hofius, Otfried: Katapausis. 1970. *Vol. 11.*
– Der Vorhang vor dem Thron Gottes. 1972.
Vol. 14.
– Der Christushymnus Philipper 2,6–11.
1976, ²1991. *Vol. 17.*
– Paulusstudien. 1989, ²1994. *Vol. 51.*
– Neutestamentliche Studien. 2000. *Vol. 132.*
– Paulusstudien II. 2002. *Vol. 143.*
– Exegetische Studien. 2008. *Vol. 223.*
– and *Hans-Christian Kammler:* Johannes-
studien. 1996. *Vol. 88.*
Holloway, Paul A.: Coping with Prejudice.
2009. *Vol. 244.*
Holmberg, Bengt (Ed.): Exploring Early Chris-
tian Identity. 2008. *Vol. 226.*
– and *Mikael Winninge* (Ed.): Identity Forma-
tion in the New Testament. 2008. *Vol. 227.*
Holtz, Traugott: Geschichte und Theologie des
Urchristentums. 1991. *Vol. 57.*
Hommel, Hildebrecht: Sebasmata.
Vol. 1 1983. *Vol. 31.*
Vol. 2 1984. *Vol. 32.*
Horbury, William: Herodian Judaism and New
Testament Study. 2006. *Vol. 193.*
Horn, Friedrich Wilhelm and *Ruben Zim-
mermann* (Ed.): Jenseits von Indikativ und
Imperativ. Vol. 1. 2009. *Vol. 238.*
Horst, Pieter W. van der: Jews and Christians
in Their Graeco-Roman Context. 2006.
Vol. 196.
Hultgård, Anders and *Stig Norin* (Ed): Le Jour
de Dieu / Der Tag Gottes. 2009. *Vol. 245.*
Hvalvik, Reidar: The Struggle for Scripture and
Covenant. 1996. *Vol. II/82.*
Jackson, Ryan: New Creation in Paul's Letters.
2010. *Vol. II/272.*
Janßen, Martina: see *Frey, Jörg.*
Jauhiainen, Marko: The Use of Zechariah in
Revelation. 2005. *Vol. II/199.*

Jensen, Morten H.: Herod Antipas in Galilee. 2006; ²2010. *Vol. II/215.*

Johns, Loren L.: The Lamb Christology of the Apocalypse of John. 2003. *Vol. II/167.*

Jossa, Giorgio: Jews or Christians? 2006. *Vol. 202.*

Joubert, Stephan: Paul as Benefactor. 2000. *Vol. II/124.*

Judge, E. A.: The First Christians in the Roman World. 2008. *Vol. 229.*

Jungbauer, Harry: „Ehre Vater und Mutter". 2002. *Vol. II/146.*

Kähler, Christoph: Jesu Gleichnisse als Poesie und Therapie. 1995. *Vol. 78.*

Kamlah, Ehrhard: Die Form der katalogischen Paränese im Neuen Testament. 1964. *Vol. 7.*

Kammler, Hans-Christian: Christologie und Eschatologie. 2000. *Vol. 126.*

– Kreuz und Weisheit. 2003. *Vol. 159.*

– see *Hofius, Otfried.*

Karakolis, Christos: see *Alexeev, Anatoly A.*

Karrer, Martin und *Wolfgang Kraus* (Ed.): Die Septuaginta – Texte, Kontexte, Lebenswelten. 2008. *Vol. 219.*

– see *Kraus, Wolfgang.*

Kelhoffer, James A.: The Diet of John the Baptist. 2005. *Vol. 176.*

– Miracle and Mission. 1999. *Vol. II/112.*

Kelley, Nicole: Knowledge and Religious Authority in the Pseudo-Clementines. 2006. *Vol. II/213.*

Kennedy, Joel: The Recapitulation of Israel. 2008. *Vol. II/257.*

Kensky, Meira Z.: Trying Man, Trying God. 2010. *Vol. II/289.*

Kieffer, René and *Jan Bergman* (Ed.): La Main de Dieu / Die Hand Gottes. 1997. *Vol. 94.*

Kierspel, Lars: The Jews and the World in the Fourth Gospel. 2006. *Vol. 220.*

Kim, Seyoon: The Origin of Paul's Gospel. 1981, ²1984. *Vol. II/4.*

– Paul and the New Perspective. 2002. *Vol. 140.*

– "The 'Son of Man'" as the Son of God. 1983. *Vol. 30.*

Klauck, Hans-Josef: Religion und Gesellschaft im frühen Christentum. 2003. *Vol. 152.*

Klein, Hans, Vasile Mihoc und *Karl-Wilhelm Niebuhr* (Ed.): Das Gebet im Neuen Testament. Vierte, europäische orthodox-westliche Exegetenkonferenz in Sambata de Sus, 4. – 8. August 2007. 2009. Vol. 249.

– see Dunn, James D.G.

Kleinknecht, Karl Th.: Der leidende Gerechtfertigte. 1984, ²1988. *Vol. II/13.*

Klinghardt, Matthias: Gesetz und Volk Gottes. 1988. *Vol. II/32.*

Kloppenborg, John S.: The Tenants in the Vineyard. 2006, student edition 2010. *Vol. 195.*

Koch, Michael: Drachenkampf und Sonnenfrau. 2004. *Vol. II/184.*

Koch, Stefan: Rechtliche Regelung von Konflikten im frühen Christentum. 2004. *Vol. II/174.*

Köhler, Wolf-Dietrich: Rezeption des Matthäusevangeliums in der Zeit vor Irenäus. 1987. *Vol. II/24.*

Köhn, Andreas: Der Neutestamentler Ernst Lohmeyer. 2004. *Vol. II/180.*

Koester, Craig and *Reimund Bieringer* (Ed.): The Resurrection of Jesus in the Gospel of John. 2008. *Vol. 222.*

Konradt, Matthias: Israel, Kirche und die Völker im Matthäusevangelium. 2007. *Vol. 215.*

Kooten, George H. van: Cosmic Christology in Paul and the Pauline School. 2003. *Vol. II/171.*

– Paul's Anthropology in Context. 2008. *Vol. 232.*

Korn, Manfred: Die Geschichte Jesu in veränderter Zeit. 1993. *Vol. II/51.*

Koskenniemi, Erkki: Apollonios von Tyana in der neutestamentlichen Exegese. 1994. *Vol. II/61.*

– The Old Testament Miracle-Workers in Early Judaism. 2005. *Vol. II/206.*

Kraus, Thomas J.: Sprache, Stil und historischer Ort des zweiten Petrusbriefes. 2001. *Vol. II/136.*

Kraus, Wolfgang: Das Volk Gottes. 1996. *Vol. 85.*

– see *Karrer, Martin.*

– see *Walter, Nikolaus.*

– and *Martin Karrer* (Hrsg.): Die Septuaginta – Texte, Theologien, Einflüsse. 2010. *Bd. 252.*

– and *Karl-Wilhelm Niebuhr* (Ed.): Frühjudentum und Neues Testament im Horizont Biblischer Theologie. 2003. *Vol. 162.*

Krauter, Stefan: Studien zu Röm 13,1-7. 2009. *Vol. 243.*

– see *Frey, Jörg.*

Kreplin, Matthias: Das Selbstverständnis Jesu. 2001. *Vol. II/141.*

Kuhn, Karl G.: Achtzehngebet und Vaterunser und der Reim. 1950. *Vol. 1.*

Kvalbein, Hans: see *Ådna, Jostein.*

Kwon, Yon-Gyong: Eschatology in Galatians. 2004. *Vol. II/183.*

Laansma, Jon: I Will Give You Rest. 1997. *Vol. II/98.*

Labahn, Michael: Offenbarung in Zeichen und Wort. 2000. *Vol. II/117.*

Lambers-Petry, Doris: see *Tomson, Peter J.*

Lange, Armin: see *Ego, Beate.*

Lampe, Peter: Die stadtrömischen Christen in den ersten beiden Jahrhunderten. 1987, ²1989. *Vol. II/18.*

Landmesser, Christof: Wahrheit als Grundbegriff neutestamentlicher Wissenschaft. 1999. *Vol. 113.*

– Jüngerberufung und Zuwendung zu Gott. 2000. *Vol. 133.*

Lau, Andrew: Manifest in Flesh. 1996. *Vol. II/86.*

Lawrence, Louise: An Ethnography of the Gospel of Matthew. 2003. *Vol. II/165.*

Lee, Aquila H.I.: From Messiah to Preexistent Son. 2005. *Vol. II/192.*

Lee, Pilchan: The New Jerusalem in the Book of Relevation. 2000. *Vol. II/129.*

Lee, Sang M.: The Cosmic Drama of Salvation. 2010. *Vol. II/276.*

Lee, Simon S.: Jesus' Transfiguration and the Believers' Transformation. 2009. *Vol. II/265.*

Lichtenberger, Hermann: Das Ich Adams und das Ich der Menschheit. 2004. *Vol. 164.*

– see *Avemarie, Friedrich.*

– see *Frey, Jörg.*

Lierman, John: The New Testament Moses. 2004. *Vol. II/173.*

– (Ed.): Challenging Perspectives on the Gospel of John. 2006. *Vol. II/219.*

Lieu, Samuel N.C.: Manichaeism in the Later Roman Empire and Medieval China. ²1992. *Vol. 63.*

Lindemann, Andreas: Die Evangelien und die Apostelgeschichte. 2009. *Vol. 241.*

Lincicum, David: Paul and the Early Jewish Encounter with Deuteronomy. 2010. *Vol. II/284.*

Lindgård, Fredrik: Paul's Line of Thought in 2 Corinthians 4:16–5:10. 2004. *Vol. II/189.*

Loader, William R.G.: Jesus' Attitude Towards the Law. 1997. *Vol. II/97.*

Löhr, Gebhard: Verherrlichung Gottes durch Philosophie. 1997. *Vol. 97.*

Löhr, Hermut: Studien zum frühchristlichen und frühjüdischen Gebet. 2003. *Vol. 160.*

– see *Hengel, Martin.*

Löhr, Winrich Alfried: Basilides und seine Schule. 1995. *Vol. 83.*

Lorenzen, Stefanie: Das paulinische Eikon-Konzept. 2008. *Vol. II/250.*

Luomanen, Petri: Entering the Kingdom of Heaven. 1998. *Vol. II/101.*

Luz, Ulrich: see *Alexeev, Anatoly A.*

– see *Dunn, James D.G.*

Mackay, Ian D.: John's Raltionship with Mark. 2004. *Vol. II/182.*

Mackie, Scott D.: Eschatology and Exhortation in the Epistle to the Hebrews. 2006. *Vol. II/223.*

Magda, Ksenija: Paul's Territoriality and Mission Strategy. 2009. *Vol. II/266.*

Maier, Gerhard: Mensch und freier Wille. 1971. *Vol. 12.*

– Die Johannesoffenbarung und die Kirche. 1981. *Vol. 25.*

Markschies, Christoph: Valentinus Gnosticus? 1992. *Vol. 65.*

Marshall, Jonathan: Jesus, Patrons, and Benefactors. 2009. *Vol. II/259.*

Marshall, Peter: Enmity in Corinth: Social Conventions in Paul's Relations with the Corinthians. 1987. *Vol. II/23.*

Martin, Dale B.: see *Zangenberg, Jürgen.*

Mayer, Annemarie: Sprache der Einheit im Epheserbrief und in der Ökumene. 2002. *Vol. II/150.*

Mayordomo, Moisés: Argumentiert Paulus logisch? 2005. *Vol. 188.*

McDonough, Sean M.: YHWH at Patmos: Rev. 1:4 in its Hellenistic and Early Jewish Setting. 1999. *Vol. II/107.*

McDowell, Markus: Prayers of Jewish Women. 2006. *Vol. II/211.*

McGlynn, Moyna: Divine Judgement and Divine Benevolence in the Book of Wisdom. 2001. *Vol. II/139.*

Meade, David G.: Pseudonymity and Canon. 1986. *Vol. 39.*

Meadors, Edward P.: Jesus the Messianic Herald of Salvation. 1995. *Vol. II/72.*

Meißner, Stefan: Die Heimholung des Ketzers. 1996. *Vol. II/87.*

Mell, Ulrich: Die „anderen" Winzer. 1994. *Vol. 77.*

– see *Sänger, Dieter.*

Mengel, Berthold: Studien zum Philipperbrief. 1982. *Vol. II/8.*

Merkel, Helmut: Die Widersprüche zwischen den Evangelien. 1971. *Vol. 13.*

– see *Ego, Beate.*

Merklein, Helmut: Studien zu Jesus und Paulus. Vol. 1 1987. *Vol. 43.* – Vol. 2 1998. *Vol. 105.*

Merkt, Andreas: see *Nicklas, Tobias*

Metzdorf, Christina: Die Tempelaktion Jesu. 2003. *Vol. II/168.*

Metzler, Karin: Der griechische Begriff des Verzeihens. 1991. *Vol. II/44.*

Metzner, Rainer: Die Rezeption des Matthäusevangeliums im 1. Petrusbrief. 1995. *Vol. II/74.*

– Das Verständnis der Sünde im Johannesevangelium. 2000. *Vol. 122.*

Mihoc, Vasile: see *Dunn, James D.G.*

– see *Klein, Hans.*
Mineshige, Kiyoshi: Besitzverzicht und Almosen bei Lukas. 2003. *Vol. II/163.*
Mittmann, Siegfried: see *Hengel, Martin.*
Mittmann-Richert, Ulrike: Magnifikat und Benediktus. *1996. Vol. II/90.*
– Der Sühnetod des Gottesknechts. 2008. *Vol. 220.*
Miura, Yuzuru: David in Luke-Acts. 2007. *Vol. II/232.*
Moll, Sebastian: The Arch-Heretic Marcion. 2010. *Vol. 250.*
Morales, Rodrigo J.: The Spirit and the Restorat. 2010. *Vol. 282.*
Mournet, Terence C.: Oral Tradition and Literary Dependency. 2005. *Vol. II/195.*
Mußner, Franz: Jesus von Nazareth im Umfeld Israels und der Urkirche. Ed. von M. Theobald. 1998. *Vol. 111.*
Mutschler, Bernhard: Das Corpus Johanneum bei Irenäus von Lyon. 2005. *Vol. 189.*
– Glaube in den Pastoralbriefen. 2010. *Vol. 256.*
Myers, Susan E.: Spirit Epicleses in the Acts of Thomas. 2010. *Vol. 281.*
Nguyen, V. Henry T.: Christian Identity in Corinth. 2008. *Vol. II/243.*
Nicklas, Tobias, Andreas Merkt und *Joseph Verheyden* (Ed.): Gelitten – Gestorben – Auferstanden. 2010. *Vol. II/273.*
– see *Verheyden, Joseph*
Niebuhr, Karl-Wilhelm: Gesetz and Paränese. 1987. *Vol. II/28.*
– Heidenapostel aus Israel. 1992. *Vol. 62.*
– see *Deines, Roland.*
– see *Dimitrov, Ivan Z.*
– see *Klein, Hans.*
– see *Kraus, Wolfgang.*
Nielsen, Anders E.: "Until it is Fullfilled". 2000. *Vol. II/126.*
Nielsen, Jesper Tang: Die kognitive Dimension des Kreuzes. 2009. *Vol. II/263.*
Nissen, Andreas: Gott und der Nächste im antiken Judentum. 1974. *Vol. 15.*
Noack, Christian: Gottesbewußtsein. 2000. *Vol. II/116.*
Noormann, Rolf: Irenäus als Paulusinterpret. 1994. *Vol. II/66.*
Norin, Stig: see *Hultgård, Anders.*
Novakovic, Lidija: Messiah, the Healer of the Sick. 2003. *Vol. II/170.*
Obermann, Andreas: Die christologische Erfüllung der Schrift im Johannesevangelium. 1996. *Vol. II/83.*
Öhler, Markus: Barnabas. 2003. *Vol. 156.*
– see *Becker, Michael.*

Okure, Teresa: The Johannine Approach to Mission. 1988. *Vol. II/31.*
Onuki, Takashi: Heil und Erlösung. 2004. *Vol. 165.*
Oropeza, B. J.: Paul and Apostasy. 2000. *Vol. II/115.*
Ostmeyer, Karl-Heinrich: Kommunikation mit Gott und Christus. 2006. *Vol. 197.*
– Taufe und Typos. 2000. *Vol. II/118.*
Pao, David W.: Acts and the Isaianic New Exodus. 2000. *Vol. II/130.*
Park, Eung Chun: The Mission Discourse in Matthew's Interpretation. 1995. *Vol. II/81.*
Park, Joseph S.: Conceptions of Afterlife in Jewish Insriptions. 2000. *Vol. II/121.*
Parsenios, George L.: Rhetoric and Drama in the Johannine Lawsuit Motif. 2010. *Vol. 258.*
Pate, C. Marvin: The Reverse of the Curse. 2000. *Vol. II/114.*
Paulsen, Henning: Studien zur Literatur und Geschichte des frühen Christentums. Ed. von Ute E. Eisen. 1997. *Vol. 99.*
Pearce, Sarah J.K.: The Land of the Body. 2007. *Vol. 208.*
Peres, Imre: Griechische Grabinschriften und neutestamentliche Eschatologie. 2003. *Vol. 157.*
Perry, Peter S.: The Rhetoric of Digressions. 2009. *Vol. II/268.*
Philip, Finny: The Origins of Pauline Pneumatology. 2005. *Vol. II/194.*
Philonenko, Marc (Ed.): Le Trône de Dieu. 1993. *Vol. 69.*
Pilhofer, Peter: Presbyteron Kreitton. 1990. *Vol. II/39.*
– Philippi. Vol. 1 1995. *Vol. 87.* – Vol. 2 ²2009. *Vol. 119.*
– Die frühen Christen und ihre Welt. 2002. *Vol. 145.*
– see *Becker, Eve-Marie.*
– see *Ego, Beate.*
Pitre, Brant: Jesus, the Tribulation, and the End of the Exile. 2005. *Vol. II/204.*
Plümacher, Eckhard: Geschichte und Geschichten. 2004. *Vol. 170.*
Pöhlmann, Wolfgang: Der Verlorene Sohn und das Haus. 1993. *Vol. 68.*
Poirier, John C.: The Tongues of Angels. 2010. *Vol. II/287.*
Pokorný, Petr and *Josef B. Souček:* Bibelauslegung als Theologie. 1997. *Vol. 100.*
– and *Jan Roskovec* (Ed.): Philosophical Hermeneutics and Biblical Exegesis. 2002. *Vol. 153.*
Popkes, Enno Edzard: Das Menschenbild des Thomasevangeliums. 2007. *Vol. 206.*

– Die Theologie der Liebe Gottes in den johanneischen Schriften. 2005. *Vol. II/197.*

Porter, Stanley E.: The Paul of Acts. 1999. *Vol. 115.*

Prieur, Alexander: Die Verkündigung der Gottesherrschaft. 1996. *Vol. II/89.*

Probst, Hermann: Paulus und der Brief. 1991. *Vol. II/45.*

Puig i Tàrrech, Armand: Jesus: An Uncommon Journey. 2010. *Vol. II/288.*

Rabens, Volker: The Holy Spirit and Ethics in Paul. 2010. *Vol. II/283.*

Räisänen, Heikki: Paul and the Law. 1983, ²1987. *Vol. 29.*

Rehkopf, Friedrich: Die lukanische Sonderquelle. 1959. *Vol. 5.*

Rein, Matthias: Die Heilung des Blindgeborenen (Joh 9). 1995. *Vol. II/73.*

Reinmuth, Eckart: Pseudo-Philo und Lukas. 1994. *Vol. 74.*

Reiser, Marius: Bibelkritik und Auslegung der Heiligen Schrift. 2007. *Vol. 217.*

– Syntax und Stil des Markusevangeliums. 1984. *Vol. II/11.*

Reynolds, Benjamin E.: The Apocalyptic Son of Man in the Gospel of John. 2008. *Vol. II/249.*

Rhodes, James N.: The Epistle of Barnabas and the Deuteronomic Tradition. 2004. *Vol. II/188.*

Richards, E. Randolph: The Secretary in the Letters of Paul. 1991. *Vol. II/42.*

Riesner, Rainer: Jesus als Lehrer. 1981, ³1988. *Vol. II/7.*

– Die Frühzeit des Apostels Paulus. 1994. *Vol. 71.*

Rissi, Mathias: Die Theologie des Hebräerbriefs. 1987. *Vol. 41.*

Röcker, Fritz W.: Belial und Katechon. 2009. *Vol. II/262.*

Röhser, Günter: Metaphorik und Personifikation der Sünde. 1987. *Vol. II/25.*

Rose, Christian: Theologie als Erzählung im Markusevangelium. 2007. *Vol. II/236.*

– Die Wolke der Zeugen. 1994. *Vol. II/60.*

Roskovec, Jan: see *Pokorný, Petr.*

Rothschild, Clare K.: Baptist Traditions and Q. 2005. *Vol. 190.*

– Hebrews as Pseudepigraphon. 2009. *Vol. 235.*

– Luke Acts and the Rhetoric of History. 2004. *Vol. II/175.*

– see *Frey, Jörg.*

Rüegger, Hans-Ulrich: Verstehen, was Markus erzählt. 2002. *Vol. II/155.*

Rüger, Hans Peter: Die Weisheitsschrift aus der Kairoer Geniza. 1991. *Vol. 53.*

Sänger, Dieter: Antikes Judentum und die Mysterien. 1980. *Vol. II/5.*

– Die Verkündigung des Gekreuzigten und Israel. 1994. *Vol. 75.*

– see *Burchard, Christoph*

– and *Ulrich Mell* (Ed.): Paulus und Johannes. 2006. *Vol. 198.*

Salier, Willis Hedley: The Rhetorical Impact of the Semeia in the Gospel of John. 2004. *Vol. II/186.*

Salzmann, Jorg Christian: Lehren und Ermahnen. 1994. *Vol. II/59.*

Sandnes, Karl Olav: Paul – One of the Prophets? 1991. *Vol. II/43.*

Sato, Migaku: Q und Prophetie. 1988. *Vol. II/29.*

Schäfer, Ruth: Paulus bis zum Apostelkonzil. 2004. *Vol. II/179.*

Schaper, Joachim: Eschatology in the Greek Psalter. 1995. *Vol. II/76.*

Schimanowski, Gottfried: Die himmlische Liturgie in der Apokalypse des Johannes. 2002. *Vol. II/154.*

– Weisheit und Messias. 1985. *Vol. II/17.*

Schlichting, Günter: Ein jüdisches Leben Jesu. 1982. *Vol. 24.*

Schließer, Benjamin: Abraham's Faith in Romans 4. 2007. *Vol. II/224.*

Schnabel, Eckhard J.: Law and Wisdom from Ben Sira to Paul. 1985. *Vol. II/16.*

Schnelle, Udo: see *Frey, Jörg.*

Schröter, Jens: Von Jesus zum Neuen Testament. 2007. *Vol. 204.*

– see *Frey, Jörg.*

Schutter, William L.: Hermeneutic and Composition in I Peter. 1989. *Vol. II/30.*

Schwartz, Daniel R.: Studies in the Jewish Background of Christianity. 1992. *Vol. 60.*

Schwemer, Anna Maria: see *Hengel, Martin*

Scott, Ian W.: Implicit Epistemology in the Letters of Paul. 2005. *Vol. II/205.*

Scott, James M.: Adoption as Sons of God. 1992. *Vol. II/48.*

– Paul and the Nations. 1995. *Vol. 84.*

Shi, Wenhua: Paul's Message of the Cross as Body Language. 2008. *Vol. II/254.*

Shum, Shiu-Lun: Paul's Use of Isaiah in Romans. 2002. *Vol. II/156.*

Siegert, Folker: Drei hellenistisch-jüdische Predigten. Teil I 1980. *Vol. 20* – Teil II 1992. *Vol. 61.*

– Nag-Hammadi-Register. 1982. *Vol. 26.*

– Argumentation bei Paulus. 1985. *Vol. 34.*

– Philon von Alexandrien. 1988. *Vol. 46.*

Simon, Marcel: Le christianisme antique et son contexte religieux I/II. 1981. *Vol. 23.*

Smit, Peter-Ben: Fellowship and Food in the Kingdom. 2008. *Vol. II/234.*

Snodgrass, Klyne: The Parable of the Wicked Tenants. 1983. *Vol. 27.*

Söding, Thomas: Das Wort vom Kreuz. 1997. *Vol. 93.*

– see *Thüsing, Wilhelm.*

Sommer, Urs: Die Passionsgeschichte des Markusevangeliums. 1993. *Vol. II/58.*

Sorensen, Eric: Possession and Exorcism in the New Testament and Early Christianity. 2002. *Vol. II/157.*

Souček, Josef B.: see *Pokorný, Petr.*

Southall, David J.: Rediscovering Righteousness in Romans. 2008. *Vol. 240.*

Spangenberg, Volker: Herrlichkeit des Neuen Bundes. 1993. *Vol. II/55.*

Spanje, T.E. van: Inconsistency in Paul? 1999. *Vol. II/110.*

Speyer, Wolfgang: Frühes Christentum im antiken Strahlungsfeld. Vol. I: 1989. *Vol. 50.*

– Vol. II: 1999. *Vol. 116.*

– Vol. III: 2007. *Vol. 213.*

Spittler, Janet E.: Animals in the Apocryphal Acts of the Apostles. 2008. *Vol. II/247.*

Sprinkle, Preston: Law and Life. 2008. *Vol. II/241.*

Stadelmann, Helge: Ben Sira als Schriftgelehrter. 1980. *Vol. II/6.*

Stein, Hans Joachim: Frühchristliche Mahlfeiern. 2008. *Vol. II/255.*

Stenschke, Christoph W.: Luke's Portrait of Gentiles Prior to Their Coming to Faith. *Vol. II/108.*

Sterck-Degueldre, Jean-Pierre: Eine Frau namens Lydia. 2004. *Vol. II/176.*

Stettler, Christian: Der Kolosserhymnus. 2000. *Vol. II/131.*

Stettler, Hanna: Die Christologie der Pastoralbriefe. 1998. *Vol. II/105.*

Stökl Ben Ezra, Daniel: The Impact of Yom Kippur on Early Christianity. 2003. *Vol. 163.*

Strobel, August: Die Stunde der Wahrheit. 1980. *Vol. 21.*

Stroumsa, Guy G.: Barbarian Philosophy. 1999. *Vol. 112.*

Stuckenbruck, Loren T.: Angel Veneration and Christology. 1995. *Vol. II/70.*

–, *Stephen C. Barton* and *Benjamin G. Wold* (Ed.): Memory in the Bible and Antiquity. 2007. *Vol. 212.*

Stuhlmacher, Peter (Ed.): Das Evangelium und die Evangelien. 1983. *Vol. 28.*

– Biblische Theologie und Evangelium. 2002. *Vol. 146.*

Sung, Chong-Hyon: Vergebung der Sünden. 1993. *Vol. II/57.*

Svendsen, Stefan N.: Allegory Transformed. 2009. *Vol. II/269.*

Tajra, Harry W.: The Trial of St. Paul. 1989. *Vol. II/35.*

– The Martyrdom of St.Paul. 1994. *Vol. II/67.*

Tellbe, Mikael: Christ-Believers in Ephesus. 2009. *Vol. 242.*

Theißen, Gerd: Studien zur Soziologie des Urchristentums. 1979, ³1989. *Vol. 19.*

Theobald, Michael: Studien zum Römerbrief. 2001. *Vol. 136.*

Theobald, Michael: see *Mußner, Franz.*

Thornton, Claus-Jürgen: Der Zeuge des Zeugen. 1991. *Vol. 56.*

Thüsing, Wilhelm: Studien zur neutestamentlichen Theologie. Ed. von Thomas Söding. 1995. *Vol. 82.*

Thurén, Lauri: Derhethorizing Paul. 2000. *Vol. 124.*

Thyen, Hartwig: Studien zum Corpus Iohanneum. 2007. *Vol. 214.*

Tibbs, Clint: Religious Experience of the Pneuma. 2007. *Vol. II/230.*

Toit, David S. du: Theios Anthropos. 1997. *Vol. II/91.*

Tolmie, D. Francois: Persuading the Galatians. 2005. *Vol. II/190.*

Tomson, Peter J. and *Doris Lambers-Petry* (Ed.): The Image of the Judaeo-Christians in Ancient Jewish and Christian Literature. 2003. *Vol. 158.*

Toney, Carl N.: Paul's Inclusive Ethic. 2008. *Vol. II/252.*

Trebilco, Paul: The Early Christians in Ephesus from Paul to Ignatius. 2004. *Vol. 166.*

Treloar, Geoffrey R.: Lightfoot the Historian. 1998. *Vol. II/103.*

Troftgruben, Troy M.: A Conclusion Unhindered. 2010. *Vol. II/280.*

Tsuji, Manabu: Glaube zwischen Vollkommenheit und Verweltlichung. 1997. *Vol. II/93.*

Twelftree, Graham H.: Jesus the Exorcist. 1993. *Vol. II/54.*

Ulrichs, Karl Friedrich: Christusglaube. 2007. *Vol. II/227.*

Urban, Christina: Das Menschenbild nach dem Johannesevangelium. 2001. *Vol. II/137.*

Vahrenhorst, Martin: Kultische Sprache in den Paulusbriefen. 2008. *Vol. 230.*

Vegge, Ivar: 2 Corinthians – a Letter about Reconciliation. 2008. *Vol. II/239.*

Verheyden, Joseph, Korinna Zamfir and *Tobias Nicklas* (Ed.): Prophets and Prophecy in Jewish and Early Christian Literature. 2010. *Vol. II/286.*

– see *Nicklas, Tobias*

Visotzky, Burton L.: Fathers of the World. 1995. *Vol. 80.*

Vollenweider, Samuel: Horizonte neutestamentlicher Christologie. 2002. *Vol. 144.*

Vos, Johan S.: Die Kunst der Argumentation bei Paulus. 2002. *Vol. 149.*

Waaler, Erik: The *Shema* and The First Commandment in First Corinthians. 2008. *Vol. II/253.*

Wagener, Ulrike: Die Ordnung des „Hauses Gottes". 1994. *Vol. II/65.*

Wagner, J. Ross: see *Wilk, Florian.*

Wahlen, Clinton: Jesus and the Impurity of Spirits in the Synoptic Gospels. 2004. *Vol. II/185.*

Walker, Donald D.: Paul's Offer of Leniency (2 Cor 10:1). 2002. *Vol. II/152.*

Walter, Nikolaus: Praeparatio Evangelica. Ed. von Wolfgang Kraus und Florian Wilk. 1997. *Vol. 98.*

Wander, Bernd: Gottesfürchtige und Sympathisanten. 1998. *Vol. 104.*

Wardle, Timothy: The Jerusalem Temple and Early Christian Identity. 2010. *Vol. II/291.*

Wasserman, Emma: The Death of the Soul in Romans 7. 2008. *Vol. 256.*

Waters, Guy: The End of Deuteronomy in the Epistles of Paul. 2006. *Vol. 221.*

Watt, Jan G. van der: see *Frey, Jörg*

Watts, Rikki: Isaiah's New Exodus and Mark. 1997. *Vol. II/88.*

Webb, Robert L.: see *Bock, Darrell L.*

Wedderburn, A.J.M.: Baptism and Resurrection. 1987. *Vol. 44.*

Wegner, Uwe: Der Hauptmann von Kafarnaum. 1985. *Vol. II/14.*

Weiß, Hans-Friedrich: Frühes Christentum und Gnosis. 2008. *Vol. 225.*

Weissenrieder, Annette: Images of Illness in the Gospel of Luke. 2003. Vol. II/164.

–, and *Robert B. Coote* (Ed.): The Interface of Orality and Writing. 2010. *Vol. 260.*

–, *Friederike Wendt* and *Petra von Gemünden* (Ed.): Picturing the New Testament. 2005. *Vol. II/193.*

Welck, Christian: Erzählte ‚Zeichen'. 1994. *Vol. II/69.*

Wendt, Friederike (Ed.): see *Weissenrieder, Annette.*

Wiarda, Timothy: Peter in the Gospels. 2000. *Vol. II/127.*

Wifstrand, Albert: Epochs and Styles. 2005. *Vol. 179.*

Wilk, Florian and *J. Ross Wagner* (Ed.): Between Gospel and Election. 2010. *Vol. 257.*

– see *Walter, Nikolaus.*

Williams, Catrin H.: I am He. 2000. *Vol. II/113.*

Wilson, Todd A.: The Curse of the Law and the Crisis in Galatia. 2007. *Vol. II/225.*

Wilson, Walter T.: Love without Pretense. 1991. *Vol. II/46.*

Winn, Adam: The Purpose of Mark's Gospel. 2008. *Vol. II/245.*

Winninge, Mikael: see *Holmberg, Bengt.*

Wischmeyer, Oda: Von Ben Sira zu Paulus. 2004. *Vol. 173.*

Wisdom, Jeffrey: Blessing for the Nations and the Curse of the Law. 2001. *Vol. II/133.*

Witmer, Stephen E.: Divine Instruction in Early Christianity. 2008. *Vol. II/246.*

Wold, Benjamin G.: Women, Men, and Angels. 2005. *Vol. II/2001.*

Wolter, Michael: Theologie und Ethos im frühen Christentum. 2009. *Vol. 236.*

– see *Stuckenbruck, Loren T.*

Wright, Archie T.: The Origin of Evil Spirits. 2005. *Vol. II/198.*

Wucherpfennig, Ansgar: Heracleon Philologus. 2002. *Vol. 142.*

Yates, John W.: The Spirit and Creation in Paul. 2008. *Vol. II/251.*

Yeung, Maureen: Faith in Jesus and Paul. 2002. *Vol. II/147.*

Zamfir, Corinna: see *Verheyden, Joseph*

Zangenberg, Jürgen, Harold W. Attridge and *Dale B. Martin* (Ed.): Religion, Ethnicity and Identity in Ancient Galilee. 2007. *Vol. 210.*

Zimmermann, Alfred E.: Die urchristlichen Lehrer. 1984, ²1988. *Vol. II/12.*

Zimmermann, Johannes: Messianische Texte aus Qumran. 1998. *Vol. II/104.*

Zimmermann, Ruben: Christologie der Bilder im Johannesevangelium. 2004. *Vol. 171.*

– Geschlechtermetaphorik und Gottesverhältnis. 2001. *Vol. II/122.*

– (Ed.): Hermeneutik der Gleichnisse Jesu. 2008. *Vol. 231.*

– see *Frey, Jörg.*

– see *Horn, Friedrich Wilhelm.*

Zugmann, Michael: „Hellenisten" in der Apostelgeschichte. 2009. *Vol. II/264.*

Zumstein, Jean: see *Dettwiler, Andreas*

Zwiep, Arie W.: Judas and the Choice of Matthias. 2004. *Vol. II/187.*

For a complete catalogue please write to the publisher
Mohr Siebeck • P.O. Box 2030 • D–72010 Tübingen/Germany
Up-to-date information on the internet at www.mohr.de